Ottoman Turkey, Atatürk, and Muslim South Asia

Ottoman Turkey, Atatürk, and Muslim South Asia

PERSPECTIVES, PERCEPTIONS, AND RESPONSES

M. Naeem Qureshi

UNIVERSITY PRESS

OXFORD
UNIVERSITY PRESS

Oxford University Press is a department of the University of Oxford.
It furthers the University's objective of excellence in research, scholarship,
and education by publishing worldwide in

Oxford New York

Auckland Cape Town Dar es Salaam Hong Kong Karachi
Kuala Lumpur Madrid Melbourne Mexico City Nairobi
New Delhi Shanghai Taipei Toronto

With offices in

Argentina Austria Brazil Chile Czech Republic France Greece
Guatemala Hungary Italy Japan Poland Portugal Singapore
South Korea Switzerland Turkey Ukraine Vietnam

Oxford is a registered trademark of Oxford University Press
in the UK and in certain other countries

Published in Pakistan by Oxford University Press

© Oxford University Press 2014

The moral rights of the author have been asserted

Database right Oxford University Press (maker)

First published 2014

All rights reserved. No part of this publication may be reproduced, translated,
stored in a retrieval system, or transmitted, in any form or by any means,
without the prior permission in writing of Oxford University Press.
Enquiries concerning reproduction should be sent to
Oxford University Press at the address below.

You must not circulate this work in any other form and you
must impose this same condition on any acquirer.

ISBN 978-0-19-906634-6

Typeset in Adobe Garamond Pro
Printed in Pakistan by
Union Enterprises, Karachi.
Published by
Ameena Saiyid, Oxford University Press
No. 38, Sector 15, Korangi Industrial Area, PO Box 8214,
Karachi-74900, Pakistan.

To my wife Ghazala

Contents

List of Maps		ix
Preface		xi
Introduction		xix
1.	Bibliographic Soundings in Nineteenth-Century Pan-Islam in South Asia	1
2.	The Balkan Crisis of 1912–1913 and Muslim India	23
3.	Pan-Islam and the Caliphate Question Revisited	47
4.	Pleading the Case of The Ottoman Caliphate: Indian Khilafatists' Endeavours in Europe	76
5.	Atatürk's Impact on Muslim India, 1919–1938	143
6.	Images of Atatürk and Turkey in Urdu Literature	161
7.	Armstrong's Grey Wolf and the 'Real' Atatürk	189
8.	Atatürk's Reforms and the Muslim World Bordering South Asia	216

CONTENTS

9. The Kemalist Model of State and Ayub Khan's Structural Reforms in Pakistan ... 236

Epilogue ... 251

Appendices

   (i) Misak-i Milli, 28 January 1920 ... 273

   (ii) Brief Diary of the Khilafat Delegation's Proceedings, 1920 ... 275

   (iii) Extracts from Mohammad Iqbal's Sixth Lecture ... 280

   (iv) M. A. Jinnah's Tribute to Atatürk ... 293

Glossary ... 294

Biographical Sketches ... 298

Selected Bibliography: Unpublished Sources ... 312

Index ... 345

List of Maps

Maps

1 The Ottoman Empire at its zenith in the sixteenth century   xv

2 Turkey after 1923   xvi

3 South Asia Today   xvii

Preface

Whenever I visited Turkey over the years, and it has been quite a few times, I was always received with open arms. Still, I tell my Turkish friends that the younger generations of Turks and Muslim South Asians—Pakistanis, Indians, and Bangladeshis—hardly realize how deeply their grandparents or great-grandparents were concerned about the other country's well-being. These writings, I hope, will bring back memories from the pages of history and serve as a reminder of the mutual empathy of the yesteryears. The late nineteenth and early twentieth centuries were particularly difficult times for the Ottomans for they were faced with enormous challenges, both from within and outside. The Ottoman Empire had been rendered vulnerable by years of shoddy governance, occasional rebellions, and slithering intrusions by western imperial powers. The Young Turks meant well but the fateful decision to enter the First World War on Germany's side produced ominous results. The situation, however, was retrieved by a spurt of sound engineering by Mustafa Kemal Atatürk and his nationalists who won some of the lost ground back for the Turks. Mustafa Kemal was now the man of the hour and the hero of millions both inside and outside Turkey. The abolition of the caliphate and the fast pace of modernization did raise some eyebrows, but business soon returned to normal.

Since the establishment of Pakistan, there have been occasional calls for adopting tailored versions of the Turkish model of state, as was suggested in muffled tones during Ayub Khan's regime in the late 1950s through the 1960s and was asserted more vociferously by Pervez Musharraf in the 1990s, but they were never followed up in any concrete shape. The following pages carry, in some detail, the story of the enigma called pan-Islam and its impact on the Muslims of South Asia in the context of the British and Allied policies towards Turkey. They also examine the enduring relevance of pan-Islam as a political tool and ventures to measure its trajectory in the future, especially when Turkey today is gradually moving away from Atatürk's model of state and society.

I would like to take this opportunity to thank those who have helped me in the preparation of this book. In particular, I would like to mention my old friends Mehmet Saray and Azmi Özcan. Mehmet and I shared the same hall of residence in London in early 1970s, while with Azmi, I shared the same school (SOAS)—only that he followed me there several years later. Mehmet went on to teach at Istanbul University and later shifted to Ankara as Head of the Atatürk Araştırma Merkezi (AAM), retiring from there in 2006. Azmi joined the Islam Araştirmalari Merkezi (ISAM) in Istanbul and then moved to Sakarya University in the Marmara Region. These days, he is busy administering Bilecik University in Midwest Turkey as Rector. Both of them have always been very good hosts and helped me constantly with Turkish sources. I must also express my gratitude to Tufan Buzpinar, now Deputy Rector of Istanbul 29 Mayis Universitesi, for his kindness and help. Similarly, I have enjoyed, on several occasions, the proverbial Turkish hospitality of several directors of the AAM, from Azmi Süslü to Cezmi Eraslan; of Reşat Genç and Sadik Tural, the two successive heads of the Atatürk Kültür, Dil ve Tarikh Yüksek Kurumu in Ankara; and of Akif Aydin, the ISAM's Director, in Istanbul. Mustaf Budak, Deputy Director-General

PREFACE

of the Başbakanlık Osmanlı Arşivi (BOA) in Istanbul, and his colleague Mustafa Küçük, have also been extremely forthcoming in extending their help and hospitality. In addition, my thanks go to Halit Eren, Director-General of the Research Centre for Islamic History, Art and Culture (IRCICA), located in the ideal environs of the Yildiz Palace heights in Istanbul, for his inimitable geniality. His rich library is worth a visit.

In Britain, Avril Ann Powell of the University of London has been very prompt in sending the required material whenever I needed it. Having lived in Lahore as a faculty member of Kinnaird College, she was my contemporary at SOAS. I cannot thank her enough for help and companionship over the years. In Pakistan, I would like to mention Rafique Afzal and Ilhan Niaz, my former colleagues at the Quaid-i-Azam University, Islamabad, and Muzaffar Mahmood Qurashi, a former Federal Secretary to the Government of Pakistan, for making valuable comments. I owe them a lot. To Muhammad Qasim Zaman, now at Princeton, I am indebted to him for his help in the preparation of an earlier draft of one of the articles now merged with chapter five. Imtiaz Begum of the Turkish Department at the National University of Modern Languages, Islamabad, helped me with the Turkish sources, and Necla Yildizgördü of the same university downloaded some material for me from the internet. I am grateful to both of them. For logistics support, I must thank Razia Sultana, Altaf Bajwa, Zahid Amin, Qaim Shah, and Afzal Sowern of the Departments of History and Physics at the Quaid-i-Azam University, Islamabad. For help in acquiring the photographs, I am grateful to the custodians of Islamic Research Institute (Islamabad), ISAM (Istanbul), IRCICA (Istanbul), Iqbal Academy of Pakistan (Lahore), and the National Archives of Pakistan (Islamabad). To my son, Sheharyar Qureshi, I owe thanks for solving many of my problems of technical nature that I faced during the preparation of the manuscript of this book.

Last but not least, I would like to record my thanks to two well-known academics, Sharif al Mujahid and Hamida Khuhro, for their perceptive

PREFACE

inputs as reviewers, and to Moazzam Wasti, Ghousia Ali, Rida Iqbal, and Sana Shaikha for giving the text the benefit of their editorial expertise. Without their professional skill, this book would not have been in the shape it is at present. I am also indebted to Ameena Saiyid, OBE, Managing Director of the Oxford University Press, for accepting the manuscript. To Fayyaz Raja, the OUP's Regional Sales Director in Islamabad, I owe thanks for his willing assistance whenever needed.

It remains for me, now, to thank the custodians and staff of the following archives and libraries: Oriental and India Office Collection at the British Library (London); National Archives UK (London); Senate House Library, University of London; School of Oriental & African Studies Library (London); Beaverbrook Library (London); University of Cambridge Library (Cambridge); Bodleian Library of the University of Oxford (Oxford); Makerere University Library (Kampala, Uganda); Islam Araştirmalari Merkezi Library (Istanbul); Başbakanlık Osmanlı Arşivi (Istanbul); IRCICA Library at Yildiz Palace (Istanbul); Jamia Millia Islamia Library (New Delhi); Archives of the Freedom Movement, University of Karachi (Karachi); Quaid-i-Azam Academy Library (Karachi); Lahore Museum Library (Lahore); Punjab Public Library (Lahore); University of the Punjab Library (Lahore); National Archives of Pakistan (Islamabad); National Institute of Historical and Cultural Research Library (Islamabad); Islamic Research Institute Library (Islamabad); Dr Raziuddin Siddiqui Library of the Quaid-i-Azam University (Islamabad), and the Department of History Library of the same university.

M. Naeem Qureshi
Islamabad
July 2013

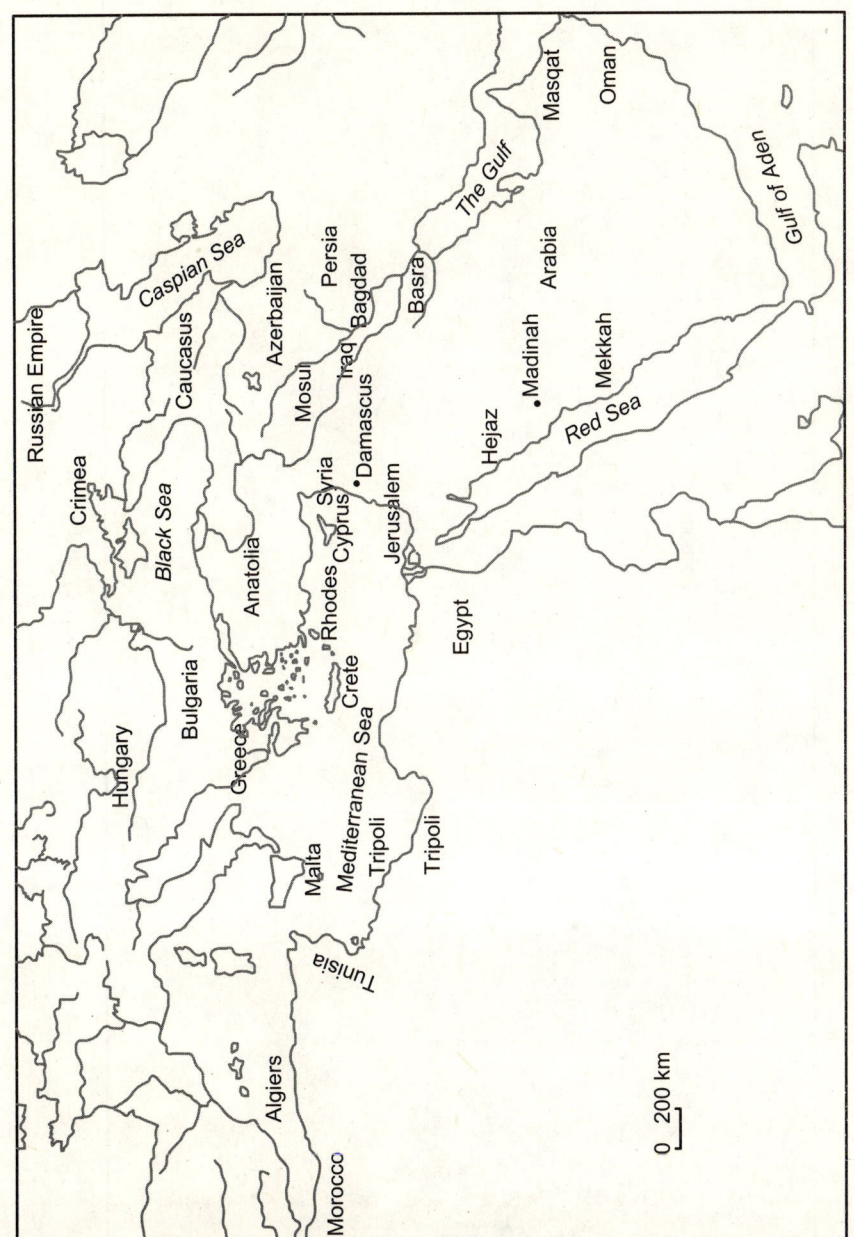

Map 1: The Ottoman Empire at its zenith in the sixteenth century

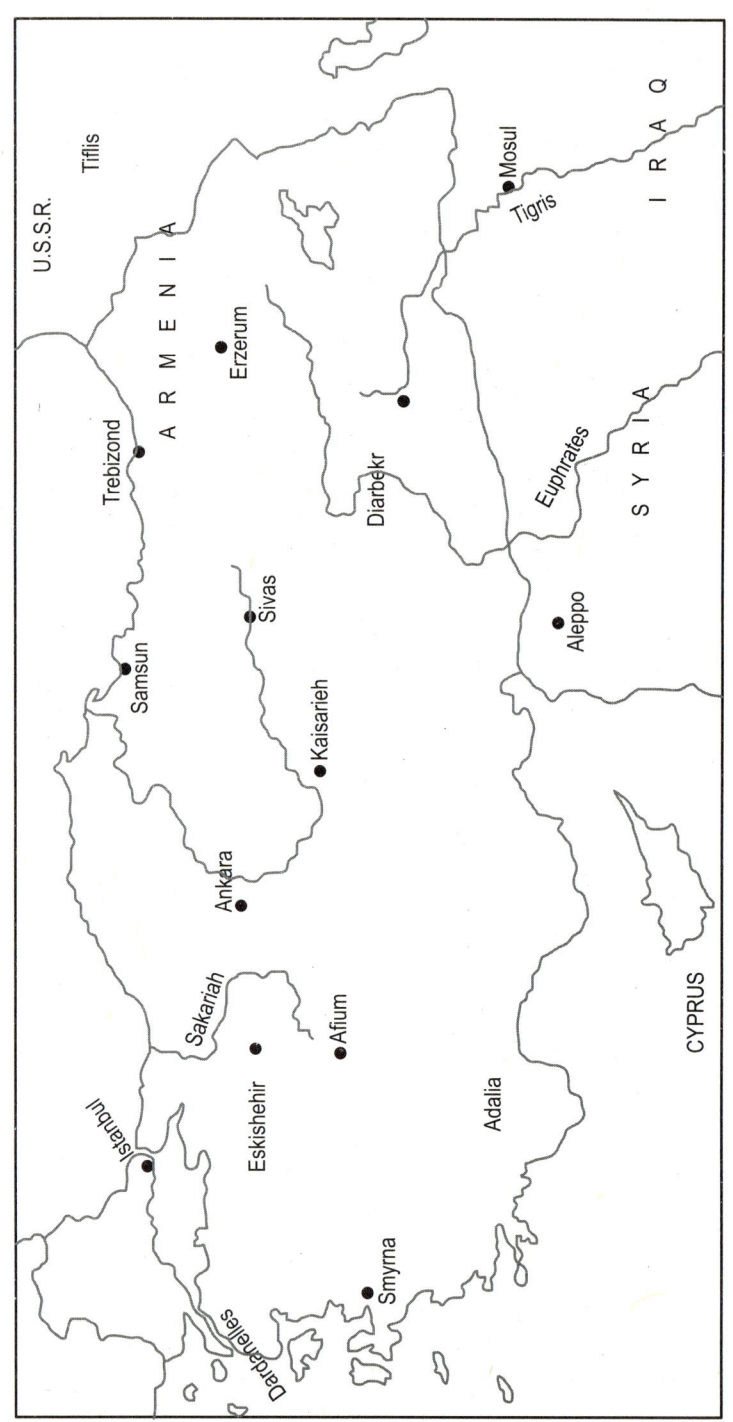

Map 2: Turkey after 1923

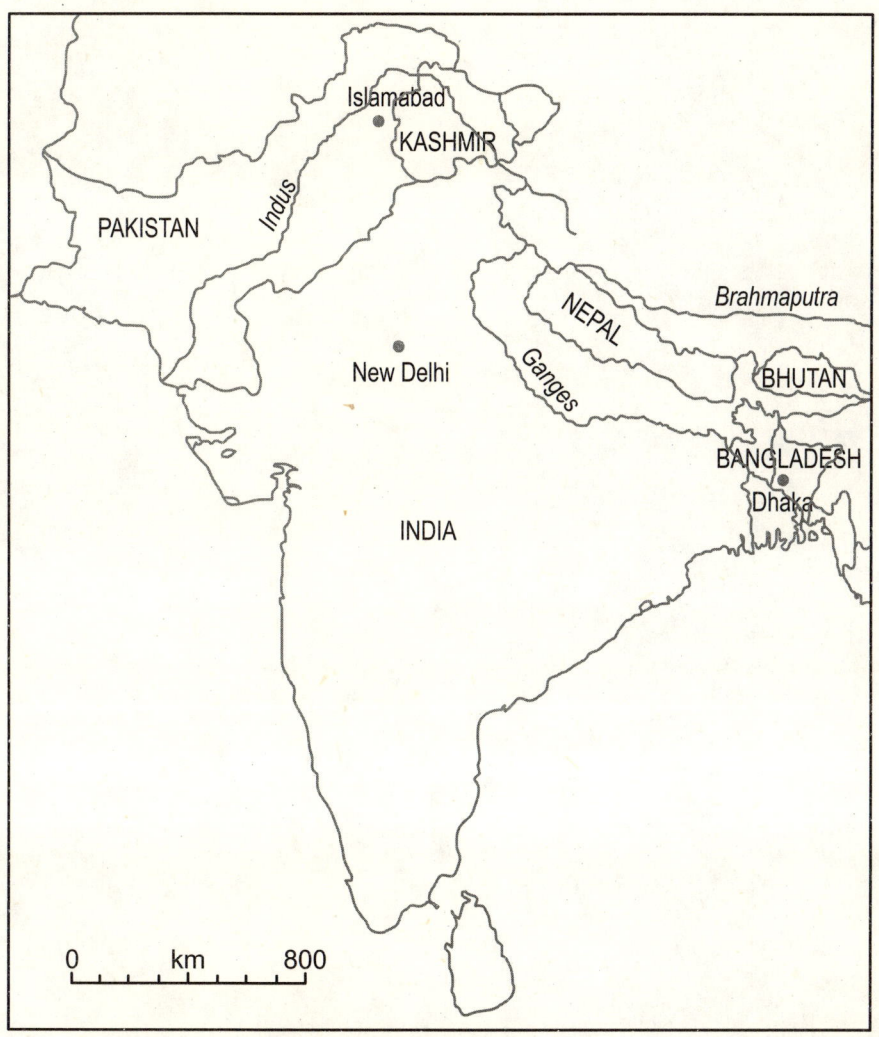

Map 3: South Asia Today

Introduction

At its zenith, around the middle of the sixteenth century, the Ottoman Empire was a traditional bureaucratic system that covered a sprawling land mass on the three continents of Asia, Africa, and Europe, acquired at different times through measured spurts of conquests. Starting from the Anatolian Peninsula and yonder to the Caspian Sea, the Empire spread in different directions and came to include Albania, Bosnia-Herzegovina, Bulgaria, Croatia, Greece, Kosovo, Macedonia, Montenegro, Romania, Serbia, and Slovenia in the Balkan Peninsula; the Ionian islands of Crete and Cyprus; parts of Hungary, Austria, and southern Russia; Syria, Iraq, Palestine, and Egypt; North Africa, as far west as Algeria; and parts of Arabia. It lasted until November 1922 when Turkey became a republic. However, the Ottoman caliphate survived the sultanate by another two years before being abolished in March 1924 by Mustafa Kemal (1881–1938). As one of the many consequences, the last of the caliphs, 56-year old Abdülmecid II (r. 1922–24), was banished along with the entire ruling family.

The turmoil, the panic, and the gloom that struck the Ottomans in the aftermath of this momentous exercise has been graphically captured

INTRODUCTION

from inside the palace by Kanizé Mourad, a great-granddaughter of Murad V, in the memoirs of her mother, Princess Selma, and remains unsurpassed in its sweep.¹ The breathtaking expansion of the old Ottoman Empire, however, was not due to a string of lucky breaks or the blunders of its enemies. It was the result of the sustained efforts of gifted rulers fortified by a certain enterprise associated with strident empire-builders. Indeed, by the time of the reigns of Sultans Mehmed I (r. 1413–21) and Süleyman 'Kanuni' (r. 1520–66), a visible sense of belonging to an 'Ottoman universe' had emerged.² This Turco-Islamic empire was the grandest, as also the most powerful, of its time and had a splendid state system organized on units of autonomous *millet*s under the sultan-caliph. The grand vizier headed a highly bureaucratized civil-military governing class while the *'ulama* under the shaikhu'l-Islam formed another important pillar of the system because, officially, the law of the land was the Islamic *shari'at* with a clear demarcation of the globe into two parallel divisions, namely the *daru'l-Islam* and the *daru'l-harb*.³ And, though there were no deliberate lines of exclusion for non-Muslims, generations of Ottomans who grew up in the shadow of this reality often displayed real arrogance when visiting the 'infidel' lands.⁴ Surely, they were proud and confident on account of their splendid inheritance but, unfortunately, also held the rest of the world in contempt. The Turks struck awe and terror in Europe—as far as the shores of Britain where Ottoman and Muslim seafarers stalked the British waters, made Britons captive, and sometimes converted them to Islam.⁵ And, though the Ottomans had inevitably earned Europe's undying contempt and hostility for themselves and their religion,⁶ they were, nevertheless, able to develop an enduring, 'well-balanced socio-economic and political structure and a pluralistic cultural-religious corporatist' construct.⁷

But, then, from the catastrophic reversal at the gates of Vienna in 1683 began the phase of defeats and territorial withdrawals that somehow never seemed to pause—resulting in the general dismantling of the

INTRODUCTION

achievements reaped over the previous two and a half centuries. Between the military disaster at Slankamen (1691) and the Balkan Wars (1912–13), the Ottoman Empire had shrunk to virtually a foothold in Europe. The major chunk of its territories, however, was sliced off during the latter half of the nineteenth century when the resurgent Europeans made devastating inroads into the Ottoman possessions. So thorough was the spoliation that not a single Muslim country on the fringe of the hitherto expansive Islamic crescent, from Algeria in the west to the distant East Indies, was left independent. The only territories of the *daru'l-Islam* that escaped subjugation were those in the altogether restricted 'core', and they, too, were now threatened. A number of Ottoman possessions, including Bulgaria, Serbia, Romania, Montenegro, Bosnia-Herzegovina, Tunisia, and Egypt, either came under European domination or became independent.[8]

The reasons for this massive withdrawal can be explained in terms of the shifting of the military balance away from the Ottomans when the West acquired better military technology, better warfare techniques, and better ways of sustaining the high costs of warfare through riches amassed from the New World. Moreover, Europe saw the rise of centralized monarchies that grew more confident.[9] What saved the Ottomans from absolute humiliation, however, was the factor of *ittihad-i Islam,* or pan-Islam, which furnished them the necessary leverage while dealing with the European powers. The other factors were the rivalry among the European states and the tri-phased reinvigorating endeavours of the Young Ottomans/Young Turks (1889–1918) who were propelled by the spirit of the French Revolution and its positivist philosophy that reshaped the history of the Ottoman Empire. Theirs, however, was a two-way struggle—among themselves over the nuances (read 'inconsistencies') of ideology and methodology, and with the autocratic regimes of despotic sultans who held the reins.[10]

INTRODUCTION

The reform and revolution (1908) spearheaded by the 'new' Ittihat ve Terakki Cemiyeti, or the Committee of Union and Progress (CUP), helped the Ottoman Empire project itself as an important power until the end of the First World War, when its decayed limbs were easily severed by the Allied Powers who devoured them through the Treaty of Sèvres (1920). In Istanbul, a compliant sultan began to warm up to the occupation forces as the only viable option. But, a small group of defiant former Young Turks of the CUP, and a few brave army commanders, showed how, with peoples' support, national resistance could still be developed and territories won back and revived for the Turkish 'fatherland'.

The credit for engineering the resistance and for creating modern Turkey from the ashes of the Ottoman Empire goes largely, though not entirely, to Mustafa Kemal and his associates. They frustrated the designs of the Allied powers that were about to perform the last rites of the 'Sick Man of Europe' and carve up its assets among themselves. Born to a lower-middle class Turkish family of settlers in Ottoman Salonika (then part of its Macedonia region and now in Greece), Mustafa Kemal rose to the pinnacle of the imperial Ottoman army through sheer professional competence during the last and third phase of the Young Turk era (1908–18), when politics and soldiering went side by side. He did not like Turkey's entry in the First World War, but fought gallantly to win laurels at Çanakkale (Gallipoli) in 1915–16, the event that cost Winston Churchill (1874–1965) his job at the Admiralty. Following the Armistice and the Allied plans to partition the old Ottoman Empire, Mustafa Kemal shifted to Anatolia and organized resistance to secure objectives outlined in the Misak-i Milli (National Pact) of January 1920. It is significant that initially Mustafa Kemal used pan-Islam and the caliphate as symbols to promote his movement but later, owing to the changed situation and hostility from Istanbul, reversed his policy.[11] In a bitter three-year armed struggle, the nationalists emerged victorious and forced the Allies to renegotiate the terms they had previously imposed on

INTRODUCTION

Turkey as the price for peace. The Treaty of Lausanne (1923), thus, replaced the humiliating Treaty of Sèvres, which restored Turkish sovereignty and cleared the way for the reconstruction of the devastated country.

Mustafa Kemal's defining moment came with his election as president of the Turkish republic—which he had proclaimed in October 1923. He initiated what is retrospectively called 'Kemalism', a process of pragmatic reform aimed at transforming Turkey into a modern westernized society in every respect. Inspired by certain overriding concepts, the ideologists of the Republican Peoples' Party perfected the process. Between 1924 and 1938, a steady stream of enactments resulted in the abolition of the caliphate, exile of the Ottomans, liquidation of religious institutions, emancipation of women, codification of laws, 'democratization' of political parties, Latinization of the Turkish script, and westernization of the Turkish culture.[12] Simultaneously, he purged, from the system, those sceptics who disagreed with him. Though at times harsh and arbitrary, Mustafa Kemal left behind a reasonably stable state. But, his reforms were not the result of any impulsive decision. There was a certain historical connection and a definite intellectual base that displayed both indigenous and foreign influences. Unfortunately, however, the mantle of guardianship of Kemalism came to be assumed by the armed forces, which, it is contended, was a distortion of Atatürk's original idea.[13] But since then, the military has staged as many as four coups in fifty years, supposedly to save the state from internal threats. In the process, they have been very critical of any party that has, at its roots even a semblance of Islamic religion and culture. The ugly turn in the present crisis in Turkey is the result of this historical fault line.

Recep Tayyip Erdoğan's (b. 1954) mildly-Islamic ruling Justice and Development Party (Adalet ve Kalkinma Partisi, or the AKP) is popular among the masses but its discordant right-wing policies have sent shivers down the spines of the secularists who fear an Islamic relapse. The wheel seems to have come full circle since the Young Turks revolution of 1908, and Turkey once again finds itself at the crossroads.[14] But, hopes of real democracy replacing the 'tutelary' system depend on how the AKP manages to steer clear of the pitfalls. With an emergent economy, shrewd foreign policy, and confident leadership, Turkey seems destined to achieve another rebirth.

To the Muslims of South Asia, the Ottoman Empire had always symbolized an unbroken emotional-psychological link in the chain of Islamic caliphate that was powerful enough to brave the western (Christian) peril. In the classical Sunni theory of an Islamic state, the caliphate holds a pivotal position. As the vicegerent of God on earth, the caliph (*khalifa*) exercises power and authority delegated to him within the guidelines laid down in the *shari'at*.[15] But, with the downfall of the 'righteous' caliphate and the rise of the dynastic sultans, the jurists were brought face-to-face with the reality of adjusting to innovations in Islam's religio-political fabric. The solution was sought in accommodating the sultan in the system so long as he operated within the jurisdiction of the *shari'at*.[16] Thus, wrapped in theoretical exegesis, the fiction of the 'universal' caliphate as the ideal centre, was sustained by a polity under siege. But, there is a vast difference between the ideal and reality. The reality was that the worldwide Islamic community had become weak, divided, and threatened with extinction by the economic and political ascendancy and military prowess of the western imperial powers. But the weaker the sultan-caliph's position in Turkey became, the more earnestly he appealed to the Muslim communities abroad to sustain the myth of the 'universal' caliphate. This fiction, at least from Murad I (r. 1362–89) onwards, became a regular feature that reached a high point in 1774 when, in the Treaty of Küçük Kaynarca with the Russians, the negotiators of Abdülhamid I (r. 1774–89) got him the much-desired recognition as the 'Caliph of all Muslims'.[17] During the latter half of the nineteenth century, especially with Abdülaziz (r. 1861–76) and Abdülhamid II (r. 1876–1909) as the high priests of pan-Islam, the

INTRODUCTION

Indian Muslims got drawn into the movement that essentially had its origins in the Indian environment.[18]

This effervescence came to notice more prominently in the early part of the twentieth century when it culminated in the Khilafat movement (1918–24), launched by the Muslims of South Asia specifically to obtain lenient terms for the Turks in their negotiations with the Allies while claiming self-rule, and even independence, for India. The significant feature was the way the Khilafatists changed their allegiance from the Ottoman caliph to Mustafa Kemal when the centre of power shifted from Istanbul to Ankara. Evidently, what drove the Indian pan-Islamists was the desire to strengthen the political power of Islam, and not really to perpetuate the Osmanlis as such. They did not, however, fully realize that the Young Turks, and then Mustafa Kemal, had already opted out of pan-Islam (as well as Ottomanism and pan-Turkism) in favour of nationalism based on a peculiar mix of secularism, positivism, and, above all, 'an organic view of "Turkish culture"', rejecting all irredentist claims.[19] The Indian and Turkish perceptions about the caliphate were seriously at odds with one another, but pragmatism rehabilitated Mustafa Kemal among the Muslims of South Asia even after he abolished the institution in March 1924, a response that took a definite shape and acquired a compelling dimension as time passed.

This book has evolved from several articles that I contributed at various times to different journals, or which were presented at international conferences, or formed part of an edited work. However, all of them are based on original archival material or contemporary published sources available in Pakistan, India, Turkey, and Britain. Somehow, these articles had remained largely inaccessible to those who are interested in the subject. This collection, I trust, will ensure a wider circulation for those fascinated by aspects of Indo–Turkish relations in history. I have tried, as far as possible, to look at the events in their historical context and

INTRODUCTION

not use hindsight for my analysis. Nor have I formulated any hypothesis to suit any pre-conceived notions. I let the facts speak for themselves.

The common theme running through these articles is the pan-Islamic indulgence of the Muslim South Asia for the Ottoman Empire and, on its fall, a dramatic shift of preferences from the Ottomans to Mustafa Kemal and his republican Turkey. The period covered in these studies starts from the latter half of the nineteenth century but concentrates, more specifically, on the events of the early decades of the twentieth century when historic changes were taking place in the aftermath of the First World War at the expense of the Ottoman Empire. Its dismemberment, however, was the result of a series of interconnected events that stemmed primarily from the West's insatiable imperial appetite for power and glory that had begun a century earlier. As these articles were independent studies, they have been edited to string them together in a coherent story as well as to achieve uniformity in transliteration, style, and format. Inevitably, in a book of this kind, there is bound to be an overlap of events and details but, hopefully, they will not be too jarring. The Turkish names of persons and places follow the pattern used in that language while the words in Urdu have been transliterated according to Ferozsons' *Urdu-English Dictionary* (Lahore, n.d.). A glossary has been added at the end of the text that further explains words and terms used in these languages. It may be noted, however, that in Turkish 'c' is pronounced as 'j', while 'ç' is 'ch', 'ğ' sounds like 'ain' in Urdu, 'ş' is 'sh', and 'ö' and 'ü' carry hard sounds as in German.

The first chapter, 'Bibliographic Soundings in Nineteenth-Century Pan-Islam in South Asia', emphasizes the problems associated with finding the precise source material for the study of the pan-Islamic phenomenon in its South Asian context. Here, I have identified nearly two hundred sources, not only in western languages but also in Urdu, which can be helpful in studying various aspects of the subject in focus. They include

INTRODUCTION

contemporary works, pamphlets, and polemics, as well as serious research contributions in the shape of academic books and articles. Opinions on 'pan-Islam' vary so radically that finding an appropriate definition of the term becomes challenging. However, a careful examination of the available material on the subject reveals that the expression had a European derivation, originally employed to profile Muslim responses to western encroachments on the *daru'l-Islam*. Essentially, the movement was viewed in the milieu of the 'Eastern Question', but this Eurocentric construct provoked contrary explanations from Muslims whose attachment to the Ottoman caliphate and its sprawling Empire had enduring psychological and emotional undertones.

If one looks objectively at the South Asian perspectives of Islamic history, Muslims appear to have a linear view of historiography beginning from Arabia and continuing down the line right up to Muslim rule in India. In between this stretch, the Ottomans were the shining beads of the Islamic rosary. Haunted as they were by a minority syndrome, the Muslims of British India were attracted to the concept of *ittihad-i Islam* and the idea of a 'universal' caliphate as the symbol of Islam's splendour and glory. This provoked mixed reactions from the western imperial powers, depending on the circumstances prevalent at the time—from open resentment to expedient manipulation of the Ottoman credentials. But, it must be remembered that the South Asian Muslims were not the only ones parading their Ottoman predilections; parallel waves of pan-Islamic fervour were discernable among Muslims of Central Asia and the Far East as well.

Since the publication of this article several new works have appeared on pan-Islam. I would like to mention at least four indispensable publications. They are: Naimur Rahman Farooqi's 'Pan-Islamism in the Nineteenth Century', *Islamic Culture* (Hyderabad), 57/4 (1983), 283–96; Jacob Landau's *Politics of Pan-Islam: Ideology and Organization*

INTRODUCTION

(Oxford: Clarendon Press, 1990); Azmi Özcan's *Pan-Islamism: Indian Muslims, the Ottomans & Britain (1877–1924)* (Leiden: Brill, 1997); and my own *Pan-Islam in British Indian Politics: A Study of the Khilafat Movement, 1918–1924* (Leiden: Brill, 1999), whose revised edition has since appeared as *Pan-Islam in British India: The Politics of the Khilafat Movement, 1918–1924* (Karachi: Oxford University Press, 2009). Taken together, these books provide a comprehensive study of pan-Islam through various phases of its complex progression from the 1870s to the 1980s. The result is the unfolding of a fascinating account of how the yearnings for Muslim unity and solidarity were mobilized for political gains in the broader context of Ottoman-European rivalries, together with its huge impact on South Asia.

The second chapter, 'The Balkan Crisis of 1912–1913 and Muslim India', looks at the disastrous impact of those fateful events on Turkey, and the enormous wave of pan-Islamic sympathy that helped to soften the shock of the defeat. It attempts to explore the depth and extent of Muslim India's empathy for Turkey, and the manner in which the moral and material support was proffered in the wake of the Balkan aggression. The credit for building up the pro-Turkish pan-Islamic movement goes to the young modernist politicians who, in concert with the madrasah-bound traditional *'ulama*, developed a solid pressure group for the benefit of the Young Turks in Istanbul. Some of them, like Mushir Hosain Kidwai (1878–1938) and Abdul Bari (1878–1926), had already established direct contacts with the Turks while others, like Mohamed Ali (1878–1931), Abul Kalam Azad (1888–1958), and Zafar Ali Khan (1873–1956), were professional politicians-journalists who bolstered Turkey's image in the public eye through favourable news and reviews in popular journals like the *Comrade*, *Al-Hilal*, and the *Zamindar*. Thus, this was the first time that the two powerful sections of Muslim society in India had come together on an issue that concerned the world of Islam. As part of their multi-pronged strategy, they arranged well-attended rallies and public meetings all over India to condemn the Balkan aggression. As practical displays of their sympathy, the Indian Muslims remitted generous sums of money to Turkey and also sent a 26-member medical mission, under Dr Mukhtar Ahmad Ansari (1880–1936), to render assistance to the Ottoman sick and wounded. How far these efforts were able to sustain Ottoman Turkey can be discerned from the fact that the British and French governments were not very happy at this sudden spurt of effervescence, immediately after a similar eruption during the Tripolitan war of 1911. But, the Balkan crisis had made the Young Turks rethink their policy and, from then on, they began to rely more fervently on the pan-Islamic support than they had done previously, since the ouster of Abdülhamid II. From that point on, their contact with the Indian pan-Islamists noticeably increased.

The third chapter, 'Pan-Islam and the Caliphate Question Revisited', takes a fresh look at the sprawling Islamic polity in which the ideal and reality co-existed only for a short time, and yet survived for centuries as the fictional 'central' caliphate before fragmenting into disparate parts under different dynasties. The *coup de grâce* came in the eighteenth century when the western imperial powers began to launch their aggressive economic and military forays into the *daru'l-Islam*. The internal disruption gave rise to movements for reform, ranging from a puritanical model in Arabia to a modernist variety in India. Externally, it triggered the ideology of *ittihad-i Islam*, or a pan-Islamic union around the Ottoman caliphate in Istanbul, as the last wall of defence against the West. In this connection, I have questioned the role of Jamaluddin 'al-Afghani' (1838–97) as the originator of the movement because his impact on the contemporary world of Islam was never precise or specific. At least the Indian variety had been in play long before 'al-Afghani' appeared on the scene. In any case, pan-Islam did not assume a precise shape until the Young Ottoman intellectuals began to patronize it in an attempt to fix the structural faults of the Empire. Abdülhamid II cashed in on this, but his despotism had the better of him and led to his exit. Subsequent events leading up to the First World War and the end of the Ottoman Empire changed the scenario and resulted in the rise of Mustafa Kemal which brought about the demise of the caliphate and the birth of the Turkish republic. The abolition was the drop scene of a long play that was being enacted since the sheikhu'l-Islam's *fatwa* declaring Mustafa Kemal a rebel. The two-stage Ankara-Istanbul sparring took almost four years to reach its denouement, when the last of the Osmanlis was exiled to Europe. The abolition ended the tussle between the competing centres of power and changed the rules of the game from pan-Islam to nationalism in Turkey. But, in the rest of the Muslim world it raised all manners of alarm bells, occasionally prompting theorists such as Barakatullah Maulavie (1859–1927) and Ali Abd al-Raziq (1888–1966) to propose solutions that did not really prevent pretenders, like Hussein ibn Ali (1853–1931) of the Hejaz and Fuad (1868–1936) of Egypt, to lay claim to the dysfunctional office. Naturally, the Turks could not remain unconcerned and whenever such an attempt seemed plausible, they would jump in to thwart it. Since then, the caliphate has remained a cherished dream of the pan-Islamists who keep ruminating about ways of resurrecting it.

The focus of the fourth chapter, 'Pleading the Case of the Ottoman caliphate: The Endeavours of the Indian Khilafatists in Europe', is on the Indian Muslims' efforts in obtaining lenient terms for the Ottomans after the First World War without jeopardizing their own political interests in India. This was an arduous task because European public opinion, as reflected in the press and by the declarations of its statesmen, was highly critical of the Turks, especially concerning the alleged Armenian massacres. Yet, the Indians took up the Turkish cause, appealed directly to the Allied statesmen and mobilized public support to gain *status quo ante bellum* for Turkey and *swaraj* for India. The main argument put forward by Mohamed Ali, the leader of the Khilafat delegation, was that since the Ottoman sultan was also the caliph of all

INTRODUCTION

the Muslims, it was religiously incumbent upon the Muslims to save the caliphate, and therefore the caliph's position as well, from the humiliation of dismemberment. To study the activities of the Indian delegation, I have followed it from place to place, recording its every meeting and analysing its every move. What emerges from its sojourns is a riveting story of political manoeuvring and intrigue spanning several countries and organizations. Of course, the Indians called upon Lloyd George (1863–1945), Etienne Millerand (1859–1953), and Geovanni Giolitti (1842–1928) to press their demands and also sought out the support of various political parties and groups; but, more significant were their contacts with the *émigré* Turks in Versailles, Geneva, Montreaux, and Territet. They also parleyed with Arabs of all descriptions, including Emir Faisal ibn Hussein (1885–1933). Equally important was Mohamed Ali's ambitious scheme, which he planned with Mehmed Talat Paşa (1874–1921), for the alleged invasion of India, through Afghanistan, with Bolshevik help. But, the Indians failed to achieve anything substantial during their trip to Europe. The Allies had no patience for anyone seeking clemency for the Turks, and the Indian issues attracted even less attention. Thus, the Indians returned home empty-handed, wholly convinced that the fate of Turkey and India would have to be decided in Anatolia and the subcontinent, respectively.

The fifth chapter, 'Atatürk's Impact on Muslim India, 1919–1938', deals with the Indian Muslims' response to the changing fortunes of the Ottoman Empire following the First World War, which led to the rise of Turkish nationalists under Mustafa Kemal. The argument is that the Indian Muslims saw the Turkish leader and his nationalists as saviours of Islam and gradually came to pin their hopes on them as a 'strong enough argument' against the Allied powers. From the middle of 1920, Mustafa Kemal was definitely their hero, and his victorious march was celebrated in India with great enthusiasm. Even Abul Kalam Azad—for whom the entire worldwide pan-Islamic polity rested on the institution of the caliphate—had no objection to the rise of Mustafa Kemal in the emerging scenario. Mustafa Kemal was given laudatory titles and vernacular newspapers glorified his exploits in prose and poetry. The differences in outlook surfaced only when Mustafa Kemal decided to clip the wings of the meddling sultan in Istanbul, who appeared to be behaving like a puppet of the Allied governments. When the Khilafatists realized that a rift with the Turks would benefit none but their enemies, they tried to repair the damage. It was mainly due to the influence of leaders like Muhammad Iqbal (1877–1938) and Muhammad Ali Jinnah (1876–1948), who understood and appreciated the nationalists' predicament, that Mustafa Kemal's popularity with the Indian masses was restored during the period 1924–1938. This was precisely the period when the republican government in Turkey had embarked on an ambitious programme of rapid modernization, touching almost every facet of life there. While the majority of the Khilafatists expressed reservations, Iqbal and Jinnah were quite receptive. Iqbal, in particular, was deeply touched by the Turkish revolution, though he did not agree entirely with all the measures taken by Atatürk. Yet, the reforms appeared to him to be quite consistent with the spirit of Islam and, therefore, he wanted the Indian Muslims to emulate the Turks and re-evaluate their intellectual heritage through *ijtihad*. Jinnah, on the other hand, found a kindred spirit in Atatürk, under whose spell he had fallen since 1932. The two leaders shared the basic elements of the traits they both became known for: will power, perseverance, and realism. When Atatürk died in November 1938, Jinnah ordered the Muslims of India to observe a 'Kemal Day', in order to express their feelings of sorrow and sympathy with the Turkish nation on the passing away of 'one of the greatest sons of Islam and a world figure'. With this as the background, when the Indian Muslims' dream of Pakistan became a reality in August 1947, the two states came even closer to each other. But, though Mustafa Kemal had been a source of inspiration for Jinnah, he could not be a model for imitation.

INTRODUCTION

'Images of Atatürk and Turkey in Urdu Literature' is the sixth chapter of the book. It highlights, more fully, the Indian Muslims' adulation of Mustafa Kemal, as reflected in Urdu prose and poetry. The Urdu language itself is the product of the synthesis of many cultures in the cauldron called India, especially in an environment where dynasties with Turkic origins had ruled over the subcontinent for nearly two centuries. Urdu was refined from a blend of local and foreign elements in the royal armies, and was enriched by words borrowed from Turkish in addition to ones from Persian and Arabic. The evolution and development of Urdu, however, is a controversial subject and, though experts in linguistics subscribe to diverse views, they generally agree that a form of the dialect existed in the Indus Valley; it gradually developed from the twelfth century on but, more visibly, from the fourteenth century onwards with considerable input from the Sufi *masha'ikh* and the Turkish/Persian-speaking officers and men of the imperial armies. Gradually, Urdu developed into a literary language and, by the twentieth century its prose and poetry had become an effective means of political mobilization. I have highlighted both the genres, covering newspapers, journals, pamphlets, biographies, and works of literature published during the 1920s and 1930s, and some even later. The review of literature includes the works of the well-known and the not so well-known poets and prose writers, such as Muhammad Iqbal, Zafar Ali Khan, Tegh Ansari, Iqbal Ahmad Suhail, Sufi Tabassum, Mansur Ahmad, Majid Atiqi, and Bashir Ahmad and his wife, Gaiti Ara. The most important feature of these writings in Urdu was the veneration that these writers displayed for Atatürk and Turkey. Their main emphasis was on the fact that Atatürk was a reformer who had modernized Turkey through a sustained programme of reforms that did not clash with the spirit of Islam. Those who disagreed with him also generally accepted Kemalism as a *fait accompli*.

The seventh chapter in the series, 'Armstrong's *Grey Wolf* and the "Real" Atatürk', is an in-depth study of H. C. Armstrong's controversial

INTRODUCTION

biography of Mustafa Kemal which he subtitled, 'An Intimate Study of a Dictator'. Foreign writers of the time had an unusually keen interest in Atatürk, but none as intense as this British author. Captain Armstrong had been a prisoner of war in Turkey during the First World War, which qualified him to be posted to the British Embassy in Istanbul as an intelligence officer with the Allied forces after the hostilities ended. But, with his wartime baggage, Armstrong had developed a strong hatred for the Turks and, in the process, had lost objectivity. When published, his *Grey Wolf* was an instant success in England—four editions appeared within the first four months—but his slanted portrayal of the Turkish leader almost created a diplomatic crisis between the two countries. Independent observers agreed that he had gone too far in parading Atatürk's personal shortcomings and, resultantly, had produced a distorted portrayal of the Turkish leader. Armstrong claimed candour founded on reliable informants but mentioned none for the readers to verify this claim. As expected, the Turkish government banned the book and prohibited its translation, but Mustafa Kemal, though furious, made no public comment. However, he arranged with a trusted journalist and member of the Türkiye Büyük Millet Meclisi, or the Grand National Assembly (GNA), to serialize a sharp retort in the daily *Akşam*. The controversy went on for a long time and, even today, a full translation of the *Grey Wolf*, is unavailable in Turkish. The chapter analyses the *Grey Wolf* and attempts to discover whether Armstrong had been able to capture the true magic of the 'real' Atatürk—this has not been an easy task. The chapter ends with a study of the response the book evoked in British official and private circles, including its impact on Jinnah, the future founder of Pakistan, who was living in London at the time.

'Atatürk's Reforms and the Muslim World', the eighth chapter, examines the impact the Kemalist reforms had on the Muslim countries bordering India, especially Afghanistan and Iran where the two modernizing monarchs, Amanullah (r. 1919–29) and Reza Shah (r. 1925–41), respectively, chose to imitate Atatürk. In his reform programme,

INTRODUCTION

Amanullah placed a great deal of emphasis on education. With the help of Egyptian, Turkish, and Indian Muslim experts, he embarked on a crash-programme establishing state-sponsored schools and sending boys and girls abroad for the same purpose. He also regulated the health services, expanded the telephone service, strengthened trade and commerce, and modernized his army on Turkish and German lines. In the second phase, he toured Europe, especially Turkey, to observe progress first hand. Mustafa Kemal received him with unusual warmth and signed a treaty of friendship. Having received red-carpet receptions everywhere, Amanullah thought that he would be able to replicate the Turkish model but Afghanistan was far more conservative than Turkey. His rapid socio-economic reforms, especially his emphasis on the western mode of dress for men and women, provoked considerable trouble. The mullahs declared him a *kafir*, allegedly for leading the country astray. Rebellions broke out and he was forced to abdicate, plunging the country into chaos.

In Iran, Reza Shah did what Amanullah had done in Afghanistan. He established schools and colleges, expanded communications, improved the economy, reduced corruption, and bettered the health services. He also paid a visit to Atatürk's Turkey to obtain direct information about how reforms were working there. But, as in the case of Afghanistan, Iran, too, was a traditional society that could not accept rapid modernization, particularly the European mode of dress. Conflicts and tensions led to protests and violence. The *'ulama* proved to be the main obstacle. The end was exactly like that of Amanullah; Reza Shah, too, was forced out of power, though much later and after several tumultuous upturns. It is interesting to note why modernization succeeded in Turkey, but failed in Afghanistan and Iran. The answer lies in the fact that Turkey had been a European power in its own right since the Congress of Vienna (1815) and had a long history of experiments with reforms. Atatürk's reforms were meant to re-establish the severed connection and mould Turkish society into the new European cultural matrix. Essentially sound, and with a strong intellectual base, the reforms were enthusiastically backed by Turkey's nationalist elite. Above all, Ataturk's charisma worked like a charm.

The focus of the ninth and last chapter of this book, 'The Kemalist Model of State and Ayub Khan's Structural Reforms in Pakistan', is about the programme of modernization, set in motion by President Ayub Khan of Pakistan (r. 1958–69) that betrayed traces of Atatürk's design. The similarities in the case of the Turkish archetype and Ayub Khan's follow-up experiment are to be found not just in the apparent nature of the two military oligarchies but also in the respective thrusts of their reforms. Even the electoral college system, spun around the 'Basic Democracies', bore an uncanny resemblance to the Turkish practice that enabled the local élite to maintain their power and influence in the federal assembly. The difference was that while the land reforms were an important part of Ayub Khan's reforms, the Turks did not touch that segment at all.

It is difficult to place the Ayubian scheme in a theoretical strait-jacket by classifying it as one of the models of nation-building. The position was, in fact, far more complex. The Ayub Khan regime was the outcome of the politics of sectional, regional, and group conflicts that characterized the post-independence scene. The path that Ayub Khan took was clearly defined by a policy of political integration, stimulation of national consciousness, and initiatives for material development of the country. Islam ceased to be his central concern as he proceeded to secularize the processes of government and make them acceptable to the people. But, after the initial spurt of reform when he tried to defy the traditionalists by changing the rules of the game and even altering the nomenclature of the state from the 'Islamic Republic of Pakistan' to just the 'Republic of Pakistan', Ayub Khan was forced by the opposition to revert to a more conventional stance with familiar nuances. Thereafter, the emphasis was more on a synthesis of religious and secular ideals than

INTRODUCTION

a concern for realism, which required shifting the weight of political authority whenever and wherever it appeared advantageous. But, his failure lay in the fact that, in spite of the backing of a strong military-bureaucratic nexus, Ayub Khan was unable to commend himself to the people as Pakistan's Atatürk.

Permissions for the publication of the above-mentioned articles with new titles were readily granted by the following publishers/editors and are duly acknowledged here: The Islamic Cultural Centre (London), and editor, M. A. Zaki Badawi, for 'Bibliographic Soundings in Nineteenth Century Pan-Islam in South Asia', in *The Islamic Quarterly*, 24/1–2 (1980), 22–34; Da Yayıncılık (Istanbul), for 'Islamic Polity, Pan-Islam and the Caliphate Reconsidered', in Halil Bal and Muhammet Erat (eds.), *Prof. Dr. Mehmet Saray'a Armağan: Türk Dünyasina Bakişlar* (Istanbul, 2002), 521–45; The Pakistan Historical Society (Karachi), and editors, Moinul Haq and Ansar Zahid Khan, for 'Mohamed Ali's Khilafat Delegation to Europe (February–October 1920)', in *Journal of the Pakistan Historical Society*, 28/2 (1980), 79–117 and 28/3 (1980), 157–85; Boğaziçi University (Istanbul), for 'The Rise of Atatürk and its Impact on Contemporary Muslim India: The First Phase', in *Proceedings, International Conference on Atatürk, 9–13 November 1981, Istanbul*, 3/55 (Istanbul, 1981), 1–9; Atatürk Araştirma Merkezi (AAM) (Ankara), and editor, Azmi Süslü, 'Muslims of British India and the Kemalist Reform in Turkey: Iqbal, Jinnah and Atatürk, 1924–1938', in *Atatürk Araştirma Merkezi Degisi*, 12/35 (1996), 379–86; AAM, and editors, Azmi Süslü/Mehmet Saray/Cezmi Eraslan, 'Images of Atatürk and Turkey in Urdu Literature', in *The Third International Symposium on Atatürk, 3–6 October, 1995, Gazi Mağusa, Turkish Republic of Northern Cyprus*, i (Ankara, 1998), 257–82; 'Atatürk and Armstrong's *Grey Wolf*: Myth and Reality', in *Fifth International Congress on Atatürk, 8–12 December 2003*, ii (Ankara, 2005), 973–90; 'The Kemalist Model of State and Ayub Khan's Structural Reforms in Pakistan', in *Fourth Atatürk International Congress, 25–29 October 1999, Turkistan, Kazakhstan*, ii (Ankara, 2000),

INTRODUCTION

1089–99; 'Atatürk's Reforms and their Impact on the Muslim World', in *Doğumunun 125. Yilinda Mustafa Kemal Atatürk* (Ankara, 2011), 523–42; and, lastly, 'The Balkan Crisis of 1912–1913 and Turkey', presented at the 7th International Atatürk Congress held at Skopje, Macedonia, on 17–22 October 2011, organized jointly by the AAM and the Macedonian Academy of Sciences and Arts, Skopje.

NOTES

1. Kanizé Mourad, *Memoirs of an Ottoman Princess*. Tr. Sabine Destrée and Anna Williams (Islamabad, 2001), esp. 175–82.
2. See Donald Quataert, *The Ottoman Empire, 1700–1922* (Cambridge, 2000), 13–34. The full sweep of the Ottoman expansion between 1359 and 1683 can be gleaned from the map accompanying Feridun Emecen's contribution, 'Osmanlilar', in *Islam Ansiklopedisi*, xxxiii, 488–9.
3. Stanford J. Shaw, 'Ottoman Empire', in John L. Esposito (ed.), *The Oxford Encyclopedia of the Modern Islamic World* (New York & Oxford, 1995), 269–76.
4. For European and other images of the Ottomans, see Suraiya Faroqhi, *The Ottoman Empire and World Around It* (London & New York, 2004), esp. 2 ff.
5. See Richard Knolles, *The General Historie of the Turks* (London, 1603), cited in Kemal H. Karpat (ed.), *Studies on Ottoman Social and Political History* (Leiden, 2002), 489. This often forced the raising of collections in Britain to pay ransom for their release. See Nabil Matar, *Islam in Britain, 1558–1685* (Cambridge, 1998), esp. 4–20.
6. See Daniel J. Vitkus, 'Early Modern Orientalism: Representations of Islam in Sixteenth-and Seventeenth-Century Europe', in Michael Frassetto and David R. Blanks (eds.), *Western Views of Islam in Medieval and Early Modern Europe: Perception of Other* (Houndmills & London, 1999), 207–30; and Asli Cirakman, *From the 'Terror of the World' to the 'Sick Man of Europe': European Images of the Ottoman Empire and Society from the Sixteenth Century to the Nineteenth* (New York, 2001), *passim*.
7. See Kemal H. Karpat, 'The Ottoman Rule in Europe: From the Perspective of 1994', in id., *Studies on Ottoman Social and Political History*, 477–80.
8. See S. G. Wilson, *Modern Movements Among Moslems* (New York, 1916), 219; M. Naeem Qureshi, *Pan-Islam in British India* (Karachi, 2009), 23; and Barbara Jelavich, *History of the Balkans*, ii (Cambridge, 1983), 79–81.
9. Quataert, *The Ottoman Empire, 1700–1922*, 37–8.

INTRODUCTION

10. See M. Şükrü Hanioğlu, 'Ittihat ve Terakki Cemiyeti', *Islam Ansiklopedisi*, xxiii, 476–84; and id., *Preparation for a Revolution: The Young Turks, 1902–1908* (Oxford, 2001). Also see Erik Jan Zürcher, 'Young Turks, Ottoman Muslims and Turkish Nationalists: Identity Politics, 1908–1938', in Kemal H. Karpat (ed.), *Ottoman Past and Today's Turkey* (Leiden, 2000), esp. 150–9.
11. See Metin Hülagü, *Islam Birliği ve Mustafa Kemal* (Istanbul, 2008), esp. 122–5.
12. The life and times of Mustafa Kemal form the subject of a plethora of literature in many languages. In English, the most cited works are: H. C. Armstrong, *Grey Wolf* (London, 1932); Lord Kinross, *Atatürk: The Birth of a Nation* (London, 1964); Enver Ziya Karal, 'The Principles of Kemalism', in Ali Kazancigil and Ergun Özbudun (eds.), *Atatürk: Founder of a Modern State* (London, 1981), 11–35; Dankwart A. Rustow, 'Atatürk as an Institution Builder', ibid., 57–77; Şerif Mardin, 'Religion and Secularism in Turkey', ibid., 191–219; Salahi Sonyel, *Atatürk—The Founder of Modern Turkey* (Ankara, 1989); Andrew Mango, *Atatürk* (London, 1999); Paul Dumon, 'The Origins of Kemalist Ideology', in Jacob M. Landau (ed.), *Atatürk and the Modernization of Turkey* (Boulder & Leiden, 1984), 25–44; and Şerafettin Turan, 'Mustafa Kemal Atatürk', *Islam Ansiklopedisi*, xxxi, 310–31. For Mustafa Kemal's view, specifically, about Islam, see Talip Küçükcan's contribution, 'Atatürk ve Din', in ibid., 337–9.
13. Dariush Zahedi and Gokhan Bacik, 'Kemalism Is Dead, Long Live Kemalism', in *Foreign Affairs*, 23 April 2010, at http://www.foreignaffairs.com/articles/66391/dariush-zahedi-and-gokhan-bacik/kemalism-is-dead-long-live-kemalism (Accessed: 21 May 2012).
14. Gwynne Dyer, 'The Young Turks', *Dawn*, 9 July 2008.
15. See Muhammad Shafique, *Islamic Concept of a Modern State* (Lahore, 1987), 58–64.
16. Ibid.
17. Ş. Tufan Buzpinar, 'The Question of Caliphate Under the Last Ottoman Sultans', in Itzchak Weismann and Fruma Zachs (eds.), *Ottoman Reform and Muslim Regeneration: Studies in Honour of Butrus Abu-Manneh* (London & New York, 2005), 17–21.
18. See Naeem Qureshi, *Pan-Islam in British India*, 1–58.
19. See Zürcher, 'Young Turks, Ottoman Muslims and Turkish Nationalists', esp. 172–9. Zürcher discounts the traditional 'Ottomanism-Islamism-Turkism paradigm' as part of the Young Turk policy. See 157.

1

Bibliographic Soundings in Nineteenth-Century Pan-Islam in South Asia*

Pan-Islam, or *ittihad-i Islam*, has been described in various forms but generally the term is understood to be of European coinage and was probably styled after the term 'pan-Slavism', which was current in the 1870s. It could, equally, have been the result of the impact of romantic nationalism upon the world of Islam. To some observers, it signified some kind of aggressive league of Muslims against the Christian West, while to others it was no more than a Utopia, having its origin partly in European encroachments on the *daru'l-Islam* and partly in Muslims' endeavours to reassert themselves under the common umbrella of Islam. The Muslims have interpreted 'pan-Islam' as a sacred and exalted passion for that ideal universal socio-political order under a common leadership which had been their cherished dream for centuries. Whatever its historic, semantic content may be, one thing is certain: the movement for pan-Islam tended to envisage some kind of a supranational *Pax-Islamica*, with the Ottoman caliphate as its rallying-point.

---

*Originally published as 'Bibliographic Soundings in Nineteenth Century Pan-Islam in South Asia', in the *Islamic Quarterly* (London), 24/1–2 (1980), 22–34.

The bibliographic problems emanating from the study of pan-Islam in South Asia are many: contemporary sources in the vernaculars are almost non-existent, and relevant literature in European languages is both scarce and scattered. Yet, with all the limitations, the present work endeavours to examine material that has any relevance to the main theme. The first use of the term 'pan-Islam', thus far discovered, is by Franz von Werner in *Turkische Skizzen*, published in 1877 but written before July 1876.[1] Later, in 1881, Gabriel Charmes borrowed the term for an article in the *Revue de deux Mondes*, and popularized it in various writings, especially, *L' Avenir de la Turquie: Le Pan-Islamisme* (Paris, 1883).[2] In Britain, the term was first used by Wilfred Scawen Blunt in an article written in 1881, which was published in the *Fortnightly Review* of January 1882.[3] Later that year, this five-part article was issued in book form, entitled *The Future of Islam*.[4] Among later works, *The Rise of Islam and the Caliphate: The Pan-Islamic Movement*,[5] an official handbook prepared under the direction of the historical section of the British Foreign Office, is a useful survey of the subject. However, a fuller explanation of the divergent theories about the origin and character of pan-Islam can be found in various articles by well-known writers like Carl H. Becker,[6] Edward G. Browne,[7] Arminius Vambéry,[8] Valentine Chirol,[9] A.R. Colquhoun,[10] Behdjet Wahby Bey,[11] H. Marchand,[12] Snouck C. Hurgronje,[13] D.S. Margoliouth,[14] Celal Nuri Bey,[15] Albrecht Wirth,[16] George Young,[17] Dwight E. Lee,[18] Jacob M. Landau,[19] Sharif al Mujahid,[20] Nikki R. Keddie,[21] and Majid Khadduri.[22] G.W. Bury's *Pan-Islam*[23] and H.A.R. Gibb's *Whither Islam?*,[24] are other useful explanations. Similarly, Shaikh Mushir Hosain Kidwai's *Pan-Islamism*[25] deals with the subject in its Indian environment, whereas X's (Sayyid Hasan Taqizade's 'Le panislamisme et le panturquisme',[26] and C.W. Hostler's *Turkism and the Soviets*,[27] have been written in the Central Asian context. Khushwant Singh's 'Pax Islamica (A Study of Pan-Islamic Movements)',[28] reflects a Marxist interpretation of pan-Islam: that it was the reaction of a decadent Muslim world against the encroachments of non-Muslims.

BIBLIOGRAPHIC SOUNDINGS

Until recently, the legend of Jamaluddin 'al-Afghani' as the originator of the pan-Islamic movement, had been widely accepted and sustained by, among others, Edward G. Browne in his *The Persian Revolution of 1905–1909*,[29] and in Blunt's *Secret History of the English Occupation of Egypt: Being a Personal Narrative of Events*.[30] The same view is to be found in Blunt's note on 'al-Afghani' in Browne's above-mentioned work.[31] Ignáz Goldziher's 'Djamal al-Din al-Afghani' in the *Encyclopaedia of Islam*,[32] Qazi Abdul Ghaffar's *Asar-i Jamalu'd-Din Afghani*,[33] and A. Hottinger's *The Arabs: Their History, Culture and Place in the Modern World*,[34] also perpetuate the myth. But recent works such as Niyazi Berkes' *The Development of Secularism in Turkey*,[35] Nikki R. Keddie's *An Islamic Response to Imperialism: Political and Religious Writings of Sayyid Jamal ad-Din al-Afghani*[36] and *Sayyid Jamal ad-Din "al-Afghan": A Political Biography*,[37] and Aziz Ahmad's *Islamic Modernism in India and Pakistan, 1857–1964*[38] and his scholarly contribution, 'Afghani's Indian Contacts',[39] have exploded the popular 'al-Afghani' myth, arguing that the pan-Islamic movement in India had developed long before 'al-Afghani' appeared effectively on the Indian scene.

Since pan-Islam revolves around the institution of the caliphate, the study of its religio-political import seems imperative. The sources on the caliphate may be classified into three sections: the first category consists of those writings which delineate the classical view of Muslim jurists like al-Mawardi and al-Ghazali. Generally, al-Mawardi's *Ihkam al-Sultaniyya*[40] is accepted as the most authoritative exposition of the Sunni theory of the caliphate. Among modern writings, H.A.R. Gibb's 'al-Mawardi's Theory of the Khilafat'[41] and 'Some Considerations on the Sunni Theory of the Caliphate',[42] are very good references. Al-Ghazali's views are scattered throughout his work but *Nasihat al-Muluk*, or *al-Tibr al-Masbuk*,[43] and *Ihya 'ulum al-din*,[44] are more significant. His political theory, however, finds better articulation in A.K.S. Lambton's 'The Theory of Kingship in the *Nasihat ul-Muluk* of Ghazali',[45] and Leonard Binder's 'al-Ghazali's Theory of Islamic Government'.[46] Haroon Khan

Sherwani's *Studies in the History of Early Muslim Political Thought and Administration*[47] and E.I.J. Rosenthal's *Political Thought in Medieval Islam*[48] are other useful discussions.

The second category of sources on the caliphate comprises works that were written not only with the intention of justifying the necessity of the institution in Islam, but also of supporting the Ottoman claim to the 'universal' caliphate. Among these, Abul Kalam Azad's scholarly treatise in Urdu, *Mas'ala-i Khilafat wa Jazira-i 'Arab*,[49] is essential reading. Similarly, Ameer Ali's 'The Caliphate, a Historical and Juridical Sketch',[50] is an excellent exposé of the Ottoman claim to the caliphate. Other comprehensive discussions on the subject include Shah Abdul Hayy's *al-Khilafah*,[51] Abul Hasanat Nadwi's *Khilafat-i 'Usmaniyya aur Turk*,[52] Sayyid Sulaiman Nadwi's 'Khilafat and the Koreish',[53] Maulawi Muhammad Talha's *Mas'ala-i Khilafat aur ahkam-i shari'yyat*,[54] Malik Muhammad Tufail's *al-Khilafat*,[55] Mufti Muhammad Habibur Rahman Qadiri's *Ayat-i Khilafat*,[56] Muhammad Ali's *The Khilafat in Islam*,[57] Muhammad Iqbal's *Khilafat-i Islamiyya*,[58] and Mohammad Barakatullah's *The Khilafet*.[59] More recently, the subject has been exhaustively dealt with in Abul-Ala Maududi's commendable work *Khilafat wa Mulukiyyat*.[60] The Shi'a point of view is represented in Shamsu'l-'Ulama Allama Hairi's *Khilafat-i Qur'ani*,[61] Sayyid Nasim Hasan's *Istikhlaf*,[62] and Sayyid Najmul Hasan's *al-Nabuwwat wa'l-Khilafat*.[63]

The third category includes the works of western Orientalists who have discussed the subject from their own particular angle, either to support the Ottoman pretensions to the caliphate or to oppose them. In fact, the story about the transfer of the caliphate from the Cairene Abbasid al-Mutawakkil to the Ottoman Salem I originated with a western source; otherwise, no contemporary Ottoman or Arab chronicler except, perhaps, Ibn Iyas[64] even refers to the event. The first mention of the transfer episode, according to G.W.F. Stripling's *The Ottoman Turks and the Arabs, 1511–1574*,[65] was made by Fabricius and Rosinus in the late seventeenth century. Later, Mouradgea d'Ohsson in his monumental work *Tableau général de l'Empire Othoman*,[66] enunciated a similar story. D'Ohsson's authority was accepted blindly by F.A. von Kremer,[67] G. Weil,[68] and August Müller,[69] without even attempting to test the validity of his assertion. But Carl H. Becker[70] and Wilhelm Barthold[71] vigorously refuted d'Ohsson's story, as did T.W. Arnold later in his 'Khalifa' in the *Encyclopaedia of Islam*[72] and, more particularly, in *The Caliphate*.[73] C.A. Nallino's *Appunti sulla natura del 'Califfato' in genere e sul presento 'Califfato Ottomano'*,[74] later issued in 1919 by the Italian Foreign Office for propaganda against the Ottomans, is another useful source on the thinking of the European Orientalists. Stanley Lane-Poole's 'The Caliphate',[75] A.H. Lybyer's 'Caliphate',[76] D.S. Margoliouth's *The Caliphate, Yesterday, Today and Tomorrow*,[77] and F.A. von Kremer's *Culturgeschichte des Orients unter den Chalifen*,[78] are other important references. A very good account of the sultan's claim can be found in D.B. MacDonald's *Development of Muslim Theology, Jurisprudence, and Constitutional Theory*.[79] Incidentally, the Turkish point of view, in retrospect, is well represented in N. Ahmet Asrar's *The Myth About the Transfer of the Caliphate to the Ottomans*,[80] wherein he denies that the caliphate was ever transferred to the Ottomans.

The historical perspective about pan-Islam in South Asia can be gleaned from a number of sources. Four excellent works, two by Pakistani historians and two by Muslim scholars of India, are indispensable to an understanding of the different ways in which Muslim history in the Indian subcontinent has been viewed. Aziz Ahmad's *Studies in Islamic Culture in the Indian Environment*,[81] and Ishtiaq Husain Qureshi's *The Muslim Community of the Indo-Pakistan Subcontinent, 610–1947*,[82] furnish different interpretations than do either Muhammad Mujeeb in *The Indian Muslims*[83] or S. Abid Husain in *The National Culture of India*.[84] The latter's *The Destiny of Indian Muslims*,[85] is no less important. Dr K.M. Karim's 'Pakistan's Historical and Cultural Ties with Iran and Turkey through the Ages',[86] as the title suggests, is a useful piece for the early contacts between India and Turkey. Aziz Ahmad's above-mentioned work[87] is an excellent review of relations between the sultans of Delhi and the caliphate in Baghdad. Sidi Ali Reis Effendi's *Mir'at al-Mumalik*[88] is an important contemporary source which throws light on the Ottoman impact on sixteenth-century Gujarat and parts of the Deccan. Banarsi Prasad Saksena's *History of Shahjahan of Dihli*[89] deals with the Ottoman relations with the Mughals.

Another good source is Hammer-Purgstall's 'Memoir on the Diplomatic relations between the Courts of Delhi and Constantinople in the Sixteenth and Seventeenth Centuries'.[90] Abdur Rahim's 'Mughal Diplomacy: Akbar–Aurangzeb',[91] is the best modern account based on Persian and Turkish sources. Bernard Lewis's 'The Mughals and the Ottomans'[92] is a tidy but brief account of the Mughal-Ottoman relations. Iftikhar Ahmad Ghauri's 'The Sunni Theory of Caliphate and its Impact on the Muslim History of India'[93] is another good contribution. Tipu Sultan's efforts to establish friendly relations with the Ottomans is the subject under study in Y. Hikmet Bayur's 'Maysor Sultani Tipu ile Osmanlı Padşahlarindan I Abdul Hamid ve III Selim arasindaki Mektuplasma',[94] and in I.H. Qureshi's 'The Purpose of Tipu Sultan's Embassy to Constantinople',[95] and M.H. Khan's *History of Tipu Sultan*.[96] Similarly, [R.] M. Martin's edited work, *The Despatches, Minutes, and Correspondence of the Marquess Wellesley, K.G., During his Administration in India*,[97] shows how the British utilized Tipu's known reverence for the Ottoman caliph to their own advantage in India.

These early contacts with the Ottomans gradually paved the way for deeper Indian Muslim involvement with the caliphate at Istanbul—then known as Kostantiniyye, an adaptation from Constantinople. But its impact did not crystallize until the early nineteenth century when the Mughal central authority in India had weakened beyond hope. The breakdown of traditional society, under pressure of the British conquest, encouraged and strengthened the pan-Islamic orientation of the Indian Muslims. Though Abul Kalam Azad[98] has argued that Shah Waliullah had tacitly accepted the Ottoman caliphate during the eighteenth century, on the basis of the latter's *Tafhimat-i Ilahiya*,[99] it was in the wake of Shah Abdul-Aziz's famous *fatwa* (1803) declaring India under the British *daru'l-harb*[100] that one looks at the pro-Ottoman attitude of the Indo-Muslim orthodoxy. Ubaidullah Sindhi's *Shah Waliu'llah aur unki siyasi tahrik*[101] and Aziz Ahmad's *Islamic Modernism in India and Pakistan*[102] are particularly valuable in this respect, especially with regard to Shah Muhammad Ishaq who was the first Indian *'alim* to migrate to Mecca in 1841 and support the Ottoman political policies.

It is, however, Syed Ahmed Khan's 'Khutba men Badshah ka nam',[103] that reveals, for the first time, how the Ottoman sultans came to be regarded as caliphs in Muslim India during the twilight of the Mughal rule. His testimony falsifies the commonly held notions of western writers such as F.W. Buckler[104] and George Birdwood,[105] that Indian interest in the Ottoman caliphate was a post-1857 phenomenon. Nonetheless, Lord William Bentinck's papers in the Portland Collection at Nottingham University contain the earliest contemporary reference to the presence of a general sympathy among the Indian Muslims for the Ottomans, around the 1820s. A selection from Bentinck's papers has been edited by C.H. Philips as *The Correspondence of Lord William Cavendish Bentinck, Governor-General of India, 1825–1835*.[106] I.H. Qureshi's 'Two Newspapers of Pre-Mutiny Delhi',[107] has similar references for 1844. The correspondence of the Marquess of Dalhousie, edited by J.G.A. Baird as *Private Letters of the Marquess of Dalhousie*,[108] points towards Indian Muslim sympathy for the Ottomans during the 1850s. J.W. Redhouse's *A Vindication of the Ottoman Sultan's Title of 'Caliph': Shewing its Antiquity, Validity, and Universal Acceptance*[109] is another extremely important source. George Birdwood's above-mentioned communication to *The Times*[110] of London suggests that, from the time of the Crimean War in 1854, the British had themselves begun to bolster Turkey in the eyes of the Indian Muslims for reasons of political expediency. In fact, Anglo-Russian rivalry in the Near East and Central Asia during the latter half of the nineteenth-century was an important factor in the development of pan-Islam and can be followed in the British Foreign Office Files Series 65 and 78 at the National Archives in London,[111] Benedict H. Sumner's *Russia and the Balkans, 1870–1880*,[112] L.E. Frechtling's 'Anglo-Russian Rivalry in Eastern Turkistan, 1863–1881',[113] and M. Anwar Khan's *England, Russia and Central Asia (A Study in Diplomacy), 1857–1878*.[114] Other good references are W.E. Baxter's *England and Russia in Asia*,[115] D.C. Boulger's *England and Russia in Central Asia*,[116] and M.A. Terentyef's *Russia and England in Central Asia*.[117] Mustafa Kamil Paşa's *Mas'ala-i Sharqiyya*,[118] Sayyid Sulaiman Nadwi's *Khilafat aur Hindustan*,[119] and Syed Mahmud's *Khilafat aur Inglistan*[120] bear ample testimony to the fact that the British used the Ottoman sultan's influence with the Indian Muslims to their advantage during the fateful crisis of 1857. Rahman Ali's *Tazkira-i 'ulama-i Hind*,[121] Mufti Intizamullah Shahabi's *Ist Indiya kampni aur baghi 'ulama*,[122] and Muhammad Miyan's *'Ulama-i Haq*,[123] and *'Ulama-i Hind ka shandar mazi*[124] are other good references about the *ulama* who migrated to Ottoman Arabia in the aftermath of the Revolt of 1857, though only Rahmatullah Kairanwi actually made any direct contact with Istanbul.

The extent of the western encroachments on the *daru'l-Islam*, which was largely responsible for heightening the pan-Islamic fervour in India, has been well brought out by S.G. Wilson, in a detailed chronological table in his *Modern Movements Among Muslims*.[125] M.A. Anderson's *The Eastern Question, 1774–1923*[126] is the best outline on the subject though J.A.R. Marriot's *The Eastern Question*,[127] Allan Cunningham's 'The Wrong Horse?—A Study of Anglo-Turkish Relations Before the First World War',[128] Uriel Heyd's 'The Later Ottoman Empire in Rumelia and Anatolia',[129] and P.M. Holt's 'The Later Ottoman Empire in Egypt and the Fertile Crescent',[130] in *The Cambridge History of Islam*, also have good references. Another factor in the spread of pan-Islam was the general European hostility towards Islam, treating it as a world religion in continuous confrontation with Christendom. L. Stoddard's *The New World of Islam*[131] deals with the reaction of Christian missionaries to the spread of Islam in Asia, Africa, and the Balkans, whereas P. Hardy's *The Muslims of British India*[132] outlines the typical examples of European scholasticism against that religion. George Birdwood's[133] and G.P. Badger's[134] communications to *The Times*, and the latter's 'Precedents and Usages Regulating the Muslim Khalifate',[135] as well as the Parliamentary Debates in *Hansard* of 1877,[136] and J.W. Redhouse's already-mentioned valuable work,[137] point to the controversy that raged in Britain over the Ottoman title to the caliphate. The same controversy was revived in the 1890s with even greater ferocity; Typical examples are Malcolm MacColl's 'The Musalmans of India and the Sultan'[138] and H.A. Salmone's 'Is the Sultan of Turkey the True Caliph of Islam?'.[139]

The cumulative effect of the various contributory factors was that by the early 1870s, the pan-Islamic movement in India was fairly well-rooted and the sultan's pretensions to the 'universal' caliphate were widely accepted. The progressive Indian Muslim involvement with Ottoman Turkey, during the latter half of the nineteenth century, is faithfully reflected in contemporary writings and private papers. Syed Ahmed Khan's contributions to the *Tahzibu'l-Akhlaq*[140] provide valuable information. Some of the more important articles were later collected and published as *Akhiri Mazamin*.[141] A further selection of his views on the caliphate was rendered into English by Kazi Siraj-ud-din as *The Truth About the Khilafat*.[142] But, a more comprehensive collection of Syed Ahmed Khan's works was edited by Ismail Panipati as *Maqalat-i sar Sayyid*[143] in sixteen volumes. Another important source on Syed Ahmed Khan, vis-a-vis the Ottomans, is Aziz Ahmad's 'Sayyid Ahmad Khan, Jamal al-Din al-Afghani and Muslim India'.[144] Cheragh Ali's *The Proposed Political, Legal and Social Reforms in the Ottoman Empire and Other Mohammedan States*,[145] which was dedicated to *'amiru'l-mu'minin'* Sultan-Caliph Abdülhamid II, indicates the trend of opinion among the educated groups of Indian Muslims. Garcin de Tassy's *La Langue et la litterature hindoustanies en 1871*,[146] and W.S. Blunt's *India Under Ripon*,[147] written after his visit to India during the winter of 1883–4, have some important references about the growing pan-Islamic feeling among Indian Muslims. Altaf Husain Hali's *Madd-o Jazr-i Islam*, known as *Musaddas-i Hali*,[148] expresses the Indian Muslims' nostalgia for Islam's past glory and power. The Lytton Papers,[149] at the British Library's Oriental and India Office Collections in London, are yet another important source for the study of the development of pan-Islam in the Indian subcontinent. They also indicate how vehemently pro-Turk the Indian Muslims were at the time of the Russo-Turkish War of 1877. Contemporary journals, such as the *Qaisaru'l-Akhbar Hind* (Allahabad)[150] and *Ahsanu'l-Akhbar* (Allahabad),[151] confirm this trend. S.R. Mehrotra's *The Emergence of the Indian National Congress*[152] is important as a reference concerning Hindu sympathy for the Muslims during the 1877–78 crisis.

An important feature of the pan-Islamic movement in South Asia was that it ran parallel to similar waves of pan-Islamic fervour among Muslims in other parts of the globe. S.A. Zenkovsky's *Pan-Turkism and Islam in Russia*[153] describes the movement in Central Asia, while

BIBLIOGRAPHIC SOUNDINGS

Anthony Reid's commendable article, 'Nineteenth Century Pan-Islam in Indonesia and Malaysia',[154] provides a valuable account with reference to South-East Asia. Within the Ottoman Empire itself, the pan-Islamic movement was sustained by the Young Ottomans though Halil Inalcik's 'The Rise of the Ottoman Empire',[155] finds its roots in the Ottoman treaties with the Persians (1727) and the Russians (1774). Werner Caskel's 'Western Impact and Islamic Civilisation',[156] Bernard Lewis's *The Middle East and the West*,[157] and 'The Ottoman Empire in the Mid-Nineteenth Century: A Review',[158] as well as Niyazi Berkes's *The Development of Secularism in Turkey*,[159] give ample information on the efforts of the Ottoman pan-Islamic ideologues, especially Namik Kemal. The same movement was carried to its perfection by Sultan Abdülhamid II, who sent his emissaries far and wide to push his claim to the ecumenical authority. The subject has been referred to by Edwin Pears in *Life of Abdul Hamid*,[160] A.J. Toynbee in his *Survey of International Affairs, 1925*,[161] Arminius Vambéry in his 'Pan-Islamism and the Sultan of Turkey',[162] and Hans Kohn in *A History of Nationalism in the East*.[163] Additional information in relation to internal discontent and external (western) intervention in Ottoman affairs, has been provided by Ahmed Emin in his *Turkey in the World War*.[164] A further reference to internal compulsions is contained in Constantine K. Zurayk's 'The National and International Politics of the Arab States'.[165] J. Holland Rose's '1815 and 1915'[166] and W.W. Cash's *The Moslem World in Revolution*[167] show how the Germans under Kaiser Wilhelm II, like their British rivals, actively encouraged the pan-Islamic orientation during the 1890s in order to advance their own economic and political interests.

Another important aspect is that in South Asia pan-Islam had created such a consciousness of affinity that, combined with other factors such as the anti-Turkish policies of the British, it led to serious unrest, especially on British India's north-west frontier. G.R.G.

Hambly's 'Unrest in Northern India during the Viceroyalty of Lord Mayo, 1869–72'[168] and J.R.M. McLane's *Indian Nationalism and the Early Congress*[169] have some good references on the subject. W.G. Palgrave's *Essays on Eastern Question*[170] discusses 'the Mahometan "Revival"' in the backwash of the Eastern Question. A memorandum on the pan-Islamic movement, in the Political and Secret Letters and Enclosures Received from India series in the Oriental and India Office Collections,[171] gives some valuable inside information from official agencies. Syed Ahmed Khan's *Akhirii Mazamin*[172] is another good contemporary source. Mirza Ghulam Ahmad's *Gornamint angrezi aur jihad*[173] suggests that many *ulama* were actively disaffected towards the British rule in India. Shibli Nomani's *Maqalat*[174] is important for his pan-Islamic progression while his *Safarnama-i Rum-o Sham*[175] throws light on his activities in Istanbul. Some Indian newspapers of the 1890s, such as *Akhbar-i 'Am* (Lahore),[176] the *Paisa Akhbar* (Lahore),[177] the *Sada'-i Hind* (Lahore),[178] and the *Rahbar-i Hind* (Lahore),[179] faithfully reflected these feelings. Fazlur Rahman's 'Internal Religious Developments in the Present Century Islam'[180] refers to Muslim reaction to Christian missionary activity. P. Hardy's already-mentioned work[181] analyses the reaction among educated Indian Muslims, like Syed Ameer Ali, Shibli Nomani, and Abdul Halim Sharar, who glorified and defended Islam. Arminius Vambéry's *Western Culture in Eastern Lands*[182] shows how, in 1886, the Muslims in London founded a pan-Islamic society called the Anjuman-i Islam for safeguarding Islamic interests. Qeyamuddin Ahmad's *The Wahabi Movement in India*[183] deals more extensively with the religio-political developments in India than Hambly's above-mentioned article.[184] Ghulam Rasul Mihr's *Jama'at-i Mujahidin*,[185] *Sarguzasht-i Mujahidin*,[186] and *Sayyid Ahmad Shahid*[187] are also valuable sources.

The apprehensions of the collaborating Indians, that the anti-British and pro-Turkish fervour of their co-religionists might actually harm their interests instead of helping the Turks, is apparent from a number of writings. For instance, Karamat Ali Jounpuri's argument that British India was *daru'l-Islam* and, therefore, *jihad* was unlawful is evident from the *Abstract of the Proceedings of the Mahomedan Literary Society of Calcutta: Lecture by Moulvie Karamat Ali (of Jounpore) on a Question of Mahomedan Law Involving the Duty of Mahomedans in British India towards the Ruling Power*.[188] Syed Ahmed Khan's *Review on Dr Hunter's Indian Musalmans: Are They Bound in Conscience to Rebel against the Queen?*[189] and *Akhiri Mazamin*[190] follow Jounpuri in preaching loyalty to the British by maintaining that the Ottoman sultan was not the caliph of the Indian Muslims. Cheragh Ali's already-mentioned panacea for reforms,[191] and *A Critical Exposition of Popular Jihad*,[192] try to justify a compromise with the British rulers. Rafiuddin Ahmad's 'A Moslem's View of Pan-Islamic Revival'[193] and 'Is the British "Raj" in Danger?'[194] point towards his efforts to convince the British rulers of India that pan-Islam was not dangerous. Mirza Ghulam Ahmad's above-mentioned work [195] contains a list of some forty works that had been written to prove that *jihad* against the British was unlawful.

Such opposition to the Ottoman pretensions, however, did not have much effect on the thinking of the Indians at large, whose pan-Islamic enthusiasm kept pace with the mounting intensity of the European thrusts against the Ottoman Empire. Internal political developments following readjustments with the British rulers and the Hindu compatriots, and the consequent growth of Muslim separatism, were other contributory factors. In fact, it was the interplay of these factors which turned pan-Islam into proto-nationalism by the dawn of the twentieth century. The Khilafat movement of the 1920s, and the pattern of politics that emerged in its wake, were expressions of the continuation of nineteenth century pan-Islam.

NOTES

1. Franz von Werner (Murad Effendi, pseud.), *Turkische Skizzen* (Leipzig, 1877).
2. See A.R. Colquhoun, 'Pan-Islam', *North American Review* (Boston), 182/6 (1906), 906–18.
3. W.S. Blunt, 'The Future of Islam', *Fortnightly Review*, 30 (Aug.–Nov.1881), 204–23, 315–32, 441–58 and 585–602; and 31 (Jan. 1882), 32–48.
4. Id., *The Future of Islam* (London, 1882).
5. *The Rise of Islam and the Caliphate. The Pan-Islamic Movement* in OIOC, Political and Secret Department Library Series.
6. Carl H. Becker, 'Panislamismus', *Archiv fur Religionswissenschaft* (Leipzig), 7 (1904), 169–92.
7. Edward G. Browne, 'Pan-Islamism', in F.A. Kirkpatrick (ed.), *Lectures on the History of the Nineteenth Century* (Cambridge, 1904), 306–30.
8. Arminius Vambéry, 'Pan-Islamism', *Nineteenth Century and After*, 60 (July—Dec. 1906), 547–58; and 61 (Jan.—June 1907), 860–72.
9. Valentine Chirol, 'Pan-Islamism', *Proceedings of the Central Asian Society* (London), 14 November 1906, 1–28.
10. A.R. Colquhoun, 'Pan-Islam', *North American Review* (Boston), 182/6 (1906), 906–18.
11. Behdjet Wahby Bey, 'Pan-Islamism', *Nineteenth Century and After*, 61/363 (1907), 860–72.
12. H. Marchand, 'Un coup d'oeil sur l'Islam: Panislamisme et modernisme', *Renseignemens coloniaux et Documents* (Paris), suppl. *L'Afrique Française* (1909), 146–52.
13. Snouck C. Hurgronje, 'Over Panislamisme', *Archives du Musée Teyler* (Haarlem), 3rd Sér. i (1912), 87–105.
14. D.S. Margoliouth, 'The Caliphate, Yesterday, Today and Tomorrow', in J.R. Mott (ed.), *The Moslem World of To-day* (London, 1925), 31–44.
15. Celal Nuri Bey, *Ittihad-i Islam* (Istanbul, 1912).
16. Albrecht Wirth, 'Panislamismus', *Deutsche Rundschau* (Berlin), 163 (1915), 429–40.
17. George Young, 'Pan-Islamism', *Encyclopaedia of the Social Sciences*, 11 (1935), 542–4.
18. Dwight E. Lee, 'The Origins of Pan-Islamism', *American Historical Review* (Washington DC), 47/2 (1942), 278–87.
19. Jacob M. Landau, 'al-Afghani's Pan-Islamic Project', *Islamic Culture* (Hyderabad), 26/3 (1952), 50–4.
20. Sharif al Mujahid, 'Pan-Islamism', *A History of the Freedom Movement*, iii, Part i, Pakistan Historical Society (Karachi, 1961), 88–117.

21. Nikki R. Keddie, 'Pan-Islamism as Proto-Nationalism', *Journal of Modern History* (Chicago), 41/1 (1969), 17–28.
22. Majid Khadduri, 'Pan-Islamism', *Encyclopaedia Britannica*, xvii (Chicago, 1966), 227–8.
23. G. Wuman Bury, *Pan-Islam* (London, 1919).
24. H.A.R. Gibb (ed.), *Whither Islam?* (London, 1932).
25. Shaikh Mushir Hosain Kidwai (of Gadia), *Pan-Islamism* (London, 1908).
26. 'X' (Sayyid Hasan Taqizadeh), 'Le panislamisme et le panturqisme', *Revue du Monde Musulman*, 22 (1913), 179–220.
27. C.W. Hostler, *Turkism and the Soviets: The Turks of the World and their Political Objectives* (London, 1957).
28. Khushwant Singh, 'Pax Islamica (A Study of Pan-Islamic Movements)', *Journal of the Punjab University Historical Society* (Lahore), 9 (Apr. 1946), 27–42.
29. Edward G. Browne, *The Persian Revolution of 1905–1909* (Cambridge, 1910).
30. W.S. Blunt, *Secret History of the English Occupation of Egypt: being a personal narrative of events, Part II, India* (London, 1907).
31. Blunt in Browne, *Secret History of the English Occupation of Egypt*.
32. Ignaz Goldziher, 'Djamal al-Din al-Afghani', *Encyclopaedia of Islam* (1913), 1008–11.
33. Qazi Muhammad Abdul Ghaffar, *Asar-i Jamalu'd-Din Afghani* (Delhi, 1940).
34. Arnold Hottinger, *The Arabs: Their History, Culture and Place in the Modern World* (London, 1963).
35. Niyazi Berkes, *The Development of Secularism in Turkey* (Montreal, 1964).
36. Nikki R. Keddie, *An Islamic Response to Imperialism: Political and Religious Writings of Sayyid Jamal ad-Din "al-Afghani"* (Berkeley & Los Angeles, 1968).
37. Id., *Sayyid Jamal ad-Din "al-Afghani": A Political Biography* (Los Angeles, 1972).
38. Aziz Ahmad, *Islamic Modernism in India and Pakistan, 1857–1964* (London, 1967).
39. Id., 'Afghani's Indian Contacts', *Journal of the American Oriental Society* (Boston), 89/3 (1969), 476–504.
40. Ali ibn Muhammad al-Mawardi, *Ihkam al-Sultaniyya* (Cairo, 1881).
41. H.A.R. Gibb, 'al-Mawardi's Theory of the Khilafat', *Islamic Culture*, 11/3 (1937), 291–302.
42. Id., 'Some Considerations on the Sunni Theory of the Caliphate', *Archives d'historie du droit oriental* (Wetteren-Paris), 3 (1984), 401–10.
43. Abu Hamid Muhammad Al Ghazali, *Nasihat al-Muluk*. Arabic tr. *al-Tibr al-Masbuk* Eng. tr. F.R.C. Bagley, *Ghazali's Book of Counsel for Kings* (London, 1964).

44. Id., *Ihya 'ulum al-din*. Fr. tr. G.H. Bousquet (Paris, 1953). Ger. tr. H. Kindermann, (Leiden, 1962).
45. A.K.S. Lambton, 'The Theory of Kingship in the *Nasihat-ul-Muluk* of Ghazali', *Islamic Quarterly*, 1/1 (1954), 47–55.
46. Leonard Binder, 'al-Ghazali's Theory of Islamic Government', *Moslem World*, 45/3, (1955), 229–41.
47. Haroon Khan Sherwani, *Studies in the History of Early Muslim Political Thought and Administration* (Lahore, 1942).
48. Edwin I.J. Rosenthal, *Political Thought in Medieval Islam* (Cambridge, 1958).
49. Abul Kalam Azad, *Mas'ala-i Khilafat wa Jazira-i 'Arab* (Calcutta, 1920).
50. Ameer Ali, 'The Caliphate, a Historical and Juridical Sketch', *Contemporary Review* (London), 107/594 (1915), 681–94.
51. Shah Abdul Hayy, *al-Khilafah* (Delhi, 1909).
52. Abul Hasanat Nadwi, *Khilafat-i 'Usmaniyya aur Turk* (Delhi, 1920).
53. Sayyid Sulaiman Nadwi, 'Khilafat and the Koreish', *Foreign Affairs* (London), 2 (July 1920), Special Supplement, vi–ix.
54. Maulawi Muhammad Talha, *Mas'ala-i Khilafat aur ahkam-i shari'yyat* (Lucknow, 1922).
55. Malik Muhammad Tufail, *al-Khilafat* (Amritsar, 1920).
56. Mufti Muhammad Habibur Rahman Qadiri, *Ayat-i Khilafat* (Badaun, 1922).
57. (Maulawi) Muhammad Ali, *The Khilafat in Islam* (Lahore, 1920).
58. Muhammad Iqbal, *Khilafat-i Islamiyya*. Urdu tr. Choudhry Muhammad Husain (Lahore, 1923).
59. Mohammad Barakatullah (maulavie), *The Khilafet* (London, 1924).
60. Abul-Ala Maududi, *Khilafat wa Mulukiyyat* (Lahore, 1966).
61. Shamsu'l-'Ulama Allama Hairi, *Khilafat-i Qur'ani* (Lahore, 1927).
62. Sayyid Nasim Hasan, *Istikhlaf* (Amroha, 1919).
63. Sayyid Najmul Hasan, *al-Nabuwwat wa'l-Khilafat*. Eng. tr. L.A. Haidari (Lucknow, 1924).
64. Ibn Iyas, *Bada-i al-Zahur fi waqa'-i al-duhur* (Boulak, 1893–95). Eng. tr. W.H. Salmon, *An Account of the Ottoman Conquest of Egypt in the Year A.H. 922 (A.D. 1516)* (London, 1921).
65. G.W.F. Stripling, *The Ottoman Turks and the Arabs, 1511–1574*, iii (Urbana, 1942).
66. Mouradgea d'Ohsson, *Tableau général de l'Empire Othoman* (Paris, 1778).
67. F.A. von Kremer, *Geschichte der Herrschenden Ideen des Islams* (Leipzig, 1868).
68. G. Weil, *Geschichte des Abbasidenchalifats in Egypten*, ii (Stuttgart, 1860).
69. August Müller, *Der Islam* (Berlin, 1885–87).

70. Carl H. Becker, 'Panislamismus', *Archiv fur Religionswissenschaft* (Leipzig), 7 (1904), 169–92.
71. Wilhelm Barthold, 'Khalif i Sultan', *Mir Islama* (St Petersburg), i (1912), 202–26 and 345–400.
72. T.W. Arnold, 'Khalifa', *Encyclopaedia of Islam*, ii (Leiden, 1927), 881–5.
73. Id., *The Caliphate* (Oxford, 1924).
74. C.A. Nallino, *Appunti sulla natura del 'Califfato' in genere e sul presento 'Califfato Ottomano'* (Rome, 1916). Eng. tr. *Notes on the Nature of the 'Caliphate' in general and on the Alleged 'Ottoman Caliphate'* (Rome, 1919).
75. Stanley Lane-Poole, 'The Caliphate', *Quarterly Review*, 224/444 (1915), 162–77.
76. A.H. Lybyer, 'Caliphate', *Encyclopaedia of the Social Sciences*, iii (New York, 1935), 145–49.
77. D.S. Margoliouth, 'The Caliphate, Yesterday, Today and Tomorrow', in J.R. Mott (ed.), *The Moslem World of To-day* (London, 1925), 31–44.
78. F.A. von Kremer, *Culturgeschichte des Orients unter den Chalifen* i–ii (Vienna, 1875–77). Eng. tr. S. Khuda Bukhsh, *The Orient under the Caliphs* (Calcutta, 1920).
79. D.B. MacDonald, *Development of Muslim Theology, Jurisprudence, and Constitutional Theory* (New York, 1903).
80. N. Ahmet Asrar, 'The Myth about the Transfer of the Caliphate to the Ottomans', *Journal of the Regional Cultural Institute* (Tehran), 5/2–3 (1972), 111–20.
81. Aziz Ahmad, *Studies in Islamic Culture in the Indian Environment* (Oxford, 1964).
82. Ishtiaq Husain Qureshi, *The Muslim Community of the Indo-Pakistan Subcontinent (610–1947)* (The Hague, 1962).
83. Muhammad Mujeeb, *The Indian Muslims* (London, 1967).
84. S. Abid Husain, *The National Culture of India* (Bombay, 1956).
85. Id., *The Destiny of Indian Muslims* (London, 1965).
86. K.M. Karim, 'Pakistan's Historical and Cultural Ties with Iran and Turkey Through the Ages', *Journal of the Regional Cultural Institute* (Tehran), 2/2 (1969), 91–5.
87. See n. 81 above.
88. Sidi Ali Reis Effendi, *Mir'at al-Mumalik* (ed.), Jevdet (Istanbul, 1895). Eng. tr. A. Vambéry (London, 1899).
89. Banarsi Prasad Saksena, *History of Shahjahan of Dihli* (Allahabad, 1932).
90. Freiherr von Joseph, Hammer-Purgstall, 'Memoir on the Diplomatic relations between the Courts of Delhi and Constantinople in the Sixteenth and

Seventeenth Centuries', *Transactions of the Royal Asiatic Society*, 2 (London, 1830).
91. Abdur Rahim, 'Mughal Diplomacy: Akbar–Aurangzeb', unpublished Ph.D. thesis (London University, 1932).
92. Bernard Lewis, 'The Mughals and the Ottomans', *Pakistan Quarterly* (Karachi), 3/2 (1958).
93. I.A. Ghauri, 'The Sunni Theory of Caliphate and its Impact on the Muslim History of India', *Journal of the Punjab University Historical Society*, 13 (Dec. 1961), 93–9.
94. Y. Hikmet Bayur, 'Maysor Sultani Tipu ile Osmanlı Padşahlarindan I Abdul Hamid ve III Selim arasindaki Mektuplasma', *Belleten*, 47 (1948), 619–54.
95. I.H. Qureshi, 'The Purpose of Tipu Sultan's Embassy to Constantinople', *Journal of Indian History*, 24 (1945), 77–84.
96. M.H. Khan, *History of Tipu Sultan* (Calcutta, 1951).
97. [R.] M. Martin (ed.), *The Despatches, Minutes, and Correspondence of the Marquess Wellesley, K.G., During his Administration in India*, i–v (London, 1836–7).
98. Abul Kalam Azad, *Mas'ala-i Khilafat wa Jazira-i 'Arab* (Calcutta, 1920). Aziz Ahmad, however, disagrees with Azad's contention. See his 'An Eighteenth-Century Theory of Caliphate', *Studia Islamica* (Paris), 28 (1968), 135–44.
99. Shah Waliullah, *Tafhimat-i Ilahiyya* (Delhi, 1906).
100. Shah Abdul Aziz, *Fatawa-i 'Aziziyya* (Delhi, 1904).
101. Ubaidullah Sindhi, *Shah Waliu'llah aur unki siyasi tahrik* (Lahore, 1952).
102. Aziz Ahmad, *Islamic Modernism in India and Pakistan, 1857–1964*, esp. 123.
103. Sir Syed Ahmed Khan, 'Khutba men Badshah ka nam', *Tahzibu'l-Akhlaq* (Aligarh), 7/11 (1876), 154–5.
104. F.W. Buckler, 'The Historical Antecedents of the Khilafat Movement', *Contemporary Review*, 121/677 (1922), 603–11.
105. *The Times* (London), 12 June 1877.
106. C.H. Philips (ed.), *The Correspondence of Lord William Cavendish Bentinck, Governor-General of India, 1825–1835*, i–ii (Oxford, 1977).
107. I.H. Qureshi, 'Two Newspapers of Pre-Mutiny Delhi', *Indian Historical Records Commission Proceedings of Meetings, XVIII, (Eighteenth Meeting Held at Mysore, January 1942)* (Delhi, 1942), 258–60.
108. J.G.A. Baird (ed.), *Private Letters of the Marquess of Dalhousie* (London, 1910).
109. J.W. Redhouse, *A Vindication of the Ottoman Sultan's Title of 'Caliph', Shewing Its Antiquity, Validity, and Universal Acceptance* (London, 1877).
110. *The Times*, 12 June 1877.

BIBLIOGRAPHIC SOUNDINGS

111. National Archives (London), Foreign Office Files, Series 65 (Russia) and 78 (Turkey).
112. Benedict H. Sumner, *Russia and the Balkans, 1870–1880* (Oxford, 1937).
113. L.E. Frechtling, 'Anglo-Russian Rivalry in Eastern Turkistan, 1863–1881', *Journal of the Royal Central Asian Society* (London), 26/3 (1939), 471–98.
114. M. Anwar Khan, *England, Russia and Central Asia (A Study in Diplomacy), 1857–1878* (Peshawar, 1963).
115. W.E. Baxter, *England and Russia in Asia* (London, 1885).
116. Demetrius Charles Boulger, *England and Russia in Central Asia*, i–ii (London, 1879).
117. M.A. Terentyef, *Russia and England in Central Asia*. Eng. tr. F.C. Daukes (Calcutta, 1876).
118. Mustafa Kamil Paşa, *Mas'ala-i sharqiyya* (Cairo, 1898). Urdu tr. (from Arabic) Maulana Niaz Muhammad Khan Niaz Fatehpuri (Pindi Bahawuddin, n.d.).
119. Sayyid Sulaiman Nadwi, *Khilafat aur Hindustan* (Azamgarh: Nadwah, 1921).
120. Syed Mahmud Sahib, *Khilafat aur Inglistan*, 3rd edn. (Patna, 1921).
121. Rahman Ali, *Tazkira-i 'ulama-i Hind* (Lucknow, 1914). Urdu tr. Muhammad Ayub Qadiri (Karachi, 1961).
122. Mufti Intizamullah Shahabi, *Ist Indiya kampni aur baghi 'ulama* (Delhi, n.d.).
123. Muhammad Miyan, *'Ulama-i Haq* (Muradabad, n.d.).
124. Id., *'Ulama-i Hind ka shandar mazi*, i–iv (Delhi, 1957–60).
125. S.G. Wilson, *Modern Movements Among Moslems* (New York, 1916).
126. M.A. Anderson, *The Eastern Question, 1774–1923* (New York, 1966).
127. J.A.R. Marriot, *The Eastern Question: An Historical Study in European Diplomacy* (London, 1917).
128. Allan Cunningham, 'The Wrong Horse?—A Study of Anglo-Turkish Relations Before the First World War', in Albert Hourani (ed.), *St. Anthony's Papers No.17, Middle Eastern Affairs, Number Four*, i (Oxford, 1965), 56–76.
129. Uriel Heyd, 'The Later Ottoman Empire in Rumelia and Anatolia', in P.M. Holt, Ann K.S. Lambton and Bernard Lewis (eds.), *The Cambridge History of Islam*, i (Cambridge, 1970), 354–73.
130. P.M. Holt, 'The Later Ottoman Empire in Egypt and the Fertile Crescent', in ibid., 374–93.
131. Lothrop Stoddard, *The New World of Islam* (London, 1921).
132. P. Hardy, *The Muslims of British India* (Cambridge, 1972).
133. See *The Times*, 12 June 1877.
134. Ibid., 12 October 1877.
135. George Percy Badger, 'The Precedents and Usages Regulating the Muslim Khalifate', *Nineteenth Century*, 2/9 (1877), 274–82.

136. Great Britain, Parliamentary Papers, *Hansard*, Parliamentary Debates of the House of Lords and the House of Commons for 1877.
137. See n. 109 above.
138. Malcolm MacColl, 'The Musalmans of India and the Sultan', *Contemporary Review*, 71/374 (1897), 280–94.
139. H.A. Salmone, 'Is the Sultan of Turkey the True Caliph of Islam?', *Nineteenth Century*, 39 (1896), 173–80.
140. See Syed Ahmed Khan's *Tahzibu'l-Akhlaq* (Aligarh), 1876–96.
141. Sir Syed Ahmed Khan, *Akhiri mazamin* (Lahore, 1898).
142. Id., *The Truth About Khilafat*. Eng. tr. Kazi Siraj-ud-din Ahmad (Lahore, 1916).
143. Muhammad Ismail Panipati (ed.), *Maqalat-i sar Sayyid*, i–xvi (Lahore, 1961–5).
144. Aziz Ahmad, 'Sayyid Ahmad Khan, Jamal al-Din al-Afghani and Muslim India', *Studia Islamica*, 13 (1960), 55–78.
145. Moulavi Cheragh Ali, *The Proposed Political, Legal and Social Reforms in the Ottoman Empire and Other Mohammedan States* (Bombay, 1883).
146. Garcin de Tassy, *La Langue et la litterature hindoustanies en 1871* (Paris, 1872).
147. W.S. Blunt, *India Under Ripon* (London, 1909).
148. Altaf Husain Hali, *Madd-o Jazar-i Islam* known as *Musaddas-i Hali* (Delhi, 1879).
149. OIOC, Lytton Papers. Papers of the First Earl of Lytton as Viceroy of India, 1876–80. OIOC, MSS Eur. E. 218.
150. *Qaisaru'l-Akhbar-i Hind* (Allahabad), weekly (ed.), Munshi Sirajuddin Ahmad Khan.
151. *Ahsanu'l-Akhbar* (Allahabad), weekly (ed.), Haji Kabiru'l-Haq.
152. S.R. Mehrotra, *The Emergence of the Indian National Congress* (Delhi, 1971).
153. S.A. Zenkovsky, *Pan-Turkism and Islam in Russia* (Cambridge, Mass., 1906).
154. Anthony Reid, 'Nineteenth Century Pan-Islam in Indonesia and Malaysia', *Journal of Asian Studies*, 26/2 (1967), 267–83.
155. Halil Inalcik, 'The Rise of the Ottoman Empire', *The Cambridge History of Islam*, i, 295–323.
156. Werner Caskel, 'Western Impact and Islamic Civilisation', in G.E. van Grunebaum (ed.), *Unity and Variety in Muslim Civilisation* (Chicago, 1955), 335–60.
157. Bernard Lewis, *The Middle East and the West* (London, 1963–4).
158. Id., 'The Ottoman Empire in the Mid-Nineteenth Century: A Review', *Middle Eastern Studies* (London), 1/3 (1965), 283–95.
159. Niyazi Berkes, *The Development of Secularism in Turkey* (Montreal, 1964).
160. Edwin Pears, *Life of Abdul Hamid* (London, 1917).
161. A.J. Toynbee, *Survey of International Affairs, 1925*, i (London, 1927).

162. Arminius Vambéry, 'Pan-Islamism and the Sultan of Turkey', *Asiatic Quarterly Review and Oriental and Colonial Record* (London), 3rd series, 23/45–6, (1907), 1–11.
163. Hans Kohn, *A History of Nationalism in the East* (London, 1929).
164. Ahmed Emin, *Turkey in the World War* (New Haven, 1930).
165. Constantine K. Zurayk, 'The National and International Relations of the Arab States', in T. Cuyler Young (ed.), *Near Eastern Culture and Society* (Princeton, 1951), 205–24.
166. J. Holland Rose, '1815 and 1915', *Contemporary Review*, 107 (Jan. 1915), 12–18.
167. W. Wilson Cash, *The Moslem World in Revolution* (London, 1925).
168. G.R.G. Hambly, 'Unrest in Northern India During the Viceroyalty of Lord Mayo, 1869–72', *Journal of the Royal Central Asian Society*, 48/1 (1961), 37–55.
169. J.R.M. McLane, *Indian Nationalism and the Early Congress* (Princeton, 1977).
170. W.G. Palgrave, *Essays on Eastern Question* (London, 1872).
171. OIOC, Political and Secret Letters and Enclosures Received from India (L/P&S/7).
172. See n. 141, above.
173. Mirza Ghulam Ahmad, *Gornamint angrezi aur jihad* (Qadian, 1900). Eng. Tr. *Jehad and the British Government* (Lahore, n.d.). Its later version, as published by Al Islam, the official website of the Ahmadiyya Community, is titled *The British Government and Jihad* (Tilford, Surrey, 2006). http://www.alislam.org/library/browse/volume/Ruhani_Khazain/book/Government_Angrezi_Aur_ (Accessed: 30 May 2012).
174. Shibli Nomani, *Maqalat-i Shibli*, i–iv (Azamgarh, 1930–4).
175. Id., *Safarnama-i Rum-o Sham* (Agra, 1894).
176. *Akhbar-i 'Am* (Lahore), tri-weekly/daily, publisher, Pandit Mukand Ram.
177. *Paisa Akhbar* (Lahore), weekly/daily, publisher, Munshi Mahbub Alam.
178. *Sada'-i Hind* (Lahore), weekly, publisher, Din Muhammad.
179. *Rahbar-i Hind* (Lahore), bi-weekly, publisher, Sayyid Nadir Ali.
180. F. Rahman, 'Internal Religious Developments in the Present Century Islam', *Journal of World History* (Paris), 2/1 (1954), 862–79.
181. See n. 132 above.
182. Arminius Vambéry, *Western Culture in Eastern Lands* (London, 1906).
183. Qeyamuddin Ahmad, *The Wahabi Movement in India* (Calcutta, 1966).
184. See, n. 168, above.
185. Ghulam Rasul Mihr, *Jama'at-i mujahidin* (Lahore, 1955).
186. Id., *Sarguzasht-i Mujahidin* (Lahore, 1956).
187. Id., *Sayyid Ahmad Shahid* (Lahore, 1952).

188. Mahomedan Literary Society, *Abstract of the Proceedings of the Mahomedan Literary Society of Calcutta. Lecture by Moulvie Karamat Ali (of Jounpore) on a question of Mahomedan Law Involving the Duty of Mahomedans in British India towards the Ruling Power* (Calcutta, 1871).
189. Sir Syed Ahmed Khan, *Review on Dr Hunter's Indian Musalmans: Are They Bound in Conscience to Rebel Against the Queen?* (Benares, 1872).
190. See n. 141, above.
191. See n. 145, above.
192. Cheragh Ali, *A Critical Exposition of the Popular Jihad* (Calcutta, 1885).
193. Rafiuddin Ahmad, 'A Moslem's View of the Pan-Islamic Revival', *Nineteenth Century* (London), 42/248 (1897), 517–26.
194. Id., 'Is the British "Raj" in Danger?', ibid., 42/247 (1897), 493–500.
195. See n. 173 above. This portion has been omitted from the later version of the work.

2

The Balkan Crisis of 1912–1913 and Muslim India*

In its heyday, the Ottoman Empire was spread over the three continents of Europe, Asia, and Africa—from Hungary to the Yemen and from Algiers to Mesopotamia. In this sprawling landmass, with Istanbul as its centre, lived an enormous conglomeration of races, ethnic groups, nationalities, and religious communities. The Ottoman state, though technically Muslim, had established a novel system by which its non-Muslim citizens prospered in self-governing *millet*s. The sultan's position in the larger world of Islam (*daru'l-Islam*) was pre-eminent, largely, because of his esteemed status as the caliph of all Muslims, demanding allegiance even from those who were under the temporal rule of non-Muslim sovereigns. From the seventeenth century, the decline of the empire became a disturbing concern. Apart from the weakening of the sultan's authority, the major cause of the fall was the breakdown of the state institutions, heightened by corruption and inefficiency among the officials. The unchecked growth of the population led to social

---

*Originally presented as 'The Balkan Crisis of 1912–1913 and Turkey: The Impact of Muslim India' at the Seventh International Congress on Atatürk held at Skopje, Macedonia, under the auspices of the Atatürk Araştirma Merkezi of Ankara, 17–22 October 2011.

imbalance and disorder. Terminal financial problems, unchecked inflation, and fresh taxation created additional difficulties. This, in turn, affected the Ottoman army, which was the backbone of the empire. Furthermore, military and naval reverses began to shrink the frontiers in Europe and elsewhere. A complete setback was only a matter of time.[1]

The Balkan region in south-eastern Europe had been a part of the Ottoman Empire for almost five centuries, until the territorial re-arrangements of the Treaties of London (1912) and Bucharest (1913) greatly reduced its size and cut its population drastically. This happened as a result of the general decline that followed the creeping rise of nationalism among the non-Muslim subjects of the empire. Already by the end of the eighteenth century, the Ottomans had realized that it would be difficult to survive without British and Russian help as they were the ones who were actually encouraging the various Balkans nationalities to revolt and had even devoured some Ottoman territories. With the dawn of the nineteenth century, this factor assumed greater seriousness. The Ottoman dominions in Europe were overwhelmingly non-Turkish and non-Muslim. Religiously and culturally, they stood apart from the Ottomans as they had neither been absorbed nor assimilated. The *millet* system had helped them to hold on to their separate identities without arousing any feelings of loyalty to the empire. Over time, this generated ideas of nationalism in them which found staunch support from the rest of the Christian Europe. The Ottoman response was slow. The *Tanzimat* reforms (1839–76), modelled on the theories of Austro-German positivists but anchored in Islamic values and ethos, were a sure step forward towards reform and modernization, synonymous with the westernization at that time. The Young Ottomans—a new breed of secular intellectuals, writers, and journalists who spearheaded the change—were intent on creating Muslim-Ottoman nationalism within the ambit of a revivified Turkish Islamic exceptionalism synchronized with European liberal ideas and institutions.[2] But the very nature of the Ottoman state, as a Muslim power holding on to the *shari'at* as its law, did not allow a complete change-over to a system whereby the Christian subjects would feel comfortable within the overall dominance of the Muslim majority.³

The intellectual confusion over the best way to tackle the internal and external pressures led to calls for the classical prescription of *ittihad-i Islam*, which the European publicists from the 1870s onwards labelled as pan-Islam, believing it to be anti-Christian in its conception and anti-colonial in its thrust.⁴ To the Muslim intellectuals and potentates in India, Indonesia, and Central Asia, *ittihad-i Islam* was an attractive ideal that held out the possibility of the coming together of Muslims politically under the aegis of the Ottoman caliphate. But, they rejected the European slant on the meaning and objective of pan-Islam: Barrister Syed Ameer Ali (1849–1928), underscored it as an 'invention to cover up attacks upon Moselm states'⁵ and journalist Zafar Ali Khan pointedly called it 'a scurvy pretext for the spoliation of the fast decaying Moslem States'.⁶ However, the concept did not become a movement until the Young Ottomans themselves had begun to push *ittihad-i Islam* as an alternative to the flopped 'Ottomanism' under the *Tanzimat*. Their option was to appeal to the Muslim world as a panacea for the ills of internal disruption and external encroachments. Accordingly, the press became abuzz with discussions that led to a proliferation of books and treatises on the subject, such as Esad Effendi's undated late nineteenth-century pamphlet, *Ittihad-i Islam*.⁷ Within a couple of years, Islamic patriotism had overwhelmed public opinion, and pan-Islam had become a force in the Ottoman state policy.⁸ Especially passionate was the response of Abdülhamid II who, rather eagerly assumed the role of the 'Green Sultan' as well as that of the 'Caliph of all Muslims'.⁹ This was his way of dealing with problems, especially in the Balkan provinces where a Russian-inspired pan-Slavic movement for independence had reared its head following the Russo-Turkish War of 1877. Soon, there was a string of rebellions in Herzegovina, Bulgaria, Serbia, and Montenegro. The suppression of these resurrections, particularly in Bulgaria, led to an anti-Turk outcry in Europe, especially in Britain where the agitation had found support among high churchmen, non-conformists, radicals, and liberal intellectuals, all led by Gladstone, the former Liberal prime minister.[10] The outcry in Europe produced an equally strong backlash in the Ottoman Empire, and also sent Abdülhamid's stock soaring in the Muslim world. Solidarity of Islamic faith became his motto and an effective double-edged weapon against internal dissent and external designs. He sent his emissaries to India, Turkistan, and Africa, and patronized 'al-Afghani' whom he put in charge of his pan-Islamic mission.[11] To dismiss this enthusiasm as an 'inconsistent policy of expediency', as some tend to do,[12] is debatable.

Pan-Islam, however, could not stop the Ottoman Empire from shrinking to a fraction of its former size and strength and was left with just a small percentage of its population. What remained were the Syrian territories, the Iraqi region, the Arabian provinces, as well as the European territories that comprised only southern Bulgaria, Macedonia, and Albania. All the other regions had been devoured by the European powers under one pretext or another.[13] More problems were in store. The rise of the Young Turks of the CUP, structured on the pattern of the Masonic orders, particularly complicated matters.[14] Their hide and seek with Abdülhamid II, and a series of reversals in the Balkans including the separation of Bulgaria, led to the sultan's removal and exile, and Mehmed V's (r. 1909–18) accession as sultan-caliph under the CUP's control.[15]

Initially, the CUP leaders, despite the pan-Islamic thrust of certain Ottoman intellectuals, did not identify themselves with *ittihad-i Islam*.[16] But, they were soon forced to eat their words and incorporate this concept in their agenda of modernization, Ottomanism, and pan-Turkism.[17] Circumstances had largely dictated this change. The situation that developed in the Balkans between 1908 and 1910, especially the

THE BALKAN CRISIS OF 1912-1913 AND MUSLIM INDIA

absorption of Bosnia-Herzegovina by Austria, the independence of Bulgaria, the union of Crete with Greece, and the separation of Montenegro, together with anxiety over their worsening image in the empire and the Muslim world, had a lot to do with this. Then there was the Tripolitan crisis of 1911 which forced them to use pan-Islam to rouse support against the Italian aggressors. This reached a crescendo during the Balkan Wars of 1912-13 and finally bound them to the ideology of their former nemesis.

The latest crisis in the Balkans began in 1912 when Bulgaria, Greece, Montenegro, and Serbia ganged up on an enfeebled Ottoman Empire in a grand alliance called the Balkan League. Roused to frenzy by jingoism and religious fanaticism, their objective was to secure territorial gains in Ottoman Rumelia, Albania, Macedonia, and Thrace, which had been missed out in the earlier hostilities. Their move was not sudden but the Young Turks were too engrossed in their domestic troubles to respond promptly. Taking advantage of the situation, the Balkan League issued a joint ultimatum demanding radical reforms that, in essence, implied renunciation of Ottoman sovereignty over its European possessions. Naturally, the Porte declined to accept. The hostilities that began on 8 October 1912 ended rather badly for the Ottoman Empire with the Treaty of London in May 1913: Albania became autonomous; Montenegro, Serbia, and Romania extended their territories; Greece acquired Epirus, Crete, and some Aegean islands; and Macedonia was divided among Greece, Serbia, and Bulgaria. The latter also obtained most of Thrace. Luckily for the Ottomans, when the Second Balkan War broke out in June 1913 among the former Balkan allies themselves over the distribution of spoils, they were able to retrieve eastern Thrace, including Edirne (Adrianople). Thus, the Ottomans actually managed to acquire more area in Europe than originally intended.[18] But, the retreating Bulgarians perpetrated untold atrocities on the Turkish population and caused massive destruction to property and food grains.[19]

The Balkan crisis of 1912–13 sent an unprecedented wave of indignation through the Muslim world; the emotional response was more noticeable than at the time of the Turco-Italian crisis of 1911.[20] The reaction among the Muslims of British India was particularly effervescent because their relations with the Ottomans stretched back into history. Having been familiar with the fiction of the 'central' caliphate from the Abbasid times, the Indian Muslims had gradually gravitated towards the Ottoman caliphs in Istanbul.[21] The provincial rulers of the Deccan and Gujarat were the first to establish political relations with the Ottomans in the fifteenth and the sixteenth centuries, when they approached Muhammad the Conqueror (r. 1451–81), Beyazit II (r. 1482–1512), and Selim I (r. 1512–20).[22] But these early contacts were in the nature of diplomatic and commercial ties, and the claim of the Ottoman naval commander, Sidi Ali Reis, that Indian obedience was widespread, was rather exaggerated.[23] However, improvement in communications repeated waves of fresh immigration from Central Asia, and the spread of interlocking Sufi networks across the *daru'l-Islam* encouraged better relations with the Ottomans.[24]

During the eighteenth century, there were definite signs of pan-Islamic activity on the Malabar Coast, and in Mysore where Tipu Sultan (1749–99) attempted to establish closer links with the Ottomans. This ensured, for Tipu, the title to his throne from Abdülhamid I (r. 1774–89), but the military alliance that he desired did not take place.[25] The first definite reference that the Ottoman sultan's name was mentioned in the Friday *khutba* in some Indian mosques dates to the reign of the Mughal ruler Shah Alam II (r. 1759–1806), whose period coincided with three Ottoman Sultans—Mustafa III, Abdulhamid I, and Selim III.[26] From then on, especially after 1857, when India passed under the direct rule of the British Crown, the Indian Muslims began to hold Abdülmecid I (r. 1839–61), and later Abdülhamid II, as the rightful caliph.[27] Indian effervescence was often exhibited at times of various crises, such as the Crimean War (1854), the Russo-Turkish War (1877), the Bulgarian tragedy (1890s), the Young Turk revolution and its aftermath (1908–9), and Italy's attack on Ottoman Tripolitania (1911).[28]

Naturally, when the news of the latest crisis in the Balkans (October 1912) first reached India, there was a reflex reaction in favour of the Ottomans and universal condemnation of the Balkan League. The Muslim press took the lead and, in an effort to support the Ottoman Empire, began publishing news and views from Istanbul and the war front. In the vanguard were Mohamed Ali's *Comrade* (Calcutta/Delhi), Abul Kalam Azad's *Al-Hilal* (Calcutta), Mahbub Alam's *Paisa Akhbar* (Lahore), Muhammad Inshaullah's *Vatan* (Lahore), and Zafar Ali Khan's *Zamindar* (Lahore). Mohamed Ali, a scion of a well-off family of Rampur, was a graduate of Aligarh and Oxford. He was a staunch pan-Islamist and a vociferous critic of British rule in India.[29] Abul Kalam Azad came from a long line of *'ulama* who fervently believed in the doctrine of *jihad* and *ittihad-i Islam*. He started his *Al-Hilal* in July 1912 from Calcutta; its biting views and reviews, couched in rhetoric, shook the educated elite and inspired feelings of *ittihad-i Islam* in them.[30] Muhammad Inshaullah, of the *Vatan*, was a forceful journalist from Lahore who had collected money for the Hejaz Railway project and, indeed, claimed that it was he who had initiated the scheme.[31] Mahbub Alam (1863–1933) was another Punjabi pan-Islamist who visited Istanbul in 1900 and later wrote a travelogue praising whatever he had witnessed there.[32] He started the *Paisa Akhbar* in 1888 as an attempt to reach the common people. Zafar Ali Khan also belonged to the Punjab province and had remitted large sums of money to Istanbul during the Tripolitan crisis. His newspaper, the *Zamindar*, was a popular journal for advanced pan-Islamic views.[33] Fed by these journals, general public opinion especially amongst the Muslims, was bound to be pro-Turkish and stridently open about it.[34]

Another feature of the situation was that the *'ulama* joined the politicians and general public to voice their concerns. The two most important orthodox religious seminaries of the Indian *'ulama*, the Deoband and the Farangi Mahal, jumped into the foray and gave some sort of a religious sanction to the protest movement. The Deobandi *'ulama*, in particular, made it obligatory upon Muslims to give money to the Ottoman Red Crescent Society, and even authorized the rerouting of *zakat* money to the Balkan funds.[35] But, a more prominent role was played by Abdul Bari, head of the Farangi Mahal madrasah in Lucknow. Not only was he an influential pan-Islamist *'alim*, but he was also a revered *pir*. He had already been in contact with the Ottomans, and had also visited Istanbul following the trip undertaken by his collaborator, Barrister Mushir Hosain Kidwai, and now played an important part in consolidating the prestige of the Ottomans in India.[36] But, the Bareilly School of Ahmad Riza Khan (1856–1921), because of its doctrinal objections to the Ottoman pretensions to the caliphate, decided to keep aloof.[37] However, Shibli Nomani (1857–1914), the head of the Nadwatu'l 'Ulama (established 1891), did renounce his earlier objections on this issue after a visit to Istanbul.[38] He now decided to support the Ottomans through his heart-warming elegiac renderings, especially *'Hangama-i Balkhan'* that became immensely popular.[39] According to an intelligence report, the venerated *imam* of the Jamia Masjid in Delhi was reported to have told his congregation that they should not believe in the accounts of Turkish reverses because 'they were greatly exaggerated and totally incompatible with the past history of Turkey.'[40] But it was Azad, Shibli's rising young ward, who devoted successive issues of his *Al-Hilal* to the theme of *ittihad-i Islam* around the Ottoman caliphate and publicly declared that the time for *jihad* had come.[41] During a public meeting in Calcutta on 27 October 1912, he declared:

> Our relations with Muslims the world over are based on a solitary bond: that of religious affinity or 'Pan-Islamism'. But with the Turks we have a dual connection. The first is the ties of religious brotherhood for they, too, are Muslims [and] as such God [Almighty] has forever made us partners in

anguish as well as in repose. The second and even stronger connection is that of the Caliphate and [its status as] Islam's ultimate political centre and the fact that the Turks alone hold the last sword in the defence of Islam's *kalima*. If Islamic rule comes to an end in any part of the world we lament that our limb is severed but when the Turks are made to face a calamity we writhe in anguish and our heart is tormented. When we are agitated for the Turks, our perturbation is not for Muslims but for Islam itself. . . . I say [with conviction] that it is incumbent upon every believer who has faith in Allah, His Prophet and His Book, to rise and declare *jihad* in the name of God. The first [type] of *jihad* is the sacrifice of worldly possessions and thereafter, if need be, comes *jihad* of life and soul. Send away your money and goods [to Turkey] and keep yourselves in readiness! It matters not if today the occasion does not arise for there shall be another chance tomorrow. It is not the kind of an asset groundwork for which would go waste.[42]

At another level of the pan-Islamic appeal, the poet-philosopher, Muhammad Iqbal, wrote exciting poems on Ottoman Turkey. In November 1912, he recited one of them, *'Jawab-i Shikwa'* or *'Answer to the Complaint'*, at a gathering in Lahore's Municipal Gardens outside the Mochi Gate in order to raise funds for the Turks wounded in the war.[43] Intended as an answer to *'Shikwa'* or *'The Complaint'*, that he had written earlier and which was now recited by Zafar Ali Khan as an 'appetizer', Iqbal attempted to awaken Muslims to the reality of their moral and political confusion: they were themselves responsible for their decadent situation because they had assumed a path quite opposite to that of Prophet Muhammad (*sal'am*) to the extent of becoming faithless and had thus become utterly divided.[44] A CID officer of the Punjab Police reported that before Iqbal stood up to recite his poem, Ghulam Mohy-ud-din of Kasur put up the twenty-page long printed version for sale page by page that raised Rs. 1,000. A large number of other copies of the poem were then purchased by the audience at the rate of one rupee per copy, and some by poor people for four annas (quarter of a rupee) each. The total amount subscribed to the Turkish Relief Fund on that occasion, including some other contributions, was Rs4,301.[45]

The *'Jawab-i Shikwa'* had such great an impact on the people that a poet of Rampur, Sahibzada Mustafa Khan Sharar, especially wrote a poem in praise of Iqbal.[46] Another poet of repute, Saiyid Hashmi Faridabadi of the United Provinces, in a passionate appeal in *'Chal Balqan Chal'*, exhorted the Indian Muslims to march to the Balkans and taste an honourable death if they had any self-respect left in them.[47] Niaz Fatihpuri and Hasrat Mohani, two well-known figures of Urdu literature, published laments on the troubles of the Ottoman Empire in *Al-Hilal*.[48]

Mohammad Ali Jinnah (1876–1948), the young Congress leader and the future founder of Pakistan, also tried to drum up support for the Ottomans. He was a consistent but pragmatic supporter of the Ottoman Empire and often donned a Turkish *fez* to display his Ottoman sympathies. When the Balkan crisis began he organized relief supplies for the Turkish sick and wounded.[49] He also helped arrange a well-attended public meeting in Bombay (Mumbai) to demonstrate sympathy for the Ottomans. On that occasion a resolution was moved by Jinnah in which he expressed the hope that Britain, as 'the greatest Mahomedan power in the world', would help preserve the integrity of the Ottoman Empire 'with which the sentiments of the Moslem world, both political and religious, are so deeply and indissolubly tied up'.[50]

A general appeal was launched for the collection of the 'Turkish Relief Fund'. At least three newspapers—*Comrade*, *Paisa Akhbar*, and *Zamindar*—and several public organizations began raising funds for the purpose. However, the *Zamindar*'s venture proved more successful because it had proposed a 120-member board of trustees with such names as Ameer Ali and Nawab Viqarul Mulk (1841–1917), to work as a sort of a regulatory body. Naturally, the figures showed a steady progress as more and more contributions poured in.[51] Major donations had come from Malik Mubaraz Khan, Pir Mihr Ali Shah (1859–1939) of Golra, and the *pir*s of Kaliar Sharif.[52] Public meetings were arranged at such far separated places as Lahore, Kasur, Lyallpur, Peshawar, Quetta, and Calcutta, where speakers delivered stirring pro-Ottoman speeches and the audience demonstrated great deal of interest in the Balkan crisis, especially on the occasion of the *'Eid* celebrations towards the end of November 1912.[53] At Lahore's famed Badshahi Masjid, subscriptions were collected as an ''*Eid* gift' for the Turks.[54] Those who did not fall in line were declared *kafir*s.[55]

Overall, in the country, such was the appeal that even the poor donated,[56] and women took a leading part in raising subscriptions.[57] Various *anjuman*s issued fervent appeals for funds.[58] Barrister Abdulla al-Mamun Suhrawardy (1875–1935) who, in 1903, had resurrected the dormant Anjuman-i Islamia as 'The Pan-Islamic Society of London' and had become its president,[59] proposed diverting the funds collected for the Aligarh University to Turkey.[60] Mahomed Ali supported the suggestion in his *Comrade*, and Azad in his *Al-Hilal*, but the Aga Khan (1877–1957) intervened to prevent it, possibly on a nod from the government.[61] However, the Government of India was wise enough not to raise any objection to the raising of the loan.[62] Viceroy Hardinge of Penshurst (1858–1944) and several officials expediently contributed to the funds raised for Turkey, but the commander-in-chief instructed his officers to discourage such collections.[63] Similarly, when Shaukat Ali (1873–1938), the elder brother of Mohamed Ali of the *Comrade*, decided to organize a volunteer corps to fight against the Balkan League, the government saw to it that it did not succeed.[64]

Among the Muslim organizations, the All India Muslim League, though struggling to find its feet politically, still did not lag behind in whipping up support for the Ottoman cause.[65] At its Lucknow sessions on 22 March 1913, Muhammad Shafi, its president, lamented the hostile attitude of the British government towards the Ottoman Empire and expressed spontaneous sympathy for the Turks in their hour of trial. From the Near Eastern crisis, he drew a lesson for the Muslims of India that 'in self-reliance alone lies the secret of national success'.[66] Already, the League's provincial branches had been doing whatever they could to express solidarity with the Turks and collect funds for them. But, more active was the League's London branch under Ameer Ali's guidance. Despite being a Shia Muslim, Ameer Ali subscribed to the Sunni theory of the caliphate and because of his writings on Islamic history, he had earned the respect of all around for his mission to bring about an understanding between Islam and Christianity and other religions.[67] In politics, Ameer Ali was a moderate and tried not to be on the wrong side of the government. Thus, he along with his London Muslim League did everything in their power to help the Ottomans through memorials to the British government and letters to the press. Simultaneously, they persevered in countering the hostile propaganda being conducted by the British Balkan Committee and the British press led by *The Times*. Kazim Husain, the London League's secretary, was quite energetic in his efforts to save the only independent Muslim state from annihilation.

The London League also kept the All India Muslim League well-informed about the trends of policy in the European capitals.[68] They had sent a British Red Crescent Mission to help the Ottoman wounded during the Tripolitan War; now, they fitted out another mission to Turkey for the same humanitarian purpose. This was necessary as most of the well-equipped European medical missions were working in the Balkan states and Greece. The Aga Khan, as usual, acted as the Society's godfather and donated a handsome amount of £2,000. He also purchased bonds worth Rs25,000 and invested another Rs90,000 in Turkish bonds. British donors also contributed generously. An appeal was addressed to the people of India, and donations started to pour in from there as well. The British mission stayed in Turkey for six months and did a wonderful job.[69]

Meanwhile, in India, the proposal to send an All-India Medical Mission was mooted by Shaukat Ali in his brother's *Comrade* which had, by then, moved to Delhi.[70] The appeal was met with considerable enthusiasm; and Dr Mukhtar Ahmad Ansari, a Delhi-based physician and a former resident medical officer at the Charing Cross Hospital in London, agreed to lead the mission.[71] Funds were not a problem but the personnel had to be arranged. Dr Ansari visited Aligarh and with the help of Abdur Rahman Siddiqui (1887–1953), president of the students' union club, scoured the college and school there for male nurses. Among the early volunteers were Choudhry Khaliquzzaman (1889–1973), Shoaib Qureshi (1891–1962), and Abdur Rahman Peshawari (1886–1925) who, at a later stage, was destined to play an important role for Turkey as its emissary to Kabul. Dr Ansari also visited Lahore with Mohamed Ali and addressed a public meeting there. The latter told his audience that he had brought a message from his elder brother, Shaukat Ali, that, at a time when the Turks were sacrificing their lives for the holy places, it was incumbent on Indian Muslims to take up the cause of guarding the Ka'ba.[72] When ready, the 26-member mission comprised seven qualified doctors, five pharmacists, twelve medical attendants and two managers. It enjoyed the full support of the Government of India (even though the provincial officers seemed uncooperative): Lord Hardinge, the viceroy, bid them farewell when they went to see him in New Delhi.[73] On 3 December 1912, Mohamed Ali had informed the Ottoman Red Crescent Society (Osmanlı Hilal-i Ahmer Cemiyeti, founded June in 1868) that the mission was ready to sail with a hundred-bed mobile hospital and a subsequent provision of ten thousand pounds sterling at its disposal.[74]

The mission sailed from Bombay on 15 December on the Italian liner, S.S. *Sardinia*, and were seen off at the Victoria Docks by a large number of dignitaries, including Mohamed Ali, Zafar Ali Khan, Mian Muhammad Haji Jan Muhammad Chotani (1873–1932), Fazalbhai M. Chinoy, Currimbhai Adamji Pirbhai, and the Turkish Consul General. The members of the mission were all dressed in khaki uniforms following the style of the Turkish military medical staff.[75] At Alexandria, the mission changed to another ship and, passing through Çanakkale in the Dardanelles, reached Istanbul on 9 January 1913. They were received by Dr Besim Ömer Paşa (1862–1940), the head of the Hilal-i Ahmer, along with other officials at the Kadirga Hospital. By this time, the Turks had suffered a defeat at Kirkareli and had retired to Lüleburgaz and thence to Çatalja about sixty miles from Istanbul. Then came the Armistice; the Indian mission was asked to establish its hospital two miles behind the Çatalja Lines, at Ömerli village. It was a particularly cold winter but the mission performed its duties bravely, day and night in deep snow and howling winds. Meanwhile, as a price for peace, Kamil Paşa's (1833–1913) government agreed to cede Edirne to the Bulgarians. Before the deal was signed, however, there was coup in which Nazim Paşa (d.1884–1913), the commander-in-chief, was assassinated. Kâmil Paşa was confined to his house, and the agreement with Bulgaria remained unsigned. But then, Sultan Rişad brought Mahmud Şevket Paşa (1856–1913) in as the grand vizier/war minister, and Ahmed Izzet Paşa (1864–1937) as the army chief, to finalize matters.[76]

By the time the mission arrived at Ömerli, the armistice had expired and the heavy guns had opened up again with thunderous roars. The mission started receiving the wounded from the frontline in their hospital. The more serious cases were sent on to Istanbul after first aid but the remaining were treated at Ömerli. A few days later, at the request of the Hilal-i Ahmer, Dr M.A. Ansari divided his mission into two groups. One group, under Dr Naim Ansari, and with Shoaib Qureshi as its manager, remained at Omerli with three other doctors, while the other group, headed by Dr M.A. Ansari himself, and with Khaliquzzaman as its manager, was sent to Istanbul with three other doctors for placement at Çanakkale, where they arrived in June 1913 and established a mobile hospital. Abdur Rahman Siddiqui, however, remained in Istanbul as the general manager of both the groups. Dr Tevfik Rüştü Aras (1883–1972), who later became a foreign minister in Mustafa Kemal's cabinet, was the overall in charge at the Çanakkale hospital. The mission remained at its designated location until a separate hospital was established for it in a Greek school building. Both the groups of the mission did a commendable job that was much acknowledged and appreciated by the Turks. Having wound up their hospitals on 22 May 1913, they headed for Istanbul on different dates amidst emotional scenes.[77] The mission had remained in Turkey for about eight months (December 1912 to July 1913) and was among a dozen other mercy missions that had come from abroad, including the one from London sent by Ameer Ali's Red Crescent Society.[78] The Turks genuinely appreciated their help and the sultan received them at his palace personally to thank them for their work.[79]

Before starting on his return journey, Dr M.A. Ansari donated the entire equipment of the mission (except fifty beds) to the Ottoman Hilal-i Ahmer. He was more than satisfied with the outcome of his mission, especially gratifying was the fact that the comparative statistics showed that the Indian mission had achieved much better results than the others. Unfortunately, Dr M.A. Ansari was caught up in an unseemly controversy with Ameer Ali when he tried to run down the work of the latter's British Red Crescent mission. It was probably the fallout of old squabbles between Ameer Ali and Mohamed Ali, but Dr M.A. Ansari never realized how unpleasant its consequences would be.[80] Kazim Husain, the secretary of the British Red Crescent Society, defended his mission and obtained the services of the *Paisa Akhbar* of Mahbub Alam for this purpose. But the controversy that followed Dr M.A. Ansari's accusations, coupled with the news of suspected missionary work in relief camps, definitely left an unfortunate imprint.[81]

This undesirable controversy apart, the mercy missions rendered commendable service to Ottoman Turkey. Dr M.A. Ansari was quite pleased with what the mission had achieved. But, 'the most important result', in his opinion, 'was the formation of a bond of union between the Turkish nation and the Indians'.[82] Izzet Paşa, the commander-in-chief, also gave expression to similar views at the farewell in honour of the mission: that though the Ottomans were passing through a bad patch, the Indian Muslims, by their help and practical expression of Islamic solidarity, had instilled a new hope in them which the Turks would never be able to repay.[83] Indeed, during its sojourn in Turkey, the mission was able to establish contacts with not only Lt. Col. Enver Bey (1881–1922) and other Young Turk leaders, but also with the Egyptian nationalists, notably, Abdul Aziz Shawish (1872–1929).[84] With the latter's collaboration, Ansari and Zafar Ali Khan (who was then visiting Istanbul to deliver funds collected by him) put forward, in early 1913, various schemes of development that envisaged a rehabilitation colony in Anatolia for Muslim refugees from Macedonia, a university in Madinah, an Islamic bank, and a co-operative society that would be solely financed by the Indian Muslims.[85] The documents in the Ottoman archives bear testimony to the money received in Istanbul for the purpose of settling Macedonian refugees in Anatolia.[86] The projects were actively supported by the *Comrade*, which also encouraged the Indian Muslims to purchase Turkish security bonds issued by the Ottoman Treasury.[87] It was, therefore, no coincidence that, in May 1913, the Turkish Consul in Bombay received Ottoman bonds worth £200,000 in several parcels from home. Out of these, a sum of £28,000 was deposited in the banks of Bombay alone.[88]

A few members of the mission, including Abdur Rahman Siddiqui, Shoaib Qureshi, Khaliquzzaman, and Abdur Rahman Peshawari, stayed behind for some months to oversee the projected schemes. But, though both the Indians and the Ottomans appeared enthusiastic, unfortunately, the schemes fizzled out after some initial planning.[89] Despite this, the Balkan crisis, especially the loss and recapture of Edirne, created such pro-Turkish furore as had never been witnessed before.[90] Henceforward, Enver Paşa, Talat Paşa, Ahmed Cemal Paşa (1872–1922), and Mahmud Şevket Paşa became popular names in India and their pictures adorned almost every Muslim house or a shop.[91]

THE BALKAN CRISIS OF 1912–1913 AND MUSLIM INDIA

Mustafa Kemal was not known in India at that time. He became famous later, during the First World War. During the Balkan War, Major Kemal Bey was on his Libyan tour where he had been fighting against the Italians as 'a patriotic duty and a political necessity'. He had developed a lasting friction with Enver Paşa, who was then the overall commander in Cyrenaica. Kemal Bey returned to Istanbul in December 1912—when the First Balkan War had already come to an end—grieving over the loss of Edirne.[92] As an offspring of Turkish settlers in Macedonia, he could not have but deeply lamented the loss of the Ottoman territories in the Balkans that were so dear to him. The impact of the Balkan crisis on the Ottoman Empire was disastrous. In another spell of tragedies, Mahmud Şevket Paşa lost his life to an assassin's bullet. But, the empire, placed on a secure foundation in Europe, has more or less remained unchanged since then. Even after the upsetting outcome of the First World War, the situation in European Turkey stayed almost the same. The next round of ethnic pogroms in the Balkans would take place some seventy-seven years later after the breakup of the Soviet Union satellites in Eastern Europe—in which Turkey was involved only indirectly.

The empire's next heartache would come from its Arab provinces, following a revolt by Sharif Hussein ibn Ali of Makkah and his sons. Immediately, however, the Ottoman Empire was able to invoke the pan-Islamic sympathy of the Muslim world, especially in British India where the Muslim community was intensely pro-Turkish, which helped them sustain their political inertia and satisfy their pan-Islamic drive without initiating a clash with their colonial rulers. Nawab Viqarul Mulk was right when he stated that 'the seeds sown by Dr M.A. Ansari and Zafar Ali Khan in Istanbul with the help of their Ottoman friends would soon grow into a sturdy tree if the Indian Muslims continued watering it with their monetary help'.[93]

When Dr M.A. Ansari's mission returned home on 4 July 1913, it was received with extraordinary enthusiasm. The newspapers, especially Azad's *Al-Hilal*, published laudatory articles accompanied by photographs of the mission with Dr Besim Ömer Paşa, Enver Bey, and members of the Ottoman Hilal-i Ahmer, taken earlier in Turkey.[94] The Government of India had remained 'neutral' so long as the British policy was pro-Turkish.[95] When that changed, the Indian Muslims' extra-territorial loyalty became an eyesore to the British, especially during the Khilafat movement when their aspirations clashed with British imperial policy.[96] Nevertheless, the Balkan crisis helped the Indians and Turks evolve a lasting friendship that has stood the test of time. An important outcome was the foundation, in May 1913, of a society called the Anjuman-i Khuddam-i Ka'ba.[97] Abdul Bari was its president, and Mushir Kidwai along with the Ali brothers, its other supporters. Originally conceived in December 1912, it is believed that the Anjuman derived its inspiration from Ottoman sources. Its genesis can be traced to Turkey's inability to effectively ward off the dangers threatening the *daru'l-Islam*. The two-fold solution was: (i) to organize Muslims to fend off any non-Muslim invasion, and, (ii) to make Turkey strong enough to sustain its hold over the holy places of Islam. Several branches emerged in Europe, the Middle East, and the Far East, with growing membership and handsome funds.[98] Its emissaries actively encouraged solidarity between the Indian Muslims and the Turks through measures such as commercial links, an Indo-Turco-Arabian steamship company, and the exchange of language instructors, in addition to efforts towards the promotion of Turco-Arab solidarity.[99] It is not surprising to find Haji Musa Khan (1872–1944), the prominent Muslim League leader, arguing for the launching of permanent offshoots of a sister pan-Islamic organization, like the Hilal-i Ahmer.[100] Over the years, several Turks, principally Admiral Hüseyin Rauf (Orbay) (1881–1964) of the *Hamidia* fame and Halidé Edib (1883–1964), were invited to India and welcomed evocatively. Continuing on those lines, Pakistan and Turkey to this day have sustained this relationship through cooperation in such organizations as the RCD and the OIC.

NOTES

1. See Inalcik, 'The Rise of the Ottoman Empire'; and id, 'The Heyday and Decline of the Ottoman Empire', in *The Cambridge History of Islam*, i, 295–353.
2. Şerif Mardin, 'Turkish Islamic Exceptionalism Yesterday and Today: Continuity, Rupture and Reconstruction in Operational Codes', in Ali Çarkoğlu and Barry Rubin (eds.), *Religion and Politics in Turkey* (London & New York, 2006), esp. 6 ff. For fuller details on the Young Ottomans see Şerif Mardin, *The Genesis of Young Ottoman Thought: A Study in the Modernization of Turkish Political Ideas* (Princeton, 1962), *passim*.
3. For details, see Heyd, 'The Later Ottoman Empire in Rumelia and Anatolia'; Inalcik, 'The Rise of the Ottoman Empire'; and P.M. Holt, 'The Later Ottoman Empire in Egypt and the Fertile Crescent', in *The Cambridge History of Islam*, i, 354–73 and 374–93.
4. See Landau, *Politics of Pan-Islam*, 1–8; Özcan, *Pan-Islamism*, 23 ff.; and Naeem Qureshi, *Pan-Islam in British India*, 1–3.
5. Ameer Ali, 'Pan-Islamism', *The Times*, 11 Jan. 1912, quoted in M.Y. Abbasi, *London Muslim League (1908–1928): An Historical Study* (Islamabad, 1988), 267.
6. Zafar Ali Khan, 'Indian Musalmans and Pan-Islamism', *Comrade*, 14 June 1913, in Rais Ahmad Jafari (ed.), *Selections from Moulana Mohamed Ali's Comrade* (Lahore, 1965), 297. Originally, this article appeared as a separate chapter in Nuri Bey's *Ittihad-i Islam*.
7. Özcan, *Pan-Islamism*, 37.
8. Ibid., 30–40.
9. On this, see Cezmi Eraslan, *II. Abdülhamid ve Islam Birliği* (Istanbul, 1992), *passim*.
10. Qureshi, *Pan-Islam in British India*, 14–16.
11. Caesar E. Farah, *Abdulhamid II and the Muslim World* (Istanbul, 2008), 19–24 and 164–227.
12. Özcan, *Pan-Islamism*, 63.
13. Reinhard Schulze, *A Modern History of the Islamic World*. Tr. Azizeh Azodi (London & New York, 2000), 22–3.
14. See E.E. Ramsaur, Jr., *The Young Turks: The Prelude to the Revolution of 1908* (Beirut, 1965), 14–51; Feroz Ahmad, *The Young Turks: The Committee of Union and Progress in Turkish Politics, 1908–14* (Oxford, 1969), *passim*; Aykut Kansu, *The Revolution of 1908 in Turkey* (Leiden, 1997), 1–27 and 73–192; and Bernard Lewis, *The Emergence of Modern Turkey*, 2nd edn. (London, 1968), 210–38.

15. Farah, *Abdulhamid II*, 25–40.
16. Landau, *Politics of Pan-Islam*, 73–87. These intellectuals included Mehmed Âkif, Ahmed Hilmi, Celal Nuri Bey, and Said Halim Paşa.
17. Ibid., 88 ff.
18. Heyd, 'The Later Ottoman Empire in Rumelia and Anatolia', 361; and Erik Jan Zürcher, *Turkey: A Modern History*, 3rd edn. (London & New York, 2004), 106.
19. See Abdur Rahman Siddiqui's eyewitness account of the destruction in Edirne and the countryside just after the Ottoman reoccupation in *Comrade*, 12 Sept. 1913.
20. Landau, *The Politics of Pan-Islam*, 92 and 125.
21. Aziz Ahmad, *Studies in Islamic Culture in the Indian Environment*, 10; Nadwi, *Khilafat aur Hindustan*, 9–24 and 32–45; and Arnold, The *Caliphate*, 82–105.
22. Anonym, *Turkey and Pakistan: Relations Between Turkey and Muslims of Indo-Pakistan Sub-continent*, Govt. of Pakistan, (Karachi, n.d.), 5–6; G.M. Nizamuddin Maghrabi, 'The Ottoman-Gujarat Relations', in *Studies in the Foreign Relations of India—Prof. H.K. Sherwani Felicitation Volume* (Hyderabad, n.d.), 185, cited in N. Akmal Ayyubi, 'A Proposal for Research on Indo-Turkish Relations', *Belleten*, Turk Tarikh Kurumu (Ankara), 46/181 (1982), 69; and Özcan, *Pan-Islamism*, 4.
23. Bernard Lewis, 'The Mughals and the Ottomans', 4–5; and Suraiya Faroqhi, *The Ottoman Empire and the World Around It*, esp. 184.
24. Naeem Qureshi, *Pan-Islam in British India*, 4–6.
25. M.H. Khan, *History of Tipu Sultan*, 132–8. Also see I.H. Qureshi, 'The Purpose of Tipu Sultan's Embassy to Constantinople', 77–84.
26. See Syed Ahmed Khan, 'Khutba men badshah ka nam', *Tahzibu'l-Akhlaq*, 155.
27. Naeem Qureshi, *Pan-Islam in British India*, 7 ff.
28. Ibid., 14–36.
29. For details, see Mohamed Ali, *My Life: A Fragment* (ed.), Afzal Iqbal (Lahore, 1942), *passim*.
30. I.H. Qureshi, *Ulema in Politics* (Karachi, [1974]), 234–5. Some important works on Azad are: Syeda Saiyidain Hameed, *Islamic Seal on India's Independence: Abul Kalam Azad—A Fresh Look* (Karachi, 1998); Ian Douglas, *Abul Kalam Azad: An Intellectual and Religious Biography* (ed.), Gail Minault (Delhi, 1988); and Khaliq Anjum, *Maulana Abu'l-Kalam Azad: shakhsiyyat aur karname* (Karachi, 1988).
31. For more details see Muhammad Inshaullah, *The History of the Hamidia Hedjaz Railway Project* (Lahore, 1908).
32. Mahbub Alam, *Safarnama: yurup bilad-i Rum Sham wa Misr* (1908).
33. See his biography by Ghulam Husain Zulfikar, *Maulana Zafar 'Ali Khan: hayat, khidmat-o asar* (Lahore, 1993), *passim*.
34. See various telegrams and copies of resolutions in OIOC, L/P&S/10/306.
35. *Paisa Akhbar*, 5 Nov. 1912.

36. Gail Minault, *The Khilafat Movement: Religious Symbolism and Political Mobilization in India* (New York, 1982), 34 and 136–7. For Abdul Bari and his *madrasah* see Francis Robinson, *The 'Ulama of Farangi Mahall and Islamic Culture in South Asia* (Lahore, 2002), esp. 1–3 and 69–176.
37. See Murtaza Hasan to Ahmad Riza Khan, 31 Oct. 1912, *Nuqush* (Lahore), 109 (Apr.–May, 1968), 113–14; M. Ahmad to Abdul Bari, 10 Nov. 1912, ibid., 119; and Saiyid Hasan Musana Anwar, 'Imam Ahmad Riza: ek mazlum Islami mufaqqir', *al-Mizan*, 6/6–8 (1976), 254–5.
38. See Shibli Nomani, *Maqalat-i Shibli*, i, 184.
39. See id., *Kulliyat-i Shibli*, 4th edn. (Azamgarh, 1954), 53–60; K.A. Khan (ed.), *Maqalat yaum-i Shibli* (Lahore, 1961), 7–17, 27–45 and 122–9; and S.M. Ikram, *Yadgar-i Shibli* (Lahore, 1971), 355–6.
40. Delhi Report, 9 Nov. 1912, Special Branch Records (SBR), Punjab Police Abstracts of Intelligence, 34/44, 16 Nov. 1912, para. 2514.
41. *Zamindar*, 5 Nov. 1912.
42. *Al-Hilal*, 6 and 13 Nov. 1912. Eng. tr. mine.
43. See Report dated 4 Dec. 1912, SBR, Punjab Police Abstract of Intelligence, 34/47, 7 Dec. 1912, para. 2627. The text of the '*Jawab-i Shikwa*' is available in Mohammed Iqbal, *Bang-i Dara* (Lahore, n.d.) 222–4. The English rendering of both the poems is in Raja Sultan Zahur Akhtar, *Shikwah and Jawab-i-Shikwah (Representation and Reply)* (Lahore, 1998).
44. Reference about Zafar Ali Khan is in SBR, 34/47, above. Also see Ayesha Jalal, *Self and Sovereignty: Individual and Community in South Asian Islam Since 1850* (London & New York, 2000), 173–4; and Khurram Ali Shafique, *Iqbal: An Illustrated Biography*, 2nd edn. (Lahore, 2007), 58 and 206.
45. Report dated 4 Dec. 1912, SBR, Punjab Police Abstracts of Intelligence, 34/47, 7 Dec. 1912, para. 2627.
46. *Al-Hilal*, 26 Feb. 1913.
47. *Al-Nazir* (Lucknow), Dec. 1912, in Rais Ahmad Jafari (ed.), *Auraq-i Gumgashta* (Lahore, 1968), 350.
48. *Al-Hilal*, 22 and 29 Jan. 1913.
49. See M. Naeem Qureshi, '(Quaid-i-Azam) Jinnah and the Khilafat Movement (1918–1924)', in A.H. Dani (ed.), *World Scholars on Quaid-i-Azam Mohammad Ali Jinnah* (Islamabad, 1979), 151.
50. *Bombay Gazette*, 11 Nov. 1912.
51. *Zamindar*, 2 Dec. 1912; and Report dated 5 Nov. 1912, SBR, Punjab Police Abstracts of Intelligence, 34/43, 9 Nov. 1912.
52. Ibid., 29 Nov. and 3 Dec. 1912 and 6 March 1913.

53. Ibid., 8, 13 and 20 Nov., 15 Dec. 1912, and 13 Feb. and 9 March 1913; and Report dated 2 Nov. 1912 and the subsequent days in SBR, Punjab Police Abstracts of Intelligence, 34/43–6, 9–30 Nov. 1912, paras. 2400, 2408–9, 2463 and 2514–30.
54. Report dated 25 Nov. 1912 in SBR, Punjab Police Abstracts of Intelligence, 34/46, 30 Nov. 1912, para. 2575.
55. For instance, at Kasur, Zulfikar Khan is reported to have declared: 'We are all Muhammdans: We are the offspring of the same Prophet. Those who do not follow the Prophet Muhammad [sal'am] are *Kafirs* and should be destroyed'. See ibid., 34/43, 9 Nov. 1912, para. 2408.
56. *Paisa Akhbar*, 28 Nov. 1912.
57. *Zamindar*, 2 Dec. 1912.
58. Ahmad Saeed, *Anjuman-i Islamiyya Amritsar* (Lahore, 1986), 190–2.
59. Since 1907/8, the society had been known as the 'Islamic Society'. It was then that Syed Ameer Ali had succeeded Suhrawardy as its president, and Hafiz Mahmud Shirani (1880–1946), the well-known scholar of Urdu literature, had become joint secretary. Apart from establishing direct contacts with Turkey, the society rendered valuable service in focussing, especially through its journal *Pan-Islam*, Muslim feelings on questions affecting Turkey and Islam. See A. Vambéry, *Western Culture in Eastern Lands*, 351–2; M.H. Kidwai, *Pan-Islamism*, 1; *Theosophist* (Madras), Nov. 1907, 98–9; Mazhar M. Shirani (ed.), *Maqalat-i Hafiz Mahmud Shirani*, i (Lahore, 1966), 49; Majid Khadduri, 'Pan Islamism', *Encyclopaedia Britannica*, xvii, 227; and Mirza Jalaluddin, 'Mera Iqbal', in Mahmud Nizami (ed.), *Malfuzat* (Lahore, n.d.), 64.
60. *Zamindar*, 8 Nov. 1912.
61. *Comrade*, 2 Nov. 1912; *Al-Hilal*, 6 Nov. 1912; and Aga Khan to Hardinge, 11 Dec. 1915, Hardinge Papers, Cambridge University Library.
62. Mohamed Ali to Private Secretary to Hardinge, Telegram 1 Nov. 1912; and Private Secretary to Viceroy to Mohamed Ali, 1 Nov. 1912, ibid.
63. See General Sir O'Moore Creagh, *The Autobiography of General Sir O'Moore Creagh* (London, 1924), 287.
64. *Comrade* (Delhi), 12 Oct. 1912. Also see Abu Salman Shahjahanpuri, *Maulana Muhammad 'Ali aur unki Sahafat* (Karachi, 1983), 10–128 and 131–95.
65. See Syed Wazir Hasan's appeal in *Zamindar*, 20 Nov. 1912.
66. Syed Sharifuddin Pirzada (ed.), *Foundations of Pakistan*, i (Karachi, 1969), 274–9.
67. Ameer Ali, 'Pan-Islamism', *The Times*, 11 January 1912; and id., 'Moslem Feeling', in Sir Thomas Barclay, *The Turco-Italian War and its Problems* (London, 1912), 101–8.
68. Abbasi, *London Muslim League*, 267–81.

69. Ibid., 281–304.
70. *Comrade*, 12 Oct. 1912.
71. Choudhry Khaliquzzaman, *Pathway to Pakistan* (Lahore, 1961), 20–6. For Ansari's biographical sketch, see Halidé Edib, *Inside India* (London, 1937), 30.
72. Report dated 27 Nov. 1912, SBR, Punjab Police Abstracts of Intelligence, 34/46, 30 Nov. 1912, para. 2576.
73. For details, see Extract, Bombay Abstract, 21 Dec. 1912, para. 1957 (iii), Bombay Abstract, 17 Dec. 1912, in SBR, Punjab Police Abstracts of Intelligence, 35/1, 4 Jan. 1913, para. 83; Ansari to Mohamed Ali (and enclosure), 28 Nov. 1912 in Mushirul Hasan (ed.), *Muslims and the Congress: Select Correspondence of Dr M.A. Ansari, 1912–1935* (Lahore, 1980), 1–3; Khaliquzzaman, *Pathway to Pakistan*, 20–7; and Abu Salman Shahjahanpuri, *Ghazi 'Abdu'r-Rahman shahid Peshawari* (Karachi, 1979), 119–63. For Abdur Rahman, also see Muhammed Han Kayani, 'Mezarlikta Çürüyen Tarihimiz', *Izlenim*, 20 (Nisan 1995), 52–4.
74. Mohamed Ali to Hilal-i Ahmer, 3 Dec. 1912, Türkiye Kızılay Derneği Kütüphanesi, Istanbul, HAC, 18/92–1 and 2.
75. Extract, Bombay Abstract, 21 Dec. 1912, para. 1957 (iii), Bombay Abstract, 17 Dec. 1912, in SBR, Punjab Police Abstracts of Intelligence, 35/1, 4 Jan. 1913, para. 83.
76. For information on the voyage and other details, see Khaliquzzaman, *Pathway to Pakistan*, 21–3.
77. Ibid., 23–7.
78. See Ansari's letter to *Comrade* 25 June 1913. For details of Ameer Ali's mission and the efforts of the Turcophile British, see 'Memoirs of the late Rt. Hon'ble Syed Ameer Ali', *Islamic Culture*, 6/4, (1932), 508–15.
79. See Türkiye Kızılay Derneği Kütüphanesi, Istanbul, HAC, 8/64; and Shahjahanpuri, *Ghazi 'Abdu'r-Rahman*, 159.
80. Ansari's letter dated 27 May 1913 in *Comrade*, 25 June 1913; and Abbasi, *London Muslim League*, 297–99.
81. Özcan, *Pan-Islamism*, 151–3.
82. OIOC, L/P&S/18, B. 267, 'Turkey: The Intellectual and Political Forces at Present Predominant in the Ottoman Empire, including [a] Note on German Agents and their Misdeeds and Turkish Intrigues among Indian Muhammedans. Memo prepared at the request of the Prime Minister', Dec. 1917.
83. *Comrade*, 13 July 1913.
84. For details, see Rais Ahmad Jafari (ed.), *'Ali Baradaran* (Lahore, 1963), 274–320.
85. See Ansari's letter to *Comrade*, 6 and 18 June 1913, and Nawab Viqar-ul-Mulk's article in the same journal, 29 June 1913, ibid., 274–6, and 318–20. Also see Zafar Ali Khan's autobiographical account in Sadiq Husain (ed.), *Anmol moti*, ii

(Lahore, 1968), 59–61 and 72–5; and Zulfikar, *Maulana Zafar 'Ali Khan*, 106–112.
86. See BEO, 4173/312901–1–10 dated 2, 5, 8, 14, 17 and 20 May 1913, Başbakanlık Osmanlı Arşivi, Istanbul.
87. Extract, Bombay Abstract, 17 May 1913, SBR, Punjab Police Abstracts of Intelligence, 35/20, 24 May 1913, para. 1221: and P.C. Bamford, *The Histories of the Non-Co-operation and Khilafat Movements*, Government of India (Delhi, 1925), 113.
88. Extract Bombay Abstract, 17 May 1913, para. 847, vide Punjab para. 1165, Bombay 12 May 1913, in SBR, Punjab Police Abstracts of Intelligence, 35/20, 24 May 1913, para. 1221.
89. Sadiq Husain (ed.), *Anmol moti*, ii, 72–5.
90. See, e.g., SBR, Punjab Police Abstract of Intelligence, 35/30–32, 2, 9 and 16 Aug. 1913, paras. 1888–92, 1936 and 2039–41; and Shahjahanpuri, *Ghazi 'Abdu'r-Rahman*, 138–41 and 164–70, citing contemporary evidence.
91. Interview with Malik Lal Khan, former secretary of the Punjab Khilafat Committee, at Lahore, in Sept. 1966; and my own personal recollections.
92. Andrew Mango, *Atatürk* (London: John Murray, 1999), 105–11.
93. Viqarul Mulk's contribution dated 25 June 1913 to the *Comrade*, 29 June 1913.
94. See, e.g., *Al-Hilal*, 19 March 1913.
95. At one point, when Turkey had not yet joined Germany in WWI in 1914, Mohamed Ali proposed donating the equipment of the medical mission that Dr Ansari had brought back. The condition was that the British Government did not go to war with Turkey. See Mohamed Ali's interview, dated 2 Aug. 1914, in Mushirul Hasan (ed.), *Mohamed Ali in Indian Politics: Select Writings*, i (Delhi, 1985), 70–1.
96. For details see Naeem Qureshi, *Pan-Islam in British India*, *passim*; and Gail Minault, *The Khilafat Movement*, *passim*.
97. The account of the Anjuman and its aims and objectives is based on: 'Note by the Special Branch', SBR, Punjab Police Abstract of Intelligence, 35/27, 12 July 1913, para. 1693; Extract, UP Abstract, 19 July 1913, ibid., 35/29, 26 July 1913, para. 1825; OIOC, L/P&S/20, H. 137, 'The Anjuman-i-Khuddam-i-Kaaba, 1913–1914', note by CID, India 1914; OIOC, P/Conf./50, ICH(P)P, Jan. 1919, Proc. no. 206; OIOC, L/P&S/18, B. 267; and Jafari, *'Ali Baradaran*, 221–2.
98. Nawab Maulawi Bashir-ud-din Khan of Delhi to Abdul Bari, 21 Jan. 1917, ibid., 210–11.
99. See, e.g., Shaukat Ali's letter to *Comrade*, July 1914, in Shan Muhammad (ed.), *Unpublished Letters of Ali Brothers* (Lahore, 1986), 47–52; and Ali brothers to Talat Paşa, 8 July 1914, Mushirul Hasan (ed.), *Mohamed Ali in Indian Politics*, i, 64–9.
100. *Zamindar*, 15 Jan. 1913.

3

Pan-Islam and the Caliphate Question Revisited*

1. The Ideal and the Reality of the Islamic Polity

The progress of Islam as a religio-political movement and a civilization, though not always uniformly successful, has been quite astounding.[1] It was achieved in a series of rapid bounds through *jihad*, *da'wa*, and itinerant traders who proved to be 'catalytic agents' in converting people to Islam. Internal discord and disruptive rebellions did not hamper its advance. Within two score years of the Prophet Muhammad's *(sal'am) hijrat* in CE 622, it had reached Syria-Palestine, Iraq-Mesopotamia, Armenia, Egypt, some islands in the Mediterranean, and Iran. During the next century it spread to North Africa, Central Asia, Spain, parts of France, and parts of India, though its fullest expansion in South Asia was not achieved until six hundred years later.

From the eleventh century onward, Islam had begun to take root in Africa and Asia Minor with varying degrees of success. Then, in the

---

*An earlier version of this paper appeared as 'Islamic Polity, Pan-Islam and the Caliphate Reconsidered', in Halil Bal and Muhammet Erat (eds.), *Studies on the Turkic World: In Honour of Professor Dr Mehmet Saray* (Istanbul, 2003), 521–45.

thirteenth century, Islam reached South East Asia through trading centres in Sumatra. There had been some serious retreats and withdrawals, such as the gradual loss of acquisitions in France in the eighth century, Sicily and Malta in the eleventh, and Spain some two to four centuries later, with much Christian vendetta, but this was admirably compensated when Ottoman armies crossed the Dardanelles into Europe, overran virtually the whole of the country south of the Balkans and, finally, in 1453, conquered the fabled Byzantine city of Constantinople (later renamed Istanbul) and with it the empire itself. Islam continued to penetrate deep into Christian Europe, including Hungary, but its march was effectively halted by its historical opponents at the very gates of Vienna in Austria, first in 1529, and then, conclusively, in 1683. Elsewhere, especially in South Asia, Islam continued to spread under powerful dynasties, at times by conquest but largely by peaceful and tireless efforts of scholars, saints, and Sufis. But then, from the seventeenth century, the ebb followed, slowly at first but quickened later towards the middle of the nineteenth and early twentieth centuries. The result was that the *daru'l-Islam*, which once sprawled from Poitiers and Andalusia to the shores of oriental Asia, began to shrink under pressure from the Christian West until its political power reached the diminishing point.[2]

The political system of Islam is hinged on three basic principles: *Tawhid*, *Risalat*, and *Khilafat*. But the Islamic state, unlike the medieval Christian theocracy or even the modern national state, is not a religious preserve. It is, in fact, a sort of 'theodemocracy'.[3] In the concept of an Islamic state, religion provides the foundation but there is no church or priesthood to control its destinies and no Caesar to exercise unlimited authority. Sovereignty, absolute, real and legal, belongs to God Almighty. In a derivative sense, however, it is exercised by the totality of the Muslim community as the vicegerent of God on earth. In turn, the community may install, by consensus, a representative to carry out the work of administration, which is signified by the term *Khilafat-i Ilahiya*.

The esoteric aspect, as implied in the institution of the Imamate and held sacred by the Shia, is inseparable from the caliphate. Thus, the only legitimate political authority in Islam, and the one which guarantees the unity of the community in conformity with the *shari'at*, is that of the 'universal' caliphate. And, though the democratic element is supposed to be preserved in the *ijma'*, there is no fixed system of government in Islam. The actual form of government depends on the prevailing circumstances and requirements of the time and place. But technically, once someone has been vested with authority, it becomes an overriding concern of Muslims to preserve that office, primarily to avoid civil strife and anarchy. Whenever a change did occur, whether from the republican to the dynastic form of government or from institutionalized to personal rule, it was tacitly accepted and given legitimacy even if it had no legal warrant in Islamic law. Thus, there has been certain congruence between the political system and prevailing political ideas. Henceforward, the state would be considered a trust, held by the amir in the name of the people, and the rights of either mutually reciprocal. In time to come, the organic unity of the religious and the political began to be expressed in the universality of the *ummat*.[4]

The ideal and the reality, however, were coexistent only for the short regime of the Prophet of Islam and his four 'righteous' caliphs. Thereafter, the Islamic state and society underwent a radical change. In fact, the political history of Islam followed rhythms of its own which, as Gibb maintains, were often discordant with the inner life of the community. Barely two decades after the demise of the Prophet in CE 632, the Shia and the Khwarij were disputing the basis of the Islamic state. A decade later, the democratic republic of Islam was turned into a hereditary monarchy, in the garb of the Umayyad 'caliphate' (661–750). The Abbasids, who succeeded them, tightened their hold still further. The *'ulama* hedged and fidgeted but then, after some rethinking, succumbed to the dynastic innovations. It was left to jurists, like al-Mawardi (974–1058), al-Ghazzali (1058–1111), and Ibn Taimiyya

(1263–1328), to make adjustments and bring about a compromise between the constitutional theory and political reality. Encouraged by their rulings, the Abbasids enveloped themselves in a cloak of spirituality; and even when their power waned, they kept alive the fiction of the central caliphate. Even the sack of Baghdad, by the Mongols in CE 1258, did not end this masquerade; and, twice more in succession, the caliphate changed dynasties as well as capitals. But the state was now Islamic only to the extent that the ruler professed Islam and enforced certain provisions of the *shari'at* in personal and criminal matters. In the words of S. Khuda Bakhsh:

> Islam became an Empire outwardly Islamic, but inwardly heathen, sceptical, irreligious to the core. Religion became a mere formal, meaningless observance, and ceased to be an uplifting force. . . . The essentials were lost sight of—[and] the non-essentials were given the palm and the crown. . . . Tribal jealousies set religious unity at naught; political necessities of the hour, snapped, effaced the link of Muslim brotherhood. . . . Thus religion became a mere pretence; politics, the happy hunting ground of unscrupulous adventurers. . . . Henceforward Islam enters on its downward path.[5]

The disaster was completed by a *coup de grace* from the West. The European impact was extensive, touching almost every aspect of society, but more obvious in the imperialistic encroachments on the *daru'l-Islam*. The earlier waves of these inroads, from the ninth to the fifteenth centuries, had been retaliatory in origin. The later waves, from the eighteenth century onwards were unprovoked, aggressive, and hegemonic. Then, beginning in the nineteenth century, one Muslim state after another began to pass under western control with amazing rapidity, either by direct annexation or through spheres of influence. The spoliation of the *daru'l-Islam* was such that by the early twentieth century, with the exception of the central Islamic lands, not a single Muslim state was left independent. Large chunks of Muslim territories were devoured by the European powers. The phenomenon of the shrinking frontiers of Islam, according to Aziz Ahmad's theory of phased extinction, indicates a certain pattern of cause-and-effect relationship. The pattern begins with the disintegration of a viable Muslim state when mutually warring fragmented successor-states are incapable of uniting against a rising hostile power. Consequently, a call to *hijrat* or a forced eviction or dispersal by the conqueror prompts the emigration of the élite from the threatened territories to more secure lands in the Muslim world. In due course of time, the masses are converted to the faith of the hostile, dominant political power and Islam ceases to exist. The extinction of Islam in Spain and Sicily, and later in the Balkans, and the loss of power in the Qipchaq Steppes, the Crimea, Central Asia, and elsewhere in Asia can be explained in the light of this paradigm.[6]

And yet, Islamic society, even when it moved away from its ideal substance, could survive as a religio-political force. Contrary to popular misconception, it never became static. In the words of Hossein Nasr, if Islam had decayed as the Orientalists maintain, 'it would have been impossible for Islam to continue to nurture a vast civilization and remain a living force to this day'.[7] The vicissitudes of fortune, and the internal-external pressures notwithstanding, Islam's inherent resilience to hold its own against heavy odds was displayed time and again. After every challenge, the Islamic society came back to fight and prosper. It continued, in fact, to develop in a dialectical way, says Kemal Karpat, though its intellectual appraisal did not correspond to the material change itself. According to Karpat, 'The so-called "ossification" of the thought process was due essentially to a social and political synthesis, reached after centuries of evolution, and to the resulting equilibrium, which created a long period of social and political stability beginning in the twelfth century.'[8]

In any case, the centuries of turmoil and disunity were not times of Islamic weakness. Far from that, Islam expanded greatly during this very period of supposed decline under the caliphate's three successor empires, the Ottoman, the Safavid, and the Mughal, and a host of other dynasties.

The stability was disturbed only when, after the eighteenth century, the challenges from outside became more intense and frequent. Otherwise, basic socio-cultural life had gone on unhindered. Here and there, along the way, tensions appeared which resulted in the Islamic society succumbing to pre-Islamic prejudices or non-Islamic influences but, as Khalifa Abdul Hakim points out, the ideal, overall, was achieved most successfully in the Islamic mode as compared to any other.[9] Thus, the Islamic society was able to retain some of the links that bind the *ummat* and these very links later proved to be the front for the various movements that emerged to attain the unreached goal of the ideal Islamic state and society.

2. The Ethos of Unity in Variety

The general weakening of the original momentum of the Islamic society, and the consequent disruption of its cultural integration, had created a crisis of identity and political purpose. But, already by the early eighteenth century, certain individuals had become conscious of the dangers that threatened Islam as a corporate body. The two common approaches that commended themselves to most situations were internal resurgence of the faith and external unity of the *ummat*. But the exercise of 'reform' in Islam, in the sense of the *tajdid* and *islah* tradition, has a different connotation than its accepted meaning in other religions. Here, revival and reform stem from a moral impulse and signify no new theological formulations. It means, rather, as Abul-Ala Maududi (1903–79) points out, an act of 'cleansing Islam of all the un-Godly elements. . . making it flourish more or less in its original pure form'.[10] The manifestations of this tradition were reflected in three directions: (a) a call for the return to the literal truth of the Qur'an and *sunnat*; (b) emphasis on the application of *ijtihad*; and (c) the reaffirmation of the authenticity and uniqueness of the Qur'anic experience. Within this aspect, there was a recurring similitude of behavioural pattern even where contact between various segments of the Islamic society was least discernible. An example of this trend is to be found in the eighteenth-century radical-puritanical movements which sought to reap Islamic reform of the classical hue by rejecting all accretions, whether due to endemic innovations or extraneous influences. Sometimes, these movements took the shape of pure traditionalism and at others that of Sufism but with an orthodox content. These currents, however, were not just *odium theologicum*; they were, in fact, socially retrospective. They set in motion deep currents of social revolution. Common to these movements, whether traditionalist or inspired by Sufism, was the overriding conviction that political liberation of Islam must be preceded by a profound spiritual regeneration. This entailed a return to the pristine purity of Islam by shedding superstition and emphasizing *ijtihad*, obliterating predeterminism and, if necessary, resorting to *jihad*. Thus, the Wahabis in Arabia, the Waliullahis in India, the Naqshbandis in the Caucasus, the Sanussis in Libya, the Fulanis in Nigeria, the Mahdis in Sudan, and the Salafis in Egypt, in one way or the other, had identical objectives with somewhat varying tendencies.[11]

Within this context, Islamic modernism, the alternative response to the western secularist challenge, spread across the Muslim world, especially in Turkey, Egypt, Central Asia, and the Indian subcontinent, in an attempt to reconcile Islam with modernity. It took various shapes and hues with relation to the conditions prevailing in each Muslim country, the emphasis of individual leaders, as well as to the nature and extent of the challenge from the West. And here, as Muhammad Iqbal has stated, Islam reconciled itself to the process of modernity with the greatest of ease and rapidity.[12] The hallmark of the nineteenth century modernist reformism, according to Fazlur Rahman, was a bold re-evaluation of Islamic precepts emphasizing rationalization of religious and social traditions 'with the dual purpose of accommodating modern ideas and outlooks within the framework of Islamic principles and at the same time ensuring to the Muslim[s] that Islam was capable of a modern orientation'.[13]

The modernist ideology, which was more an individual thought than a popular movement, developed in a two-way process: the religious approach tended to revive the glorious spirit of pristine Islam while the apologetic expression reaffirmed the faith by castigating various aspects of the western society and its criticism of Islam. In politics, the modernists affirmed the restoration of pan-Islamic fraternity of the *ummat*—barring, perhaps, Syed Ahmed Khan (1817–98) who thought otherwise—and advocated the liberal democratic elements in the Islamic model in terms of jargons borrowed from the West. This did not mean that allusions to democracy were a modern phenomenon and that the traditional Muslim juridico-political theory was least concerned with democracy as a form of government, or that the *falasifa* had treated the whole thing almost as 'a regime in error'.[14] Far from that, the democratic spirit of Islam was reflected in the very fact that the vicegerency of God on earth was vested not just in an individual but in the entire Islamic polity. Besides, such Qur'anic concepts as *ijma'*, *shura*, and the ouster of an erring *ulu'l-amr* (those in authority), even though conditional, were perceived as explicit elements of the democratic polity of Islam. In this context, instances of personalized rule in the long sweep of Islamic history were dismissed as deviations from the ideal. Though Islamic modernism helped to reinforce, among Muslims under colonial rule, a certain consciousness which had disappeared under the impact of imperialism, Islam was flexible enough to adjust itself adequately to the changing conditions.[15]

As regards the factor of the *ittihad-i Islam*, or pan-Islam as the western Orientalists and administrators in the East have dubbed it, it was no more than a pious wish for Islamic solidarity in contradistinction of the western concept of nationalism that emphasized language, culture, history, and territory as unifying factors. Undefined feelings of Islamic fraternity were, indeed, noticeable early in the nineteenth century in regions as far apart as South and Central Asia and the Far East, with the institution of the caliphate symbolizing the rallying-point. The Christian West misconstrued this activity as an aggressive and co-ordinated movement against them. In fact, the concept of pan-Islam was not a new development, as its ideological rationale was rooted in Islam's instinctive symbiosis as an integrated universal socio-political order. In its nineteenth century expression, however, pan-Islam, apart from being a psychological factor, was *daru'l-Islam*'s viable construct of a defensive alliance against the increasing political and economic penetration by western powers. In this sense, the movement was tainted by elements of suspicion and distrust between Islam and the West. Otherwise, when redefined after distinguishing its religious aspects from its socio-economic and political dimensions, pan-Islam unfolds a disparate phenomenon of complex convolutions. In the words of Kemal Karpat, pan-Islam comprised

> ... a variety of ideological aspirations, which, short of secular channels of expression used the traditional-religious ways to exteriorize themselves. Thus pan-Islamism, besides being an anti-imperialist movement, also expressed the social grievances of the lower class produced by the gradual introduction of the western capitalist system into the Middle East. It also expressed the populist yearnings of some sections of the old traditionalist élites as well as of the modern élites arising among the lower classes.[16]

Arising first in South Asia in the early nineteenth century, as a sequel to British incursions against Mughal India, the pan-Islamic 'movement' spread to Central Asia in the wake of the Russian conquests. But, it did not become a consciously relevant factor until the later half of the nineteenth century when the Ottomans themselves, spurred by various pressures, began to ride its waves in the backwash of the Eastern Question and the general discord then prevailing in the Empire. And, for a time, the Ottoman pretensions to their ecumenical authority over all Muslims were widely accepted; even the European powers had begun, erroneously, to acknowledge the sultan as a kind of 'Pope' of Islam.

The pan-Islamic movement, thus, was already in existence when the charismatic figure of Jamaluddin 'al-Afghani' made his appearance. An Iranian by birth, and an Afghan by design, 'al-Afghani''s contribution to modern Islamic political thought has been profound though his actual impact on the contemporary situation is still a matter of controversy. While he became a champion of the pan-Islamic creed only after 1881, he appears to have formulated his views much earlier during the fateful days of 1857–58 when, while living in India, he witnessed how religious emotions were used as an effective means of mobilization against the foreign 'infidels'. Therefore, 'al-Afghani' responded to a trend as much as initiated it. 'al-Afghani''s panacea for the ills of the *daru'l-Islam* was centred on an interlinked programme of internal reform, national liberation, and Islamic integration. But, in spite of his political acumen, 'Al-Afghani' was unable to evolve an effective *modus operandi*. The fact that he adapted his views at different times to different political settings, and was ultimately a sort of Islamic 'cosmopolitan', clearly hindered him from organizing his political interests into any coherent political programme.

Pan-Islam, therefore, could not become a dominant political force in his lifetime, especially since the original concept of the Islamic polity had blurred. Besides, the Ottoman caliphate, which 'al-Afghani' had chosen as the rallying-point, was a weak and embarrassing link. The sultan-caliph was usually more interested in enhancing his own political power and using it as an instrument of foreign policy. Further, at that particular point in time, the political supremacy of the western world was at its zenith. Most of the Muslim lands were its colonial possessions and, therefore, could hardly unite without first attaining their political independence. And here, 'al-Afghani' could not convince his audience that pan-Islam and territorial nationalism were not mutually exclusive.

It did not register with the Muslims that their solidarity was a premium for the territorial integrity of the Muslim countries, and that a nationally coherent and strong Muslim world could play a meaningful role in promoting Muslim solidarity. It is precisely for these reasons that 'al-Afghani's impact on the contemporary world of Islam was variable.[17]

Erratically pursued through the nineteenth century, the pan-Islamic movement did not achieve the desired results. This was largely because the pattern of its development, both in motivation and ideology, was affected by the personal whims and political expediencies of the ruling élite in various Muslim countries. And, since the process of modernization in the Muslim world was then being evolved within the perimeters of national aspirations, no appreciable synthesis between western socio-political concepts and Islamic traditions could be developed. Therefore, the Islamic movements, in spite of being pan-Islamic in essence, could not effectively wean Muslims away from moving into nationalistic channels, which eventually led them to arrive at 'Muslim nationalism'. It was a compromise whereby the concept of nationalism was declared compatible with Islam. In this way, territorial nationalism and Islamic universalism were merged together in one political process. This whole activity, from modernist reform to pan-Islam to Muslim nationalism, was a difficult exercise but was made possible because of Islam's internal dynamism and external stimuli. These same advantages helped to overcome challenges and to adjust to socio-political changes in a variety of ways in each Muslim society.[18] More far-reaching changes, however, were still to come.

3. The Caliphate and the Ottomans

As a consequence of the political vicissitudes of the *daru'l-Islam* and the halo of 'spirituality' that surrounded the caliphate, the institution took on a new and revivified image in modern times. This was particularly so because, with every fresh encroachment on the *daru'l-Islam*, there was a corresponding call for the protection of the caliphate, the symbol of Islam's splendour and glory. Basically, it reflected a yearning for that ideal universal socio-political order under one leader which transcends barriers of race, language, environment, and custom. Sunni jurists have not only interpreted the *shari'at* as the basis of the caliphate but, with some exceptions, have arrived at a consensus regarding the religious necessity of the institution. The recognition of, and submission to, the caliph or the *ulu'l-amr* was considered binding on the faithful except when the former deliberately flouted the *shari'at*. Thus, the caliph, as the *Khalifat-Allah* (and not just the *Khalifatu'r-Rasul-Allah*), was the centre of gravity in the Islamic system and combined in his person religious as well as political authority. He was the defender of the faith, the protector of the *daru'l-Islam*, and the enforcer of the *shari'at*. The esoteric aspect, as the Shia believe, was embodied in the 'apostolic' *imam* who was inseparable from the 'pontific' caliph. It is, however, another matter that this ideal state had never had more than a brushing contact with reality. Yet, large portions of the Sunni Muslim world continued to submit to the Ottomans in Istanbul as they had done to the Abbasids (750–1258) at Baghdad or the Fatimids (969–1171) in Egypt, mainly as a result of their successful religious pretensions.[19]

By the early 1850s, the Ottomans, realizing the structural weakness of their empire, were themselves reported to be pushing Sultan Abdülmecid's (1839–61) claim as caliph through their emissaries. Visitors to Turkey, during that period, found the presence of distinct signs of pan-Islamic activity. In their designs to exalt themselves in the eyes of the Muslim world, the Ottomans were fervently encouraged by the European powers; after the Crimean War, especially, the British did everything to inflate the sultan's image as a counterpoise to Russian expansion in Central Asia, which was then threatening their empire in India. But pan-Islam, which had almost coincided with similar waves among the Muslims of India, Central Asia, Indonesia, and Malaysia, did not become a conscious movement until the early 1870s. It was then that the Ottomans themselves, under various pressures (chiefly military, political, and economic), began to emphasize the sultan's ecumenical jurisdiction over Muslims under the political suzerainty of other governments more strongly. Its initiation, however, can be traced to the eighteenth century when Sultans Ahmed III in 1727 and Mustafa III in 1774, had pushed their claims to be the 'Caliphs of all Muslims' in their treaties with the Persians, the Central Asian Khanates, and the Russians, respectively. Later, in the 1780s, the sultans started invoking the notion of *ittihad-i Islam* and mobilizing religious dignitaries, especially in the Central Asian Khanates. But in practical terms, neither could they save their brethren from western subjugation nor could they put together an effective pan-Islamic union until the late nineteenth century.[20]

It fell to the lot of the Young Ottoman intellectuals, particularly Namik Kemal (1840–88), to inspire this union under Ottoman leadership. The Young Ottoman philosophy had been culled from the western ideal of liberalism but its genesis lay in the prevalent dissatisfaction with the Porte's policies, especially with regard to the *Tanzimat* doctrine of Muslim-non-Muslim fusion. In the process, it had dealt a tremendous blow to the traditional Ottoman society and its *millet* system of administration. The result was an aggressive programme of pan-Islamic ideology disseminated through publications such as the *Ibret* and the *Besiret*, and the equally emotive undated treatise by Esad Efendi, *Ittihad-i Islam*. Additional stimuli came from the influx of thousands of Muslim refugees, especially intellectuals, from Central Asia in the wake of the Russian onslaught and the movements of unification among the Germans and the Italians in the 1860s and the 70s.

The government of Sultan Abdülaziz (1861–76), in the strict tradition of Sultan Ahmed III (1703–30), began to push this sentiment though its thrust remained largely socio-cultural and religious in nature and only marginally political. It was carried to perfection by his successor,

Abdülhamid II, who, in spite of his autocratic disposition at home, extended his pan-Islamic subvention throughout the Islamic world. Pressure from populist-traditionalist Islamic groups had forced him to take refuge in pan-Islam. Broadly speaking, Abdülhamid's policy was centred on the exultation of the halo surrounding his office and exerting influence on the European powers through their Muslim populations. He accomplished this through an elaborate system of consulates, missions, and emissaries, and by patronizing and funding various sinews of propaganda—the press, publications, associations, and fraternities—supervised directly by him from the Yildiz Kösk in Istanbul.[21]

The primary aim in mobilizing the forces of Islam was to strengthen the position of the Ottoman Empire, which had almost been reduced to the status of 'a tributory state' by the European powers through direct intervention, manipulations, and Capitulations. With its history of anti-Turk belligerency dating from the Ottoman conquest of Istanbul in the fifteenth century, the western onslaught was perceived in the popular mind as an attempt to destroy Islam. Partly, pan-Islam was intended to divert the attention of the Turkish people from internal unrest, and that of the subject nationalities from entertaining any political aspirations. The pan-Islamic orientations were also encouraged by the Germans, and, to a lesser degree, by the Russians and the French, particularly in the 1880s and 1890s, in an attempt to advance their political and economic interests at each other's expense. Thus, the 'Sick Man of Europe' was able to get another lease of life and its sultan, almost furtively, came to be regarded as a kind of a Muslim 'Pope', having 'spiritual' authority over all the Muslims. His claim was duly acknowledged in the subsequent treaties by Austria-Hungary (1908), Italy (1912), and Greece and Bulgaria (1913)—an error that the Allies later strove to undo in the abortive Treaty of Sèvres (1920) and the definitive Treaty of Lausanne (1923).[22]

PAN-ISLAM AND THE CALIPHATE QUESTION REVISITED

For Ottoman Turkey, the watershed was the First World War. In November 1914, when it entered the war, it was still a sprawling empire, of which a fertile portion was located in Europe. By the end of the hostilities in October 1918, it had been reduced to a small country facing the threat of complete dismemberment. The Armistice, negotiated by Hüseyin Rauf Orbay on board a British carrier, envisaged *inter alia*, (i) a partial demobilization of the Turkish armed forces and their withdrawal from Transcaucasia to pre-war borders; and (ii) occupation of the Straits and other strategic points, including the *vilayet*s by the Allies. In the changed circumstances, Sultan Vahdeddin Mehmed VI (r. 1918–22), who had succeeded to the throne only a few months earlier, thought it wise to revert to a policy which envisaged total dependence on Britain in the hope of salvaging whatever he could from the mess created by the defeat. But there was hardly any hope as the Allies had made it quite clear that Turkey had been beaten completely and it must, therefore, face the consequences. Secret treaties and other wartime arrangements had committed the Allied policy to devouring the Ottoman Empire. When the war ended, the Entente powers, with remarkable rapidity, began to secure their respective spheres of economic and strategic interests in the Ottoman Empire.[23]

What followed the trauma of defeat was an arduous journey to national regeneration and the emergence of modern Turkey, in which Mustafa Kemal's role was crucial. But, fortunately for the Turks, the Allies could not agree on how to divide their kill. They were more interested in preventing each other from obtaining an advantage than in securing an equitable settlement. The driving force of the Turkish national movement, however, was the Allied-backed Greek invasion of İzmir (15 May 1919), in the heartland of Turkey. The deliberations at Amasaya in June, and, at Erzurum in July–August 1919, outlined the irreducible minimum of the nationalists' demands: that the eastern provinces of Erzurum, Sivas, Diyarbekir, Elazig, Van, Bitlis, Trabzon, and the district of Çanak (Samsun), were an integral part of the Ottoman territories within the national boundaries. Equally important was the fact that Mustafa Kemal had come to power partly with the support of the religious groups and, therefore, the nationalists initially invoked the inviolability of the sultanate-caliphate along with the national independence.

The Sivas Congress of September 1919 amended the Erzurum decisions and delimited the boundaries of the new Turkey inhabited by a Muslim majority, united in religion, culture, and race. These principles were later embodied in the Misak-i Milli of 1920 that became the basis of the nationalist diplomacy and the rallying-point for the Turks. But the rise of the nationalists militated against the plans of the Istanbul government. It could survive only if the movement was to fail, and Damad Ferid Paşa used the weight of the sheikhu'l-Islam's religious authority to seek his aims. He accused the nationalists of fomenting trouble and obtained a *fatwa* from the new sheikhu'l-Islam declaring Mustafa Kemal and his associates rebels and liable to be put to death. This became the basis of the sultan's official death warrant of 24 May against Mustafa Kemal. Stung by the *fatwa*, the nationalists hit back and obtained a counter-*fatwa* from the official mufti of Ankara—and got it attested by 153 *'ulama* throughout Anatolia—that indicted the grand vizier and his colleagues of high treason and appealed to Muslims 'to do all to liberate the Caliph from captivity'. This was the beginning of the struggle with the sultan-caliph which later led to the establishment of a parallel government in Ankara and, eventually, to the abolition of the caliphate. But, for the present, their chance came in March 1920 when, consequent to the uprising in Cilesia, the Allies occupied Istanbul. Describing the sultan-caliph as a captive and the government of Damad Ferid Paşa as too subservient to the Allies, the nationalists built up their organization to oppose the annexation of western Anatolia and the creation of Armenia and the Kurdish state in the east.[24]

Meanwhile, Turkey's fate was sealed on 11 May 1920 when devastating peace terms were imposed. Turkey was made to cede Thrace, Tenedos, and Imros to Greece. A large area in Asia Minor, including Smyrna, was also placed under Greek administration. Turkey was compelled to recognize the independence of Armenia, Syria, Mesopotamia, Palestine, and the Hejaz, and the autonomy of Kurdistan. She was also to recognize the British protectorate over Egypt and Sudan, British sovereignty over Cyprus, and a British mandate for Palestine and Mesopotamia. Similarly, Turkey was to recognize French protectorate over Syria and Tunisia and a French zone in Morocco, and Italian sovereignty over Libya and the Dodecanese. Turkey was also to renounce her rights, secured by the Suez Canal Treaty of 1888, in favour of Britain. The Straits and the Dardanelles were internationalized, and a zone of the Straits was created which was to be controlled by a commission appointed by the League of Nations. The Turkish army was to be reduced drastically, the navy was to be abolished and the Turkish air force was to be disbanded. The proposals also contained stringent financial clauses. The Capitulations were also re-established.[25]

There was a chorus of condemnation against the proposals; even the Porte, at first, hesitated to sign. It finally did so under great pressure from the Allies. But, the nationalists refused to bow. In fact, the Treaty of Sèvres instilled, among them, a fresh will to stand and fight. In August 1920, the Greek forces were routed and driven across the Straits into Europe. Within a fortnight, Greece was begging the Allies to negotiate an armistice on its behalf. By 8 September, Mustafa Kemal's forces had occupied Smyrna and their pacification of Anatolia was practically complete. This, however, brought the Turks almost into a clash with Britain. But, since the French and the Italians were not willing to get involved, the Turks were able to get away with an armistice. Thrace was now theirs and a conference for a treaty to replace the Treaty of Sèvres was proposed to be held at Lausanne sometime in November 1922.[26]

Turkey had been rescued by the genius of Mustafa Kemal but it took the demise of an empire to register the fact that, in order to survive, Turkey must reject pan-Islam and Ottomanism. The separation of religion and the state was but a natural corollary of the prolonged friction that existed between the puppet sultan in Istanbul and the *de facto* government in Ankara. The matter had been precipitated by the Allied action of extending separate invitations to Istanbul and Ankara to attend the peace conference at Lausanne. This gave Mustafa Kemal his much-awaited chance to settle his old score with the sultan. On 1 November 1922, he manoeuvred the GNA to take over the ultimate powers of the government while the caliphate still remained in the House of Osman, but the right to select a caliph was given to the assembly. Thus, the Turkish government was made to appear as the chief bulwark of the caliphate. More concerned about his safety than the loss of power, the sultan fled, took asylum on board a British battleship, and was escorted to Malta from where he proceeded to Makkah as the guest of King Hussein ibn Ali. On the contention that the fugitive monarch had forfeited his position by taking refuge with a non-Muslim power, the GNA, on 18 November, following a *fatwa* from the commissar for religious affairs, proclaimed the deposition of Mehmed VI as caliph and elected his cousin Abdülmecid II, a 54–year old son of the late Sultan Abdülaziz, as his successor with 'spiritual' powers only.[27]

The Ankara Law of 1 November 1922 provoked a strong reaction among Muslims everywhere, except perhaps in a few places. But the Turkish nationalists were justified in trying to establish their own national sovereignty against all enemies, whether the Allies, the Greeks, or the Turks, including the sultan-caliph at Istanbul. And here lay the justification for what the nationalists had done. The final showdown, however, was postponed until after the Treaty of Lausanne (24 July 1923), which once more made Turkey the chief power in the Near East. In fact, when the republic was born, the caliphate had lost its reason to exist. In Mustafa Kemal's opinion, it had become irrelevant and obsolete, and indeed, a nuisance for the Turkish republic. Therefore, the caliphate and all religious institutions must be dealt with in a radical manner. By abolishing the caliphate, the Ankara leaders also hoped to allay British suspicions of pan-Islam, and thereby soften their attitude towards the question of Mosul. The matter was precipitated by an innocuous letter from the Aga Khan (1877–1957) and Ameer Ali—two well-known Indian Muslims—which they wrote from London in November 1923 to Ismet Inönü (1884–1973), prime minister of Turkey, entreating that the Turks reconsider their decision with regard to the caliph and maintain 'the religious and moral solidarity of Islam' by re-establishing the powers of the Sunni caliphate-imamate.[28] The genesis of the letter was the authors' personal anxiety over the fate of the caliphate, but the nationalists, in the prevailing atmosphere of suspicion, took it as part of a big British conspiracy. Thus, the fate of the caliphate was sealed.

By February 1924, the Ankara leaders had definitely decided to abolish the caliphate and expel the imperial household from Turkey. In order to prepare public opinion, Mustafa Kemal took the editors of several Turkish dailies into confidence, conferred with his senior military commanders, and held long consultations with Mustafa Fevzi, the minister of religious affairs. On 2 March, the draft laws on the abolition of the caliphate were considered and endorsed by the Halk Firkasi (Peoples' Party), which was determined to go through with its professed philosophy of nationalism and secularism. As approved by the party, the bills were finally passed by the GNA on 3 March 1924 abolishing the caliphate and deposing the caliph. Within hours of the decision, Abdülmecid II and his family were put on a train to Territet in Switzerland. The nationalists then expelled the rest of the imperial dynasty with the utmost effectiveness.[29]

4. The Caliphate Question and the Muslim World

The crisis in Turkey, generated by the abolition of the caliphate, had wide repercussions in the Muslim world. Its impact on the neighbouring Arab countries was particularly sharpened by the feelings of alienation that had existed against the Turks since the Arab Revolt of 1916. Contrary to popular misconception, nationalistic aspirations among the Arabs were deep-rooted and genuine. But the British backing of Sharif Hussein ibn Ali, and the promise of a Quraishite caliphate, had turned the majority of the Muslims away from Husain who, however, had never forgotten its possibility and had kept making unsuccessful bids for it. But, in March 1924, when the Turks abolished the caliphate, he could restrain himself no longer. Husain manipulated requests from leading Arabs to assume the office, which he did on 5 March, and was recognized as the caliph on 11 March in Shuneh, Jeddah, Aleppo, Damascus, and Beirut. In Egypt his assumption was disapproved of and attributed to British intrigues. However, it was in British India that it encountered the strongest opposition. A vast majority detested him for his alleged dependence on the British and his betrayal of Turkey in the War. There was even a suggestion that killing Husain was a legal obligation. The few isolated cases of support, such as from Maulana Abdul Bari (1879–1926), the well-known *'alim* of the Farangi Mahal madrasa, could not help diminish the feelings of hatred towards him.[30]

But the lingering sore point for the Indian Muslims was not so much the Arab claim as the abolition of the caliphate by the Turks. For six long years since the Armistice, the Indians had conducted a relentless agitation on their behalf in order to save them from the ignominy of dismemberment. Now, they had even been deprived of the plank on which they had stood so far. The Khilafat movement had largely been an expression of their veneration for the sultan-caliph who symbolized the power of Islam. But, quite apart from being a romantic ideal and a psychological leverage, pan-Islam was a means for acquiring national entity in a composite society. Raised first by a small body of pan-Islamists, the Khilafat issue was quickly grabbed by western-educated professional politicians to force the British to leave India. The *ulama* joined hands with them and built up a pervasive agitation. Support from M.K. Gandhi (1869–1948), the rising Hindu leader, brought about the much-needed backing of the Indian National Congress. The result was a movement, the like of which had never been witnessed in the annals of India.[31]

But, in spite of its wide support and multilateral activities, the Khilafat movement failed to achieve its twin objectives, i.e. the preservation of the Ottoman caliphate and the freedom of India. Secret wartime treaties, a strong anti-Turk bias of the Allied governments, and the inherent limitation of the complex movement itself blended to cause this failure. But the major setback came in March 1924, when the Turks abolished the caliphate altogether. Obviously, the professed aims of the Khilafat movement were in direct contradiction with the nationalistic aspirations of the Turks. In the years that followed the abolition, the Indian Muslims did try to divert their attention from extra-territorial matters to domestic issues but found no workable solution. Besides, the Khilafat organization had become so faction-ridden that the rejuvenated All India Muslim League under Mohammad Ali Jinnah seemed to be the only alternative for facing the new challenge.[32]

The question of the reinstatement of the caliphate, however, continued to haunt the Muslim world for a long time. The natural inclination of the Muslim intellectuals, *ulama,* and politicians involved was to advance various suggestions. Among the first was the one put forward by Mohammad Barakatullah Moulavie (1859–1927), a prominent pan-Islamist émigré revolutionary who was working to bring about the fall of the British in India. Barakatullah articulated his views in a book entitled *The Khilafet*, which he published in London in 1924. Written in the aftermath of the abolition crisis, the book aimed at influencing

Muslim opinion to find an amicable solution to the caliphate question. Barakatullah maintained that Mustafa Kemal's action was merely an acknowledgement of the established fact that Turkey was no longer able to maintain the dignity of the sultan-caliph. If someone was to be invested with the high office of the caliphate, then he should only be given spiritual powers. The new caliph must 'shun politics like poison' and eschew interference in political affairs generally. In any case, no despotic king or autocratic priest should be allowed to take control of the people's lives. It was a historical fact that temporal power had always failed to maintain the union of the Muslim nations, and the representatives to the forthcoming Cairo conference had to keep this in mind. Barakatullah proposed a completely new set-up for the caliphate. The governing body was to be the supreme council, the president of which was to be the caliph. The members of this council were to head various administrative departments and the future caliph was to be chosen from among them. The central point in Barakatullah's argument was that the caliphate, being a permanent institution, was meant to perpetuate the mission of the Prophet, i.e. the dissemination of the divine message. Barakatullah recommended Sheikh Ahmad Sanussi for the office of the caliph. As to the seat of the caliphate, he suggested Istanbul or, failing that, Cairo.[33]

The debate thus charted by Barakatullah was next taken up in Egypt by Ali Abd al-Raziq, a professor at the famous al-Azhar University. He was thoroughly conversant with Islamic political philosophy as well as with the Qur'an and the *hadis*. In his book, *al-Islam wa usul al-hukm*, published in Cairo in 1925, Abd al-Raziq made a distinction between spiritual and temporal aspects of the caliphate, but questioned the revival of an institution whose very form he considered defective. The core of Abd al-Raziq's philosophy was that the caliphate was a form of government. In Islam, the caliphate had always been based on brute force, except in rare cases. The caliphs had consolidated their power through coercion and thus obtained legitimacy. The powerful empire that grew in the course of time was Arab in nature, and Islam could not to be held responsible for whatever transgressions took place thereafter. It had nothing to do with the misdeeds and tyranny of individual rulers. Basically, Abd al-Raziq's view was a secularist contention and was too revolutionary for the *'ulama* at al-Azhar. He was declared a heretic, stripped of all his academic titles, and removed from office.[34] Closer to Barakatullah's proposals were those by another Egyptian, A. Sanhoury, who published a work in French in Paris in 1926. Sanhoury also suggested the election of a caliph by a general assembly of the caliphate. The only addition he made was that a smaller supreme council was to meet more often. Both the bodies were to be presided over by the caliph, who was to combine in his office both the spiritual and the temporal powers.[35]

Meanwhile, the political scenario changed towards the end of 1924 after Ibn Saud ousted Husain from the Hejaz. Ibn Saud, in spite of his success, had preferred to crown himself king. It was in Egypt that the patter for the claim to the caliphate became audible. But the Egyptian case for King Fuad's candidature, supported as it was by the *'ulama* under Muhammad Mustafa al-Maraghi (1881–1945), cut at the very basis of the Ottoman-centred pan-Islam of Mustafa Kamil Paşa (1874–1908) and his followers. Al-Maraghi had at first been opposed to the abolition of the caliphate as he was contemptuous of the likely contenders, especially Hussein ibn Ali. Gradually, he had come round to the idea of an Arab Egyptian caliphate.[36] However, the decision had been deferred to the Cairo conference of world Muslim representatives which was scheduled for early 1925. As it turned out, the conference could not be held until May 1926, and even when it assembled, most of the Muslim countries chose to ignore it. Only thirty-nine delegates representing non-official organizations in Egypt, Palestine, Tripolitania, Tunisia, Morocco, Hejaz, Yemen, Iraq, Poland, the Dutch Indies, the Sultanate of Johur, and South Africa attended. Turkey furiously opposed the convening of the conference, as did the deposed caliph then living in Switzerland. Algeria,

Iran, and Afghanistan refused to attend. The Indian Central Khilafat Committee (CKC) also refrained from sending any representative. The latter feared that if a British vassal like the Egyptian monarch was to become the caliph, he would indirectly enhance Britain's 'power of mischief' in the Muslim world. Even the Khaksar leader, Inayatullah Khan Mashriqi (1888–1963), who attended the conference in his individual capacity, chose to speak out against King Fuad's candidature. The resultant controversy forced the organizers to shelve the question of electing a new caliph. The greater part of the deliberations was wasted in procedural matters and, beyond giving a theoretical definition of the caliphate or laying down the procedure of nomination, no definite declaration was made. The question was left wide open for a future convention to decide.[37]

The second moot, the conference at Makkah, opened on 6 June 1926 but, like the Cairo conference, proved a failure. Of course, there were far more, and more celebrated, delegates at this conference than at Cairo, including those from Turkey, Afghanistan, and India, but Ibn Saud cleverly excluded any discussion of the caliphate issue from the agenda. He was only interested in obtaining the recognition of his conquest of the Holy Places. Most of the seventy-five delegates were extremely disappointed. The proceedings, therefore, turned to discussing pan-Islamic matters. The Ali brothers, who represented the CKC, tried to persuade the conference to decide on guarantees for the independence of Arabia. But this did not suit Ibn Saud. Dissension became quite apparent under the thin veil of the slogans of solidarity. The delegates returned home without achieving any solid results.[38]

The matter, however, did not end there. The supporters of the caliphate system continued to cherish the revival of the institution, at least in an ornamental form. As time passed, the number of aspirants increased. Apart from King Fuad of Egypt, Ibn Saud of the Nejd-Hejaz, Emir/King Faisal of Iraq, Imam Muhammad Hamid ed-Din Yahya (1869–1948) of Yemen, and even the Nizam Mir Osman Ali Khan (1886–1967) of Hyderabad, were reported to be desirous of becoming the caliph, to the detriment of each other, as none would concede primacy to the other. Yet, of all the contenders, ex-Caliph Abdülmecid II was still the favourite. Already, in May 1930, General Cherif Paşa, the well-known Turk of Kurdish origin who was then living in Paris, had floated the idea of settling Abdülmecid II in India so that his acceptance as caliph might become easier.[39] But, when, a conference was convened in Jerusalem in 1931 through the efforts of the Mufti of Palestine, Amin al-Huseini (1897–1974), and Shaukat Ali, the caliphate issue was not discussed at all. It appeared to have lost its relevance. The pan-Islamic conference held in Geneva in 1935 also took no notice of its reinstatement. Later, in March 1937, when Abdülmecid became seriously ill, young King Faruq's name began to crop up through various sources. The Egyptians conveniently forgot that Abdülmecid had as many as three legal successors who were waiting in the wings: Prince Selim (1870–1937), the eldest son of Abdülhamid II, then in Syria; Prince Ziaeddin, the eldest son of Murad V, then in Egypt; and Prince Ahmed Nihad (1883–1954), grandson of Murad V, then in Syria. He could also nominate his own successor—his son, King Farouk (1936–52), or the Nizam whose eldest son was married to his daughter. Al-Maraghi, who was supporting Farouk, maintained that he was proposing only a territorial or local title for the Egyptian ruler and not a universal appellation. And since the Aga Khan was also backing al-Maraghi on this issue, it created an impression that the British were behind Farouk's candidature.[40]

In the controversy that ensued, the Turkish government could not remain unconcerned about the proposal of reviving the caliphate, even if it were to be a local title. Perhaps it was not clearly understood that the caliphate question was not just an issue of Egyptian party politics, as it concerned the entire Muslim *ummat*. Informed opinion, however, knew that the neutrality of the European powers was an essential ingredient in any solution, especially when leaders like Benito Mussolini

(1883–1945) were believed to be toying with the idea of exploiting the issue. But it was forgotten that the office of the caliphate could not be assumed by simply desiring it. None of the Muslim countries wielded enough power to lay an effective claim. Nor was there any consensus among Muslim countries on this issue. In fact, informed circles considered the whole idea absurd. Even if the Indian Muslims were to have supported a candidate, the Turks would not relent their pressure. Yet, the Egyptians continued to chase the shadow. The charade lasted until the 1940s when the inauguration of the Arab League changed the slogan from pan-Islam to a pan-Arab union. Only then, says a perceptive writer, 'the ambition of an Egyptian caliphate died a most reluctant death',[41] but not before another congress was proposed in Cairo soon after the conclusion of the Second World War in 1945. Again, the figure of the Aga Khan was seen to be lurking in the shadows[42] but, like many other proposals, this one, too, remained a mere dream.

Since then, the revival of the institution of the caliphate has remained a top item on the agenda of the pan-Islamists. It is an article of faith with the leaders of the Islamic resurgence. In Pakistan, especially, the *'ulama* and the traditionalist Muslims, from the very early days of independence, demanded for the establishment of a truly world-wide Islamic *ummat* which in effect meant a reversion to the early days of the Islamic caliphate. Various leaders, from time to time, have craved indulgence for its revival. In the wake of Gen. Ziaul Haq's (1924–88) Islamization programme, in particular, the search for a viable political system brought round the *'ulama* and their political collaborators to demand the re-establishment of the Islamic caliphate. Its political overtones became quite apparent when the *'ulama* agreed that the caliph thus chosen would rule uninterrupted and unchallenged throughout his mortal life.[43] Similar dreams have haunted the ruling élite in other Islamic countries. Whether these can be brought to fruition is the question, but the existence of a pan-Islamic organization like the Mu'tamar al-Alam al-Islami (World Muslim Congress), with its headquarters in Karachi and branches and affiliations in all six continents, shows that the dream for a worldwide Islamic polity continues to haunt the Muslims of the world.

NOTES

1. For more concise information on Islam and Islamic civilization, see Fazlur Rahman, 'Islam', *Encyclopaedia Britannica*, ix, 1981, 911–26; and—*Islam*, 2nd edn. (Chicago, 1979); H.A.R. Gibb, *Islam* (Oxford, 1975); L. Gardet, 'Islam', *Encyclopaedia of Islam*, iv, 1978, 171–4; and Abdo A. Elkholy, 'The Concept of Community in Islam', in Khurshid Ahmad and Zafar Ishaq Ansari (eds.), *Islamic Perspectives* (London, 1979), 171–81.
2. The full sweep of Islamic expansion can be followed in Gibb (ed.), *Whither Islam?*, 15 ff; J. Jomier, 'Islam', *Encyclopaedia of Islam*, iv, 174 and 177; and Reuben Levy, *The Social Structure of Islam*, 2nd edn. (Cambridge, 1979), 4–52.
3. Abul-Ala Maududi, *Islamic Law and Constitution* (tr. and ed.), Khurshid Ahmad (Lahore, 1960), 148.
4. For a discussion of the state and society in Islam see, e.g., Sherwani, *Studies in the History of Early Muslim Political Thought and Administration*, 254–74; Rosenthal, *Political Thought in Medieval Islam*, 7–8 and 21–7; Hasan Askari, *Society and State in Islam* (Lahore, 1979), esp. 70 and 120; and Sadiq al-Mehdi, 'The Concept of an Islamic State', in Altaf Gauhar (ed.), *The Challenge of Islam* (London, 1978), 122 ff.
5. S. Khuda Bukhsh, *Studies: Indian and Islamic* (London, 1927), 23–5.
6. Aziz Ahmad, 'Shrinking Frontiers of Dar al-Islam', Quaid-i-Azam Memorial Lectures Series (Islamabad 1975), 1–32.
7. Seyyed Hossein Nasr, *Ideals and Realities of Islam*, 2nd edn. (London, 1975), 36.
8. Kemal H. Karpat, *Political and Social Thought in the Contemporary Middle East* (New York, 1982), 90.
9. Khalifa Abdul Hakim, *Islamic Ideology*, 3rd edn. (Lahore, 1980), 132.
10. Sayyid Abul-Ala Maududi, *A Short History of the Revivalist Movement in Islam*, 2nd Eng. edn. (Lahore, 1972), 35.
11. See J.O. Voll, *Islam: Continuity and Change in the Modern World* (Boulder, 1982), 35; Fazlur Rahman, 'Islam: Challenges and Opportunities', in Alford T. Welch and Pierre Cachia (eds.), *Islam: Past Influence and Present Challenge* (Edinburgh, 1979), 317; Alexander Bennigsen and Marie Broxup, *The Islamic Threat to the Soviet State* (London, 1983), 73–7, and Albert Hourani, *The Emergence of Modern Middle East* (London, 1981), 76.

12. Mohammad Iqbal's views can best be followed in his *The Reconstruction of Religious Thought in Islam*, reprint (Lahore, 1982).
13. F. Rahman, 'Islam', *Encyclopaedia Britannica*, ix, 924; and id., 'Roots of Islamic Neo-Fundamentalism', in Philip H. Stoddard (ed.), *Change and the Muslim World* (Syracuse, 1981), esp. 28.
14. Fauzi M. Najjar, 'Democracy in Islamic Political Philosophy', *Studia Islamica*, 51 (1980), 120–2.
15. Carlo Caldarola, *Religion and Societies: Asia and the Middle East* (Berlin, 1982), 15–16.
16. Karpat, *Political and Social Thought*, esp. 91 ff; and Landau, *Politics of Pan-Islam*, passim.
17. Nikki R. Keddie, *An Islamic Response to Imperialism*, 22–8; id., *Sayyid Jamal ad-Din "al-Afghani": A Political Biography*, 57 ff; and Landau, *Politics of Pan-Islam*, 13 ff.
18. C.V. Findley, 'The Advent of Ideology in the Islamic Middle East', *Studia Islamica*, 55 (1982), 140–51, n. 3; Shaukat Ali, *Pan-Movements in the Third World* (Lahore, 1976), 119. ff; and Stoddard (ed.), *Change and the Muslim World*, 19.
19. The more important discussions on the theory and practice of the Caliphate are by Ameer Ali, 'The Caliphate, a Historical and Juridical Sketch', 681–94; Azad, *Mas'ala-i Khilafat wa Jazira-i 'Arab*; Arnold, *The Caliphate*; and Syed Aziz-al Ahsan, 'State, Legitimacy, and Succession: Sunni Political Traditions and Colonial Heritage', *Journal of South Asian and Middle Eastern Studies*, 16/3, (Spring 1993), 1–24.
20. See Naeem Qureshi, *Pan-Islam in British India*, 12–13; and Özcan, *Pan-Islamism*, 25 ff.
21. Özcan, *Pan-Islamism*, 35–40; and Landau, *Politics of Pan-Islam*, 36–72.
22. Feroz Ahmad, 'The Late Ottoman Empire', in Marian Kent (ed.), *The Great Powers and the End of the Ottoman Empire* (London, 1989), 6–14; and Ahmed Emin, *Turkey in the World War* (New Haven, 1930), 26–7 and 34–9.
23. Britain moved in to control the Straits, Mesopotamia, and the Arabian Peninsula. France manoeuvred to preserve her privileges in Syria. Italy was intent on holding on to the Dodecanese and the *vilayet* of Adalia. The United States, though unwilling to accept any territorial reward, nevertheless advocated the dismemberment of the Ottoman Empire. See Feroz Ahmad, 'The Late Ottoman Empire', 8–18; H.N. Howard, *The Partition of Turkey* (Norman, 1931), 181–213; J. Nevakivi, *Britain, France and the Arab Middle East, 1914–1920* (London, 1969), 95 ff.; and Naeem Qureshi, *Pan-Islam in British India*, 60.
24. Feroz Ahmad, *The Making of Modern Turkey* (London & New York, 1993), 47–9; Dankwart A. Rustow, 'Politics and Islam in Turkey, 1920–1955', in Richard N.

Frye (ed.), *Islam and the West* (The Hague, 1957), 76; and R.S. Salahi, *Turkish Diplomacy, 1918–1923* (Abingdon, 1975), 14–30.
25. Naeem Qureshi, *Pan-Islam in British India*, 113–14.
26. Ibid., 203–4 and 246–9.
27. Ibid., 251–5.
28. Ibid., 279–81.
29. Ibid., 284–6; and Mim Kemal Öke, *Tahrik-i Khilafat*. Urdu tr. Nisar Ahmad Asrar (Karachi, 1991), 174–202.
30. Ibid., 380–1.
31. For details, see M. Naeem Qureshi, 'The Indian Khilafat Movement (1918–1924)', *Journal of Asian History*, 12/2 (1978), 152–68.
32. Ibid., 167.
33. Barakatullah Maulavie, *The Khilafet*, passim.
34. Bassam Tibi, *Arab Nationalism*. Eng. tr., Marion Farouk-Sluglett and Peter Sluglett (London, 1981), 148–9.
35. Landau, *Politics of Pan-Islam*, 222.
36. See Denis Walker, 'Pan-Islam as a Modern Ideology in Egyptian Independence Movement of Mustafa Kamil', *Hamdard Islamicus*, 17/1 (Spring 1994), 57–109; and Elie Kedourie, 'Egypt and the Caliphate, 1915–1946', *Journal of the Royal Asiatic Society*, 95/3–4 (1963), 214.
37. Landau, *Politics of Pan-Islam*, 237–8; and Naeem Qureshi, *Pan-Islam in British India*, 306–7.
38. Naeem Qureshi, *Pan-Islam in British India*, 306–7.
39. OIOC, L/P&S/10/1314, files P&J(S), 1784/31 and 1367/31 with 1449/31 and file PZ 3265/30 with PZ 2934/1937.
40. Landau, *Politics of Pan-Islam*, 240–5; OIOC, L/P&S/12/230, files PZ 2934/37, PZ 3000/37, PZ 2401/38 and PZ 2471/38.
41. Elie Kedourie, 'Egypt and the Caliphate', 242. Also see OIOC, file PZ 4483/38.
42. OIOC, L/P&S/12/1022, file 4195/45.
43. See *Jang* (Magazine section), 30 Sept.–6 Oct. 1988.

4

Pleading the Case of The Ottoman Caliphate: Indian Khilafatists' Endeavours in Europe*

Part 1

For the Muslims of British India, Ottoman Turkey, with its pretence of being the last great Muslim power and claimant to the 'universal' caliphate of Islam, had always had a special attraction. Whenever the Ottoman Empire was threatened by western encroachments, reverberations in Muslim India were prompt and intense.[1] This pan-Islamic reaction reached its climax after the First World War when the Allied statesmen gathered round the conference table to divide the severed limbs of the Ottoman Empire among themselves. Thus began, in December 1918, the famous Khilafat movement in India that attempted to save Turkey from the ignominy of spoliation.[2] The movement—led originally by Abdul Bari, the head of the Farangi Mahal seminary in Lucknow, and two Delhi-based physician-politicians, Dr M.A. Ansari and Hakim Ajmal Khan (1865–1927)—was born in the embryo of the

---

*Originally published as 'Mohamed Ali's Khilafat Delegation to Europe, 1920', in the *Journal of Pakistan Historical Society* (Karachi), 28/2 (Apr. 1980), 79–117 and 28/3 (July 1980), 157–85.

All India Muslim League (founded in 1906). But, soon, a separate body, known as the Central Khilafat Committee or the CKC, was formed in Bombay under a wealthy businessman, Seth Jan Muhammad Chotani, to concentrate solely on the Turkish issue. Mohamed Ali and his elder brother, Shaukat Ali, the two firebrand brothers who later took over and led the movement, were at that time in British captivity—undergoing the rigours of detention for their pan-Islamic exuberance since 1915.

It was under these trying circumstances over the Turkish peace settlement that the CKC decided, in November 1919, probably on the advice of M.A. Jinnah,[3] to send an Indian Muslim delegation to Britain to canvass support on the question of the caliphate and the Holy Places of Islam.[4] The decision was affirmed by the first All-India Khilafat Conference, held at Delhi (23 November) under the chairmanship of Abul Kasem Fazlul Haq (1873–1962). The objective was to lay the sentiments of the Indian Muslims before the British cabinet and, if necessary, to do the same in the United States.[5] The second Khilafat Conference, held at Amritsar in the last week of December 1919, reaffirmed this resolution and decided to dispatch the delegation forthwith. Another delegation was to visit Turkey, ostensibly to tender 'sentiments of Islamic brotherhood' to the caliph on behalf of Indian Muslims.[6] The conference also authorized a deputation of prominent Hindu-Muslim leaders to wait on the viceroy of India, Lord Chelmsford (1868–1933), and seek his permission and assistance for the delegations.[7] Subsequently, in January 1920 when the viceroy was approached in this regard, he promised to do all that he could to assist and enable the mission to Europe to represent the views of the Indian Muslims while in Paris and London. But, he expressed his apprehension that the delegation might be too late as the peace terms were about to be announced.[8]

Originally, the Khilafat delegation was to consist of seventeen well-known leaders. Prominent among those nominated were the Raja of Mahmudabad (1877–1931; UP), Abdul Bari of Farangi Mahal (UP),

Syed Reza Ali (1880–1949; UP), Syud Hossain (1888–1949; UP), Seth Chotani (Bombay), Mirza Sir Abbas Ali Baig (1858–1932; Bombay), Sir Fazulbhoy Currimbhoy (b. 1872; Bombay), Dr Ansari (Delhi), Seth Haji (Sir) Abdoola Haroon (1872–1942; Sind), Fazlul Haq (Bengal), Abul Kasem (1871–1936; Bengal), Syed Hasan Imam (1871–1933; CP), and Mian (Sir) Fazl-i-Husain (1879–1936; Punjab), with the power to add to their number.[9] But, by the time the arrangements were finalized, a much smaller delegation was selected. The leader of the delegation was none other than Mohamed Ali, the fiery journalist-politician who had, in 1913, led a two-member delegation to Britain to secure redress in the famous Kanpur (Cawnpore) Mosque affair.[10] Educated at Aligarh and Oxford, Mohamed Ali had a brief initial career in the states of Rampur and Baroda before embarking on a brilliant journalistic venture. He edited two well-known journals of Indian opinion, the *Comrade* and the *Hamdard*, which were later banned for their pan-Islamic fervour; the editor was interned at Chindwara in the CP, along with his elder brother Shaukat Ali.

The First World War ended in October/November 1918 but it took the government almost a year to release the Ali brothers along with the other detainees. The CKC lost no time in asking Mohamed Ali to lead the delegation to Europe.[11] The other members of the delegation were also chosen with care and commissioned to perform specific duties. For instance, Abu Najib Anisu'l-Hasan, better known as Syed Sulaiman Nadwi (1884–1953), the head of the Shibli Academy in Azamgarh and the editor of *al-Nadwa*, was to represent the *'ulama* of India, who had re-emerged after their absence from the public scene since the cataclysm of 1857. He was also required to answer any criticism of religious or historical nature, secure support from Muslims of Islamic countries, and send home weekly reports of the delegation's activities abroad.[12] Syud Hossain, the thirty-two year old editor of Pandit Motilal Nehru's *Independent* (Allahabad), was to emphasize Indian feelings concerning the Khilafat question.[13] Hassan Muhammad Hayat, who later entered the service of the Nawab of Bhopal, was to act as the secretary to the delegation.[14] Abul Kasem, the Bengal legislator, and Mushir Hosain Kidwai, the well-known pan-Islamist barrister and the head of the Islamic Information Bureau in London, were to join the delegation in Britain later that summer.[15]

Prior to the delegation's departure for Europe, Mohamed Ali, accompanied by his brother Shaukat Ali, who as honorary secretary of the CKC had become the most powerful leader of the Khilafat movement, undertook a whirlwind tour of the principal centres of political activity in northern India in order to raise funds for the expenses of the delegation. They were given rousing receptions in most places, particularly in Delhi, but the amount of money collected by them fell considerably short of the target of one million rupees in spite of the fact that the Ali brothers contributed the entire sum of money presented to them at public meetings for their personal use.[16] Nevertheless, on 1 February 1920, the Khilafat delegation left Bombay for Europe by the Italian steamer S.S. *Hungaria*.[17] The members were given a hearty send-off and Abdul Bari and Seth Chotani were there at the quayside to bid them farewell.[18]

On board the ship, Mohamed Ali tried to learn spoken Arabic; and Sulaiman Nadwi occupied himself by taking English lessons as he was not fluent in the language.[19] Syud Hossain kept himself busy with his books.[20] After passing Karachi, they briefly stopped at Aden, Massawa, and Port Said, mingling with the local population at each stop and explaining the purpose of their mission to them. At Massawa, they also met Mushir Kidwai and Lala Lajpat Rai (1865–1928), who were on their way to India by another ship.[21] They wanted to visit Cairo from Port Said but could not get a suitable train connection.[22] At the Italian port of Brindisi in the Adriatic the ship's employees staged a strike and were persuaded, with much difficulty, to take the ship to Venice.[23]

When the delegation disembarked at Venice on the evening of 21 February 1920, they learnt from the local newspapers that the Peace Conference regarding the future of the Ottoman Empire had already started its deliberations in London. Fearing that a decision would be taken before they reached London, the delegation cabled the Allied governments and, in particular, David Lloyd George, the British prime minister, and Edwin S. Montagu (1879–1924), the British secretary of state for India, requesting them to postpone a verdict until after the delegation had been given the opportunity to explain the Muslim case.[24] Pending the submission of a detailed memorial on arrival in London, they briefly outlined the Indian Muslim view on the question of the Khilafat.[25] The telegram was repeated to a number of leaders of the Labour Party, the Reuters news agency, and principal British newspapers.[26] From Venice, they left for France on 23 February by way of Switzerland, reaching Paris two days later. Then, on the evening of 26 February 1920, in spite of a rail-strike in France, the delegation managed to reach London.[27]

On their arrival in London, the members of the Khilafat delegation went straight to Parliament where a debate had been forced in the House of Commons by anti-Turkish circles against the Supreme Council's decision, on 14 February 1920, to leave Istanbul with Turkey.[28] By the time the Indians took their seats in the gallery, the debate was halfway through. The prime minister had already spoken, and although he had fought tooth and nail against the decision on Istanbul in the Council, in Parliament he defended the Allies' verdict as a political expedient.[29] Most of the remaining speakers had relentlessly attacked the decision. Sir Donald Maclean (1864–1932), Lord Robert Cecil (1864–1958), T.P. O'Connor (1848–1929), S.F. Ormsby-Gore (1863–1950), and Sir Charles Oman (1860–1946) were vociferous in advocating the expulsion of the Turks from Europe.[30] 'What we want', cried Lord Robert Cecil, 'is to put an end to Turkish rule in Constantinople.'[31] A telegram— allegedly sent to France from Alexandria—was read out to the House and purported to warn against the danger of a massacre of the entire Armenian population in Marash (Cilicia) at the hands of the Turks.[32] The debate in the Commons was an unmistakable indication of the trend of prevailing public opinion which Mohamed Ali and his companions discovered they would have to face.

In fact, Britain was in the grip of a highly prejudiced propaganda against the Turks who were depicted as villainous butchers and incapable rulers. The critics ranged from those who were opposed to them as a matter of policy to distinctly anti-Islamic groups.[33] The fact of the matter is that ever since the reversal of the pro-Turkish policy by the Marquess of Salisbury (1830–1903) in the 1870s, British public opinion had been ill-disposed towards the Ottoman Empire.[34] Mild at first, this hostility had become extremely aggressive since the First World War.[35] As time passed, the clamour for vengeance intensified. Since early 1919, a movement had been afoot to secure the expulsion of the Ottomans from Europe as well as to obtain the 'redemption' of the 'cathedral' of Hagia Sophia (built CE 532–37) to Christianity.[36]

In order to force the hands of the Allies, Lord Robert Cecil and Viscount James Bryce (1838–1922), the two most vehement critics of Turkey, organized several protest meetings.[37] While Lord Cecil demanded the end of Turkish rule over other races 'once and for all',[38] Lord Byrce insisted that 'no Turkish control east of the Taurus mountains' must be the principle while dealing with Turkey.[39] A number of parliamentarians, intellectuals, and Orientalists lent their willing support. Ormsby-Gore, Donald Maclean, O'Connor, and Charles Oman left no opportunity either inside or outside Parliament to condemn the Turks.[40] Historian Arnold J. Toynbee (1889–1975) wrote a series of articles in favour of the argument.[41] Rev. William Holden Hutton (1860–1930), Dean of Winchester and Reader in Indian History at Oxford, claimed that Indian Muslim opinion regarding the Turkish question was exaggerated and that Istanbul should not be given to the Turks.[42] Professor D.S. Margoliouth

(1858–1940), at one time Mohamed Ali's tutor at Oxford,[43] even questioned the Ottoman claim to the Islamic caliphate and sought to prove that the title was of a comparatively recent origin.[44] A pamphlet in wide circulation in Britain, entitled *Sultan as Caliph*, written by Professor Carlo Nallino (1872–1938) of the Royal University of Rome, argued that the caliphate as an institution was non-existent since the fall of the Abbasids.[45] One, P. Tonapetean, described the sultan as a 'heretic and an impostor' who owed his title of caliph to the 'British friends of Turkey', and who enjoyed little support among the Muslims themselves. Tonapetean maintained that the Turk, as a ruler, had been criminal throughout and unless his empire was brought under the control of 'a civilized strong power' there was little chance of reform.[46] An Arab caliphate in the person of Sharif Hussein ibn Ali of Makkah was enthusiastically advocated and accepted.[47] In the same way, pro-Greek circles, led by the Anglo-Hellenic Society, pushed the claim of a revived empire of ancient Greece embracing Asia Minor and the East. The acquisition of Smyrna was considered the first stage in this direction.[48]

The British Press, led by Viscount Northcliffe's (1865–1922) *The Times* of London, lent its active support to the campaign. 'Europe can never again know lasting peace until the Turks return to the uplands of Anatolia from where they came', wrote the journal in one of its issues.[49] 'If the Turkish administration is not now uprooted from Europe', warned the same paper in a different issue, 'another war will have to be fought in the future in order to evict the Turks from their last lodgement on European Soil'.[50] Another London Journal, the *New Europe*, lamented the Allied decision on Istanbul as 'a dangerous attempt to settle a fundamental European problem for purely Asiatic reasons'.[51] The press generally exhibited extreme partisanship by highlighting every bit of news derogatory to Turkey but suppressing any which was even remotely favourable.

To reinforce their demand for Turkish eviction from Europe, the anti-Turk faction magnified the alleged Armenian massacres said to have been perpetrated by the Turks during the war, and later in early 1920 in Marash by the Turkish nationalists.[52] An exceedingly vigorous and systematic propaganda, backed by large funds, was conducted on behalf of the Armenians through such media as the cinema, the theatre, and the press. The 'massacres' were termed 'the blackest page in modern history'[53] and described as the result of careful planning, the order for which had originated from Istanbul.[54] *The Treatment of Armenians in the Ottoman Empire, (1915–1916)*,[55] a document prepared by Arnold Toynbee and Lord Bryce in 1916 and presented to the British Parliament, was often cited as an indictment against the Turks.[56]

Horrifying details of alleged murders of defenceless Armenian men, women, and children, based on the accounts of American and European missionaries who had worked in Asia Minor, found their way into the press and works of fiction.[57] Particularly scandalous was a novel entitled *Auction of Souls*, which depicted harrowing details of alleged Turkish atrocities on Armenians. It became so popular that, within a few months of its initial publication, it went into four editions.[58] Its stage and film versions, which drew large crowds in the theatres and cinemas of Britain and America, were equally effective in creating anti-Turk sentiment.[59] Another book entitled *The Memoirs of Naim Bey*, supposedly written by an Ottoman ex-chief secretary to the 'deportations committee' of Aleppo, was circulated in support of the argument. It contained facsimiles of 'documents' claiming to be orders for massacres from Talat Paşa and Enver Paşa, two of the triumvirate then ruling Turkey.[60] As a result, the British public, which was already anti-Turk, was roused beyond recall. A mere mention of Armenia in a British gathering was enough to defeat the Turkish case.[61]

A forceful sustenance to the campaign came from the Anglican Church, which treated a purely political problem as a religious issue, representing it as a struggle between the Cross and the Crescent. For instance, Dr Cosmo Gordon Lang (1864–1945), the Archbishop of York, for instance, speaking at the York Diocesan conference on 19 February 1920, declared that 'some way must be found if the conscience of Christendom is to be satisfied for protecting those to whom we have given our solemn bond and promise'.[62] Dr John Clifford (1826–1923), the British Nonconformist minister, propagandist, and Liberal politician, advocated 'a clean and complete settlement' of the problem by carrying out the 'bag and baggage' policy of the Victorian premier William Gladstone (1809–98) as 'the imperative demand of civilization.'[63] Dr Arthur Winnington-Ingram (1858–1946), and Edmund Arbuthnott Knox (1847–1937), Bishops of London and Manchester, respectively, were equally in the forefront.[64] But, by far the most implacable adversary was Dr Randall Thomas Davidson (1848–1930), the Archbishop of Canterbury. In his support for the Armenian and Greek causes, he was probably attracted by the possibility of enhancing the prestige of the Anglican Church.[65] In March 1920, the archbishop received a telegram from Bishop Birch of New York, on behalf of a hundred American bishops, thanking him for his leadership 'in crusade against [the] retention of Turks in Constantinople and [the] spoliation of Armenia'.[66] The archbishop, in his reply, assured them of his 'continued and cordial sympathy' in that regard.[67] Similarly, he assured the Holy Synod of the Church of Constantinople of the support of the Church of England for the 'deliverance of oppressed races and renewal of Christianity in the Near East'.[68] The archbishop's anti-Turk campaign found support from the Armenian Patriarch, the Archbishop of Trebizond, the Archbishop of Sinar, and the sister of the Patriarch of the Nestronians who especially came to London in February 1920 to plead the Armenian case.[69] Thus, there was, in the words of Lloyd George, a recrudescence of 'something of the old feeling of Christendom against the Crescent'.[70]

Such being the case, the Indian Muslims' demands found little support in Britain. The Khilafat movement was dismissed as nothing but a well-organized, lavishly financed, artificial agitation engineered by radical Muslim opinion.[71] Arnold Toynbee argued that Indian Sunni Muslims did not reflect the opinion of the Muslim world, except for its pride in Turkey as a great Muslim power. The Indian Muslims' apprehensions were uncalled for as the Allies had no intention to 'make the political subjection of Islam to Christendom', and it was also out of question 'that we should deliberately favour Moslems in the settlement in violation of our principles'.[72] He thought that the real reason behind the Indian clamour was the collapse of the Turkish Empire and, as a remedy, suggested grant of self-government to India, Egypt, Iraq, and Iran.[73] (Sir) T.W. Arnold (1864–1930), who had been associated with the University of the Punjab and the Mohammadan Anglo-Oriental College of Aligarh and, at that time, was the educational adviser to the secretary of state for India, thought that the movement had no sound religious basis; rather, it derived its strength from 'hatred of Europe and rage at the growing domination of Europe over the Oriental world'. What the Khilafatists were fighting for, maintained Arnold, was 'Mahommadan sovereignty and prestige'.[74]

The British cabinet, too, was ill-disposed towards Turkey.[75] It was hardly expected to have any sympathy for the caliphate question in view of the opinions held by Lloyd George and Lord Curzon of Kedleston (1859–1925), a former viceroy of India and the secretary of state for foreign affairs. Lloyd George was bitterly anti-Turk and equally pronounced in his pro-Greek sentiments, probably because of his attitude as a true Gladstonian liberal of the old 'bag and baggage' school. His 'romantic admiration' for ancient Greece and his adulation of Eleutherios Venizelos (1864–1936), the then Greek premier, must also have influenced his approach.[76] But, perhaps the imperial consideration of a policy of expansion as well as some latent religious prejudice played as much a part in the formation of his anti-Turk views.[77] Similarly, Lord Curzon advocated a policy that suggested the reduction of Turkey to purely an Asiatic state with the sultan and his court retiring either to Bursa or

Konya. Istanbul would then be administered through an international commission, clinching St. Sophia back as a church.[78] As regards the Khilafat movement, he brushed it aside as having been engineered from Britain by Kidwai and his associates[79]—a view that was in keeping with his ideas about the agitation against the partition of Bengal in 1905. Lord Hardinge, another former viceroy of India and the permanent under-secretary for foreign affairs at that time, was opposed to giving any weight to the Indian Muslims' feelings while dealing with Turkey.[80] Both Curzon and Hardinge lamented the 'shocking weakness' of the Indian government which they thought had rendered the agitation formidable.[81] The Government of India's representations for lenient treatment of Turkey, as a concession to Indian Muslim sentiment, therefore, fell on deaf ears.

By no means, however, was this general hostility towards the Turkish cause synonymous with the opinion of the entire British nation. There was a small minority which supported and sympathized with the Turkish and Indian aspirations, particularly from the time of the Tripolitan and Balkan Wars (1911–13), with only a temporary recession during the First World War.[82] The contemplated dismemberment of the Ottoman Empire now revived pro-Turkish sentiment among some of the British. On the floor of the House of Commons, parliamentarians like Earl Winterton (1883–1962), Col. Josiah Wedgwood (1872–1943), Brig.-Gen. H. Conyers Surtees (1858–1933), Lt. Col. Aubury Herbert (1880–1943), Lt.-Commander J.J. Kennworthy, and J.D. Rees (1854–1922) raised their voices against such an eventuality.[83] Some other eminent Englishmen, foremost among whom were Earl Abingdon (1836–1928), Lord Ampthill (1869–1935), Lord Carmichael (1859–1926), Sir Theodore Morison (1863–1936), Sir Louis Dane (1856–1946), Field Marshall Sir Charles Egerton (1848–1921), and Sir James La Touche (1844–1921) pleaded with Lloyd George that an anti-Turk policy would alienate Muslims and sow the seeds of great peril. They also urged the prime minister to abide by his pledge of 5 January

1918.⁸⁴ Sir George Roos-Keppel (1866–1921) and Professor E.G. Browne (1862–1926) were the other friends of Turkey.⁸⁵ The Anglo-Ottoman Society of Lord Mowbray (l867–1936), gave full support to the cause.⁸⁶ English Muslims like Marmaduke Pickthall (1875–1936) of Kidwai's Information Bureau, Omar Henson Flight of the Islamic Society, Khalid Sheldrake (b. 1888) of Manchester, Professor H.M. Léon/Abdullah Quilliam (1855–1932), dean of the London College of Physiology and vice-president of the Anglo-Ottoman Society, and others like them came up with all possible assistance.⁸⁷

The efforts of these prominent Britons were supplemented by the Indian Muslims residing in England who were, since the turn of the century, doing all in their power to protect Indian and Islamic interests in Britain. In the forefront was the London Muslim League, which conducted the bulk of the work. Technically, it was a subsidiary of the All India Muslim League, but for all practical purposes it used its own initiative—more like an allied organization.⁸⁸ In 1920, the London League was led, as before, by Syed Ameer Ali, the sixty-year old member of the Judicial Committee of the Privy Council and a veteran politician, who had organized, as early as 1878, the National Mahommedan Association for the uplift of the Muslims of India.⁸⁹ M. Hashim Ispahani was its honorary secretary, and the Aga Khan, who was well-connected with leaders of public opinion and ministers in Britain and Europe, did what he could to help obtain leniency for Turkey.⁹⁰

The two Islamic societies supplemented the work of the London League. Of these, the Islamic Society, established in 1886, had a somewhat of an international character as its members were drawn from various countries. Barrister Syed Abdul Majid of Monghir (India), who was one of the founder members of the Muslim League and a lecturer in Mohammadan Law at the Colonial Office, was the president of the society, while Nawab W.H.M. Jung was its honorary secretary.⁹¹ The other Islamic society was known as the Central Islamic Society, whose president in 1920 was Mushir Kidwai.[92] Along with Ispahani and Pickthall, Kidwai was also running the Islamic Information Bureau which was the principal source of pan-Islamic propaganda in Britain.[93] The Bureau published a considerable amount of miscellaneous pro-Turkish literature and, by the end of 1919, it had its own journal called the *Muslim Outlook* which, under the management of Ispahani and the editorship of Malik Abdul Qayyum (1892–1956), became the mouthpiece of the Muslims of Britain.[94] Besides these societies, there was the Woking Mission of the Lahori Ahmadis under Khwaja Kamaluddin (1870–1932). Though given chiefly to the preaching of Ahmadiyya doctrine, the Lahori Ahmadis were not yet an anathema to orthodox Muslims, and the mission was regularly utilized for the cause of the Khilafat movement in Britain. Its journal, the *Islamic Review and Muslim India* (later shortened to *Islamic Review*), did useful work in this connection.[95]

To these organizations fell the onerous task of presenting the Muslim viewpoint regarding Turkey. For this purpose, every possible means of propaganda, such as interviews, public meetings, resolutions, pamphlets, and contributions to the press, were utilized. The London Muslim League, for instance, addressed, between January 1919 and January 1920, a series of six well-argued memorials on the Turkish question to the British government. Of these, the first two were addressed to Earl Balfour (1848–1930), the then secretary of state for foreign affairs, and the remaining four to Lloyd George, the prime minister.[96] The memorials to the prime minister were signed by not only the leading Indian Muslims in Britain, but also by prominent Englishmen.[97] In addition to this, at the prompting of Sir Abbas Ali Baig, a former member of the India Council, a Khilafat Day had been organized in London in October 1919, the purpose of which was to focus attention on the Turkish question.[98] In the service, led by Marmaduke Pickthall, prayers were offered for the preservation of the Ottoman Empire and the 'undiminished power and authority' of the sultan of Turkey as the caliph of the Muslim world. Resolutions passed on that occasion emphasized the political independence of the caliph and protested 'in strongest language at its command' against the European Press for 'vilifying' the Turkish nationalists.[99] The painstaking efforts of the Indian Muslims and their British sympathizers, however, failed in their main purpose as the British government remained rigidly consistent in its anti-Turk policy.

It was in such an atmosphere that the Khilafat delegation began its work in London. Mohamed Ali's earlier optimism about the success of his mission vanished on coming face to face with the prevailing realities.[100] Moreover, the personnel of the delegation, especially the leader, had come under attack from various quarters, including some members of Parliament.[101] No doubt, Mohamed Ali led a weak delegation— Sulaiman Nadwi knew very little English and the proceedings had to be interpreted for him; Syud Hossain was constantly sulking over a broken love-affair with Motilal Nehru's daughter, Vijaya Lakshmi *(née* Swarup Kumari; 1900–90); and Abul Kasem and Kidwai had yet to join him from India—but most of the criticism was unwarranted.[102] However, Mohamed Ali was not dejected and started working with whatever support he could muster, particularly in co-operation with Syed Ameer Ali and M.H. Ispahani of the London League, B.G. Horniman (1873– 1948), the erstwhile editor of the *Bombay Chronicle*, Sarojini Naidu (1879–1949), who was then visiting Britain, and other Muslim and non-Muslim associates.[103]

Through his previous experiences in Britain, Mohamed Ali knew that the success of such missions depended on good contacts and sound propaganda. So, he lost no time in contacting all known sympathizers, both inside and outside Parliament, such as George Lansbury (1859– 1940), Arthur G. Field, Leland Buxton, and Capt. E.N. Bennet (1868– 1947).[104] At the same time, he started to revive the Islamic Information Bureau. But the difficulty was that Marmaduke Pickthall had lost all interest and he was away from London most of the time. He had also quarrelled with Ispahani. Though the latter had continued to give monetary assistance to the Bureau, he was in bad health and Mirza, who was working for the Bureau, was more devoted than he was capable.[105] In the circumstances, Mohamed Ali offered Pickthall charge of all the literary and journalistic activities of the delegation as well as the general supervision of the *Muslim Outlook*, but the remuneration that Pickthall demanded was considered to be on the higher side.[106] Therefore, Mohamed Ali undertook to pay the entire cost of the *Muslim Outlook* which, despite Yakub Hasan's (1875–1940) financial assistance, was in dire straits; he also paid a part of the expenses incurred on *India*, the journal of the British Congress Committee.[107] Further, he looked for an opportunity to financially help any publication that was in need of assistance and was willing to throw its columns open to the delegation. This had become necessary since *The Times* and other notable publications had refused to publish even their well-paid notices. An opportunity was found very soon when Mohamed Ali bought £10,000 worth of shares of George Lansbury's *Daily Herald*, which had been founded in 1911 as a strike sheet but had survived to furnish an outlet to Syndicalist views.[108] These efforts resulted in a modest success and the delegation's activities began to be noticed.[109] In its work, the delegation also found the willing co-operation of some Indian students, including Abdur Rehman Siddiqui, Shoaib Qureshi, and Muhammad Habib.[110]

Meanwhile, the delegation did not have to wait too long to explain the Indian Muslim case to the British government. The delegation had two meetings: the first on 2 March 1920, with H.A.L. Fisher (1865–1940), president of the board of education, who received them on behalf of the indisposed Montagu, and the second on 19 March with Lloyd George at 10 Downing Street.[111] In the meetings, Mohamed Ali, as the spokesman of the Khilafat delegation, disavowed that there was any question of Indian Muslims attempting to dictate to, or threaten, the British government or the Allies.[112] He said that they had chiefly come in connection with a religious question of great importance. There were certain clear obligations imposed on Muslims by their faith, and among those was the question of the caliphate. The Islamic outlook on life being supranational rather than national, Muslims had always had two centres—personal and local. The personal centre was the caliph, the successor of the Prophet of Islam; the local was the *Jaziratu'l-'Arab* ('Island of Arabia') which, as defined and delimited by Muslim geographers, included the Hejaz, together with Transjordan, Syria, Palestine, and Iraq. The institution of the caliphate united in itself temporal as well as spiritual duties and it was incumbent upon the entire Muslim nation to preserve it. This was the basis of the Indian Muslim connection with the Ottoman caliphate. As 'the Commander of the Faithful', the caliph's temporal power, especially after the Balkan wars, had been reduced to a minimum with which he could maintain his dignity and act as the 'Defender of the Faith'; the irreducible minimum was the restoration of territorial *status quo ante bellum*.

Mohamed Ali asserted that, in consonance with the religious requirement, the caliphate should be preserved with adequate temporal power and the caliph should retain his control over the *Jaziratu'l-'Arab* and the wardenship of the Holy Places and sacred shrines. He argued that if the caliph retained his control of the *Jaziratu'l-'Arab*, and if the pledges of the British prime minister and of President Woodrow Wilson (1856–1924) of the United States were redeemed in their entirety, the restoration of the territorial *status quo ante bellum* would automatically be achieved. Within the scheme of Turkish sovereignty, he pointed out, reasonable guarantees could be taken for the autonomous development of all communities, whether Muslim, Christian, or Jewish. Mohamed Ali did not hesitate to state that their allegiance to God and His Prophet took precedence over any allegiance to an earthly sovereign. Mohamed Ali was joined by Syud Hossain and Sulaiman Nadwi in laying stress on the point, that for them and for the Indian Muslims, the question of the Khilafat was purely religious and not a political issue. Syud Hossain pointed out that Hindus had joined the movement because they had come to regard the Khilafat issue as a national rather than a sectarian question.[113]

In the short time given to the delegation, they presented their case 'very clearly and very fully'; even Fisher and Lloyd George appreciated their lucidity and moderation.[114] But, as is the case with such deputations, they are suited only to the convenience of the governments. The prime minister had been thoroughly briefed beforehand by his private secretary, Philip Kerr, later Lord Lothian (1882–1940), who had great influence over him. Even at the meeting, Lloyd George was aided by experts on Indian and Islamic affairs. He knew about the antecedents of each member of the delegation, and whom they represented. Answers to any possible arguments, as well as the general line of reply from the point of view of the Indian public opinion, had been prepared well in advance.[115] The prime minister had been advised that he should quote from the Qur'an and refer to Muslim history 'as an Oriental appreciates [such] references'.[116] Care had also been taken that the meeting would end with the prime minister's address.[117] Naturally, therefore, the results of the meetings were a foregone conclusion.

In their replies to the delegation, Fisher was non-committal and Lloyd George obdurate. With his anti-Turk bias, the British premier told the delegation that they had applied the principle of self-determination in dealing with Austria-Hungary and that the same must apply to the Ottoman Empire. Turkey was not being treated severely because it was Muslim, and Indian Muslims had to understand this. The Turk had been an intolerant and inept ruler and the interests of civilization demanded the imposition of some control over him. Therefore, Asia Minor must be supervised by the Allies. Arabia should belong to the Arabs, who had no wish to be ruled by the sultan of Turkey. Thrace should go to Greece as a reliable census had shown that the Muslim population there was 'in a considerable minority'. The same applied to Smyrna where 'a most careful investigation by a very impartial Committee' had revealed a preponderance of a non-Turk population and that the Greek Muslims preferred Greek rule to that of the Turks.[118]

Lloyd George remained unmoved by the delegation's arguments and refused to concede even a single demand. All through the meeting, he was impatient and avoided being drawn into any discussion. He touched and emphasized only those aspects that suited him and refused any discussion on the Palestinian question or on the massacre of the Turks in Smyrna.[119] He did not refer to his own pledge of 5 January 1918, which he admitted was a 'specific, unqualified, and deliberate' declaration.[120] His arguments were one-sided and he drew wrong analogies.[121] His statistics on Thrace and Smyrna were defective, and overwhelmingly Muslim-majority areas were handed over to Greece which had not even been at war with Turkey[122]—a decision that was thoroughly detested by Montagu, strongly opposed by Admiral Sir John Michael de Robeck (1862–1928), the British High Commissioner in Istanbul, and disapproved of by the General Staff.[123] The settlement of Asia Minor was based on the Armenian 'massacres', the fundamental responsibility for which had not been established by an impartial investigation.[124] There seems to be no basis for his claim that not only were the Indian Muslims heard but that the settlement was very largely affected by their opinion. The Indian delegation at the Peace Conference, to which he referred, was never treated seriously.[125] And, as for the Istanbul decision, the credit goes to Etienne Millerand and Saverio Nitti (1868–1953), the French and Italian prime ministers, respectively, who, in spite of Lloyd George's opposition, had insisted on retaining the Turk there.[126]

After the meeting, a cleverly edited summary of the proceedings was issued from 10 Downing Street. The demands of the delegation were made to look ridiculous while the prime minister's arguments were made to appear flawless. The India Office cabled this summary to the viceroy without the knowledge of Mohamed Ali, who was given a copy only after its publication in India.[127] This one-sided story was then spread widely through Reuters' seemingly reliable messages. Mohamed Ali was angry at this deliberate twist but was helpless. He hunted out the correspondents of the *Bombay Chronicle* and *India* to send amplification of what had been attributed to the delegation, but by the time he traced them out it was too late and, therefore, he decided not to spend a 'pot of money' without gaining any corresponding advantage.[128] For his part, Lloyd George was probably trying to reconcile those anti-Turk circles in Britain who were unhappy about the Istanbul decision. And, no doubt, it won him the gratitude of such sections, including *The Times* which was pleased at the prime minister's 'firmness and precision' with 'these pretenders to the representation of "Indian" feelings'.[129] However, his decision disappointed the pro-Turkish elements in Britain. Major-General Lord Edward Gleichen (1863–1937), who had retired in October 1919 after a distinguished service, wrote a very bitter letter to Lloyd George (written on his behalf by A.G. Field):

> Your reply to the Caliphate Delegation [he declared], amiable and considerate as it is, still excuses by reason of vengeance the entry of Turkey into the war against us. . . . Your reply also speaks of the destruction of Austria and the taking away of Alsace Lorraine. You have not occupied Vienna; you have not yet agreed to the treatment of Turkey as favourable as Germany.
>
> If you explain your attitude towards Turkey by the law of self-determination, apply, we beg, self-determination to all Thrace, to all Constantinople, and to the Province of Aidin (Smyrna). We would even beg that this whole principle be applied to Cilicia and Armenia, where a system of administrative sectors could easily solve the question of contiguous minorities.[130]

The strongest reaction, however, was felt in India. The nationalist press was profuse in its bitter comments. The *Bombay Chronicle*, for instance, thought that the prime minister's insistence on the principles of nationality and self-determination was incompatible with his desire for mandates, and concluded that the terms of the peace meant a dismemberment of the Turkish Empire.[131] The *Amrita Bazar Patrika* (Calcutta), generally moderate in its comments, wondered how the premier could reconcile his attitude towards the delegation with the promises made by him during the war, particularly with reference to Thrace.[132] The *Independent* (Allahabad) issued an ominous warning: 'the peace as contemplated by Mr Lloyd George will bring no peace to India'.[133] It further declared that 'the premier's pronouncement will only stiffen the back of the Mussalmans of India and the attitude of their Hindu sympathizers will remain unaltered'.[134] The Khilafatists' disappointment was even greater. More so because, after the meeting with Fisher, some of them, like Abdul Bari and Kidwai, had been well-disposed towards accepting the decision, with certain modifications, of the Supreme Council.[135] Now they felt annoyed, particularly when the verdict had come after an incessant anti-Turkish and anti-Islamic 'crusade' by certain British prelates, publicists, and statesmen. This nullified the advantages that had resulted from the Allied decision to leave Istanbul with Turkey.[136] Mohamed Ali's excited tirade against Britain, at the Woking Mosque on 21 March, must also have encouraged them further in their attitude.[137]

Towards the end of March 1920, a meeting was hastily convened at Ajmal Khan's residence in Delhi which was attended by all the prominent leaders, including Abdul Bari, Shaukat Ali, Abul Kalam Azad, M.K. Gandhi, B.G. Tilak (1856–1920), and Motilal Nehru. A secret session was also held at the meeting where non-cooperation with the government was discussed.[138] Pressure was also put on Gandhi to proceed to London immediately and, without prejudice to Mohamed Ali's delegation, place the prevalent Hindu-Muslim feelings on the question of the Khilafat before the British ministers and the public.[139] But Gandhi, perhaps realizing the futility of the measure, was reluctant to proceed to Britain[140] unless he was assured that public opinion was generally in favour of sending another delegation abroad and that it also had the permission and approval of the viceroy.[141] These were just delaying tactics for Gandhi knew that the CKC was divided in its opinion regarding the dispatch of another delegation, and Chelmsford was also sceptical of the expediency of such a mission.[142] Montagu, too, when approached by Gandhi, did not give a favourable response.[143] The India Office had no intention of encouraging 'another talker', or giving Indian agitators 'joy-rides' to Europe.[144] But the basic issue was whether the British government would recognize the rights of a non-Muslim Indian to have a special voice in matters relating to Turkey. It could have established a most embarrassing precedent for the government.[145] But in the meantime, the CKC, in deference to the wishes of the majority, had decided to drop the matter. Nevertheless, Gandhi's hesitation had created misgivings among some of the Khilafatists, particularly Azad, who had begun to suspect his motives.[146] The suspicion, however, did not last very long as Gandhi soon plunged himself vigorously into the Khilafat movement.

There were two alternatives for the delegation after the meeting with Lloyd George: either to stay on in Europe and seek fresh avenues, or to return to India as there were demands in certain sections for its recall.[147] Abul Kalam Azad, Mushir Kidwai (who was still in India), and, above all, Abdul Bari appeared to have passed hasty judgements on the performance of the delegation.[148] Even a moderate like Mohammad Iqbal, who was idolized by Mohamed Ali, was moved to ridicule the 'begging bowl' of the delegation.[149] The Indian Muslims residing in Britain were also reported as being reluctant to offer further support to the delegation.[150] They seemed particularly embarrassed by the prime minister's arguments regarding Mohamed Ali's disapproval of Arab desire for independence.[151] Syed Ameer Ali was among those who displayed, though only temporarily, a sign of irritability.[152] But, despite these disheartening circumstances, Mohamed Ali decided to stay on and continue his work on the caliphate issue.

Having failed to secure anything from the head of the British government, the delegation knocked at Montagu's door—who had resumed his duties as secretary of state for India after recovering from his recent illness. Contacting him had become all the more necessary because Montagu had sabotaged a proposal from the Aga Khan—which had the support of both Chelmsford and Sir George Lloyd (1879–1941), governor of Bombay—to send Sir Ibrahim Rahimtoola (1862–1942), member of the Bombay Legislative Council, to represent the sentiments of 'reasonable Mahomedans'.[153] Moreover, their requests for permission to explain their case before the Supreme Council at San Remo had also been turned down by the British government.[154]

Mohamed Ali was able to have two meetings with Montagu: the first on 26 April 1920, accompanied by the rest of the delegation, and the second, on 4 May, all by himself.[155] On both these occasions, the proceedings were strictly private. In the first meeting, the delegation traversed the entire ground of Lloyd George's reply and 'absolutely shattered', as Mohamed Ali put it, 'the case that Lloyd George had built up ... as [an] agent of M. Venizelos'.[156] They also raised the question of the release of Mahmud Hasan (1851–1920), the renowned pan-Islamist and former principal of the Deoband seminary in the UP who had, since 1916, been a British internee in Malta. Montagu was indeed very sympathetic and assured them of his continued personal support.[157] But he complained that Mohamed Ali was uncompromising and that the delegation's attitude vis-à-vis the maintenance of the caliphate left him, as their spokesman, with no margin for give and take.[158] For his part, Mohamed Ali argued that no compromise was possible in matters of faith, and that the Indian Muslims were defending 'only a remnant of a once great Empire'. If their demands were not satisfied, they would have recourse to *jihad* or *hijrat*.[159] The only issue Mohamed Ali did not say much about was Armenia, thinking that Mustafa Kemal, the leader of the Turkish nationalists in Anatolia, would take care of that.[160] However, one result of this meeting was that the delegation was given the impression that the San Remo decisions, as far as the Allies were concerned, were not final.¹⁶¹

In the second meeting, the question of mandates came up for discussion but yielded no positive result. Mohamed Ali also brought up the question of Mahmud Hasan's release, at which Montagu repeated his promise that he would re-examine the detained *alim's* case.¹⁶² Next, Mohamed Ali complained about the damaging questions asked about his brother and him in the House of Commons by the Indo-British group and against which he had already protested to Montagu in a long letter, denying the charges levelled against him and asking for protection against his 'cowardly calumniators'.¹⁶³ Unfortunately, in reply to a question in the Commons, Fisher had wrongly stated that Mohamed Ali had been interned during the war for 'pro-German activities'. Although Fisher retracted his statement the very next day, he had presented the Indian leader with an opportunity to challenge him.¹⁶⁴ Montagu wanted Mohamed Ali to overlook the matter and let bygones be bygones. He told Mohamed Ali that his brother and he were free for the future, subject of course to such action as their conduct might necessitate or if the Khilafat movement became unconstitutional. On being pressed by Mohamed Ali, Montagu agreed to consult the Government of India as their case involved a policy statement on the subject.¹⁶⁵

The net result of these meetings, from the delegation's point of view, was far from satisfactory. They had a staunch supporter, in Montagu, who had wholeheartedly been trying 'to get the Cabinet to accept a pro-Turkish policy which, he believed, would satisfy the agitators in India and enable the reforms to be introduced in a peaceful atmosphere'.¹⁶⁶ The same policy had, repeatedly and emphatically, been urged by Chelmsford and his Indian government on the grounds that the Muslim turbulence over the Turkish peace terms was the most serious element in the situation.¹⁶⁷ Montagu was convinced of this but he was in an unenviable position. He had to fight, almost single-handedly, against his persistently antagonistic colleagues. Viscount Milner (1854–1925) was perhaps his only supporter in the British cabinet. In the end, Montagu failed to extract any important concession and was compelled to enforce a peace that he utterly disliked.[168] It was his obsession with the Turkish treaty that ultimately cost him his happiness and health, and eventually his political career.[169]

By early May 1920, the delegation had fully realized that they were not getting anywhere with the British government and that their real work lay in India.[170] And yet, they had decided to stay on and try to reach at least that section of British public which seemed amenable. The delegation had already been seeking to enlist the support of various political parties. On 10 March, they had met Herbert Asquith (1852–1928), a former British prime minister and leader of the Liberal Party. But the meeting had come to nought. In the meeting, Asquith had given the impression that he was sympathetic to the delegation's case[171] but later, in the Commons, he declared that their 'pretensions' were entirely untenable and amounted to letting the sultan of Turkey go practically blameless.[172] Mohamed Ali had also had occasion to meet the Liberal Party as a whole, but there, too, he did not succeed.[173]

Next, the delegation turned to the Labour Party. But, in the British Parliament of 1920, the Labour Party was a small and undistinguished group. Almost all the prominent Labour leaders, including Ramsay MacDonald (1866–1937), Phillip Snowden (1864–1937), and F.W. Jowett (1864–1944), had been defeated in the last elections, as were Arthur Henderson (1863–1935) and George Lansbury.[174] However, since the parliamentary Labour party was twice the size of the Liberal Party, it was, therefore, the official opposition.[175] In its foreign policy, the Labour Party was opposed to Lloyd George as being unduly and dangerously pro-Greek, and denounced the treatment of Turkey as likely to produce repercussions throughout the Muslim world.[176] Mohamed Ali first visited the Labour Executive on 30 March and on 10 April, met the Party's advisory committee; but, as the Labour was then involved in stopping British aid to Poland against Russia, and even more in domestic issues, it seems that he failed in gaining their support.[177] Ramsay MacDonald, in particular, refused to render any assistance because he had felt insulted at being ignored by the delegation.[178] This was in spite of the fact that he was a staunch supporter of the Turkish cause and knew Mohamed Ali personally.[179] Of course, other important Labourites, such as George Lansbury, John Robert Clynes (1869–1949), Neil Maclean (1876–1953), and William Hutchinson (d. 1965), helped the delegation individually and through their Party workers who thronged the Khilafat meetings, and had even provided Mohamed Ali with an opportunity to speak at the twentieth annual conference of the Labour Party at Scarborough in June 1920. However, as a collective, the Labour Party could not be won over.[180] The delegation found the British Labour Party preoccupied in the prevailing industrial unrest, and hopelessly ignorant and narrow-minded about Indian affairs.[181]

In their efforts to influence public opinion directly, and to counter the organized propaganda prejudicial to the delegation, a series of public meetings were arranged in London and in the provinces with the assistance of the Indian Muslims in Britain and their British sympathizers, notably George Lansbury, Marmaduke Pickthall, and Arthur Field, the last named being the secretary of the Anglo-Ottoman Society. In London, three such meetings were held at the Woking Mosque (21 March), Essex Hall (23 March), and Kingsway Hall (22 April), where the delegation was attentively heard and heartily cheered by well-attended and distinguished audiences.[182] The central themes of the speeches were always the same, i.e. exposition of the Khilafat case, articulation of Indian Muslims' demands, and criticism of Lloyd George's policy. As time passed, Mohamed Ali's speeches became increasingly bitter. The delegation was able to attract some attention in London but the propaganda against them was too strong to let them create any lasting impression.[183]

The tour in the provinces was a fiasco, mostly due to incompetence and mismanagement on the part of the man entrusted with the job by Pickthall. He organized only one 'abominably mismanaged' meeting in Manchester on 30 April, while he ignored important places like Edinburgh and Glasgow.[184] Under these circumstances, members of the delegation had to arrange meetings themselves at other places such as Cambridge and Edinburgh. In Cambridge, it was purely an Indian affair with only four or five of the 'better sort' of dons.[185] At Edinburgh, the meeting was held with the help and co-operation of Lansbury and his party workers and the Indian students,[186] but the overall impact was negligible. Armenian and Greek hecklers hounded them from place to place, either to disrupt the meetings or to turn those occasions to their own advantage.[187]

Besides the public meetings, an effort was made to influence the press. A handsome amount of £500 was paid to *Foreign Affairs*, the journal of Ramsay MacDonald's Union of Democratic Control (founded 1914), to bring out a special supplement on the delegation.[188] The *Daily Herald* was already under contract to publish their news in a favourable manner, and the *Muslim Outlook* and *India* did their best to reach the British public,[189] but these efforts were not much of a success. *Foreign Affairs* was essentially a pacifist journal and did not have much appeal even in the Labour circles. The *Daily Herald* was much more interesting than the ill-fated official Labour newspaper, the *Daily Citizen,* but since it was mostly read by the *'hoi polioi',* its appeal was also limited.[190] Similarly, the *Muslim Outlook* and *India* had diminutive circulations: they were not read outside the Islamic and Indian circles; furthermore, the distribution of the former had been banned in India.[191]

Part II

Disappointment in Britain led the delegation to seek support elsewhere. Earlier, they had intended to go to Turkey and had raised the subject in their meeting with Fisher.[192] The benefit they would have derived from this visit is difficult to ascertain. Perhaps they wanted to bolster the Turkish resistance to the peace treaty. But, in any case, the visit did not materialize as the British government was unhelpful.[193] Then, in the summer of 1920, they were reported to be contemplating a trip to America and Japan. In the latter, they were supposed to work for an alliance between Nippon and the Muslim world.[194] But they reverted to their earlier programme and turned their attention to the continental European powers, notably France and Italy who were known to be favourably inclined towards a lenient treaty with Turkey.[195] Between April and September 1920, the members of the delegation crossed over to Europe on no less than six different occasions and visited Paris, Versailles, Rome, Geneva, Montreaux, and Territet.[196] The intelligence branch of Scotland Yard and the British missions in Europe kept a careful watch throughout on the delegation's movements and activities lest they steal a visit to Turkey or elsewhere.[197] The day-to-day record of their activities was scrupulously maintained and sent home.[198]

In France, the delegation worked in co-operation with the French socialists, particularly Jean Longuet (1876–1938), a grandson of Karl Marx (1818–1883), who, unlike his extremist father, Charles Longuet (1839–1903), was a moderate pacifist. His influential paper, *Le Populaire*, which had been founded during the war as a rival to Pierre Renaudel's (1871–1935) *L'Humanité*, and which, in spite of being only a weekly, had become more powerful than the daily, was also thrown open to them.[199] Ordinarily, the French Socialist Party was known for refusing participation in 'bourgeois' governments. It was also given to laying more emphasis on its pacifism and opposition to colonial domination and military adventures.[200] But, in the post-war political setting of France, the Socialist Party, which Jean Jaurès (1859–1914) had taken twenty years to build up,[201] had gone to pieces when the extremist majority sought to establish the dictatorship of the proletariat by violent means. They also denounced the peace as a capitalist contrivance for the maintenance of bourgeois supremacy, and professed allegiance to a new Third International whose headquarters were in Moscow.[202] In May 1920, Marcel Cachin (1869–1958), the new controller of *L'Humanité*, felt politically strong enough to go to Moscow and offer V.I. Lenin (1870–1924) control of the French Socialist Party on the condition that the latter would curb the activities of the French communists.[203] The Russians agreed to take the French party in the Third International but the conditions they laid down strong, including a vigorous attack on Jean Longuet and his followers and the socialist press, both *L'Humanité* and *Le Populaire*.[204] The bargain was struck but the unity of the French socialists was gone. The communists gained control of the assets of the old party, including *L'Humanité*.[205]

Thus, when Mohamed Ali's delegation arrived in Paris, the French Socialist Party was split down the middle and Jean Longuet was having his own problems with the Third International.[206] But, he still came forward to help Mohamed Ali and his pan-Islamic associates. Through Longuet and other friends like Dr Nehad Rechad, the editor of the *Echo d'Islam* (Paris), they contacted a number of influential senators, deputies, ex-ministers and other prominent Parisians.[207] They also visited M. Cauvain, the editor of *Journal des Débats*, on several occasions, and the offices of important publications like *Le Temps* and *Le Journal* and met Louis Barthou (1862–1934), a former minister of war and a well-known Anglophobe.[208] On 14 May 1920, Baron de Lormain, the representative of the Duke d'Orleans, paid a visit to the delegation on behalf of the Duke and, it was said, of the Vatican as well.[209] The same day, M. Stoiloff went to see Mohamed Ali.[210] Apart from meeting people, Mohamed Ali reorganized the Bureau d'Islamique which, like its London counterpart, was inactive and in dire straits.[211] Shariff Paşa, a former

ADC to Sultan Abdülhamid of Turkey and in charge of the bureau at that time, had stopped taking any real interest in it.[212] Mohamed Ali assisted the bureau financially and helped rejuvenate its journal, the *Echo d'Islam*, under the editorship of Dr Rechad.[213] These measures seemed to indicate a promise of success for the Khilafat delegation.

Soon after their initial arrival in Paris on 13 April 1920, the delegation was able to place their viewpoint before thirty deputies and had meetings with highly-placed officials. Longuet's newspaper gave wide publicity to the delegation and published leading articles on the caliphate and the Turkish question, and interviewed Mohamed Ali.[214] Several public meetings were arranged by, or for, the delegation where important Frenchmen spoke in their support. One such successful meeting was held on 20 April, under the chairmanship of Deputy Jules Roche (1841–1923), a former finance minister and a well-known economist.[215] On 17 May, the delegation attended a conference which included many important politicians and journalists like René Lecomte, Du Menil, Gen. Cherfils Deslailleur, Jules Roche, Baron de Lormain, Le Coconnier, Jean Meila, and M. Pathe.[216] Another such meeting was arranged by the Comité National d'Estudes where Mohamed Ali also expressed his views.[217] More meetings followed: on 27 May, at Salle de Sociétés Savantes where Longuet, Cachin and Le Coconnier spoke; and on 6 June at Salle des Ingénieurs Civils where Le Coconnier, De Kerguezec, and Claude Farrére (1876–1957) expressed their views.[218] But, by far the most successful meeting in Paris was held on 25 June 1920 in Salle Wagram, the biggest hall in Paris. The meeting was arranged by the Comité la France et l'Islam and was presided over by Senator M. de Mouzie, a former French minister of mercantile marine. Those present included M. Bourdarie, director of the *Revue Indigéne*, Xavier de Magallon, and Deputies Le Coconnier and Pillon.[219] In this way, the delegation was able to put its message across to the French public.

PLEADING THE CASE OF THE OTTOMAN CALIPHATE

The delegation was in Paris when, on the afternoon of 11 May 1920, the draft Treaty of Peace with Turkey was handed over to the Turkish plenipotentiaries—led by the seventy-seven-year old Ahmed Tevfik Paşa (1845–1936)—in the Clock Room of Le Quai d'Orsay.[220] In fact, the Indians had arrived in Paris on 8 May, explicitly to meet the Turks who had reached there three days earlier. Mohamed Ali had known Tevfik Paşa since 1913, when he was in London in connection with the Kanpur Mosque affair and the latter was Turkey's ambassador to the Court of St James's. When Mohamed Ali heard that Tevfik had arrived in Paris to receive the draft treaty, he, too, went to France. On 9 May, with much difficulty and in great secrecy, he managed to meet the Turks at a Versailles hotel in the dead of night.[221] From Tevfik, the Indians must have learnt the extent of the damage proposed by the treaty. In essence, the planned treaty was meant to confirm the death of the Ottoman Empire. The sultan-caliph was to remain in Istanbul, but he would become a virtual prisoner of the Allies. The whole of European Turkey, including Smyrna, was handed over to Greece. The eastern territories were either to be taken over by the Allies as mandates or were to be managed under their influence. The Straits and the Dardanelles were internationalized.[222] The agitation in India and representations in Europe all seemed to have gone to waste. Under the circumstances, the delegation could do little to improve the situation except beg the aged Ottoman Sultan Mehmed VI to reject the proposed treaty. This they did on the day it was handed to the Turks, in full knowledge that the sultan was no more than a dignified Allied prisoner and that the real government of Turkey was in Anatolia.[223] In a lengthy telegram to the sultan, evidently drawn up with the knowledge of the Turkish plenipotentiaries, the Indian delegation reminded him expectantly that the eyes of the whole Muslim world were turned towards Istanbul and that 'in all conceivable circumstances and at all costs' he would uphold 'the dignity of Islam' and 'remain stedfast [*sic*] in the defence of the Khilafat and of the sanctity of the Jazirat-ul-Arab in its entirety'.[224] In other words, if the claim of territorial *status quo ante bellum* was not accepted by the powers, the sultan should boldly tear up the draft treaty as 'Islam to day stands solidly by your side'.[225]

The telegram to the helpless sultan was no more than a hysterical gesture, but it aroused bitter comments from the British press, especially the *Daily Telegraph*.[226] For their part, the delegation denied that the telegram was either a comment on the peace terms or that it had been drawn up with the knowledge of the Turkish delegates. They maintained that they were primarily concerned with the future of Islam, rather than that of Turkey, and had felt it their duty, 'at this hour of grave peril to Islam', to remind the sultan-caliph, no less than the Allied statesmen, that he should do his duty 'not only by Turkey but by Islam'.[227] The delegation's action may have been quite consistent with the position they had taken throughout—that in matters of faith their allegiance to the caliph took precedence over their allegiance to the king-emperor—but the British government could not take this 'seditious document' lightly.[228] The India Office was in favour of prosecuting the members of the delegation for having written to 'an enemy sovereign'. However, the idea was dropped when Sir Edward Chamier (1866–1945), the legal adviser to the secretary of state for India, pointed out that a case could not stand against them under the Indian Penal Code and neither could they be prosecuted in Britain on the evidence of such a document alone.[229] Further, any hopes that the delegation might have entertained for a modification of the proposed treaty[230] were dashed by Lloyd George's explicit declaration that there were to be no modifications unless the Turkish reply contained substantial arguments not previously taken into account by the Peace Conference.[231] Subsequently, their entreaties, such as that from Paris on 10 July 1920,[232] in spite of Montagu's inclination for their acceptance,[233] aroused no favourable response from the British government.[234]

PLEADING THE CASE OF THE OTTOMAN CALIPHATE

During his stay in Paris, Mohamed Ali had been successful in influencing public opinion to some extent but had failed to win over the French government whose support he was reported to have tried to enlist by exploiting colonial jealousy.[235] The delegation's view was that French interests in the East were largely in accord with their own, as both were opposed to any extension of the British influence.[236] However, their much-sought-after audience with Millerand, which coincided with the signing of the Treaty of Sèvres on 11 August, was a complete failure. The French prime minister gave no encouragement to Mohamed Ali and his friends.[237] The delegation found that the French government was greatly dependent on Britain for support against German aspirations. Naturally, France was obliged to subordinate its aspirations in the East to those of Britain's.[238] The French mandate in Syria, against Arab wishes, and the delegation's support for Tunisian demands for independence, had complicated matters still further.[239] In reply to the delegation, Millerand repeated the familiar response of his British counterpart: that France had no enmity with the Muslims nor any hostility towards Islam; that it was the fundamental duty of the Allies to end, once and for all, the Turkish atrocities on their Christian subjects; that the French presence in Syria was not due to any imperialistic designs but was only a strategic necessity and as soon as the time was right they would withdraw from there; and, finally, that it was better if the delegation would subordinate their religious sentiments to dictates of reason.[240] After the speech, Millerand gestured that the meeting was over. But Mohamed Ali could not hold himself back and retorted that their religion was wholly based on reason and that none of its dictates were illogical. They would have explained the Islamic injunctions about their case in detail if only the ministers had time to listen to them. Millerand, however, did not wish to prolong the discussion. Nevertheless, when leaving, Mohamed Ali made the Indian position clear to him: that the acceptance of the draft treaty by the representatives from Istanbul did not at all mean the end of the matter for the Muslims as a whole.[241]

Despairing, first with Britain and then with France, the Indian delegation turned its full attention towards Italy. Mohamed Ali had tried to visit Rome as early as April 1920, and though the British authorities were intent on preventing the Indians from going to Italy or elsewhere the visit had been called off only because of the Italian railway strike.[242] Finally, on 23 July 1920, accompanied by H.M. Hayat, Mohamed Ali managed to visit Rome.[243] The political atmosphere in Italy, apparently, was favourable to the delegation as public opinion was generally incensed at Italy's small share in the post-war spoils, especially in Dalmatia and Africa.[244] Therefore, the Italian government had no particular liking for the treaty as it then stood. Giovanni Giolitti (1842–1928), the Italian prime minister, who had come to power only a month earlier in June 1920, had been openly opposed to Italy's entry into the war and had regarded it as an act of disloyalty to the powers to which she had been aligned.[245] The Christian Democrats of the Partito Popolare (the Popular Party), under the leadership of Don Luigi Sturzo (1871–1959), with their 'inter-class' support had also preferred to become an auxiliary of Giolitti and had joined the nationalists in demanding a better deal in the spoils of war.[246] The socialists, led by Filippo Turati (1857–1932), though they had lost their stature as the leading political party,[247] were still ready to help the Khilafatists.

The delegation's work in Rome was carried out in accordance with the programme laid down for it by the Ligue des Nations Opprimees de tout l'Orient, which had been formed in the interests of the Orient and Italy with the support of Giolitti himself.[248] Besides the Ligue, there was an anti-British bureau in Rome known as the Colonial Institute, with A. Chesaro as its president and Dr Escarpa as its secretary.[249] The Institute was a private body working on the lines of the German Oriental Bureau, but it intended to cooperate secretly with the ministries of colonies and foreign affairs. The Bureau encouraged and helped all Eastern agitators, and was trying to establish contact with workers in India, Egypt, and Turkey through the Ligue.[250] At the time of Mohamed Ali's arrival in Rome, no such contact existed with India but plans were claimed to have been afoot.[251] The delegation was also helped in its work by Ghalib Kemal Bey of Turkey, Dr Abdul Hamid Said of Egypt, Aziz Nuri Bey of Turkey, and Shaikh Khalid of Tunisia who were then living in Rome.[252]

On his arrival in Rome on 23 July 1920, Mohamed Ali sought a meeting with Prime Minister Giolitti, which was promptly granted.[253] The Italian premier expressed his whole-hearted sympathy with the aims of the delegation and pointed out that Italy had never followed a policy allowing for the disintegration of the Ottoman Empire and claimed that it had always given, and would continue to give, all possible help. This, he said, was apparent from the fact that Italy had accepted almost all the demands of the Albanians and was also thinking of granting complete autonomy to Tripoli the moment the time was ripe for that. Giolitti also agreed with Mohamed Ali that, until the eastern countries were freed from the yoke of the foreign rulers, there could never be permanent peace in the world. But, he pointed out that this could only be achieved through a combined uprising on the part of those countries themselves, and not merely through foreign assistance. Mohamed Ali argued that India was powerless owing to its poverty, ignorance, and caste prejudices and particularly for want of arms. He added that that was the reason they desired help from a 'civilized Power of Europe'. Giolitti assured Mohamed Ali that Italy was ready to help all, especially the Muslims, if they would unite. The Italian prime minister asked Mohamed Ali to keep the proceedings of the meeting secret for he did not want to create misunderstandings between himself and Britain.[254] To maintain appearances, Giolitti directed the Italian ambassador in London to convey to Lord Curzon that he had met Mohamed Ali and had told him that the Italian government had strongly advised the Turks to sign the proposed treaty, without delay, in their own interest as any other course would be suicidal.²⁵⁵ But, the British were already aware of what had passed between Giolitti and the Indians.

While in Rome, Mohamed Ali also had meetings with Count Carlo Sforza (1872–1952), the Italian foreign minister, and Dr Nikoli, the president of the Italian Chamber.²⁵⁶ In addition to his dealings with the Italian government, Mohamed Ali was in touch with some 'dangerous' revolutionary elements, and also contacted the Italian socialists under Turati.²⁵⁷ Mohamed Ali's contacts with the socialists, while carrying on negotiations with the Italian government, was interpreted by the British as consistent with his attempts to create dissension among the Allies with a view to prevent them from undertaking concerted action against Turkey. This was considered analogous to the 'double dealings' in his transactions with the French and British governments. It was reported that Mohamed Ali became somewhat cautious when the Italian government threatened to cease its support unless he broke away from the socialists.²⁵⁸ In any case, the result of Mohamed Ali's mission to Rome was encouraging. The Italian government even allowed him to correspond with the Turkish government from Rome, through the Italian diplomatic bag.²⁵⁹ Mohamed Ali was happy with the outcome of his visit to Rome and hoped that the Italian government would not range itself on the side of injustice.²⁶⁰

During his visit to Rome, Mohamed Ali also wished to have an audience with the Pope, who was regarded by the Catholic world as the Vicar of the Christ and the visible head of the Church at the Vatican. He wanted to explain, to the Pope, that the movement he represented aimed at the redress of certain grievances and that it was not, in any way, directed against the Christians.²⁶¹ Some Catholic well-wishers had also been insisting that the Indians must pay their respects to the Pope.²⁶² Mohamed Ali presumed that Giacomo Della Chiesa (1854–1922), who had succeeded to the Pontifical primacy in September 1914 as Pope

Benedict XV, was apprehensive of a union between the Protestant, Greek Orthodox, and Armenian Churches, and, as such, would prefer the Turks to any one of them.[263] Even if Mohamed Ali was being too optimistic in his calculations, the Pope could not have approved of Lloyd George's sinister reference to the dwindling power of the Pope.[264] Moreover, there had been a lingering rupture between Benedict XV and the Allies because of the former's efforts, during the war, to prevent the spread of a conflict that had set Catholic against Catholic and for his unsuccessful attempt at mediation in 1917. The Allies had neither forgotten nor forgiven him, and they saw to it that he was excluded from the peace negotiations despite the Papal relief work for prisoners of war and war victims.[265]

On 30 July 1920, Pope Benedict XV received Mohamed Ali and H.M. Hayat in a private audience. During the audience, the Pope is reported to have heard the Khilafat case with consideration. Mohamed Ali pointed out that Britain had not honoured her pledges to the Muslims. On the contrary, it had practically abolished the caliphate and had brought the Holy Places of Islam directly or indirectly under its control. Mohamed Ali also protested against the British and French mandates in Palestine, Iraq, and Syria.[266] The Pope, in his reply, reportedly expressed pleasure at the spirit of religious tolerance shown by the Ottoman Turks and their government to which, he said, the Nuncios in Istanbul had borne testimony in their despatches.[267] He added that the Turkish treaty had brought no peace to the world and hoped that the objectives of the Muslims, for which the delegation had come to Europe, would be secured peacefully. The Pontiff recognized that if the hostilities were to continue, the responsibility would lie squarely on the authors of the treaty and not on the Muslims. He assured the delegation that the Catholic world stood for peace with Islam, and underlined the fact that the last war had not been a conflict between Islam and Christianity. The Pope is said to have authorized Mohamed Ali to convey an assurance of his cordial sympathy with the delegation's brief and good wishes to the people of India and to the Muslims of the world.[268] Before the Pope's audience with Mohamed Ali, Cardinal Pietro Gasparri (1852–1934), the Pontiff's secretary of state, had consulted Count de Salis (1864–1939), the British ambassador at the Vatican, as a matter of protocol. Though neither the India Office nor the Foreign Office wished to raise any objection, Montagu wanted the Pope to be informed of Mohamed Ali's 'disloyal past', which rendered him unsuitable as the true representative of India and of the Indian Muslims. On a suggestion from the India Office, the Foreign Office directed Count de Salis to inform the Pope of Mohamed Ali's credentials.[269] In the meantime, perhaps to uphold his motto that 'Everyone has the right to see the Pope',[270] Benedict XV had already committed to give audience to Mohamed Ali. When the India Office came to know of the audience through a report in the *Muslim Outlook*, it immediately asked the Foreign Office to ascertain whether the Pope had really given utterance to the sentiments attributed to him. Count de Salis, who was asked to find out the facts, was told at the Vatican that 'the article does not in its essential parts correspond in anything to what was really said on the occasion in question'.[271] However, this contradiction was 'authoritative' only at second- and third-hand and was not very specific. Cerretti Bonaventura (1872–1933), the papal secretary for external affairs since 1917, who supplied the information, was not present at the audience and the note which he sent to Count de Salis, after making enquiries, did not specify which parts did not correspond with the published account.[272] Curzon was in favour of issuing an authoritative denial of the statement,[273] but the India Office did not approve of the idea as it would not be possible to express the denial in very categorical terms on the basis of the Papal response to de Salis.[274]

By early August 1920, a change had gradually come about in the thinking of the delegation, primarily because of their continuous disappointments. Already, Mohamed Ali had been saying that their real work lay in India.[275] Then, in July of the same year, in an interview to the press in Rome, he had stated that India intended to follow a line of its own and was determined to sever connections with the British government through a phased programme of non-cooperation.[276] But, this did not mean that the Khilafatists had given up on pan-Islam. On the contrary, pan-Islam and Indian independence were still their cherished twin objectives. Mohamed Ali's primary aim, it was reported, 'was the independence of India, more especially Mohammedan India, with the object of uniting it [ultimately] to a revived Islam'.[277] Thus, Islamic solidarity remained an important part of his programme. In consequence, Mohamed Ali and his colleagues seldom missed an opportunity to establish rapport with Muslims from other countries who had come to Europe either as political exiles or as representatives of their respective countries. As early as April 1920, while in London, Mohamed Ali and Sulaiman Nadwi (Syud Hossain was then in Paris) had called on Nuri As-Said (1888–1958), the agent and adviser of Emir Faisal, and other Arabs of the Hejaz delegation.[278] Their purpose was to effect reconciliation between the Arabs and the Turks; but, when the Indians realized that the former were unresponsive to their proposal of a 'federation' of Arab territories under the nominal suzerainty of the caliph on the model of the Commonwealth of Britain, Canada, and Australia, they wisely concluded that it was better if the matters were settled coolly, in their true perspective.[279] At least Sulaiman Nadwi admitted that he had become partial towards the Arabs.[280] In a subsequent meeting, the Arabs advised the Indians to send a deputation to Sharif Hussein and discuss the entire problem directly with him.'[281] Later, however, instead of sending a delegation, it was agreed that a memorial would be addressed to Sharif Hussein but that, too, was not sent due to the political changes brought about by the Treaty of Sèvres.[282]

In the same context, Mohamed Ali met Mohammed Ali Paşa, the brother of Abbas Hilmi, who as the Khadive of Egypt (1892–1914) had tried, unsuccessfully, to rid his country of British control. The Paşa was in Paris and had himself sought out the delegation through Shariff Paşa of the Bureau d'Islamique. The meeting was later described as 'very interesting'. The Paşa assured the Indians of the support of the Egyptian Muslims in their efforts to preserve the caliphate and sanctity of the *Jaziratu'l-'Arab*.[283] Similarly, the Khilafatists established contact with the Egyptian nationalists. On 16 April 1920, the Egyptian delegation under Saad Pasha Zaghloul (1857–1927) hosted a dinner in honour of the Indian delegation. Zaghlul assured Mohamed Ali of their fullest support for the Khilafat cause. The Egyptians told him that they were not demonstrating pro-Turkish feelings publicly because they wanted to avoid giving the impression that their agitation for independence was inspired by the Turkish agents, as was being done in the case of India.[284] In their attempt to woo Muslims from other countries, the delegation also met the Tunisians under Abdul Aziz Taalby, who had visited India during the Balkan crisis (1913). Among others, they met the Tartars, Chinese, Russians, and Iranians as well.[285]

More important, however, were the delegation's contacts with the *émigré* Turkish CUP leaders, who had taken refuge in various European capitals, as well as with Mustafa Kemal and his Anatolia-based adherents. Mohamed Ali had been in contact with the CUP Turks all this time through Khalil Khalid Bey, whom he had known since the latter's posting as the Ottoman consul in Bombay before the war.[286] Similarly, he was in contact with Ghalib Kemal Bey, Mustafa Kemal's agent in Rome, and later communicated directly with the nationalist leader through the Italians.[287] The idea, it seems, was to carry out some kind of concerted action against the British with the help of the Bolsheviks. An indication of this came in June 1920 when Alitcha Zade Harun, an associate of former Turkish ministers, Mehmed Cavid Bey (1875–1926) and Ahmed Cemal Paşa, informed Mohamed Ali that Talat Paşa, who was then living in Berlin, wanted to meet him in Switzerland.[288] Talat Paşa, in fact, had been endeavouring since April 1920, to establish contact with Mohamed Ali.[289] It was believed that the Turks intended to persuade Mohamed Ali to remain in Europe to supervise pan-Islamic and anti-British propaganda. In the event of his declining the offer, he was to be asked to precipitate an agitation in India.[290]

Mohamed Ali, who was dejected by his lack of success with the Allied governments and was already on the lookout for other avenues, was happy to oblige. Accordingly, on or about 31 July 1920, he arrived in Territet, a small Swiss town near Montreaux, on his way back from Rome. On arrival, he first met Mohammad Fahmy of Egypt and discussed 'important matters relating to the Khilafat question' with him.[291] He also established contact with other pan-Islamic exiles, especially Selim Bey Hejazi, formerly the Turkish minister at Berne, and Dr Behdjet Wahby Bey, Alitcha Harun, Chirin Beg, and other Egyptian nationalists who had gathered in Territet.[292] Since Talat Paşa had not arrived there due to his preoccupations in Lucerne, Mohamed Ali returned to Geneva on 2 August and thence to Paris. Three days later, on 5 August, he was again in Geneva where he took time off to explain his case to the socialists and communists of Europe who had gathered there for an international conference. For this purpose, he elicited the willing assistance of Neil Maclean and other British socialists.[293]

On 6 August 1920, Mohamed Ali and Talat Paşa had a long meeting in Territet. By this time, it appears that an understanding had been reached between the CUP and the Turkish nationalists.[294] The Indians, too, had realized that the effective government of Turkey was in Ankara and not in Istanbul.[295] Mohamed Ali, therefore, approved of the tactics of Mustafa Kemal whose military prowess, he believed, would achieve what others had failed to accomplish.[296] He was reported to have repeated to Talat Paşa the suggestion of a world Muslim congress for intra-Islamic issues which he had proposed earlier to Mustafa Kemal and Muhammad Fahmy.[297] Apparently, the two men also prepared an ambitious plan for the invasion of India by an army composed of Afghans, Indian *muhajirin*, and tribesmen on the Indo-Afghan border.[298] The funds for organizing this force were to be provided by, among others, the CKC. The Bolsheviks were expected to help launch the offensive. For the proper execution of the plan, it was reported that Talat Paşa was to move to Moscow, Enver Paşa was to go to Tashkent, and Cemal Paşa was to raise the army of invasion in Afghanistan. Mohamed Ali was expected to synchronize it with a revolt in India.[299]

Some efforts seemed to have been made to carry out the plan which, however, fell through in the end due to various reasons—particularly, the collapse of the Indian *hijrat*, the withdrawal of the Afghans and the Bolshevik support, and above all, the deaths of Talat, Enver, and Cemal Paşas. The details are outside the scope of this study and the information is also scant, but the plan shows the anxiety of the Indians to turn to any direction that appeared to offer some benefit. A significant aspect of the situation was the change that came about vis-á-vis the thinking of the delegation after they had established contact with the Ligue des Nations Opprimees de tout l'Orient and with Talat Paşa. Mohamed Ali was flattered into believing that he was a *persona grata* in world affairs and, from that time on, there was a noticeable change in the tone of the speeches and writings of the members of the mission. They talked of cooperation with the Bolsheviks with whom Mohamed Ali corresponded through V.N. Chattopadhyaya (1883–1937), Sarojini Naidu's revolutionary brother, who was then in Sweden and formed a link between Moscow and Berlin. Mohamed Ali was also reported to be receiving funds from Bolshevik sources.[300]

So far as the Turkish nationalists were concerned, it was no mere coincidence that, in September 1920, Mustafa Kemal informed his army corps commanders that Britain could not take offensive action against them as the Indian troops had been forbidden to fight against the Anatolian forces by Indian leaders.[301] This is directly traceable to Mohamed Ali's correspondence with Mustafa Kemal and to the delegation's efforts to start a campaign against all wars.[302] The idea, it seems, was to have a link with all pacifist and socialist groups, and subsequently to influence the war-weary public to oppose any military campaign whatsoever, subsidising anti-militarist bodies whenever and wherever possible.[303] They were also to try and stop the dispatch of Indian troops outside India and, if possible, to divert them from their allegiance to the British Crown.[304] The object appears to be two-fold: first, to obstruct any possible military intervention against the Turkish nationalists and, secondly, to hamper the authorities in India from using military force in suppressing the Indian nationalist movement. Further evidence of the growing reliance on each other came just before Mohamed Ali's departure for home, when he received a communication from Mustafa Kemal asking the former how much money he would require for propaganda work in India. Mohamed Ali replied that he would let him know after his return to India.[305] But the Khilafatists' dealings with the nationalists, like those with the CUP Turks or the Arabs, produced no lasting associations. It is true that the delegation had based its demands for lenient treatment for Turkey on purely religious arguments,[306] but the fact remained that the Indian Muslim leaders were defending the caliphate only to uphold the political dominance of Islam. The Turkish nationalists, on the other hand, were fighting merely to secure their national sovereignty in accordance with the terms of the Misak-i Milli of 1920, without any claim to *Republica Moslemica*.[307] With this divergence in their aims, they slowly moved further apart until they broke away completely in March 1924 following the abolition of the Ottoman caliphate by Mustafa Kemal.

By mid August 1920, having failed to achieve anything regarding the Turkish treaty, the delegation seriously contemplated sailing back to India.[308] Just then, a telegram was received from the CKC which stated that it was the opinion of Abdul Bari, Gandhi, Chotani, and other Khilafat leaders that the delegation should visit the United States for a month.[309] The members were divided in their opinion about the utility of their mission across the Atlantic. While Mohamed Ali was in its favour, H.M. Hayat was non-committal and Abul Kasem and Sulaiman Nadwi were opposed to the idea. Nadwi, in particular, was of the view that in the anti-Turk bias America had taken such firm root that their visit was bound to prove ineffective. If they were still intent on going, then only Mohamed Ali and Syud Hossain should visit the States for a month or two while the others should return to India. An 'angry scene' was said to have followed, but in the end the idea was dropped altogether.[310]

Before their departure for home, the delegation asked Nagai San, the Imperial Japanese chargé d'affaires in London, for a meeting. H.M. Hayat, the secretary, wrote to Nagai explaining that since it had not been possible for them to visit Japan, they were desirous of presenting their case to him to communicate to his government in Tokyo.[311] But the Japanese chargé d'affaires did not wish to get entangled in diplomatic impropriety with Britain. Therefore, on 24 August, he personally went to the British Foreign Office to ascertain whether he would have any problem if he agreed to the meeting.[312] The Foreign Office certainly did not wish for the Japanese diplomat to receive the delegation, but it also did not want to appear to be raising any hurdles. As a way out, they informed Nagai a few days later that the delegation had no credentials to represent either the caliph or the Indian nation, nor even the Muslims among them. Above all, after the ratification of the Treaty of Sèvres, they had been left with no legitimate *raison d'etre*.[313] Nagai took the hint and refrained from receiving the delegation. The Indians also attempted to arrange another meeting with Montagu but failed.[314]

On 1 September 1920, the delegation finally left London for Paris, on their way to India. Kidwai, who wanted to settle the Information Bureau's affairs, and Syud Hossain, for whom India without his love seemed to be an empty place, decided to stay on in Britain for the present. After two days' stay in Paris, Mohamed Ali and friends proceeded to Territet in Switzerland on 3 September, and then on 7 September arrived in Milan in Italy. There they received the news from their travel agents, Thomas Cook, that their voyage on the liner s.s. *Cracovia,* on which they were due to sail on 10 September from Venice, had been cancelled. They were, therefore, forced to delay their departure and decided to head for Rome. On arriving in Rome on 9 September, Mohamed Ali, with much difficulty, was able to secure four seats in another Lloyd-Trustino liner, s.s. *Graz,* which was expected to sail on 17 September from Brindisi. This time, there was no hitch and they all embarked for home on the due date, visiting Port Said, Massawa, Perim, and Aden on the way. On 4 October 1920, the delegation arrived back safely in Bombay.[315] They had been away from India for nearly eight months; during that time, the Khilafat movement in India had taken on a much more aggressive pace.

From an examination of the delegation's activities, utterances, and writings, it is evident that not only had they gone to Europe to plead the cause of the Ottoman caliphate, but also to advance the nationalist interests of India. In the first place, Mohamed Ali and his associates sought to approach the British government but, unfortunately, the interests of imperial policy clashed with those of its subject people. Of course, the Government of India tried to present their case with sympathy but the British government dealt with the problem in a typically imperialistic manner. And the British Labour Party, towards which the Khilafatists looked indulgently for support, appeared to them to be too nationalistic to think internationally.[316] At their farewell dinner on 30 August 1920, George Lansbury unsuccessfully tried to pacify the Khilafatists by telling them that if they had accomplished little for the present, they had sown the seeds that would bear fruit when Labour came to power.[317]

Having failed to achieve anything substantial in Britain, the Indians naturally turned to France and Italy. In France, they sought to enlist sympathy by playing upon colonial jealousies but did not succeed. They found the French government, particularly in colonial matters, subservient to the British. As for the French socialists and the public at large, they evoked some favourable response but that did not affect the Allied policy towards Turkey in any way. In Italy, however, Mohamed Ali's endeavours seemed to have been more fruitful. But, there, too, the promised assistance was dependent on the remote possibility of the eastern people uniting among themselves. The only visible outcome in Italy was their permission to use their diplomatic bag from Rome for correspondence with the anti-British elements.

Failure with the Allies compelled Mohamed Ali to look elsewhere for assistance. It was then that he turned to the Bolsheviks and revived his contacts with the CUP and the Turkish nationalists, and even the Arabs, for the 'regeneration of all Mohamedan Powers in the East aided by the Bolsheviks'.[318] But, here, he ignored the contemporary international situation. The Bolsheviks, on whose support everything depended, were neither interested nor even capable of 'liberating' India.[319] Collusion between the CUP and the nationalists was also impossible as the Arab question was their weakest point. The Arab revolt against the Turks, though British-instigated, had been an armed expression of their desire for national independence and stemmed from their utter dislike of pan-Turanianism. Indian Muslim hostility to Arab aspirations, deliberate as it may seem, arose from their apprehension of an ominous schism in the Muslim world and from their fear of non-Muslim encroachments into the heartland of Islam. Naturally, when the Indians met the Hejaz delegation in London in the summer of 1920, and later held discussions with Emir Faisal bin Hussein in Milan towards the end of their tour, they could not conceal their anger towards them.[320] However, at the same time when reconciliation between the Arabs and the Turks failed, they wisely did an about-face and raised the slogan of an independent Arabia, free from all non-Muslim control.[321]

glorious end an enterprise which absorbed the chivalry of Europe for centuries. We forget now that the military strength of Europe was concentrated for generations upon this purpose, and concentrated in vain. A British Army under the command of General Allenby achieved it and achieved it finally.' Parl. Papers, 1919, *Hansard,* 119, H.C. Deb. 5S, col. 418. Emphasis added.

78. OIOC, L/P&S/18, B. 310 (a). The difference between the views of Lloyd George and Curzon was that while the former advocated a total destruction of the Ottoman Empire and Turkey's existence as a sovereign state, the latter was prepared to leave Turkey as a purely Asiatic state. See Earl Ronaldshay, *Life of Lord Curzon,* iii (London, 1928), 259–68.
79. Curzon to Sir Eyre Crowe, Paris Peace Delegation, No. 7289, 30 Oct. 1919, encl., Foreign Office to India Office, No. 145162/ME/44A, OIOC, File 6818/1920 in L/P&S/10/797.
80. See his note in OIOC, L/P&S/10/796.
81. See Curzon's minute in NAUK, FO, 371/E 2505/139/44. Hardinge thought that the Government of India was paying too much attention to the Muslims' feelings. See his undated minute (presumably of 12 May 1920) in NAUK, FO, 371/E 4935/139/44.
82. Prominent among them were Lord Charles Lamington (1860–1940), Sir Mortimer Durand (1850–1924), Sir J.D. Rees, Edward Delgado, Dr Elis Schaap, Aubury Herbert, and Bedwin Sands. Their efforts resulted in the formation of the Anglo-Ottoman Society in Aug. 1913, of which Lord Mowbray was the president, and Elis Schaap its hon. secretary. See OIOC, File 4431/1912; *Civil and Military Gazette* (Lahore), 4 Feb. 1912; *Asiatic Quarterly Review* (Woking), Oct. 1913; and *Asiatic Review,* Feb.-Apr. 1914.
83. Parl. Papers, 1919, *Hansard.* 113 H.C. Deb. 5S, cols. 2370 and 2379; 115 H.C., Deb. 5S, cols. 1868–9; 116 H.C. Deb. 5S, cols. 22, 794 and 1531–3; 120 H.C. Deb. 5S, cols. 1114 and 1132; and 121 H.C. Deb. 5S, cols. 739–40.
84. *The Times,* 10 Sept. 1919.
85. Ibid., 2 Feb. 1920; and Nadwi to Daryabadi, 4 Mar. 1920, *Barid-i Farang,* 20.
86. OIOC, File 4216/1919 in L/P&S/10/797.
87. Their efforts are more clearly depicted in the work of the societies they represented. When Professor Léon became a Muslim, he changed his first and middle names from 'Henri Marcel' to 'Haroun Mustafa'.
88. See Matiur Rahman, *From Consultation to Confrontation: A Study of Muslim League in British Indian Politics, 1906–1912* (London, 1970), 149. For the earlier pro-Turkish efforts of the London Muslim League see *Civil and Military Gazette,* 10 and 20 Feb. and 10 Mar. 1912; OIOC, Files 3899/1912, 66/1913,

196/1913 and 470/1913 with 4287/1912; 4265/1914, I; and 913/1919 in L/P&S/10/797.

89. For information on Ameer Ali and the National Mahommedan Association, see K.K. Aziz, *Ameer Ali: His Life And Work* (Lahore, 1968), 8 and 45–50.
90. The Aga Khan's services to Muslim India on the Khilafat question have not been properly appreciated because most of his contributions were made behind the scenes. For instance, in May 1919, it was mainly through his efforts that Indian Muslims were able to present their case before the Council of Four at Paris. Similarly, he helped the Khilafatists financially so that they could reach the British public through a journal of Muslim opinion. See *Nuqush* (Lahore), 109, Apr./May 1961, 85 and 101–9.
91. In 1920, the Islamic Society's office-bearers, besides Abdul Majid and Jung, were Fevzi Lutfi Bey, Prof. Léon, Ali Hikmet Nahid Bey, M. Kassimoff, Omar Flight, S. Khan, M. Jabir, M. Zade, M. Kibria, A. Peepardy, M. Shafee Lakhsar (vice-president), and M. Hussein Tabrizi (hon. treasurer). Its offices were located at 87, Westbourne Grove, London, W11. OIOC, Files 4287/1912, 5254/1919 and 2882/1919 in L/P&S/10/797; and 1424/1920 and l826/1920 in L/P&S/10/798.
92. The Society was located at 158, Fleet Street, London. For the Society's pro-Turkish work, see, e.g., File 4105/1919 L/P&S/10/795.
93. The Bureau had its offices at 33, Palace Street, London, S.W. 1.
94. In 1919, when Yakub Hasan (1875–1940) of Madras visited Britain as a member of the Muslim League delegation, he also joined its staff. P.C. Bamford, *The Histories of the Non-Co-operation and Khilafat Movements,* Government of India (New Delhi, 1925), 145.
95. For details, see Ashiq Hussain Batalawi, *Chand yaden chand ta'assurat* (Lahore, 1969), 399–405. The Lahori Ahmadis had split from the main Qadiani Movement in 1914 over serious doctrinal issues. This happened when Mirza Mahmud Ahmad, the son of the Movement's founder, Mirza Ghulam Ahmad, began to proclaim that his father was a true prophet, and all those Muslims who did not subscribe to this assertion, were *kafir*s. He also disallowed his followers from holding or joining the funeral prayers of all 'dissidents'. At this, a faction under Maulana Muhammad Ali separated and established the Ahmadiyya Anjuman Isha'at Islam at Lahore. Since September 1974, both of these groups have been declared 'non-Muslim' through a constitutional amendment for not subscribing to Muhammad's (*sal'am*) absolute finality as Prophet of Islam.
96. OIOC, File 1972/1920 in L/P&S/10/798.
97. Ibid.

39. Lord Bryce, 'The Settlement of the Near East', *Contemporary Review* (London), Jan. 1920, 1.
40. See Parl. Papers, 1920. *Hansard.* 116 H.C. Deb. 5S, col. 812; 117 H.C. Deb, 5S, cols. 963–4; 123 H.C. Deb. 5S, cols. 676, 752 and 723–4; 125 H.C. Deb.5S, cols. 1951–5; *New Europe* (London), 15 Jan. 1920, 5; and Sir Charles Oman, 'East and West', *Transactions of the Royal Historical Society*, 4/3 (London, 1920), 5–6.
41. See, e.g., his articles, 'A Review of the Turkish Problem', *New Europe*, 14/170, 1–5; 'The Meaning of the Constantinople Decision', ibid., 14/175, 129–31; and 'Mr Montagu's Pound of Flesh', ibid., 14/176, 145–9.
42. *The Times,* 27 Feb. 1920.
43. Mohamed Ali to Abdul Majid Daryabadi, 10 Nov. 1916, in Abdul Majid Daryabadi (ed.), *Khutut-i-Mashahir*, i (Lahore:1944), 276.
44. D.S. Margoliouth, 'The Caliphate', *New Europe*, 14/182, 294–300.
45. Originally, Nallino's pamphlet was entitled *Notes on the Nature of the Caliphate in General and on the Alleged Ottoman Caliphate,* and was published and circulated in 1919 by the Italian Foreign Ministry. Copy available in OIOC, File 3344/1923 with 3344/1920.
46. P. Tonapetean, *The Sultan is not Caliph* (London, 1920), *passim*.
47. See OIOC, File 53/1915, I.
48. Nadwi to Masud Ali, 17 Apr. 1920. *Barid-i Farang,* 55–6.
49. *The Times*, 7 Jan. 1920.
50. Ibid., 26 Feb. 1920.
51. *New Europe*, 26 Feb. 1920.
52. The Turkish action against the Armenians was neither unprovoked nor motivated by any religious animosity. The reasons were purely political. The alleged atrocities were caused by an unceasing struggle between the Armenian revolutionary societies and the Turkish government. The Armenians, with the support of the Russians, had been active belligerents and quite combative, openly claiming reward from the Allies. See *Asiatic Review,* Jan. 1916, 106; Marmaduke Pickthall, 'Massacres and the Turks: The Other Side', *Foreign Affairs* (London), July 1920, xvi; and 'Q', 'Self-Determination and the Turkish Treaty', ibid., xxiii.
53. H.A. Gibbons, *The Blackest Page in Modern History: Armenian Events of 1915* (New York & London), 1916, 7–8.
54. F.R. Scatchard, 'Armenian Atrocities and Some Sceptics', *Asiatic Review,* Jan. 1916, 106.
55. Parl. Papers, 1916, Cd. 8325.
56. Nadwi to Masud Ali, 12 Apr. 1920, *Barid-i Farang,* 55.
57. Nadwi to Abdul Bari, 4 Mar. 1920, ibid., 15.

58. Nadwi to Abdul Bari, 6 May 1920, ibid., 69–70.
59. Ibid. The advertisement for the film version, then being screened at the Royal Albert Hall in London, presented it as 'The most astounding film ever produced', which had been 'acclaimed by tens of thousands of enthralled patrons as the most powerful, convincing, and memorable film ever shown.' See *The Times*, 2 Feb. 1920.
60. The *'Memoirs'*, published in London by Hodder and Stoughton in 1920, was compiled by an Armenian, Aram Andonian, and carried a foreword by Viscount Gladstone. It contained forged Ottoman 'official' documents alleging massive deportations and massacres of Armenians.
61. Nadwi to Abdul Bari, 6 May 1920, *Barid-i Farang*, 69.
62. *The Times,* 20 Feb. 1920.
63. Ibid.
64. Felix Valyi, *Spiritual and Political Revolutions in Islam* (London, 1925), 37–8.
65. Nadwi to Daryabadi, 1 Apr. 1920, *Barid-i Farang*, 35.
66. *The Times,* 3 Mar. 1920.
67. Ibid.
68. Ibid.
69. M.R. Hassan. 'Indian Politics and the British Right, 1914–1922', unpublished Ph.D. thesis (London, 1963), 344.
70. Parl. Papers, 1920, *Hansard*, 125 H.C. Deb. 5S, col. 1965.
71. T.P.O'Connor in ibid., col. 1983.
72. A.J. Toynbee, 'The Question of the Caliphate', *Contemporary Review,* 127, (Feb. 1920), 193.
73. See his communication to *The Times,* 25 Feb. 1920.
74. See his minute of 17 Mar. 1920, in OIOC, File 2021/1920 in L/P&S/10/798.
75. During the last stages of the war, a high-powered Eastern Committee appointed by Lloyd George with Lord Curzon, Viscount Balfour, Gen. Jan Smuts (1870–1950), Edwin Montagu, and Gen. Sir Henry Wilson (1864–1922) as members was asked to examine a policy for the annexation of Turkey in the event of a speedy Turkish or Russian collapse. For details see NAUK, CAB 27/24.
76. Thomas Jones, *Lloyd George* (London, 1951), 197.
77. Some of Lloyd George's statements had been particularly emotive and full of religious fervour. For instance, in Aug. 1919, while proposing a gratuity to Field Marshall Viscount Edward Allenby (1861–1936) in Parliament, he had declared: 'The name of General Allenby will be ever renowned as that of the brilliant commander who fought and won the last and most triumphant of the crusades. It was his good fortune, aided by his skill, to be able to bring to a

PLEADING THE CASE OF THE OTTOMAN CALIPHATE

be able to continue their useful propaganda network.³³³ In this way, the Khilafat issue was to be kept alive in Europe.

NOTES

1. The earliest reference in this connection can be traced to the Crimean War (1854) in the correspondence of the Marquess of Dalhousie (1812–60), the governor-general of India. See Baird (ed.), *Private Letters of the Marquess of Dalhousie*, 300.
2. For a study of the Khilafat Movement see A.C. Niemeijer, *The Khilafat Movement in India, 1919–1924* (The Hague, 1972); and the works by Gail Minault and Naeem Qureshi, already mentioned elsewhere in this book.
3. Jinnah, who had returned from Britain on the day that the meeting was held (14 Nov. 1919), made this suggestion in an interview to the press. See *Times of India* (Bombay), 17 Nov. 1919.
4. OIOC, File 186/1920 in L/P&S/10/798.
5. See Fazlul Haq to Lloyd George, Tel. 2 Dec. 1919, OIOC, L/P&S/10/796.
6. *Bombay Chronicle*, 5 Jan. 1920.
7. Ibid.
8. Ibid., 20 Jan. 1920.
9. The additional nominees were Sheriff Dewjee Canjee (Bombay), Mirza Ali Mohammad Khan (d. 1930; Bombay), Munir-uz-Zaman Islamabadi (Bengal), and Abdul Halim Sharar (1860–1926; UP). See Fazlul Haq to Lloyd George, Tel. 2 Dec. 1919, OIOC, L/P&S/10/796.
10. The other member was Saiyid Wazir Hasan (1874–1947). For Mohamed Ali's activities in Britain in connection with his 1913 mission see Muhammad Sarwar (ed.), *Maulana Mohamed Ali ke yurup ke safar (khud unke apne qalam se)* (Lahore. 1941), 19–35.
11. See Mohamed Ali, *My Life: A Fragment* (ed.), Afzal Iqbal (Lahore, 1942), 191. For a detailed study of the life and work of Mohamed Ali, see Afzal Iqbal, *The Life and Times of Mohamed Ali* (Lahore, 1974).
12. See Sayyid Sulaiman Nadwi's Introduction to his *Barid-i Farang* (Karachi, 1952), 11–12.
13. Ibid., 11.
14. Ibid., 10.
15. Ibid.
16. See Anon., *Muhammad Ali: His Life, Services and Trial* (Madras, 1922), 116–17 and 127–8. Also see Viceroy to Secretary of State for India, Tels. P., Nos. 17 and 82, 14 Jan. and 2 Feb. 1920, OIOC, Chelmsford Papers; and *Hindu* (Madras), 15 Jan. 1920.

17. Afzal Iqbal (*Mohamed Ali*, 191) has erred in suggesting that the delegation left for Europe by an Austrian-Lloyd Steamer, SS *Trestino*. In fact, the name of the liner was s.s. *Hungaria*. See, for instance, the address atop Sulaiman Nadwi's letters from aboard the ship in *Barid-i Farang* 2.
18. Nadwi to Masud Ali, 3 Feb. 1920, *Barid-i Farang*, 2.
19. Nadwi to Abdul Hakim, 3 Feb. 1920, ibid., 2.
20. Nadwi to Masud Ali, 9 Feb. 1920, ibid, 5.
21. Nadwi to Abdul Hakim, 14 Feb., and 3 Mar. 1920; and Nadwi to Masud Ali, 14 Feb. 1920, ibid., 5–11.
22. Nadwi to Abdul Hakim, 3 Mar. 1920, ibid., 10.
23. Ibid., 11.
24. OIOC, File 1434/1920 in L/P&S/10/799.
25. Ibid.
26. Nadwi to Abdul Bari, 4 Mar. 1920, *Barid-i Farang*, 14.
27. Ibid.
28. Ibid. For details of the Istanbul decision, see NAUK, CAD 29/82, ICP, 28.
29. Parliamentary Papers (Parl. Papers), 1920, *Hansard*, 125 H.C. Deb. 5S, cols., 1958–79.
30. Ibid., cols., 1949–2060, esp. cols. 1949–55, 1961–3, 1971–89, 2006–8 and 2025–8.
31. Ibid., col. 1979.
32. Ibid., col. 2061.
33. K.K. Aziz has classified the anti-Turk opinion in Britain into eight well-defined groups. See his *Britain and Muslim India* (London, 1963), 109–11.
34. Sir Thomas Barclay (1853–1941) points out that British public opinion had always been keenly on the side of the Christians and against the Muslims, and on the side of the Christian communities in the Ottoman Empire. See his 'England and Islam', *Asiatic Review* (London), 15 Aug. 1914, 147.
35. The press, in particular, took a leading part in the anti-Turk campaign and published numerous cartoons and articles derogatory to Islam and the Sultan of Turkey. See, e.g., *Punch* (London), 16 Dec. 1914.
36. See Parl. Papers, 1919, *Hansard*, 113, H.C. Deb. 5S, cols. 1054–5. 2231–2 and 2370; 114, H.C. Deb 5S, cols. 225 and 239: and 115 H.C. Deb. 5S. col. 1868.
37. As early as Feb. 1919, one such meeting where the Archbishop of Canterbury, Viscount Bryce, and the Marquess of Crewe (1858–1945) were to advocate the 're-conversion' of the Mosque was cancelled at Lord Curzon's intervention. See PRO, CAB/Minute 3 of the War Cabinet, No. 537, of 26 Feb. 1919.
38. Parl. Papers, 1919, *Hansard*, 123 H.C. Deb. 5S, col. 730.

The activities of the delegation in Europe, and their close co-operation with B.G. Horniman, Mrs Naidu, and with the British Congress Committee, further indicate that their own community was most clear in their mind. Mohamed Ali's extreme nationalism was evident from his speeches delivered in Britain and on the continent.[322] He and his associates interested themselves in the massacre at Amritsar (April 1919) almost as much as in the misfortunes of Turkey.[323] But the Khilafatists were amazed to note that purely Indian issues attracted much less attention than those concerning Turkey. This was visibly demonstrated by the thinly-attended meetings held to protest against the Amritsar killings and the Hunter Committee Report (May 1920), while the meetings called to discuss the Khilafat issue were comparatively well-attended.[324] Another outstanding feature of the situation was the delegation's connections with the Irish Sinn Feinners, though the evidence is small.[325] Still, it shows that the Indians were trying to copy the Irish catchwords, if not their methods. Propaganda against the employment of Indian troops outside India was another feature which engaged their attention as a sound tactic. The Bolsheviks, in particular, were keenly interested in this aspect.[326] One of Mohamed Ali's declared objectives was to bring about lasting peace in Iraq, Palestine, Syria and Turkey.[327] What is more significant is the fact that the delegation had come into contact precisely with those elements that had been so closely connected to the unrest in the summer of 1920 in Iraq.[328] In short, Mohamed Ali and his colleagues were closely associated with the unionist-Bolshevik-nationalist organizations in Europe and the Middle East.

The overall impact of the delegation's efforts on Allied policy towards Turkey was, however, insignificant, though the West could no longer plead ignorance of either the demands of the Indian Muslims or of their nature. The odds against the delegation were too many and too difficult to surmount. On top of this, post-war Europe was too entangled in its own difficulties to notice the problems of a distant part of the British

Empire. And all this was notwithstanding the huge sum of money that the delegation incurred on its trip to Europe, and the allegations of extravagance and misappropriation of funds which Mohamed Ali earned for himself from his more uncharitable opponents.[329] In the end, despondent at the state of affairs in Europe, the delegation orientated itself towards the complete freedom of India as a panacea. Syed Sulaiman Nadwi, in one of his letters to Abdul Bari, opened his heart thus:

> We [the Indian Muslims] . . . have spent about half a century in a way that we have had practically no concern or purpose with the politics of India and have kept wandering and straying aimlessly in the deserts and wildernesses of Africa and Asia. . . . If we want to free the *K'aba* and the Green Tomb [of the Prophet] we must [first] secure the freedom of India. The endeavour and exertion for the constitutional freedom of India is now not only a worldly affair but a religious duty and religious right as well.[330]

This change was elaborated more clearly by Mohamed Ali on his return home. He declared that he had no antipathy or superstition about the British connection which must be judged on its intrinsic merits in relation to what India would gain or lose thereby. The chief, and sole, consideration must be the Indian good. In his opinion, the attainment of *swaraj* was the ultimate goal, and non-cooperation the only sure means to realize it. Mohamed Ali laid more stress on Indian freedom than the Khilafat wrong, because, he felt, that Muslim claims could only be achieved successfully if India was in Indian hands. In other words, the freedom of India was necessary for the freedom of Islam. His message to Indian Muslims was that if they wanted to secure the freedom of Islam, they must join their Hindu brethren and work together for the freedom of India.[331] Though Mohamed Ali had realized that the real work was to be done in India itself, nevertheless, he favoured foreign propaganda side by side with the work in India.[332] Before his departure for India, Mohamed Ali had strengthened the Islamic Information Bureaus in London and Paris in order for them to

Moslem Delegation', *New Europe* 15/185, 29 Apr. 1920, 56–60; and 'Q', 'Self-Determination and the Turkish Treaty', ibid., xxiii.
182. See Indian Khilafat Delegation Publications, nos. iv and vi, n. 109, above.
183. Ibid. The delegation also attended several other gatherings. On 5 March, Mohamed Ali spoke at 3, Campden Hill Road, London. On 17 March, the delegation attended the foundation ceremony of the 'Persian Association'. On 12 August, they attended the B.G. Tilak Memorial meeting. And, on 22 August, they were present at a demonstration held at Trafalgar Square in London. See OIOC, L/P&S/18, B. 361, 10; and NAUK, FO 371/E 9954/44 and E 10825/l39/44.
184. Mohamed Ali to Shaukat Ali, 6 May 1920, n. 105, above. Also see *Indian Annual Register, 1920,* Part i, 202.
185. Ibid
186. Ibid.
187. Ibid. Also see Nadwi to Abdul Bari, 5 May 1920, *Barid-i Farang*, 77–9.
188. Jafari, *Sirat-i Mohamed Ali*, 298. The UDC, which published the journal, had been primarily formed for the purpose of propaganda against the war by MacDonald and four other anti-war Liberals, Norman Angell (1874–1967), E.D. Morel (1873–1924), Charles Travelyan (1870–1958), and Arthur Ponsonby (1871–1946). The UDC demanded democratic control of foreign policy, no annexations, and an international organization to maintain peace and disarmament. See Pelling, *A Short History of the Labour Party*, i, 37.
189. See above, nn. 107 and 108.
190. Sir Ivor Jennings, *Party Politics*, i (Cambridge, 1960), 142.
191. The *Muslim Outlook* had a chequered history since its birth. The journal had to change its name more than once because of the ban imposed on its entry into India by the Government of India, reappearing first as *Islamic News* and then as the *Muslim Standard*. See Anon., *Muhammad Ali*, 136.
192. OIOC, L/P&S/18, B. 370.
193. OIOC, ibid.; and Files 1139/1920, 1634/1920 and 2182/1920 in L/P&S/10/799.
194. OIOC, File. 5635/1920 with 1229/1920, XI.
195. The Allied rivalries over Turkey have been well summed up in H.N. Howard, *The Partition of Turkey: A Diplomatic History, 1913–1923* (Norman, 1931), 217–49.
196. OIOC, L/P&S/18, B. 370; L/P&S/18, B. 361; and *Barid-i Farang*, passim.
197. See OIOC, J&P (S), 3724/1920; L/P&S/18, B. 361; and NAUK, FO 371/E 1441/ 139/44, E 3276/139/44, E 3676/139/44, E 4286/139/44, E 4514/139/44, E 4608/ 139/44, E 4650/139/44, E 4949/139/44, E 6431/139/44, E 6757/139/44, E 7315/139/44, E 8492/139/44, E 9999/139/44, E 10082/139/44, E 10670/139/44, E 10825/139/44, and E 14492/139/44.
198. Ibid.

199. Anon., *Muhammad Ali*, 144. For Jean Longuet and his *Le Populaire*, see D.W. Brogan, *The Development of Modern France (1870–1939)*, 4th edn. (London, 1943), 532 and note.
200. Cole, *A History of Socialist Thought*, iv, Part ii, 460–8; and J.P.T. Bury, *France, 1814–1940*, 6th edn. (London, 1962), 197.
201. For Jaures's contributions to the French Socialist Party, see J. Hampden Jackson, *Jean Jaurès: His Life and Work* (London. 1943), *passim*.
202. Bury, *France, 1814–1940*, 259.
203. Carl Landauer, *European Socialism*, i (Berkeley & Los Angeles, 1959), l017; and Jackson, *Jean Jaurès: His Life and Work*, 187. Jean Longuet, who was supposed to accompany Cachin to Moscow, was deliberately ignored in favour of the extremist Louis Frossard (1889–1946). See Cole, *A History of Socialist Thought*, iv, Part ii, 474.
204. Brogan, *The Development of Modern France*, 561.
205. Cole, *A History of Socialist Thought*, iv, Part ii, 475–6. For the twenty-one conditions for affiliation as approved by the Second Congress of the Comintern (6 Aug. 1920), see Jane Degras (ed.), *The Communist International, 1919–1943: Documents*, i (London, 1956), 168–72.
206. The Communist executive had condemned Longuet as one of the 'notorious opportunists'. See Degras, *The Communist International*, i, 170.
207. OIOC, L/P&S/18, B. 361, 10.
208. Ibid., 10.
209. NAUK, FO 371/E 10670/139/44.
210. OIOC, L/P&S/18, B. 361, 10.
211. The Bureau was located at No. 3. Rue de Teheran, Paris.
212. Jafari, *Sirat-i Mohamed Ali*, 299. Also see Nadwi to Abdul Hakim, April 1920, *Barid-i Farang*, 37.
213. Ibid.
214. Anon., *Muhammad Ali*, 144.
215. Ibid., 142–4.
216. OIOC, L/P&S/18, B. 361, 10.
217. *Indian Annual Register, 1920*. Part i, 202.
218. OIOC, L/P&S/18, B. 361, 10–11.
219. Ibid. 11; and *Indian Annual Register, 1920*, Part i, 202–3.
220. *The Times*, 12 May 1920.
221. Nadwi to Masud Ali, 12 May 1920, *Barid-i Farang*, 83.
222. For details see Parl. Papers, 1920, Cmd. 964. *Treaty of Peace with Turkey*.
223. See Nadwi to Abdul Hakim, 6 May 1920, *Barid-i Farang*, 81.

that, for the first time in the history of Islam, a claim had been laid on Arabia by someone who was not a caliph. See OIOC, L/P&S/18, B. 371.
152. Ameer Ali to Duke, 25 Mar. 1920, OIOC, File 2410/1920 L/P&S/10/798.
153. Montagu had thought that the suggestion had come too late and, even if Rahimatoola were to reach Britain in time, his arguments would be familiar to the Peace Conference. See Viceroy to Sec. of State, Tel. P., 30 Mar. 1920; and Sec. of State to Viceroy, Tel. P., No. 513, 1 Apr. 1920, OIOC, Chelmsford Papers.
154. See Mohamed Ali's communication to the *Nation* (London), 29 May 1920, 279. Lloyd George had become so sensitive to the delegation's activities that, on his direction, a search was made in the Peace Conference archives to find out whether, apart from the representations made to himself and correspondence with his secretary (Philip Kerr), they had made any direct appeal to the Peace Conference. The search revealed no trace of any such appeal but it is a fact that the delegation had sent, on 24 April 1920, a lengthy telegram to the president of the Supreme Council inviting attention to the gravity of the situation in India and requesting an earnest consideration of the Turkish issue 'in the interests of justice and tranquillity in the Indian Empire'. They maintained that their action arose 'out of nothing beyond their anxiety to reconcile their loyalty to His Majesty the Emperor of India and their ardent desire for the restoration of peace in India.' See Curzon to Vansittart (Paris), No. 703, 16 June 1920, NAUK, FO 371/E 6583/139/44; Sir G. Graham (Paris) to Curzon, Tel. No. 728, 17 June 1920, NAUK, FO 371/E 6701/139/44; and *Indian Annual Register, 1920* (Calcutta, 1920), Part I, 184 *(b)*.
155. Nadwi to Abdul Bari, 6 May 1920, *Barid-i Farang*, 66–7; Mohamed Ali to Shaukat Ali, 6 May 1920, n. 105, above; and Montagu to Chelmsford, 23 June 1920, OIOC, Montagu Papers.
156. Mohamed Ali to Shaukat 6 May 1920, n. 105, above.
157. Ibid.
158. Ibid.; and Montagu to Chelmsford, 2, June 1920, OIOC, Montagu Papers.
159. Ibid.
160. Ibid.
161. Ibid. Also see Abdur Rahman to Shaukat Ali, 29 April 1920, encl. Chelmsford to Montagu, 3 June 1920, OIOC, Montagu Papers.
162. Ibid. Montagu kept his promise and, soon after, Mahmud Hasan was released from detention.
163. Mohamed Ali to Montagu, 12 Apr. 1920, OIOC, J&P, 2403/1920 with 1451/1919. His protest was against the questions of Lt. Col. James (10 and 16 Mar.), Ormsby-Gore (10 Mar.), Col. C.E. Yates (17 and 24 Mar.), and Sir Charles

Oman (31 Mar.). See Parl. Papers, 1920, *Hansard*, 126 H.C. Deb. 5S, cols. 1249–50, 2032 and 2173–4; and 127 H.C. Deb. 5S, cols. 386–7 and 1225–6.

164. Parl. Papers, 1920, *Hansard* 126 H.C. Deb. 5S, cols. 203 and 2174.
165. Mohamted Ali to Shaukat Ali, 6 May 1920, n. 105, above.
166. S.D. Waley, *Edwin Montagu: A Memoir* (Bombay, 1964), 240.
167. Ibid., 240.
168. Montagu to Chelmsford, 20 May 1920, OIOC, Montagu Papers.
169. Waley, *Edwin Montagu*, 240. For details of Montagu's controversy with Lloyd George see Montagu to Lloyd George, 15 Apr., 22 June, 26 June, 20 Aug. and 8 Sept. 1919, and 15 Apr. 1920, Beaverbrook Library, Lloyd George Papers.
170. Mohamed Ali to Shaukat Ali, 6 May 1920, n. 105, above.
171. Anon., *Muhammad Ali*, 133.
172. Parl. Papers, 1920, *Hansard,* 127 H.C. Deb. 5S, cols. 640–1.
173. Anon., *Muhammad Ali*, 133.
174. Ralph Miliband, *Parliamentary Socialism: A Study in the Politics of Labour* (London, 1961), 64.
175. Sir Ivor Jennings, *Party Politics*, ii (Cambridge, 1961), 279.
176. For details see Arthur Henderson, *Labour and Foreign Affairs* (London, 1922), 5–8; and Brand, *The British Labour Party*, 69.
177. OIOC, L/P&S/18, B. 361, 10; Nadwi to Masud Ali, 14 Apr. 1920, *Barid-i Farang*, 47–8. For the Labour Party and the Russian crisis see D.G.H. Cole, *A History of Socialist Thought: Communism and Social Democracy, 1914–1931*, i and iv (London, 1958), 427–8. For the Labour Party and the industrial unrest see Henry Pelling, *A Short History of the Labour Party* (London & New York, 1965), 48–9.
178. Jafari, *Sirat-i Mohamed Ali*, 281–2.
179. Ibid. MacDonald's pro-Turkish stance is evident from his article 'Turkey and Constantinople', in *Foreign Affairs*, Apr. 1920, 7.
180. Afzal Iqbal (ed.), *Select Writings and Speeches of Maulana Mohamed Ali*, 2nd ed. (Lahore, 1963), 49 and 144–5; Nadwi to Masud Ali, 6 May 1920, *Barid-i Farang*, 75; Labour Party, *Report of the Twentieth Annual Conference of the Labour Party* (Scarborough, 1920), 144–5; *The Times*, 24 June 1920; and Muhammad Sarwar (ed.), *Maulana Mohamed Ali* (Lahore, 1962), 181.
181. Nadwi to Daryabadi, 28 Apr. 1920, *Barid-i Farang*, 59–60; and Nadwi to Abdul Hakim, 16 June 1920, ibid., 118. Among others, the delegation met Arnold Toynbee to discuss the vexed question of the Armenian 'massacres' with him but the meeting revealed that both sides differed profoundly vis-à-vis the nature of the evidence on the subject. The delegation insisted on an impartial investigation by a mixed commission but it was never instituted. See A.J. Toynbee, 'The Indian

124. See Admiral de Robeck to Curzon, 9 Mar. 1920, n. 122, above.
125. Montagu to Curzon, 28 Aug. 1919, OIOC, File 4995/1910 with 4995/1019, III.
126. At the Allied Conference in London in February 1920, Lloyd George had made no secret of his designs and regretted missing 'a great opportunity of ridding Europe once and for all this pest and potential source of trouble [i.e., the Turk]'. But he was compelled to yield to Millerand who wanted to leave Constantinople/Istanbul with Turkey 'for very cogent reasons', and to Nitti who believed that it was useless for the Allies to demand things unless they were certain to get them. Nevertheless, Lloyd George alleged that the decision of the Conference was due to pro-Muslim prejudice and until the end tried his best to limit the Sultan's sway in Europe. See the minutes of the Allied Conference in London of 14 Feb. 1920, in NAUK, CAB 29/8, I.C.P.–28. The decision of the British Cabinet had been taken earlier on 6 Jan. 1920. On 7 January, Curzon had recorded his note of dissent with the decision. See Cabinet Minute I (20) and C.P. 407 and Appendix IV, in NAUK, CAB 23/20.
127. Sec. of State to Viceroy, Tel. P&R, dated 21 Mar. 1920, OIOC, Chelmsford Papers; and Mohamed Ali to Shaukat Ali, 6 May 1920, n. 105, above.
128. Mohamed Ali to Shaukat Ali, 6 May 1920, n. 105, above.
129. *The Times,* 22 Mar. 1920. Orientalist Margoliouth also praised the firmness of the Premier, contending that the Khilafat question was only a camouflage for plans which the civilized powers of Europe could not countenance. D.S. Margoliouth, 'The Caliphate', *New Europe,* 14/182 (1920), 294–300.
130. Letter dated 22 Mar. 1920, NAUK, FO 311/8 22091139/44.
131. *Bombay Chronicle,* 26 and 27 Mar. 1920.
132. *Amrita Bazar Patrika,* 27 Mar. 1920.
133. *Independent.* 27 Mar. 1920.
134. Ibid., 28 Mar. 1920.
135. On 9 March 1920, Abdul Bari and Kidwai had sent the following telegram to Mohamed Ali, Ameer Ali, and Ispahani: 'Interview with Fisher hopeful. Accept Montagu's formula. Countries Muslim before [the] War should remain under Muslim Government and Khalifa's S[i]ya[da]t.', See OIOC, File 2261/1920 in L/P&S/10/798.
136. See Chotani to Montagu, 27 and 28 Feb. and 6 Mar. 1920, OIOC, Files 1734/1920, 1785/1920 and 2008A/1920 in L/P&S/10/798. Early in March, Chelmsford reported to Montagu that the anti-Turk agitation in Britain had aroused 'strong resentment throughout the Indian Muslim world and widespread agitation is now being organized by Khilafat leaders to counteract English agitation [by the Church dignitaries and others] and openly preaching boycott of

Government and threatening *jihad*. See Viceroy to Sec. of State, Tel. P., No. 217, 6 Mar. 1920, OIOC, Chelmsford Papers.
137. Mohamed Ali had declared that if 'Britain sought to crush the Turk then Moslems throughout the world would fight on the side of the Turk against Britain'. For his remarks, Mohamed Ali was severely criticized by the British press and Sir Charles Oman floated a proposal in the House of Commons for legal proceedings against him. For his part, Mohamed Ali contended that he had been quoted out of context. See *Glasgow Herald*, 26 Mar. 1920; *Daily Telegraph* and *Morning Post*, 23 Mar. 1920; and Parl. Papers, 1920 *Hansard*, 127 H.C. Deb. 5S, cols 1225–6.
138. *Advocate of India*, 1 Apr. 1920.
139. Reference in Gandhi to Hignell (Pvt Sec. to Viceroy). Tel. 13 Apr. 1920, OIOC, Chelmsford Papers.
140. Gandhi to Chotani, Tel. 18 Apr. 1920, *The Collected Works of Mahatma Gandhi*, xvii, Ministry of Information and Broadcasting, Government of India (New Delhi, 1965), 322.
141. Ibid., xvii, 345–6.
142. Ibid., 346.
143. Gandhi to Montagu, Tel 22 Apr. 1920, OIOC, File 3255/1920 in L/P&S/10/799; and Hignell to Gandhi, 6 May 1920, referred to in Gandhi to Hignell, 12 June 1920, encl. Chelmsford to Montagu, 23 June 1920, OIOC, Montagu Papers.
144. See the minutes by (Sir) J.W. Hose (1865–1958), Sec., J&P Dept., and J.E. Shuckburgh, dated 27 Apr. 1920, in OIOC, File 3255/1920 in L/P&S/10/799.
145. See Shuckburgh's minute, n. 144, above.
146. Viceroy to Sec. of State, Tel. P., No. 379, 7 May 1920, OIOC, Chelmsford Papers.
147. *Nuqush*, CIX, 96.
148. Nadwi to Abdul Bari, 6 May 1920, *Barid-i Farang*, 67; and Mohamed Ali to Shaukat Ali, 6 May 1920, n.105, above.
149. Muhammad Sarwar, *Maulana Mohamed Ali ke yurup ke safar*, 36–7. See also Iqbal's 'Daryuwzah-i Khilafat' in *Bang-i Dara*, (Lahore, 1924), 236–7.
150. See James A. Malcolm to Sir John Tilley, 24 Mar. 1920, NAUK, FO 371/E 2155/139/44.
151. Ibid. In the meeting on 19 March, Lloyd George had tried to put the delegation off balance by asking Mohamed Ali whether he was opposed to Arab independence. To this question, Mohamed Ali had replied that though he was against their complete independence he did not object to Arab self-government. However, he expressed his hope of reconciling the Arabs and the Turks. Elaborating this point, Syud Hossain argued that their opposition to Arab aspirations was due to the fact

98. About the middle of 1919, Sir Abbas had written to M.H. Ispahani suggesting that 'the Muslim view of the vital problems affecting Islam should be made known to the Peace Conference' because 'the dissevered limbs of the Turkish Empire among the Christian nations', were in sight. See OIOC, File 6786/1919 in L/P&S/10/797.
99. Ibid.
100. Mohamed Ali to Chotani, Tel. 7 Mar. 1920, in Anon., *Muhammad Ali*, 129.
101. See OIOC, J&P, 2433/1920 with 1451/1919.
102. Afzal Iqbal, *Mohamed Ali*, 207–8. In Parliament, Lt.Col. James (1847–1927) had directed his criticism against Syud Hossain who, he alleged, had been accused, at the insistence of Motilal Nehru, of the abduction and forcible conversion to Islam of the latter's daughter. Montagu, however, expressed his ignorance of any information about the matter. See Parl. Papers, 1920, *Hansard*, 127 H.C. Deb. 5S, col. 1860.
103. Ameer Ali was much more co-operative than he had been in 1913. See M.Y. Abbasi, 'Jauhar is Outspoken as Ever: The 1913 Episode', *Pakistan Times* (Rawalpindi), 22 Dec. 1978. For others see Nadwi's introduction to *Barid-i Farang*, ii.
104. OIOC, L/P&S/18, B. 361, 10.
105. Mohamed Ali to Shaukat Ali, 6 May 1920, encl. Chelmsford to Montagu, 3 June 1920, OIOC, Montagu Papers.
106. Ibid.
107. Ibid. Also see Rais Ahmad Jafari, *Sirat-i Mohamed Ali* (Delhi, 1932) 297–8; and Special Bureau of Information Weekly Report No. 16 (for the week ending 5 June 1920) in OIOC, File 5635/1920 with 1229/1920, XI.
108. Mohamed Ali to Shaukat Ali. 6 May 1920, n. 105, above; and Jafari, *Sirat-i Mohamed Ali*, 298 and 302–3. For information about the *Daily Herald*, see Carl F. Brand, *The British Labour Party: A Short History* (London. 1965), 27.
109. The delegation brought out many propaganda pamphlets and similar kinds of literature. The variety of subjects included the address presented in January 1920 to the viceroy in Delhi, the Khilafat Manifesto approved by the Third Khilafat Conference at Bombay in February 1920, and important interviews and speeches. See Indian Khilafat Delegation Publications: (i) *The Turkish Settlement and the Muslim and Indian Attitude* (London, 1920); (ii) *The Secretary of State for India and the Indian Khilafat Delegation* (London, 1920); (iii) *The Prime Minister and the Indian Delegation* (London, 1920); (iv) *The Case for Turkey and the Khilafat* (London, 1920); (v) *Atrocities Committed by the Greeks in Smyrna* (London, 1920); (vi) *Justice to Islam and*

Turkey (London, 1920); and (vii) *India's Verdict on Turkish Treaty* (London, 1920).

110. Jafari, *Sirat-i Mohamed Ali,* 293; Nadwi's Introduction to *Barid-i Farang,* 11; and Nadwi to Masud Ali, 24 March 1920, ibid., 31.
111. See 'Report Submitted by the Delegation and Accepted by Mr Fisher', OIOC, L/P&S/18, B. 370; and 'Minutes of Proceeding at a Deputation from the Indian Khilafat Delegation to the Prime Minister at 10 Downing Street On Friday, 19th March 1920', OIOC, L/P&S/18, B. 371.
112. This was in answer to Col. Wedgwood's allegation in the Commons that the Indian Muslims had come to threaten the British Government. See Parl. Papers, 1920, *Hansard,* 125 H.C. Deb. 5S, col. 2023.
113. OIOC, L/P&S/18, B. 370 and B. 371.
114. Ibid.
115. See Philip Kerr's note to Sir William Duke (1863–1924), Permanent Under Sec. of State, dated 15 Mar. 1920; and minute by (Sir) John Shuckburgh (1877–1953), Sec., Pol. Dept., India Office, dated 16 Mar. 1920, in OIOC, File 2130/1920 in L/P&S/10/799.
116. See C.C. Garbett's undated minute in ibid.
117. Ibid. Emphasis added.
118. OIOC, L/P&S/18, B. 371.
119. Mohamed Ali to Shaukat Ali. 6 May 1920, n. 105, above.
120. Parl. Papers, 1920, *Hansard,* 125 H.C. Deb. 5S, cols. 1960-2.
121. For instance, in his analogy of the loss of the temporal power by the Pope to that of the Caliph, Curzon has vividly described Lloyd George's technique of intimidating others—which he seems to have used to his advantage in his meeting with the Khilafat delegation. 'On scores of occasions at Cabinets and elsewhere', Curzon recorded, 'I had listened almost with stupefaction to his amazing faculty of confusing the issues, of a calculated and overpowering irrelevance in argument, of attempts to frighten his opponent by sudden and menacing attack, also, when required, of gracious flattery and compliment and cooling apology, and of the most moving and sentimental affects'. Quoted in Leonard Mosley, *Curzon: The End of an Epoch* (London, 1960), 243.
122. See the minute by Sir John Tilley (1869–1952). Asst. Sec., FO, dated 10 Apr. 1920. NAUK, FO 371/E 2830/139/44. Also see Admiral Sir John de Robeck to Curzon, 9 Mar. 1920, ibid., 371/E 2291/56/44.
123. For Montagu, see his minute of 11 Nov. 1920 in OIOC, File 8039/1920 in L/P&S/10/796. For de Robeck, see Admiral de Robeck to Curzon, 9 Mar. 1920, n. 122, above. For the General Staff, see NAUK, FO 371/E 2207/3/44; and /E 324S/3/44.

224. Copy of the telegram enclosed in Webb to Curzon, 14 May 1920, NAUK, FO 371/E 5433/139/44. Emphasis added. Rear Admiral Sir Richard Webb (1870–1950), the acting British high commissioner at Istanbul, however, got the telegram intercepted and stopped it from being delivered to the Sultan, though he thought that the latter would probably receive a copy by mail in due course. See ibid.

225. Ibid. On 28 May 1920, the delegation followed-up the telegram with a lengthy letter to the Sultan, in which they again begged him to reject the Treaty, and assured him that not only did he have the support of Indian Muslims, but that Muslims in Afghanistan, Tunisia, Algeria, Morocco, and Egypt were also ready to support him. This confidential letter, which apparently escaped detection by the British authorities, was not published until November 1924 for fear of involving the deposed Sultan in trouble with the British. See *Comrade*, 14 Nov. 1920.

226. *Daily Telegraph*, 14 May 1920.

227. See ibid., 20 May 1920.

228. See Lord Hardinge's minute in NAUK, FO 371/E 5433/139/44.

229. See the minutes and notes by Sir Arthur Hirtzel (1870–1937), Asst. Under Sec. of State, Sir Edward Chamier, Legal Adviser, J.W. Hose and J.E. Shuckburgh of 13, 14, 17 and 20 May 1920, respectively, in OIOC, Flie 3828/1920 in L/P&S/10/799.

230. See, e.g., Mohamed Ali to Shaukat Ali, Tel. 17 June 1920, in Viceroy to Sec. of State Tel. P&R. No. 523, 28 June 1920, OIOC, Chelmsford Papers; and *Islamic Review and Muslim India*, June–July 1920, 226.

231. See Philip Kerr to Sir S.K. Brown, note dated 1 July 1920, OIOC, File 5080/1920, 7 July 1920, Chelmsford Papers.

232. See OIOC, File 5438/1920 in L/P&S/10/799.

233. See Montagu's minute of 22 July 1920, in ibid.

234. Even the India Office (excepting, of course, Montagu) was reluctant to concede any point. See, e.g., the minutes by J.E. Shuckburgh (15 and 18 July), C.C. Garbett (6 and 16 Aug.), and J.W. Hose (9 Aug.) in ibid.

235. Report W/HD (273), 24 July 1920, in OIOC, L/P&S/18, B. 361, 7; and Summary in B. 361 by Major Bray of the India Office in File 8769/1920 in L/P&S/10/799.

236. Report R/Misc. (131), 9 Sept. 1920, in ibid., 7.

237. For details of the interview, see Nadwi to Abdul Bari, 12 Aug. 1920, *Barid-i Farang*, 164–6.

238. Report R/Misc. (131), 9 Sept. 1920, OIOC, L/P&S/18, B. 361, 7.

239. Reports W/HD (273) and (279), dated 24 July and 5 Aug. 1920, respectively, in ibid., 7.

240. Nadwi to Abdul Bari, 12 Aug. 1920, *Barid-i Farang*, 164–6.

241. Ibid.
242. See Sir G. Buchanan to Curzon, No. 291, 28 Apr. 1920, NAUK, FO 371/E 4286/139/44; Hardinge's minute, probably of 5 May 1920, and the related correspondence in NAUK, FO 371/E 3276/139/44; and Mohamed Ali to Shaukat Ali, 6 May 1920, n. 105, above.
243. Report W/LH (35), 6 Oct. 1920, OIOC, L/P&S/18, B. 361, 6.
244. Richard A. Webster, *Christian Democracy in Italy, 1860–1960* (London, 1961), 63.
245. *Annual Register, 1920* (London, 1920), 169.
246. Webster, *Christian Democracy in Italy*, 62–3.
247. See ibid., 58–63.
248. Report W/LH (35), 6 Oct. 1920, OIOC, L/P&S/18, B. 361, 6.
249. Report W/LH (20), 5 July 1920, in ibid., 9.
250. Ibid.
251. Ibid.
252. Jafari, *Sirat-i Mohamed Ali*, 294.
253. Report W/LH (35), 6 Oct. 1920, OIOC, L/P&S/18, B, 361, 6.
254. Ibid.
255. Note dated 28 July 1910, NAUK, FO 371/E 9073/139/44.
256. Buchanan to Curzon, No. 617, 8 Aug. 1920, NAUK, FO 371/E 9999/139/44 and OIOC, L/P&S/18, B. 361, 5 and 11.
257. Reports W/HD (279), 5 Aug. 1920; and R/Misc. (131), 9 Sept. 1920, OIOC, L/P&S/18, B. 361, 6 and 11.
258. Report W/HD (279), 5 Aug. 1920, in ibid., 6.
259. Report W/MX (131), 31 July 1920, in ibid., 5.
260. Report W/HD (279), 5 Aug. 1920, in ibid., 6.
261. Count de Salis to Curzon, Tel. No. 31, 24 July 1920, NAUK, FO 371/E 8877/139/44.
262. Nadwi to Masud Ali, 10 Aug. 1920, *Barid-i Farang*, 160–1.
263. Mohamed Ali to Shaukat Ali, 6 May 1920, n. 105, above.
264. OIOC, L/P&S/18, B. 371.
265. Roger Aubert, 'Papacy–VII: The 19th and 20th Centuries', *Encyclopaedia Britannica*, xvi, 1972, 271.
266. OIOC, File 5767/1920 in L/P&S/10/799.
267. *Muslim Outlook,* 5 Aug. 1920, OIOC, File 6755/1920 in ibid.
268. Ibid.
269. See Count de Salis to Curzon, Tel. No. 31, 24 July 1920, above; Montagu's minute, probably of 30 July 1920, in OIOC, File 5767/1920 in L/P&S/10/799; note from India Office to Foreign Office, No. 5767, dated 3 Aug. 1920 in Ibid.;

and Curzon to Count de Salis, Tel. No. 29, 6 Aug. 1920, NAUK, FO 371/E 936/139/44.
270. W.H. Peters, 'Benedict XV', in *New Catholic Encyclopaedia*, II (New York & London, 1967), 280.
271. See note from to IO to FO, dated 10 Sept. 1920, OIOC, File 6755/1920 in L/P&S/10/799; Curzon to Count de Salis, 22 Sept. 1920, NAUK, FO 371/E 11213/139/44; and Count de Salis, to Curzon, No. 134, 16 Nov. 1920, in ibid., FO 371/E 14492/139144.
272. Count de Salis to Curzon, No. 134, 16 Nov. 1920, above.
273. See note from to FO to IO, No E 14492/139/44, dated 30 Nov. 1920, in OIOC, File 8507/1920 in L/P&S/10/799.
274. See the minutes by L.D. Wakely (2 Dec. 1920), J.W. Hose (7 Dec. 1920), and Sir William Duke (9 Dec. 1920) in OIOC, File 8507/1920 in L/P&S/10/799. Accordingly, on 16 Dec. 1920, the FO was informed by the IO that they did not intend to issue a denial. See ibid.
275. Mohamed Ali to Shaukat Ali, 6 May 1920, n. 105, above.
276. Report FO 371/E 9999/139/44 dated 24 Aug. 1920, OIOC, L/P&S/18, B. 361, 8.
277. OIOC, L/P&S/18, B. 361, 2.
278. Nadwi to Masud Ali, 14 Apr. 1920, *Barid-i Farang*, 44–7; and Nuri As-Said to Major Young, 12 Apr. 1920, NAUK, FO 371/E 3102/139/44.
279. Ibid. Also see Nadwi to Abdul Hakim, 20 May 1920, *Barid-i Farang*, 89.
280. Nadwi to Masud Ali, 17 July 1920, ibid., 128–9.
281. Nadwi to Masud Ali, 18 July 1920, ibid., 130.
282. Nadwi to Masud Ali, 10 Aug. 1920, ibid., 160.
283. Mohamed Ali to Shaukat Ali, 6 May 1920, n. 105, above; and Nadwi to Masud Ali, 28 Apr. 1920, *Barid-i Farang*, 63–4.
284. Ibid.
285. Nadwi to Abdul Hakim, 28 Apr. 1920, ibid., 65; and Nadwi to Masud Ali, 27 May 1920, ibid., 101.
286. Report W/LH (3), 30 Apr. 1920, OIOC, L/P&S/18, B. 361, 2. Khalil Khalid is also known for his *The Diary of a Turk* (London, 1903) and *The Crescent Versus the Cross* (London, 1907).
287. Reports W/MC (7), 15 June 1920 and HC/1273, 25 July and 19 Aug. 1920; and Report W/MX (131), 31 July 1920, OIOC, L/P&S/18, B. 361, 4 and 5.
288. Report W/MC (8), 17 June 1920, ibid., 2–3.
289. Report W/LH (1). 24 April 1920, ibid., 2.
290. Memo showing the movements of the delegation, Rd. 13 May 1920, NAUK, FO 371/E 4650/139/44.

291. Reports W/DR (7), 31 July and 20 Aug. 1920, OIOC, L/P&S/18, B. 361, 3.
292. Report R/Misc. (131), 9 Sept. 1920, ibid., 3.
293. See ibid., 11; and Nadwi to Masud Ali, 10 Aug. 1920, *Barid-i Farang*, 163.
294. OIOC, L/P&S/18, B. 361, 11.
295. Nadwi to Abdul Hakim, 6 May 1920, *Barid-i Farang*, 81.
296. Reports R/Misc. (131), 6 Aug. and 9 Sept. 1920, OIOC, L/P&S/18, B. 361, 4.
297. Reports W/DR (4), 20 July 1920; W/DH (7), 20 Aug. 1920; HC/1273, 25 July and 19 Aug. 1920, OIOC, L/P&S/18, B. 361, 3, 4 and 8.
298. See Iqbal Shaidai's 'Memoirs' in *Imroze* (Lahore), 25 May 1969.
299. In addition to Shaidai's 'Memoirs', this information has been pieced together from OIOC, L/P&S/18, B. 350 and B. 361; and Zafar Hasan Aybek, *Aap biti*, i (Lahore, [1964]), 221–2.
300. Ibid.
301. Reports HC/1436, 12 Sept. and 13 Oct. 1920, OIOC, L/P&S/18, B. 361, 4.
302. Reports HC/1273, 25 July and 19 Aug. 1920, ibid, 4 and 8.
303. Reports W/HD (268), 16 July 1920; and W/HD (276), 3 Aug. 1920, ibid., 8.
304. Report W/VC (14), 6 Sept. 1920, ibid., 8. The tampering with the soldiers' loyalty came to the surface in November 1920, with the *Mutafiqqa Fatwa* of the *'ulama*. It re-emerged at the Karachi Khilafat Conference of 9 July 1921, when a resolution was passed emphatically declaring that it was religiously unlawful for any Muslim to serve in the army or help or acquiesce in recruitment.
305. Report W/RW (56), OIOC, L/P&S/18, B. 361, 4.
306. Even the address presented to the viceroy in January 1920 by the Khilafatists at Delhi stated that the object of the Khilafat delegation to Europe was to explain the 'nature and [the] binding force of Islamic obligations and the true character and scope of Muslim aspirations'. See the Indian Khilafat Delegation Publications No. (i), n. 109, above.
307. The details of the Turkish Misak-i Milli can be seen in Lord Kinross, *Atatürk: The Rebirth of a Nation* (London, 1964), 531–2.
308. Basil Thomson to FO, 18 Aug. 1920, NAUK, FO 371/E 10082/139/44.
309. Nadwi to Abdul Hakim, 19 Aug. 1920, *Barid-i Farang*, 171–2; and Report dated 1 Sept. 1920, encl., Basil Thomson to Under Sec., Foreign Affairs, No. SB 18824/139/44, 2 Sept. 1920, NAUK, FO 371/E 10825/139/44.
310. Ibid.
311. See H.M. Hayat's letter to the Japanese chargé d'affaires, 13 Aug. 1920 in NAUK, FO 371/A 6J24/39/45.
312. See C.H. Bentinck's minute of 24 Aug. 1920, in ibid.

313. See letter from FO to the Japanese chargé d'affaires, 31 Aug. 1920, in ibid.
314. Report dated 28 Apr. 1920, encl., Basil Thomson to FO, No. SB 18824/4, 2 Sept. 1920, NAUK, FO 371/E 10825/139/44.
315. For details, see Nadwi to Masud Ali, 9 Sept. 1920, *Barid-i Farang*, 182–7; Nadwi to Abdul Hakim, 13 Sept. 1920, ibid., 187–94; Nadwi to Masud Ali, 15 Sept. 1920, ibid., 194–9; and Nadwi to Abdul Hakim, 28 Sept. 1920, ibid., 200–8.
316. See, e.g., Nadwi to Daryabadi, 28 Apr. 1920, *Barid-i Farang*, 59–60. Also see Nadwi to Abdul Hakim. 16 June 1920. ibid., 118.
317. *India* (London). 3 Sept. 1920.
318. See Report W/YC (14), 6 Sept. 1920, OIOC, L/P&S/18, B. 361, 3.
319. Zafar Imam convincingly argues that in 1920 no responsible Soviet leader, except perhaps Leon Trotsky (1879–1940), seriously thought of doing so by force of arms. See his *Colonialism in East-West Relations: A Study of Soviet Policy Towards India and Anglo-Soviet Relations, 1917–1947* (New Delhi, 1969), 147.
320. See Nadwi to Masud Ali, 9 Sept. 1920, *Barid-i Farang*, 185–6; and Nadwi to Abdul Hakim, 13 Sept. 1920, ibid., 189–90.
321. Ibid. The CKC's efforts to bring about reconciliation between the Arabs and the Turks did not succeed because, apart from the intransigence of the Arabs, the British government refused to give permission to its contemplated delegations to the Hejaz, Syria, Najaf, and Iraq. Similarly, a request for a Muslim mission to Smyrna was also turned down. See Viceroy to Sec. of State, Tel. P., No. 353, 2 May 1920; Sec. of State, to Viceroy, Tel. P., No. 3723, 14 May 1920; Viceroy to Sec. of State, Tel. P., No. 444, 29 May 1920; Viceroy to Sec. of State, Tel. P., No. 536, 30 June 1920; Sec. of State to Viceroy, Tel. P., No. 5427, 21 July 1920, OIOC, Chelmsford Papers; and NAUK, F.O 371/E 8753/139/44; and E 7925/139/44.
322. See the Indian Khilafat Delegation publications Nos. (iv), (vi) and (vii), n. 109, above.
323. See, e.g., Montagu to Chelmsford, 16 June 1920, OIOC, Montagu Papers.
324. Nadwi to Abdul Hakim, 10 June 1920, *Barid-i Farang*, 111–12.
325. OIOC, L/P&S/18, B. 361, 9.
326. Summary of Memo. L/P&S/18, B. 361, by Major Bray in OIOC, File 8769/1920 in L/P&S/10/799.
327. *India,* 3 Sept. 1920.
328. Summary of Memo, B. 361, n. 329, above.
329. Cited in Francis Robinson, 'The Leadership of the Professional Politicians in Muslim Politics, 1911–1923', paper presented in October 1973 at the Centre of South Asian Studies, School of Oriental and African Studies, University of

London. However, the allegations sprang mostly from the delay in submitting the accounts and due to the high cost of living in Europe. Otherwise, even Sir Basil Thomson (1861–1939), Scotland Yard's Director of Intelligence, testified to the careful manner in which Mohamed Ali spent his money. See Central Khilafat Committee, *Hisaibat-i wafd-i Khilafat-i yurup*, published by Haji Siddique Khatri, Hon. Sec., CKC (Bombay, 1923), 1–6 and 17–20; and NAUK, FO. 371/E 10670/139/44.

330. Nadwi to Abdul Bari, 26 Aug. 1920, *Barid-i Farang*, 178–9. Later, Iqbal seems to have changed his earlier disparaging views, when he complimented Nadwi for having done 'a great job' in Europe and expressed his confidence that their tour 'will yield important results'. See Iqbal to Nadwi, 10 Oct. 1920 in S. Ataullah (ed.), *Maktubat-i Iqbal*, i (Lahore, 1945), 112–13.
331. *Hindu,* 14 Oct. 1920.
332. Ibid.
333. Report dated 1 Sept. 1920, encl., Basil Thomson to FO, No. SB, 1884/4, 2 Sept. 1920, NAUK, FO 371/E 10825/139/44.

5

Atatürk's Impact on Muslim India, 1919–1938*

Even today, one is likely to find, among family memorabilia in Pakistani homes various prints and photographs of Mustafa Kemal dating back to the early twenties of the previous century. This is just an example of the impact that he had—and continues to have—on Muslims of the subcontinent. Indian involvement with Turkey is a fact of history and goes back to the latter days of the Mughal rule. Gradually, this undefined pan-Islamic feeling developed into a conscious movement and climaxed in the massive demonstration of support for Turkey after the First World War. The post-war period was crucial for the war-ravaged Near Eastern country: its army was in disarray, its economy was shattered, and its people were demoralized. Above all, the victorious Allies were well-poised to divide the prize amongst themselves. Precisely at that juncture, Mustafa Kemal instilled a new hope in his people,

---

*An amalgamated version of the two articles originally published as 'Rise of Atatürk and its Impact on Contemporary Muslim India; The First Phase', in the *Proceedings: International Conference on Atatürk*, Boğazici University (Istanbul, Turkey), 3/55, (1981), 1–9, and 'Muslims of British India and the Kemalist Reform in Turkey: Iqbal, Jinnah and Atatürk, 1924–1938', in the *Atatürk Araştirma Merkezi Dergisi* (Ankara), 12/35 (1996), 379–86.

re-organized them, and, finally, led them to victory. The facts of his rise to power are too well known to be repeated here. This chapter will concentrate, instead, on Atatürk's impact on contemporary Muslim India from the early stages of his struggle to the time he launched and perfected his extensive reforms.

To develop a correct perspective on Indian Muslim perceptions of Mustafa Kemal and of the situation in Turkey, it is imperative to view the subject in the context of three basic propositions. First, among all the Muslim peoples, those of India probably had the most pronounced sense of the international aspect of Islam.[1] This 'extra-territorial' involvement may have been a reaction against the dominant Hindu nationalism or a result of the socio-political predicament in which they found themselves under the British rule, though it is obvious why such an attitude should have led them to identify their interests with those of Ottoman Turkey. Secondly, the Indian Muslim identification with Ottoman Turkey was based on their perception of Turkey as the seat of the caliphate and the protector of Islamic interests. The threat to Turkey was, therefore, construed as a threat to Islam, so that anyone who made an effort to check this threat would be hailed as the 'saviour' of Islam. It is in terms of this second proposition that the Indian Muslims' adulation of Mustafa Kemal, in the years between 1919 and 1938, should be interpreted. Finally, the fact that the Kemalist challenge was presented in modernist terms had profound implications for Indian Muslims, especially after 1924, because of its influence on two of the most ardent pro-Turkish modernist leaders of the post-Khilafat period, Muhammad Iqbal and Mohammad Ali Jinnah. Iqbal could have taken this as a happy augury for Muslim renaissance, while Jinnah could have found a good precedent to follow in the achievements of Mustafa Kemal.

Mustafa Kemal's name was first heard in India when the details of his Çanakkale/Gallipoli exploits (1915–16) began to trickle into the Indian newspapers. Before that, hardly anyone in India knew about him.

However, it was his organization and leadership of the Turkish nationalists against the Allies that endeared him most to the Indian Muslim masses. And, since Mustafa Kemal initially posed as the saviour of the threatened caliphate, he appeared to be a symbol of Islam's resistance to western challenge. Thus, from the middle of 1920, Mustafa Kemal was a hero to the Indian Muslims. Popular poems eulogized him for his heroism and for his services to Islam and the caliphate. In such an atmosphere, when Graeco-Turkish hostilities were renewed in the summer of 1921, the Indian Muslims were stirred by the rumoured possibility of the British government rendering military assistance to the Greeks against Ankara. They were further angered by the capture, in Anatolia, of Mustafa Saghir, an Indian Muslim secret agent said to be in the service of the British Foreign Office and Military Intelligence and deputed to eliminate Mustafa Kemal.[2] This prompted some *'ulama*, notably Abul Kalam Azad and Abdul Bari, to proclaim that it had become religiously imperative to help save Mustafa Kemal and his nationalists. Therefore, they advocated the adoption of more effective measures against the British.[3] Similar views were echoed by other Indian Muslim leaders such as Mohamed Ali, and repeated at several meetings and conferences at different places.[4] In the event, the British did not involve themselves openly in the Graeco-Turkish war but, nevertheless, the Khilafatists decided on a more aggressive policy. Early in July 1921, they held a conference in Karachi under the chairmanship of Shaukat Ali, the CKC's powerful honorary secretary, and passed a resolution emphatically declaring that it was religiously unlawful for any Muslim to serve in the army or help or acquiesce in its recruitment. It further decided that:

> If the British Government directly or indirectly, openly or secretly, fights the Ankara Government, the Muslims of India will start civil disobedience and establish their complete independence at the next session of the Indian National Congress to be held at Ahmedabad and hoist the flag of the Indian Republic.[5]

This was a clear indication to the British government of how far the Indian Muslims were prepared to go in their support of Mustafa Kemal, even if it was more of a pressure tactic than a real threat. In addition to passing inflammatory resolutions, they tried to raise a loan of thirty millions rupees in order to purchase arms for Mustafa Kemal.[6] This was over and above the subscriptions to the Smyrna Fund, which had been instituted as early as 1920.[7] The arms purchase scheme had been prompted by the Supreme Council's decision in Paris on 10 August 1921, to lift the arms embargo on the Turkish and Greek belligerents.[8] The collection of such a colossal amount was too ambitious, and even Mohamed Ali was doubtful about its realization unless the ruling chiefs also contributed.[9] Nevertheless, a regular Angora Fund for the relief of Turkish sufferers was created and merged with the Smyrna Fund.[10] Eventually, by early 1923, remittances to Ankara amounted to about £160,000,[11] most of which was utilized to pay the nationalist army.[12] The British and the Indian governments were disinclined to interfere with the arms purchase scheme,[13] but they could ill-afford to disregard the attempts at tampering with the loyalty of the Indian troops. In September 1921, the Ali brothers were arrested along with some of their associates and, in November of the same year, sentenced to two years of rigorous imprisonment[14]—but the agitation continued unabated.

The summer of 1922 brought fresh reverberations to India from the Near East, mainly due to British Prime Minister Lloyd George's open encouragement of the Greeks to launch a fresh attack on the nationalists. But the hostilities that began in the middle of August resulted in a complete rout of the Greek forces, which were driven back into Europe. Within a fortnight, Mustafa Kemal's forces had occupied Smyrna and their pacification of Anatolia was practically complete.[15] The news of the nationalists' victory brought great jubilation to India. Celebrations were held throughout the country with great enthusiasm. Muslims of all shades of opinion flocked together and vied with one another in lauding the services of Mustafa Kemal, 'a hero at the head of a band of heroes', who had saved the caliphate from disaster.¹⁶ But the celebrations turned sour over the news of a possible British involvement on the side of the Greeks. For a moment, war and peace hung by a thread due to the Çanakkale crisis. This angered the Indian Muslims but, since they were unable to restrain the British, they pre-empted to forestall the use of Indian troops against Ankara in any impending Allied operation.¹⁷ The moderates pressed the government of Lord Reading (1860–1935) for the immediate withdrawal of Indian forces from the territories that were formerly within the Ottoman Empire.¹⁸ The militants, on the other hand, tried to raise an 'Angora Legion' to fight for the Turkish nationalists.¹⁹ Seth Chotani, the president of the CKC, warned Lloyd George that the volunteering would definitely proceed unless Istanbul and Thrace were immediately restored to Turkey.²⁰ But, when the Government of India threatened to implement the Foreign Enlistment Act 1870 that viewed such volunteering as illegal, the Khilafatists quietly shelved their plan.²¹

Mustafa Kemal's popularity in India grew rapidly during the months that followed. The period from the Armistice at Mudania (October 1922) to the final peace treaty at Lausanne (July 1923), saw the high watermark of his impact on Muslim India. In fact, in November 1922, this relationship had been severely tested but it had survived the crisis. This happened when Mustafa Kemal, after a prolonged friction with the puppet sultan, Mehmed VI, decided to deprive the latter of his potentially menacing temporal powers. The GNA went along with him and, through a law, separated the sultanate from the caliphate. When Mehmed VI fled and took refuge with the British, the assembly immediately appointed his cousin Abdülmecid as his successor with 'spiritual' powers only.²² The decision may have been defensible from the Turkish nationalists' point of view but it provoked a strong reaction in the subcontinent. It was especially embarrassing the Khilafatists, and they secretly tried to obtain a revision. A two-man delegation was hastily despatched to Switzerland with a message for Ismet (Inönü), then attending the Lausanne Conference, for transmission to Ankara.²³ But since the Indian leaders had by now committed themselves so deeply to the Ankara policies, they could not take any other stance publicly. Therefore, Seth Chotani had no reservation in declaring that whatever the GNA decided would be acceptable to them.²⁴ He also sent a telegram to Mustafa Kemal assuring him of the continued support of the Indian Muslims.²⁵

The CKC and the Jami'yyat al-'Ulama, the religio-political body of the Indian *ulama*, made every effort to reconcile Indian opinion to Ankara's policies.²⁶ Later that year, the Khilafat Conference lavished the titles of *Saifu'l-Islam* ('Sword of Islam') and *Mujaddad-i Khilafat* ('Restorer of the Caliphate') upon Mustafa Kemal, in recognition of his 'services to Islam'.²⁷ These titles were hardly appropriate considering the internal political situation in Turkey, but the Indians were reluctant to break openly with the Turks and, instead, delivered angry warnings to the British government for the impasse at Lausanne, and demanded a positive response.²⁸ A New Year's Day (1923) resolution of the Khilafat Conference threatened that, in the event of war with Turkey, the Khilafatists would launch civil disobedience which would include 'propaganda among Police and Army, stoppage of fresh recruitment, refusal to subscribe to war loans. [and] recruitment to [the] Angora Legion'.²⁹

It is doubtful whether such threats would have worked, but the resolution shows the extent of Mustafa Kemal's support among the Indian Muslims. This kind of an ideal situation, however, did not last for long. In October 1923, Turkey declared itself a republic and elected Mustafa Kemal as president. This rendered the status of the caliph at Istanbul to be completely anomalous and his ouster became a matter of time. What precipitated his exit was the letter that Sir Aga Khan and Syed Ameer Ali wrote to Ismet (Inönü) from London towards the end of November 1923, entreating him to maintain 'the religious and moral solidarity of Islam' by re-establishing the powers of the Sunni caliphate-imamate.[30] The letter was no more than a personal appeal from two well-known Indian Muslims, but the nationalist, erroneously perceiving it as part of some British intrigue, hurriedly moved to take appropriate measures which culminated in the abolition of the caliphate on 3 March 1924.[31]

This was something that the Khilafatists could not accept. Therefore, the Indian reaction was strong.[32] The commonly-held view was that the GNA, or any another government, had no right, jurisdiction, or power to abolish an institution that had become the integral part of the religious institutions of the Sunni world of Islam.[33] Shaukat Ali, who had succeeded Chotani as President of the CKC, sent a telegram to Mustafa Kemal pleading with him to revise the decision.[34] But the Turkish president had no intention of either rescinding his action or assuming the title of caliph for himself.[35] To him the caliphate had ceased to have any relevance for Turkey.[36] But the Indian Muslims were unable to understand this argument, as they looked at the problem from a different angle altogether. Therefore, the shock and reaction at the abolition of the caliphate was instantaneous and sharp. Its impact changed the way the Indian Muslim conceived of Turkey; Ottoman Turkey, which once symbolized the *daru'l-Islam*, was now republican Turkey, one of several parts of the Muslim world. This meant, that in future, the position of Turkey would not be that of a 'protector' but, probably, as a future model for emulation. In a sense, therefore, Kemalist Turkey represented not so much of an emotional setback as an unexpected source of psychological advantage for the Indian Muslims. Not surprisingly, after the initial shock, Indian public opinion, spearheaded by those who understood the Turkish predicament, began to tilt again in favour of the nationalists and the new situation generally came to be accepted.[37] Only the diehard Khilafatists refused to accept the *fait accompli* and persisted in their resolve to continue the movement on the secondary issue of the freedom of the *Jaziratu'l-Arab* from non-

Muslim control. But it was clear that the Khilafat movement had lost its sting.

As time passed, the impact of Mustafa Kemal on contemporary Muslim India became increasingly discernable. This was precisely the period when he had embarked on an ambitious programme of rapid modernization, touching almost every facet of national life in Turkey. Within one month of the abolition of the caliphate, the whole medieval paraphernalia of the religious government, as represented by the *shari'at* courts, the *auqaf* ministry, and the religious schools, had been swept clean with a broom. The government then pursued, with the utmost vigour and at a reckless pace, the cultural and economic transformation of the state on purely European lines. The full sweep of the Kemalist revolution has been explained elsewhere in this book. Here, only a brief mention will suffice, in the words of an official Turkish publication which proudly recalls:

> A homogeneous, unitary nation-state emerged from the ruins of a sprawling multi-national, multi-religious, multi-lingual empire. A dynasty which had ruled for more than six centuries came to an end. All power was assumed by a Republic, with its Parliament and President, representing the will of the people. Theocracy, entrenched religious institutions, Koranic education, and Islamic law, with all their 'sacred' values and symbols, were abolished and replaced by Western governmental and legal institutions, secular education, and the adapted forms of the Swiss Civil Code, Italian Penal Code, and German Business Law. The traditional fez was outlawed overnight as a symbol of backwardness and the veil removed as the first step in the Turkish women's liberation. It was perhaps the most remarkable phenomenon of 'disorientation' in the modern world...[38]

With these reforms, Mustafa Kemal hoped to achieve the transition of his state from a monarchy disguised as a caliphate to a laicized republic within the shortest possible span of time. His objective was a modern and secular Turkey completely free from retarding influences or hampering ties. With his clear vision, he saw that Turkey, in order to survive, must be brought into line with the rest of Europe in all walks of life, and pursued it with a thoroughness rarely witnessed.

What was Muslim India's reaction to Mustafa Kemal's reforms? Murray Titus, a contemporary writer, suggests that India's liberal Muslims, like their Turkish counterparts, strove to be progressive but not too progressive. The masses were led by those who had a strong aversion to radical reform and preferred adherence to stricter interpretations of Islamic injunctions.[39] Nevertheless, they helped ease the situation. Notable among them were Sahibzada Aftab Ahmad Khan (1867–1930), a former member of the India Council, Prof. Khuda Bakhsh, historian and writer, and Iqbal, and Jinnah.[40] Of all of them, Iqbal was the one who appreciated the idea of *ijtihad* in the religious and political thought of the Turkish state the most. He unreservedly agreed with the Turkish view that, according to the spirit of Islam, the caliphate or imamate could be vested in a body of persons or an elected assembly.[41] 'The republican form of government', he declared, 'is not only thoroughly consistent with the spirit of Islam, but has also become a necessity in view of the new forces that are rent free in the world of Islam'.[42] Iqbal and his friends believed that the old system had definitely broken down and that the time had come for Muslims to temporarily withdraw from universalism, acquire strength and power, and then regroup themselves in a living family of republics or a League of Muslim Nations.[43] As a corollary, Iqbal defended the nationalists' drive towards reform. He hoped that the Indian Muslims, too, would one day, just like the Turks, re-evaluate their intellectual inheritance and, if unable to make any positive contribution, would at least provide a healthy restraint to the strident Turkish liberalism.[44]

Iqbal took great pains to emphasize that the Turkish revolution was not a religious setback and, even if all the Kemalist measures could not be justified, the spirit of dynamism was worth some risk. More significantly, some of Mustafa Kemal's measures could be construed as being variants of the many principles and institutions Islam cherished the most. Since Iqbal was Muslim India's foremost intellectual, and Jinnah its pragmatic leader, it would not be unwarranted to study their responses to the events in nationalist Turkey in terms of the formulations articulated by them. But it is pertinent to ask: Did the Indian Muslims, in general, acquiesce in the way Iqbal and Jinnah interpreted Kemalist Turkey? There are two broad indications that they did. First, from the fact that both Iqbal and Jinnah confidently praised Mustafa Kemal when the Indian Muslims were themselves favourably disposed towards him, and not because Iqbal and Jinnah led them to this position. 'To explain, to expand, to write commentaries on, and to "follow" Iqbal, became almost a major profession in Indian Islam', wrote a critical observer.[45] If this was so after his death, there is no reason why his formulation should not have been widely accepted and followed in his lifetime. Secondly, it is noteworthy that, in the Muslim freedom movement in India, it was the western-educated leadership and not the *'ulama* who had influence and initiative. The *'ulama* may have had some reservations about the inspiration coming from Kemalist Turkey, but the former did not suffer from similar inhibitions. The people followed this leadership and not the *'ulama*. The similarities between Mustafa Kemal's struggle against the Allied powers and the Indian Muslim struggle against the British were always transparent. In a theoretical sense, therefore, Indian Muslims could not have reservations about Mustafa Kemal without suspecting their own leadership. And this leadership, especially Jinnah who had fallen under Mustafa Kemal's spell since 1932, never attempted to conceal its admiration for what Turkey was poised to achieve.

Iqbal's response to the changes in Kemalist Turkey, though expressed repeatedly and at great length, was not always uniform. His final stance was what he maintained in his *Reconstruction of Religious Thought in Islam*. The following passage from his lecture on 'The Principle of

Movement in the Structure of Islam', epitomizes his perception of the Turkish experience well, and, therefore, needs substantial reproduction:

> The truth is that among the Muslim nations of today, Turkey alone has shaken off its dogmatic slumber, and attained to self-consciousness. She alone has claimed her right of intellectual freedom; she alone has passed from the ideal to the real—a transition which entails keen intellectual and moral struggle. To her the growing complexities of a mobile and broadening life are sure to bring new situations suggesting new points of view, and necessitating fresh interpretations of principles which are only of an academic interest to a people who have never experienced the joy of spiritual expansion.... [M]ost Muslim countries today ... are mechanically repeating old values, whereas the Turk is on the way to creating new values. He has passed through great experiences which have revealed his deeper self to him. In him life has begun to move, change, and amplify, giving birth to new desires, bringing new difficulties and suggesting new interpretations. The question which confronts him today, and which is likely to confront other Muslim countries in the near future, is whether the Law of Islam is capable of evolution—a question which will require great intellectual effort, and is sure to be answered in the affirmative...[46]

The basic point about Iqbal's stand is that he was neither resigning himself to the *fait accompli*, nor was he offering a kind of an apologia for what was going on in Turkey. For him, the only way to understand and appreciate the dynamism of the Turkish experiment was to develop a perspective on this problem which itself was not merely pragmatic but also dynamic. This, indeed, was the way in which Iqbal viewed the measures suggested or taken in Mustafa Kemal's Turkey. The basic achievement of Turkey, in his view, was that it had passed from the ideal to the real even though the experiment had tended to deny, in many ways, the validity of the ideal itself. Considering that Iqbal, himself, reconstructed religious thought in Islam on the assumption that there was a need for such a change, and in its very nature, this enterprise was a departure from tradition, his position on theoretical grounds was, therefore, compatible, perhaps even synonymous, with that of the

Kemalist Turk. Thus, there is no reason why he should not have 'heartily welcome[d] the liberal movement in modern Islam'.⁴⁷ In fact, Iqbal hoped that the Indian Muslims, too, would one day, like the Turks, re-evaluate their intellectual inheritance and, even if unable to make any positive contribution, at least provide a healthy restraint on the rapid movement of liberalism.⁴⁸

And yet, Iqbal's position was not that of a vague theoretician. He was a firm supporter of concrete manifestations of Turkish modernism. Thus, he regarded the Turkish view as 'perfectly sound' in that the institution of the caliphate, as understood in the traditional juridical sense, was anachronistic, and that an elected assembly, which would be better suited to the needs of the time and was compatible with the spirit of Islam, should replace this institution.⁴⁹ It is remarkable that Iqbal was prepared to go even further. On the question of the separation of Church and State, a question particularly relevant in the context of Kemalist Turkey, Iqbal maintained that 'personally' he regarded ideas of separation as 'a mistake' but conceded that 'the structure of Islam as a religio-political system, no doubt, does permit such a view'.⁵⁰

On the emancipation of women, another problem addressed by Turkish modernists, Iqbal was affirmative and emphatic. The point on which he differed from the Turks was not that women are in any way inferior—for he readily conceded their equality with men—but that it is Islam that has made her so. As for the present dispensation, wherein there were cases in which Muslim women wishing to get rid of undesirable husbands were driven to apostasy, Iqbal recognized a need for reform. 'I do not know', he wrote, 'whether the awakening of women in Turkey has created demands which cannot be met without a fresh interpretation of foundational principles.'⁵¹ But, nowhere does he say that such demands and reinterpretations would not be in order. It is important at this point to be clear about one thing—Iqbal's support for the Turkish experiment was unequivocal but it was not unqualified. The fundamental clue to an understanding of Iqbal's position is this: a vigorous and dynamic worldview was, for him, the pre-requisite to this worldly salvation. Of all the Muslim peoples, the Turk alone had shown this vigour and what it could lead to. To Iqbal, this was a tremendous achievement that paved the way for the inauguration of the Islamic renaissance. But there also was some uneasiness in Iqbal's mind. He complained:

The Turk has no new melody in his lute,
His new is but Europe's old.
Originality is at the root of all creation,
Never by imitation shall life be reformed.[52]

The apprehension, therefore, was that the inner vitality of the Turkish experiment might, in its early stages, become bogged down because it was patterned on the western model. What worried Iqbal was not that Turkey had gone too far; he feared that given the potential that it had, it might—by limiting itself within the perimeters of the western framework—stop short of going further towards a balanced reform. What is remarkable about Iqbal is that all his conservatism notwithstanding, he was not worried by what many Muslims interpreted as Turkish excesses. 'We have [heard] now and then', he wrote, 'that Turks are repudiating Islam. A greater lie was never told. Only those who have no idea of the history of the concepts of Islamic Jurisprudence fall an easy prey to this sort of mischievous propaganda.'[53] For Iqbal, the spirit of dynamism was worth some risk. Indeed, Muslim intellectual tradition had stagnated because of guarding too rigidly against, and stamping out, such risks. But since modern Islam could ill-afford this stagnation, it was imperative that the spirit of dynamism be given free flow in the hope that in time the dialectic of continuity and change, of tradition and modernity, would eliminate or minimize the risk. This was how Iqbal argued. And this was the theoretical basis on which he appreciated the Kemalist enterprise.

Jinnah's appreciation was a different matter. While Iqbal was conscious and tried to make others conscious of the significance of the experience that the Turkish people were undergoing and the relevance it had for the future of Islam, Jinnah realized the importance of the precedent Mustafa Kemal had set. Kemal Atatürk, Jinnah said, 'was the foremost figure in the Muslim East. In Persia and Afghanistan, in Egypt and, of course, in Turkey, he proved to the consternation of the rest of the world, that Muslim Nations were coming into their own. . . . With the example of this great Musalman in front of them as an inspiration, will the Muslims of India still remain in quagmire?'[54] These words, which Jinnah uttered to mark the death of Mustafa Kemal, clearly indicate the terms in which he conceived of Atatürk. It is evident that for Jinnah, Mustafa Kemal was not necessarily a model for emulation because the situations in which the two men found themselves, the odds they confronted, and the ways in which they reacted were completely dissimilar. Jinnah was not an idealist: therefore, to emulate Kemal was inconceivable for him. The sense in which the Kemalist achievement was important was indicated by the resolution of the All India Muslim League on his death: '[H]is memory', the resolution stated, 'will *inspire* Muslims all over the world with courage, perseverance and manliness'.[55] Mustafa Kemal, therefore, was a source of inspiration, not a model for imitation. For, as Iqbal had already warned, inspiration reinforces vitality, but imitation dampens its spirit; Jinnah could ill-afford to dampen it in his case.

In what way could Jinnah seek inspiration from Mustafa Kemal? The answer is possible in at least three ways. First, it is important to note that, until 1937, and probably even later, Jinnah, while being one of the most prominent Indian politicians, had not been as successful in national life as he wanted to be. His frustration was considerable for a variety of reasons.[56] Indeed, as late as 1931, Jinnah had decided to quit politics; it was not until 1935 that he re-entered the political arena. But, a resumption of political life did not mean an end of the problems that had led to Jinnah's initial retreat. It is possible, therefore, that Jinnah, in this situation, may have found the experience and achievement of men like Mustafa Kemal to be a source of some psychological 'redemption'. The report that Jinnah did, in fact, come under Mustafa Kemal's spell when he read, and greatly enjoyed, H.C. Armstrong's biography, *Grey Wolf*, would reinforce this point.[57] Secondly, in so far as there was a measure of affinity in the attitude, orientation, and worldview of Mustafa Kemal and Jinnah, the suggestion that the latter should have been amenable to Mustafa Kemal's influence becomes plausible. This affinity took two forms: a strong will and strength of character; and an essentially westernized outlook. Jinnah, therefore, did not have to translate Mustafa Kemal's experience in terms of the categories that were familiar to him; he had merely to acquire the inspiration that this experience entailed. In terms of basic assumptions, Jinnah was closer to Kemal than Iqbal could ever be. Finally, it is significant that the relevance of Atatürk's achievement was two-fold: the first step was the regaining of national sovereignty; the second was that of nation-building. If Mustafa Kemal's experience was at all relevant to Jinnah, it is clear that it should have been relevant in both of its dimensions.

What, then, was the basic point of reference in the Indian Muslim perception of Mustafa Kemal? It is clear, from the preceding discussion, that his remarkable success was central, and this meant many things. To men like Iqbal, it meant that the stranglehold of tradition would be broken and Muslims would regain their initiative, and in turn reinvigorate Islam. To men like Jinnah, it meant that perseverance did indeed command success. And to the Indian Muslim at large, as to Muslims all over the world, this symbolized an invitation to a courageous struggle in the way Turkey had struggled against the odds, and even against enemies that were not dissimilar to those Turkey had fought against.

NOTES

1. Gibb (ed.), *Whither Islam?*, 73.
2. *Morning Post*, 13 May 1921; *Islamic News*, 9 June 1921; and *Bombay Chronicle*, 11 June 1921.
3. *Bombay Chronicle*, 10 and 13 June 1921.
4. Bamford, *The Histories of the Non-Co-operation and Khilafat Movements*, 168; and Viceroy to Sec. of State for India, Tel. P., No. 517, 21 June 1921, OIOC, Reading Collection.
5. *Hindu*, 14 July 1921.
6. See the substance of telegram from Chotani, the Aga Khan, Kidwai, and Ispahani, in Viceroy to Sec. of State for India, Tel. P., No. 890, 9 Sept. 1921, OIOC, Reading Collection.
7. *Hindu*, 12 July 1923. The reference is to earlier events.
8. *The Times*, 11 Aug. 1921. Also see Lloyd George's announcement in the House of Commons on 15 Aug. 1921, allowing British firms to supply arms to Greek and Turkish forces in Parl. Papers, 1921, *Hansard*, 146 H.C. Deb. 5S., col. 937.
9. See Mohamed Ali to Shaukat Ali, Tel. 1 Sept. 1921, in Viceroy to Sec. of State for India, Tel. P., No. 906, 11 Sept. 1921, OIOC, Reading Collection.
10. *Hindu*, 12 July 1923. This also refers to earlier dates.
11. Ibid.
12. Lord Kinross, *Atatürk*, 298. His figures, however, are not reliable.
13. Viceroy to Sec. of State for India, Tel. P., No. 890, 9 Sept. 1921; and Sec. of State for India to Viceroy, Tel. P., No. 1350, 27 Sept. 1921, OIOC, Reading Collection.
14. For details, see R.V. Thadani (ed.), *The Historical State Trial of the Ali Brothers and Five Others* (Karachi, 1921).
15. *Annual Register, 1922*, 208 and 211–12.
16. See Viceroy to Sec. of State for India. Tel. P & En Clair, nos. 781, 796 and 872, 28 Sept. and 3 and 17 Oct. 1922. OIOC, Reading Collection; *Times of India*, 20 Sept. 1922; and *Hindu*, 28 Sept. and 5 Oct. 1922.
17. See Abul Kalam's interview with a press correspondent dated 20 Sept. 1922 in *Hindu*, 28 Sept. 1922.
18. *Times of India*, 21 Sept. 1922; and *Hindu*, 28 Sept. 1922.
19. *Times of India*, 20 Sept., 20 and 21 Oct. 1922; and William Vincent's letter to M. Faiyaz Khan in *Madras Mail*, 30 Oct. 1922.
20. *Hindu*, 12 Oct. 1922.
21. Vincent's letter to Fayyaz Khan; and Central Khilafat Committee, *Kar rawa'i ijlas jama'at-i 'amila* (Bombay, 1923), 3.
22. 'Turkey: Annual Report, 1922', NAUK, FO 371/9176. Also see Henderson to Curzon, No. 1024 A–17 Nov. 1922 and its enclosures, NAUK, FO 371/7962.

23. NAUK, FO-141/587.
24. *Madras Mail*, 7 Nov. 1922.
25. *Times of India*, 23 Nov. 1922.
26. *Bombay Chronicle*, 24 Nov. 1922; Viceroy to Sec. of State for India, Tel. P., No. 1717, 24 Nov. 1922, OIOC, Reading Collection; and the *Indian Annual Register, 1923*, ii, 61.
27. *Hindu*, 4 Jan. 1923.
28. Ibid.
29. Ibid.
30. *The Times*, 14 Dec. 1923.
31. For details, see Naeem Qureshi, *Pan-Islam in British India*, 279–86.
32. See *Englishman* (Calcutta), 6 Mar. 1924; and *Hindu*, 13 Mar. 1924.
33. *Times of India*, 5 and 10 Mar. 1924; and *Pioneer*, 6, 9 and 14 Mar. 1924.
34. *Pioneer*, 8 Mar. 1924.
35. *Pioneer*, 13 Mar. 1924. In fact, some of the *'ulama* led by Azad had forcefully supported this idea. See OIOC, Native Newspaper Reports (UP), Nos. 20 and 21 of 1924, 1 and 2, respectively; Ghulam Rasul Mihr (ed), *Tabarrukat-i Azad* (Lahore, [1959]), 214–60; and *Pioneer*, 19 Mar. 1924.
36. *Daily Telegraph*, 4 Mar. 1924.
37. Naeem Qureshi, *Pan-Islam in British India*, 287 ff.
38. Ambassador for Cultural Affairs, Turkish Centre, *Atatürk's Republic of Turkey* (New York, 1981), 2–3.
39. Murray Titus, 'The Reaction of Moslem India to Western Islam', in Mott (ed.), *The Moslem World of To-day*, 108.
40. OIOC, Native Newspaper Reports (UP), No. 131 of 1924, 1; Ferrer, 'India', in Gibb (ed.), *Whither Islam?*, 225; and Titus, 'The Reaction of Moslem India to Western Islam', 98–9.
41. Mohammad Iqbal's essay on *ijtihad* was written sometime after the abolition of the caliphate in 1924 but it did not appear until his *The Reconstruction of Religious Thought in Islam* was published from London in 1934. The present reference is to the Lahore reprint of 1982. See 157.
42. Ibid., 157.
43. Ibid., 159.
44. Ibid., 153.
45. W.C. Smith, *Modern Islam in India: A Social Analysis*, 2nd edn. (London, 1946), 142.
46. Mohammad Iqbal, *The Reconstruction of Religious Thought in Islam* (Lahore, 1971), 162.
47. Ibid., 162.

48. Ibid., 153.
49. Ibid., 157.
50. Ibid., 153–4.
51. Ibid., 169.
52. Mohammad Iqbal, *'Javidnama'*, in *Kulliyat* (ed.), Ahmad Saroosh (Tehran, 1343 A.H. [shamsi]), 307; Tr. as in B.A. Dar, *A Study in Iqbal's Philosophy* (Lahore, 1971), 140.
53. In his view '[T]he Turks ... have not renounced Islam but reviewed it'. See Syed Abdul Vahid (ed.), *Thoughts and Reflections of Iqbal* (Lahore, 1967), 371; cf. W.C. Smith, *Islam in Modern History* (Princeton, 1957), 161.
54. Jinnah's Presidential address at the 26 Annual Sessions of the AIML at Patna on 26 Dec. 1938. S. Shamsul Hasan (ed.), *Presidential Address of Quid-e-Azam M.A. Jinnah delivered at the sessions of the All India Muslim League* (Delhi, 1946).
55. Resolution I, moved by the Chair in Syed Sharifuddin Pirzada, (ed.), *Foundations of Pakistan*, ii (Karachi, 1969), 311.
56. Cf. Jamil-ud-din Ahmad (ed.), *Speeches and Writings of Mr. Jinnah*, i (Lahore, 1960), 39.
57. Hector Bolitho, *Jinnah: Creator of Pakistan* (London, 1954), 102. For the *Grey Wolf*'s impact on, and relations with Britain, see Chapter Eight below.

1. Dr. Ansari's Balkan Medical Mission with Col. Enver Bey at Kadirgah Hospital, Istanbul.
Courtesy: Al-Hilal, Calcutta, 19 March 1913

2. Shaikh u'l-Islam Müsâ Kâzim proclaiming jihad at the Fatih Mosque in Istanbul, November 1914.
Courtesy: Research Centre for Islamic History, Art, and Culture, Istanbul

3. Mustafa Kemal Paşa offering du'a in front of the Grand National Assembly, 1920. Courtesy: Türkiye Diyanet Vakfı, Istanbul

4. The Front Page of the pro-Turkish newspaper the *Zamīndār* published in Lahore, 16 November 1920. Courtesy: The author's personal collection.

5. M. A. Jinnah (1876-1948), President of the All India Muslim League.
Courtesy: National Archives of Pakistan, Islamabad

6. Muhammad Iqbal (1877-1938), Poet-Philosopher.
Courtesy: Iqbal Academy of Pakistan, Lahore

6

Images of Atatürk and Turkey in Urdu Literature*

It is an established fact that contacts between Turkey and the Indo-Pakistan subcontinent have been thriving for a thousand years. Leaving aside the pre-Islamic Türk-Shahiya contacts, this association can be traced to the early tenth century when Turkish warriors, coming down from Afghanistan and Central Asia through the mountain passes of the north-west, established themselves as rulers in India. For several centuries thereafter, dynasty after dynasty of Turkish tribes—Ghaznavids, Khaljis, Tughluqs, Taimurid Mughals, Barid-Shahis, and Qutub-Shahis—sat on the throne of Delhi or ruled over the lesser states in an almost unbroken chain. These Turks brought with them a well-developed culture and mode of life, through which they exercised a lasting influence on the subcontinent. In fact, the lifestyle of the Muslim élite in Lahore, Delhi, and other towns of India was patterned after those of their Turkish and Iranian counterparts elsewhere in the Muslim world. They introduced Turkish traditions in government and law, language and literature, arts and architecture, and dress and diet.

---

* Published originally in the *Proceedings of the Third International Symposium on Atatürk* (Ankara, 1998), 257–82.

Out of this Turco-Persian-Islamic culture in India, a new language called Urdu was evolved, which subsequently became the new lingua franca of the Muslims of the subcontinent. Born as a result of contacts between the local and Turkish elements in the royal *ordu*, meaning a 'camp' or an 'army', the new language was enriched by an overflowing vocabulary from other languages, chiefly from Persian, Arabic, and Turkish.[1] This language of the 'camp' moved with the victorious Muslim armies, and with a little help from the Sufi saints, it spread far and wide.[2] Gradually, Urdu became a literary language and poets and writers from Amir Khusrau (1255–1325) onwards prided themselves on relying exclusively on inter-Islamic imagery for their metaphors, epithets, and poetic formulae.[3] These cultural influences, preserved and invigorated through fresh waves of immigrants, commercial contacts, Sufi orders, and annual pilgrimages to the Holy Places, paved the way for deeper Indo-Turkish involvement.

Over time, even as Urdu literature developed and came to be imbued with strong Persian traditions, especially in its classical poetic form, Turkish influences remained quite predominant.[4] This is evident from the presence of a large number of loanwords from Turkish that continue to adorn the Urdu language.[5] In its modern form, Urdu literature has freed itself from its conventional shackles and, therefore, reflects a more realistic view of life. It has gradually evolved, a more intellectual, critical, and imaginative approach, especially in poetry.[6] Political poetry in Urdu played a singular role as a vehicle of mass mobilization in the early twentieth century. No rally was complete without a poet moving the audience to a frenzy with patriotic renditions before the main speakers arrived on the stage. The cheerleaders cleverly timed each verse to build up enthusiasm. The development of modern Urdu prose, on the other hand, has been a comparatively new phenomenon as no tradition, in this particular literary form, existed before the British established themselves in India. But, from the nineteenth century onwards, Urdu prose came to be modeled on English prose. Unlike classical literature which was rather decorative, modern prose was simple, precise, direct, clear, and communicative.[7] Yet, its impact was nowhere near that of poetry because the printed word had a very limited circulation compared to the emotional appeal of a versified rendition. The newspapers, however, were an exception. The press became a far more effective medium, especially with the introduction of lithography in the early nineteenth century.[8]

This chapter attempts to analyse the various writings in Urdu on Atatürk and Turkey. These can be divided into several categories: newspaper reports, views and comments in periodicals, pamphlets in prose, poetry, and biographies. All of them faithfully record Turkey's fortunes and Atatürk's rise to power and his modernizing zeal. Since the socio-cultural fountainheads of both Urdu and Turkish were the same, it was natural that themes from one would pass to the other. But, this did not happen until the nineteenth century when India had emerged from the so-called 'medieval' to the 'modern' age under the imprint of British rule—a division arbitrarily drawn by the colonial power. As a result of the psychological trauma that followed the loss of their political power and economic privileges, the Indian Muslims, in search of a rallying-point, became involved with the Ottoman caliphate and pan-Islam. The enthusiasm for the Ottoman cause was reflected nowhere more accurately than in the vernacular press. Of course, there were delineations of pro-Turkish sentiments in the Urdu newspapers of Delhi as early as the 1840s through the 1860s, including Syed Ahmed Khan's (1817–98) *Aligarh Institute Gazette*,[9] but the real impact of the Urdu press was demonstrated during the Russo-Turkish War of 1877 for the first time. In the forefront were journals like the *Shamsu'l-Akhbar* and the *Jarida-i Rozgar* of Madras, *Awadh Punch* of Lucknow, and the *Qaisaru'l-Akhbar Hind* and the *Ahsanu'l-Akhbar* of Allahabad.[10] Even Hindu owned and edited journals, like the *Awadh Akhbar* (Lucknow) of Munshi Newal Kishore and the *Akhbar-i Am* (Lahore) of Pandit Gopi Nath, vied with the Muslim papers in their support for Turkey.[11] Only Syed Ahmed

Khan's *Tahzibu'l-Akhlaq*, in spite of its open praise for Sultan Abdülaziz's *Tanzimat* and his adoption of European ways, struck a discordant note on pan-Islam for reasons known too well.[12]

A connected strand in Urdu literature appeared in prose, poetry, plays, and novels. Romantic idealism being an essential element in national resurgence, Urdu literature helped stimulate pan-Islamic sentiment. A typical example was Ismail Meeruthi's (1844–1917) poem extolling the Ottoman *ghazi*s fighting against the invading Russians.[13] He was followed by Altaf Husain Hali (1837–1914) whose epic poem, *Madd-o Jazr-i Islam* (1879), better known as *Musaddas-i Hali*, took Muslim India by storm and created widespread pan-Islamic fervour.[14] Pandit Ratan Nath Sarshar (1845–1903), the editor of the *Awadh Akhbar*, though a Hindu was known for his *Fasana-i Azad*, a novel spun around characters from the Russo-Turkish War.[15] His successor at the *Akhbar*, Abdul Halim Sharar (1860–1926), is also remembered for his novels and plays on themes drawn from Ottoman-Islamic history. His historical romances, first serialized in the *Dil-Godaz* (founded 1887) and later published in book form, were inspired by a romantic love for Islam's glorious past.[16] *Hasan aur Angelina*, which became particularly popular, was set in the background of the Russo-Turkish War.[17]

The next spurt of pro-Turkish activity in the Urdu press was witnessed during the 1890s when British public opinion turned hostile towards the Turks on the Armenian question. The partisan European press presented it as a one-sided affair, deliberately perpetrated by the Ottoman authorities.[18] The religious dignitaries gave it a semblance of a struggle between Christianity and Islam. In turn, this religious fervour among the Europeans touched a sensitive chord in India in favour of the Ottomans. The Muslim press, led by Maulawi Mahbub Alam's *Paisa Akhbar* (Lahore), Hakim Muhammad Khan's *Akmalu'l-Akhbar* (Delhi), Sheikh Ghulam Muhammad's *Vakil* (Amritsar), and several other papers[19] reflected these sentiments and prominently displayed news from

Islamic countries with strongly-worded editorials and articles on issues confronting the Ottoman Empire.[20] Besides, material from several Turkish and Arabic newspapers, such as *al-Jawaib*, the *Tercuman-i Rum*, the *Akhbar Daru'l-Khilafat*, and the *Tercuman-i Mashriq*, was translated into Urdu and published in Indian journals.[21] Although none of these publications had an impact similar to that of the *Paik-i Islam*, an Urdu journal from Istanbul edited by an Indian Muslim during the 1880s,[22] they were able to widen the contemporary perspective. The major thrust, however, remained with the Indian papers and they never hesitated to put it in ink.[23]

This tradition was continued by other writers, such as *Shamsu'l-'Ulama* Shibli Nomani, Agha Hashr Kashmiri (1879–1935), Shaikh (Sir) Abdul Qadir (1874–1950), Sajjad Haidar Yildirim (1880–1943), and several others.[24] Yildirim, in particular, had direct contact with some of the Turkish writers of the *Tanzimat* period. While many of his writings are either adaptations or translations of Turkish works, he was not just a plain translator; he almost re-wrote the works he translated.[25] The idea was to stir up Indian Muslim fervour for Islam and Turkey.[26] Yildirim began his career by translating the writings of Halil Rüşti,[27] moving on to Namik Kemal's play *Celaleddin Harzemşah*, and then adapting Ahmed Hikmet Müftüoğlu's *Haristanve Gülistan*.[28] Sheikh Abdul Qadir, the talented young editor of Lahore's English newspaper, the *Observer*, visited Istanbul in 1900 and produced a series of articles on the cultural, social, and educational conditions prevailing in Turkey. He also published an account of his travels which he called *Maqam-i Khilafat*.[29] Earlier, he had started a journal, the *Makhzan* (April 1901), to which many prominent writers of the day contributed.[30]

The Tripolitan and Balkan crises of 1911–13 catapulted several journals into prominence. In the forefront were Mohamed Ali's *Hamdard*, Abul Kalam Azad's *al-Hilal*, and Zafar Ali Khan's *Zamindar*, which published news and views criticizing Italy and the Balkan States for their aggression against Turkey.[31] The pages of these journals were full of pro-Turkish sentiment. The poet-theologian Shibli Nomani raised the warning 'Islam in Danger' in his *Hangama-i-Balkan*, and his protégé, Azad, went a step further and proclaimed that the time had arrived for *jihad*.[32] Following Shibli, Mohammad Iqbal wrote *'Jawab-i Shikwa'* in continuation of his own *'Shikwa'* (1911) and *'Shama'-o Sha'ir'* (1912), to help raise relief funds for Turkey.[33]

The First World War and its aftermath saw the rise of the Khilafat movement which marked the zenith of Indian pan-Islam. For six long years, the Muslims of India conducted an incessant agitation with the purpose of saving the Ottoman Empire from dismemberment. In the process, pan-Islam merged with nationalism, and the Muslims, aligned with their Hindu compatriots, demanded *status quo ante bellum* for Turkey and *swaraj* or self-government for India. For this purpose, they also utilized public platforms as well as mosque pulpits. The Urdu press played a key role in this struggle. The columns of the *Paisa Akhbar*, the *Siyasat*, the *Vakil*, the *Zamindar*, the *Watan*, the *Hamdam*, the *Hamdard*, and the *Khilafat* (the official organ of the CKC) helped raise the agitation to heights previously unknown in the political history of the subcontinent. Besides these publications, thousands of pamphlets were brought out in both prose and verse to support the Khilafat movement. This vast literature throws light on the tremendous sacrifices—both in human and financial terms—that were made during the course of the Khilafat movement. Thousands went to jail for pro-Turkish and anti-British activities and some even embraced death, as in the case of the *muhajirin* who perished while undertaking *hijrat* to Afghanistan, believing that India had become *daru'l-harb*. All this was done just to save Turkey from the threatened dismemberment.[34]

Yet, in spite of all these sacrifices, it took the demise of an Empire and the valour of Mustafa Kemal and his nationalists to help raise a phoenix from the ashes. Eventually, the Treaty of Sévres (1920) was replaced by the Treaty of Lausanne (1923) and Turkey's honour was vindicated. Naturally, the Indian Muslims saw Mustafa Kemal as their hero, a symbol of Islam's challenge to western imperialism. From the middle of 1920 onwards, he became the subject of eulogy in the works of many an Urdu poet, mainly for his services to the caliphate and his military exploits against the Greeks. For instance, Tegh Ansari of Allahabad, lauded the feats of Mustafa Kemal thus:

> *Gone are the days when wolves, dogs, and hogs were bold,*
> *Enraged is now the lion of Anatolia*
> *In Ankara can be seen the grandeur of the Almighty.*
> *Embracing victory and success is Mustafa Kemal*
> *The war in Anatolia is warning Europe.*
> *Come and dye your hands red in the blood of Asia!*
> *Do not run away from the battlefield, stay for a while*
> *Or compelled you would be to beg for your life!*
> *Give battle to your opponents with courage.*
> *Well! you'll see now the cudgeled hand of Mustafa Kemal!*[35]

After recounting the tales of oppression and killing in Smyrna by the Greeks who were aided by the Allies, the poet is happy to note that the tide of the events had turned against them.

> *Now God's help is with the forlorn people*
> *A wonderful time this fourteenth century (hijra) will usher;*
> *Now the enemy is undergoing punishment for his misdeeds*
> *Now the spring is here, gone is the autumn.*
> *There is an excitement in the emotions of the people of the Ka'bah*
> *The storm is blowing to drown the unbelievers,*
> *See for yourself these strange occurrences*
> *Focus your gaze on the approaching vision of victory.*[36]

In another poem, Tegh wrote:

> *Just now the world has witnessed the excellence of Mustafa Paşa*
> *Tossing about in the battlefield is the carcass of Greece,*
> *The world of Islam is rejoicing over the conquest of Smyrna*
> *So full of joy are the young and old.*
> *The lion of Ankara has shown such courage*
> *Thrace was vacated so quickly by the cowardly adversaries,*
> *Now the Allies are about to leave Istanbul (also)*
> *The adversaries knew not that such a calamity awaited them.*[37]

Another poet, Iqbal Ahmad Suhail of Aligarh, composed a long poem called *'The Song of Felicitations'*, which ended in laudatory terms displaying imagery peculiar to Urdu poetry.

> *Time has again turned a leaf from the past*
> *Look, the standard of Islam is again fluttering over the land of Smyrna;*
> *Here, the Turkish ghazis are advancing victoriously*
> *There, a commotion is overtaking the enemy forces*
> *The hearts are full of restlessness and zealous delight,*
> *As if the surge of old wine was restless in a goblet.*[38]

Suhail continues:

> *The Islamic faith is the reflection of God's brightness in this world,*
> *How can the gusts of wind from the West extinguish it?*
> *The bounties of the Prophet would continue to protect the Ghazi;*
> *Mustafa (the Prophet) shall affirm his appreciation of Mustafa (Kemal).*[39]

Then again:

> *May God bestow on Mustafa Ghazi the rightful victory*
> *For he has fulfilled the longstanding desire of the nation;*
> *God be the friend of this captain of the nation's ship*
> *For he has saved the sinking ship of the righteous faith.*[40]

Zafar Ali Khan (1873–1956), whose compelling writings have been noted above, gave Urdu literature an expression that it had not known before. The son of a government official turned journalist, his style was excessively rhetorical and devoid of balance and restraint. It has been argued that 'he wrote like a cavalry in full charge' and, ever-ready 'to break a lance with an adversary great and small, in jest or in earnest, he was never so happy as in the thick of a fight'.[41] But, surprisingly, Zafar Ali Khan's poetry is characterized by a restraint that is lacking in his prose. His verses show the gentle currents of his thoughts and feelings couched in 'extraordinary facility' and 'dextrous manipulation of the language'.[42] Yet, the biting impact remained strong and made him a marked man for the British government. His contacts with Istanbul and the caustic effect of his writings landed him in prison during the First World War. On his release, he was re-arrested in July 1920 for another stint of several years. But, even in jail, he was unable to restrain himself at the severity of the Treaty of Sévres and involuntarily remarked:

The ground seems to be slipping from under (my) feet
The sky that shaded our heads above remains no more;
Suddenly such a wind began to blow in the world,
The gardens whose nightingales we were remain no more
The Christians are saying this today,
The traces of Islam's dominance remain no more
Even the sacred sanctuary could not remain safe from hunters,
Not even a single bird's nest remains any more
The broken heart has no hope of safety,
The tongue is so frozen that it has no courage any more
Why shouldn't the enemy be happy at the downfall of the Ottomans?
The veil that was a hindrance remains no more.[43]

Later, when the Greco-Turkish crisis of 1919–22 ended in the defeat of pan-Hellenism, Zafar Ali Khan rejoiced, especially at the re-conquest of Smyrna:

If you have the eye to see, then look at the fascinations of this world
Look at the imprints of Allah's power in the sky
How perfectly the dark night's garment has been slit!
Look, how enchantingly the sun has appeared,
How the subsided rivulet has risen (again)!
Look, in what splendour the ebb is concealed in every flow!
How the withered branches have turned green (again)!
Look, how autumn has departed from the garden;
In one single attack the Turks have gotten hold of Smyrna.
Look, how in one leap they have reached from here to there:
Again the width of the river is the same as it was before
Look, how the blending river is stretching from shore to shore,
Again there is hustle and bustle in the bazaar of Rasul of Arabia
Look at the shop of the adversaries which has been burnt to ashes,
O you denier of the complaint of the oppressed,
Look at the smoke that rises from the burning Europe.[44]

When the crisis ended in July 1923, resulting in the Treaty of Lausanne, Zafar Ali Khan expressed his exhilaration thus:

Faith has fanned the flame of honour
And has lit the lamp of the House of the Ottomans;
The stone-splitting dagger of the Ottomans
Has turned the kafirs of Europe into Muslims;
The compulsion of the exalted restorer of the true faith
Has made it the preamble of the Treaty of Lausanne;
'Today even God Almighty Himself cannot revive the East'—
This doctrine of the West has (no doubt) been falsified;
This victory, of which there is no example in the world,
Has astonished the minds of the entire world.[45]

Zafar Ali Khan saw the saviour of Islam in Mustafa Kemal:

Would there ever be the same spring in the garden?
This was my query to the bearers of the highest sphere.
They were not unanimous but I understood their meaning.
The answer to my question was Mustafa Kemal.[46]

He was full of praise for the Turkish leader for what he had achieved in Ankara. In a poem dedicated to the capital city of the nationalists, he wrote:

If Mustafa had not established the system of Angora,
It would have been almost certainly finished by Curzon,
He (Kemal) sauntered into Europe to slander the Kings
By the hooves of his fast (and) highbred horse from Angora,
Those who are proud of their democratic principles
Are captivatingly astonished at the management skills of Angora,
All worshippers of God have stood on their feet
The whole world has been given this message of Angora,
God has made it the pride of Asia
Even higher would in future be the place of Angora.[47]

Urdu poetry would be incomplete without mention of Muhammad Iqbal. His pan-Islamic, pro-Turkish stance has already been discussed in earlier chapters. Here, the focus is on his impassioned poetry in which he beseeches the Indian Muslims to override their social and geographical barriers, and unite. Since danger seemed to stem from European nationalism, Iqbal denounced it as a sinister ideology.[48] But when it came to Muslims, he did not mind nationalistic spirit developing within them. Iqbal was vociferous in his admiration for Turkey which broke with the past and was, under Mustafa Kemal's leadership, making headway towards reconstruction and reform after the debacle of its Empire. In *'Khizr-i Rah'*, he lamented the Arab betrayal of the Ottomans as exemplified by Sharif Hussein's revolt in 1916.

> *Lo! the Hashemite is selling the honour of the faith of (Prophet) Mustafa*
> *While the hardy Turkoman is besmeared with dust and blood.*
> *There is fire, the descendents of Abraham, (and) Nimrod!*
> *Is it that someone wants to test someone again?*[49]

Prophet Khizr holds out the solemn assurance in his usual serious tone:

> *What tale are you telling me of the Turks and the Arabs?*
> *Indeed the deep and silent grief of the Islamic people is not unknown to me.*
> *The sacred heritage of (Abraham) Khalil has been snatched by the sons of the Trinity!*
> *The sacred soil of the Hejaz has been turned into a foundation-stone of the church!*
> *The scarlet fez has been disgraced in the world!*
> *And those who were (once) full of pride are today compelled to do supplication.*[50]

But then Khizr gives a message to rekindle every heart by declaring that though the country had slipped out of the millet's fold, salvation for Muslims rested only on their coming together.

> *The Muslims should unite for the defence of the Sanctuary (of the Ka'bah),*
> *From the banks of the Nile to the land of Kashgar!*[51]

And again:

> *In order to establish once more the institution of the Caliphate on sure foundations*
> *Go, search somewhere and fetch the heart and soul of your great ancestors!*[52]

In Turkish heroism, he found the heartening signs of Muslim resurgence:

The dream of universal freedom that Islam envisioned,
O Muslim, see today the true interpretation of that dream.[53]

When the good news of the Turkish nationalists' victory over the Greeks reached India, Iqbal could not restrain himself from expressing his deepest emotions in *'Tul'u-i Islam'*, one of his first poems envisioning the rebirth of Islam. The emotional vibrancy of this poem is reminiscent of the 'vision of the New Jerusalem, coming from heaven, granted to John of Patmos'.[54]

Proof of the dawn is clear from the fading light of the stars
The sun rises from the horizon, gone is the time for deep slumber!
The blood of life has started to run again in the dead veins of the East
(Even) Sina and Farabi are unable to grasp this secret!
The Muslim has been turned into a (true) Muslim by the tempest of Europe;
It is from the stormy waves of the river that the pearls are cultured
The true believer is again going to be blessed at the threshold of the Almighty:
The grandeur of a Turk, intellect of an Indian (and) eloquence of a Bedouine![55]

The tribulations of Turkey were seen as the fading twinkle of stars which were followed by the dawn of a new era.[56]

If a mountain-load of sorrows crashed on Ottoman Turk, grieve not
For dawn follows in the wake of the death of myriads of stars![57]

Iqbal's confidence in the success of the Turks is evident in the following verse:

In slavery neither the sword nor prudence are of any avail
(But) if firm faith be kindled, the fetters are all shattered;

OTTOMAN TURKEY, ATATÜRK, AND MUSLIM SOUTH ASIA

Can anyone gauge the strength of his arm?
For a single glance of the true believer can change the destinies![58]

But Iqbal's feelings were torn between his deep affection for the Turks and an utter dislike of their breakneck race for reforms and modernization. He thought that the Turks had entangled themselves in a complicated situation, which had bred misunderstandings. This is apparent from the following verses:

I have heard that the Ottoman Turks are eloquent
(But) who will recite to them this humble verse of Iqbal
(That) they consider Europe as their neighbours,
From whose dwelling the stars seem much nearer![59]

This, however, was a temporary phase, as Iqbal eventually overcame his doubts and apprehensions. In his *Lectures*, he is full of praise for the Turkish nationalists for establishing democratic principles in modern Turkey.[60] But, since his English and Farsi writings are beyond the scope of the present analysis, it is difficult to draw a complete graph of Iqbal's political thought here. Suffice it to say that Iqbal represented the general thinking of the Muslim intelligentsia of the time and, most often, he moulded their opinions on various issues. The Turkish situation was one of them.

The Urdu prose was no less expressive, in its praise for Mustafa Kemal and the Turks. Foremost was the monthly *Humayun* of Lahore, founded in January 1922 by Barrister Mian Bashir Ahmad. Born in 1893, Mian Bashir Ahmad was the only son of the late Justice Shah Din. He was educated at Lahore and Oxford, and was called to the Bar in 1914. Later, he married Gaiti Ara, the daughter of Sir Muhammad Shafi, a former member of the viceroy's executive council and president of the All India Muslim League. Ahmad was a writer and poet, and a well-known politician of the Pakistan movement. Later, from June 1949 to October 1951, he served as Pakistan's first ambassador to Turkey. The *Humayun* was devoted to publishing articles in favour of Mustafa Kemal and the nationalists, and most of them were authored by Ahmad himself. The December 1922 issue, for instance, carried three articles from his pen. The first one, entitled 'Turkon ki jidd-o juhd-i azadi ke liye', juxtaposed conditions in Turkey before and after the First World War and pointed at how sullen the Turks really were in its wake and how they struggled to regain their freedom—a task which was accomplished by Mustafa Kemal who alone deserved to be called the saviour of Turkey.[61] In the second contribution, 'Daulat-i Angora', Bashir Ahmad praised the bravery and valour of the nationalists, approved the Misak-i Milli, and highlighted the exploits of Mustafa Kemal who, he believed, had infused the spirit of freedom among the Turks.[62] The third article was wholly devoted to the Turkish president. In this contribution, Ahmad traced his life and work and recounted repercussions of the revolution. The pith of the writer's argument is that Atatürk was a man with an iron will whose popularity resulted from the respect and love that he evoked among the ordinary people as well as the armed forces.[63]

The late 1920s and the early 1930s were marked by an intense period of reform in Turkey. For the Turks, it was the struggle for a new state structure and a new society on modernized lines, visualized by Atatürk as *Turkish* and *national* in essence as opposed to Ottoman and pan-Islamic. It was also the period when opposition to reforms within Turkey, and outside, created misunderstandings and dissension. During this period, the principal pro-Turkish Indian Muslim writers who contributed to *Humayun* were Mansur Ahmad and Sufi Ghulam Mustafa Tabassum. Mansur Ahmad, in his article on 'Jadid Turki' ('Modern Turkey'),[64] highlighted Turkey's progress towards modernization under Mustafa Kemal with pictorial glimpses of life in Turkey. The article was based on excerpts from the works of the British writer, Grace Ellison. Of course, Mustafa Kemal occupied centre stage for no work on Turkey was complete without his name. Mansur Ahmad argued that the imprint of his personality was apparent from every facet of Turkish life. It would be quite appropriate to call modern Turkey 'Kemalistan' because it was his creation. 'He is an extraordinary person', said the author, 'and indeed one of those magnificent men who appear at the time of adversity and with the help of their superhuman powers pull their nations out of a state of extreme disappointment and despair and lead them to prosperity.'[65]

Referring to Grace Ellison's account, Mansur Ahmad pointed out how she was almost captivated by the charismatic personality of Mustafa Kemal when she went to interview him. Still, she found the architect of modern Turkey modest enough to say that it could only have been possible with the help of the entire nation.[66] About Ankara, Mansur Ahmad wrote that the capital city was a wonderful place where there was no *hijab* or veil among women and they went about their chores freely and took part in every activity and attended mixed parties.[67] This had become possible because Mustafa Kemal had severed the diseased parts of the old system and introduced *inkilab* after *inkilab*. The caliphate was abolished, old laws were changed, and freedom for women was achieved. 'By giving the Turkish women this newly acquired honour', wrote the author, 'Mustafa Kemal has raised the standard of all women of the East.'[68] The writer also praised other reforms, like the ban on the *fez* (which he calls 'an expression of medieval mentality'); liberation of Turkey from the stranglehold of obscurantist *'ulama*; introduction of a new education system in villages and in cities; establishment of healthcare centres; promotion of arts and culture; and change of the script from Arabic to Latin. This was, according to Mansur Ahmad, 'an astonishing record, of the deeds of an amazing man'.[69]

Another contribution of interest to *Humayun* (April 1930) was 'Turki aur azadi-i niswan'[70] by Sufi Ghulam Mustafa Tabassum, a well-known figure of Urdu literature. In this article, Tabassum talks about women's freedom and rights in Turkey. Tracing the history of women's struggle in Turkey, he recorded that though women had started demanding equal rights and opportunities after the revolution of 1908, it was not until after the First World War that they met with any noticeable success. Their chance came when the Greeks invaded Smyrna, and the women began to work alongside men to fend off the enemy. Later, they took part in Turkey's struggle towards achieving modernization. The writer tells us that modern Turkey was the result of their struggle. In 1920, there were twelve women's associations working for the political, social, and educational uplift of women. However, the organized movement for women's rights started in early 1923 when the *Waqat* of 31 May announced the establishment of a women's *anjuman* named the 'Defence of Women's Rights', whose founder was Mohyuddin Hanim, the daughter of the head of the court of appeal of Mosul. But this met with little success until 1925–26 when Mustafa Kemal revoked its separate and secluded existence.[71] It was then laid down that there could be no divorce without a proper legal procedure and in matrimonial matters, civil marriage must precede the *nikah* under the *shariʿat*.

Further, the article then traces the development of the emancipation of women. After three years of struggle from 1927 onwards, three commissions were appointed to investigate the state of affairs as regards education of women, their role in the press, health matters, and interaction with women's organizations of other countries. After much hesitation, the governor of Istanbul accepted the women's associations in social affairs. But political emancipation was only secured after a long and arduous struggle. The opinion was expressed—Kazim Paşa's reportedly among them—that women were not yet mature enough for political activity.[72] Gradually, however, support began to develop for this, though not before there was a change in the personnel of the women's association itself. With Lutfi Hanim in the saddle, Sufi Tabassum tells us, things began to warm up. The unions multiplied, and their recognition followed.[73] In the post-1927 period, the women's bodies attained an increasing importance. Many positions, which were previously reserved for men, were now thrown open to women. For instance, the registrar's position at the civil chamber of Istanbul was given to Nuzhat Celil Hanim who had a law degree. Six girls obtained degrees in medicine and one of them was appointed at the naval hospital. Many others obtained degrees in the natural sciences and some entered the business sector as well. Celal Salma Darwesh and Zakrya Hanim were at the forefront. Several other women studied civil engineering. Sufi Tabassum cites the names of at least five women who attained excellence in public life: Safia Hanim was a delegate at a medical conference in Bologne, Badi'a Hanim was an advocate of the high court of Istanbul, Suriyya Hanim and Nekowar Hanim enjoyed similar status, and Şagufta Hanim obtained an LL.D. degree.[74]

Before ending his article, Sufi Tabassum informs us that the *hijab* was breaking down in Turkey and that, in 1929, a 'beauty contest' was held with great fanfare. The surprising thing was that most of the participants were Muslim women. The standard of beauty at the contest was not just the female face but the charm of the feminine personality. There were both men and women among the judges. In addition to the beauty contest, the writer goes on to inform us, Turkish women took part in sports and dances and did not lag behind the women of Europe in any way. 'It is evident from the state of affairs (in Turkey)', concludes the author, 'that whereas interest in higher education has developed among Muslim women there has also arisen among a certain class of people resistance to Islamic traditions owing to an approbation for everything western. This peculiar situation is creating concern about women's future in the hearts of every mature person.'[75]

In March 1934, Mustafa Kemal was the subject of an editorial in Zafar Ali Khan's *Zamindar*.[76] It began with the following verse:

> *It wouldn't be surprising if the Muslims are thrown into ecstasy by divine power,*
> *With the downfall of the Caliphate comes (the rise of) Kemal.*

After tracing the history of western encroachments on Turkey, Zafar Ali Khan recalls that the Europeans had always been uneasy that they would have no peace as long as Islam's flag kept flying over Istanbul. Their opportunity came when, during the First World War, men like Hussein bin Ali agreed to play their game. Arabian provinces were thus separated from Turkey, and the Holy Places of Islam were seized by the Christians. Iraq, Syria, Palestine and the Hejaz passed under European control. The Europeans had designs on Istanbul as well, and nearly had their way, when the Almighty showered his blessings on the Muslims and two illustrious personalities appeared on the scene—Ibn Saud and Mustafa Kemal—who thwarted the evil designs of the Europeans. Continuing, Zafar Ali Khan compares the military prowess of Mustafa Kemal with the exploits of Khalid bin Walid, the seventh-century Muslim warrior and companion of the Prophet of Islam, and says that his skills in war had been unhesitatingly acknowledged even by the generals of Europe. It was Mustafa Kemal who turned Turkey's defeat into victory and, at Lausanne, avenged the indignities endured by Turkey for so long. Kemal enhanced fourfold the position of his country by compelling the Allied powers to extend recognition. He reunited the scattered forces of Islam by concluding offensive and defensive alliances in Asia which would prevent the European powers from exploiting the phantom of pan-Islam. To fully record the services of Mustafa Kemal, writes Zafar Ali Khan, requires a much more comprehensive treatment than a mere editorial. He concludes:

> To strengthen his power Ghazi Mustafa Kemal had to accept the bitter expediency of abolishing the caliphate as a result of which the imperial Ottoman dynasty was deprived of the seat of power. In order to pit the modern democratic system against Europe's material forces he did some cutting and clipping of the Islamic traditions whose correctness can be questioned but the European propaganda that the [Turkish] government has begun to tread the path of *kufr* and atheism is no more than a perverse accusation in the eyes of the discerning people.[77]

But the most interesting contemporary prose work in Urdu on Kemal Atatürk, in my opinion, is a booklet by Muhammad Abdul Majid Atiqi. It is called *Turkan-i Ahrar*.[78] It went into several editions after its first appearance in 1922. Atiqi was a prolific writer who had written several books on Turkey, including *Shahidan-i Dastur* ('Martyrs of the Constitution') and *'Uruj-i Turki* ('Rise of Turkey'). *Turkan-i Ahrar* achieved special popularity because of the subject it dealt with—the life-sketches of various Turkish leaders who had helped Turkey achieve its greatness. The shining star among them, of course, was Mustafa Kemal. The eighth edition, to which the reference is being made here, carried a preface by Maulana Sulaiman Nadwi, a well-known *'alim* of the Khilafat movement fame who had accompanied Mohamed Ali to Europe in 1920 to plead the Turkish case before the British government of Lloyd George. In his writing, Nadwi was full of praise for Mustafa Kemal and his nationalists but thought that unless the *'ulama* and the younger generation worked together, Islam would not be able to benefit.[79]

The *Turkan-i Ahrar* is a straightforward account of Mustafa Kemal's life from birth to death but the interesting thing is that while describing the revolutionary reforms in Turkey, Atiqi takes several pages to defend him against the allegations that he had banished Islam from Turkey and replaced it with a regime of disbelief and irreligion.[80] In his view, the Turkish leader had neither forsaken Islam nor forbidden *namaz* (prayers) nor distorted the *shari'at*. It was all Reuters' propaganda to malign him and undermine his popularity. Otherwise, he maintains, there was no truth in these allegations. Atiqi informs us that Mustafa Kemal was writing a biography of the Prophet of Islam. Quoting from Dr Browne's article in the *Fortnightly Review* of January 1934, he says that the 'Ghazi' had firm faith in the Prophet and his heart was filled with love for Islam. However, he interpreted Islam according to his own viewpoint. His reforms were intrinsically in accordance with the *shari'at*. Contrary to European understanding, he followed in the footsteps of the Prophet.[81]

Atiqi cites a Russian visitor as stating that Europe was deliberately spreading lies about Mustafa Kemal. He also has a British general stating that the stories of Kemal's supposed atheism and irreligion originated with his western detractors. He had lived with Mustafa Kemal for six years and was prepared to affirm that the Turkish leader had full faith in God and religion and regarded Muhammad (*sal'am*) as the last of the Prophets. But he was not a narrow-minded bigot like the mullahs and wanted to purge Islam of all superstitions.[82]

Atiqi goes on to state that it was apparent, from the *khutba* which Mustafa Kemal delivered on the occasion of the 1935 *'Idu'l-fitr* in Ankara, that the Turks were resolute and firm followers of the religion of Islam and were steeped in the Prophet's traditions.[83] Atiqi refers to several other eyewitnesses who went to Turkey and were impressed by the Islamic zeal of the Turks. For instance, Sheikh Razzaq al-Azhari of Egypt gives a description of how the Turks flocked to mosques on hearing the call for prayers, and how the 'Ghazi' himself offered his prayers publicly. Similarly, Professor Amin Efendi, the editor of *al-Muqid* of Egypt who interviewed Mustafa Kemal, is cited as saying that Islam was the Turks' dearest bequeath. However, their Islam was the Islam of the Qur'an and not of the mullahs who interpreted it in a dogmatic formulation. All followers of the Majlis-i Watani believed in the Qur'an and *Sunnat*. On the testimony of a western visitor to Turkey, Atiqi portrays Mustafa Kemal as a man who loved Islam and whose countrymen were devoutly religious. The 'Ghazi' is shown as a great Muslim and a patriot whose daily life reflected the piety of Abu Bakr and Omar, the first and the second caliphs of Islam, respectively, and in whose footsteps he had chosen to follow. The mosques in Turkey are shown to be full to their capacity, and the madrasas and libraries humming with activity. In fact, the Turks, besides being good nationalists, were also good Muslims; European propaganda, according to the author, was plain lies.[84] Atiqi concludes by saying:

Mustafa Kemal was a precious commodity of great pride and glory not only for the Turks but also for the Muslims of the whole world. In spite of the fact that the Ottoman caliphate was abolished the late Ghazi raised on its ruins the fortress of democracy whose heralders are still proclaiming that Islam is their inalienable legacy. . . . This was the man whom the Turkish nation had elected president of the republic three times and had continued to honour him even when he faded away from public life due to ill health. In their eyes he had performed a miracle by bringing back to life a sick and paralysed nation in less than eighteen years.[85]

Such was Atatürk's appeal among Indian Muslims. The day he died (21 November 1938), Muslim India joined in mourning him. Mohammad Ali Jinnah, the president of the Muslim League, who had found a kindred soul in Atatürk, especially after reading H.C. Armstrong's *Grey Wolf* around 1932,[86] paid rich tribute to him and lamented the loss of a great hero of the Islamic world.[87] Bashir Ahmad published a special article on the 'Ghazi' in the *Humayun* in which he recounted the major events of his life and his achievements.[88] Even the Jam'iyyatu'l-'Ulama-i Hind, the religio-political body of the *'ulama* who had once opposed Mustafa Kemal for abolishing the caliphate, passed a most moving resolution on his death, calling him *Mufakkar-i A'zam* ('Great Thinker') and *Mujahid-i Akbar* ('Great Mujahid').[89] But it was Zafar Ali Khan who came out with the most heart-warming poem on the departed leader:

You are asking about the condition of the Prophet's followers,
Whoever you see, you'll find him burdened by sadness;
This is a sorrow that penetrates deep into our souls
From the distant parts of China to the suburbs of Portugal;
By this sadness are affected the Arabs and non-Arabs alike
O perceptive people! this sadness is the sadness for Mustafa Kemal;
The great mujahid has passed away from this world
Whose peer you will not find, strive how much you might;
He removed the millat's difficulties easily
By dint of his greatness, through the Grace of the Almighty;

The wound that had been festering for the last three hundred years,
He became the cause of the healing of that wound;
The Empire that was once the star of the world,
Its dignity he helped to establish afresh;
Incessantly he inflicted wounds on worshippers of the Cross
Whenever he advanced with a crescent-like dagger;
The kettle-drum has begun to sound in Asia
That the Kings and the Popes had heard for a thousand years,
From Kabul to Ankara (and) from Iran to Egypt,
Once more the elegance of Islam is soothing the eyes;
The system which Kemal has established,
O Lord of Ka'bah, may it never experience the shame of downfall;
(O God) the troubles of the Turks that you have already removed,
Remove them (also) from over the heads of the Muslims of India.[90]

The same trend of pro-Turkish sentiment continued after the partition of India and the creation of Pakistan in August 1947. But it was not until 1949 that the first Pakistani ambassador presented his credentials to the Turkish president in Ankara. And the person chosen was none other than Bashir Ahmad, the well-known pan-Islamic writer and editor of the *Humayun*, who had rendered useful service to Turkey during and after the First World War. Between 1949 and 1952, Bashir Ahmad contributed at least eight articles on Turkey in his journal, which varied from description of various historical towns and places in Turkey to portrayal of life in the republic generally. In 'Turkiyya ka Roznamcha' (November 1952), for instance, he recounted his experiences in Ankara as Pakistan's ambassador.[91]

Bashir Ahmad's work was supplemented by that of his wife, Gaiti Ara, who, in her articles in the same journal from 1949 onwards, depicted life in Turkey with particular reference to Turkish women. In 'Turki Khwatin', especially, she painted a very sympathetic account of Turkish women, highlighting their cheerfulness, confidence, and strength of character. She praised them for keeping the Islamic spirit alive while they worked alongside men for the regeneration of their country, particularly in professions like law and medicine.[92] She also shed light on the cultural aspects of Turkey in articles like 'Turkiyya se ek khat' and 'Cemhuriyyet Behram'.[93] What she emphasized the most was that Turkey was still an Islamic country where Islamic and Asian traditions were dominant and the Turks had a great passion for their faith in their hearts. They celebrated *'Idu'l-fitr* and *'Idu'l-azha* with great enthusiasm, and frequented mosques and tombs where vows were taken and offerings made. She noted that Turkish men and women took particular care of their dress but was amazed to find a vast cultural difference between the city folks and the villagers. In conclusion, Gaiti Ara appreciated the high standards of Turkish social etiquette and their general affability.[94]

In conclusion, one can say that the striking feature of Urdu writings on Mustafa Kemal Atatürk and Turkey, for the period under review, was the extraordinary pan-Islamic pull that the Muslims of India (and later of Pakistan) felt and displayed for the Turks. The writers generally seemed to make an extra effort to prove that there was nothing irreligious about Atatürk's reforms. In fact, the Turkish endeavour towards modernization was seen as an internal movement for reform within the ambit of Islamic religion and not just blind imitation of the West; only their interpretation was considered different from the Muslims of other countries. The Turks were believed to have suffered as much at the hands of their own caliphs as of the West. But that is not to say that everyone approved of whatever the Turks did. There were those who openly expressed reservations about them on several counts. But, generally, the *fait accompli* was accepted either as an expedient or as a reflection of a genuine understanding of the Turkish predicament. The Urdu literature for the period is very informative and analytical, and provides a deeper analysis of the contemporary Turkish scene along with an insight into the response in Turkey to what was happening in Muslim India at that time.

NOTES

1. For the evolution and development of Urdu, see Hafiz Mahmud Shirani, *Punjab men Urdu* (Lahore, 1928), 21–23; and Mohammad Sadiq, *A History of Urdu Literature*, 2nd edn. (Karachi, 1985), esp. ch. I. Also see G.H. Zulfikar, 'Urdu Language in the Background of Pak-Turkish Cultural Relations', *Journal of the Research Society of Pakistan*, 23/4 (1986), 5 ff.
2. F. Halidé Dolu, 'Some Similarities in the Turkish and Urdu Languages', *Peshawar University Review*, 1/1 (1974-75), 84; and Akmal Ayyubi, 'Urdu men Turki zaban ke alfaz', *Ma'araf*, 104/6 (Dec. 1969), 460–1.
3. Aziz Ahmad, *Studies in Islamic Culture in the Indian Environment*, 252–3.
4. Sadiq, *A History of Urdu Literature*, 14–18.
5. See Dolu, 'Some Similarities in the Turkish and Urdu Languages', 78–110; Otto Spies, 'Turkisches Sprachgut im Hindustani', *Studia Indologica* (1955), 321–43; Erkan Türkmen, 'Turkish Elements in Urdu', *Journal of Ottoman Studies*, 6 (1986), 1–30; and Akmal Ayyubi. 'Urdu men Turki zaban ke alfaz', 460–5.
6. Sadiq, *A History or Urdu Literature*, 320–5.
7. Ibid., 328–9.
8. See Abdus Salam Khurshid, *Sahafat: Hind-o Pak men* (Lahore, 1963), 191–8.
9. See I.H. Qureshi, 'Two Newspapers of Pre-Mutiny Delhi', 258–60; Rafiq Zakaria, *Rise of Muslims in Indian Politics* (Bombay, 1970), 211–12; and Panipati (ed.), *Maqalat-i Sar Sayyid*, xiii, 419–24, 441–6 and 450–63.
10. Khurshid, *Sahafat*, 273–6, 283–4 and 316 ff.
11. Ibid., 179–200, 233–51 and 307–16.
12. Panipati (ed.), *Maqalat-i Sar Sayyid*, xiii, 405–18, 425–40, 447–9 and 464–6.
13. Government of Pakistan, Ministry of Information, *Turkey and Pakistan: Relations Between Turkey and Muslims of Indo-Pakistan Sub-continent* (Karachi, n.d.), 20-1.
14. Sadiq, *A History of Urdu Literature*, 347–51; and S.M. Ikram, *Modern Muslim India and the Birth of Pakistan*, 2nd edn. (Lahore, 1970), 62 ff.
15. Sadiq, *A History of Urdu Literature*, 417–24 and 427–8.
16. Ibid., 339-44. Also see M.M.K. Shihab Malirkotli, 'Maulana 'Abdu'l-Halim Sharar ke nawal', *Humayun* (Lahore), 44/6, (1943), 466–9.
17. Sadiq, *A History of Urdu Literature*, 431–5.
18. See S.R. Sonyel, *The Ottoman Armenians* (London, 1987), esp. 168.
19. Aziz Malik, *Sahafat aur tahrik-i azadi*, 65; and Khurshid, *Sahafat*, 338–41, 346–73, and 385–97.
20. Ikram Ali Malik (ed.), *Punjab Muslim Press and the Muslim World, 1888–1911* (Lahore, 1974), esp. 9–11.
21. Khurshid, *Sahafat*, 291–3; and Aziz Malik, *Sahafat aur tahrik-i azadi*, 28.

22. Özcan, 'The Press and Anglo-Ottoman Relations, 1876–1909', *Middle Eastern Studies*, 29/1 (Jan. 1993), 111 ff.
23. Aziz Malik, *Sahafat aur tahrik-iazadi*, 23.
24. Ram Babu Saksena, *A History of Urdu Literature* (Lahore, 1927), 287–8; Sadiq, *A History of Urdu Literature*, 358–60; Muhammad Shafi, *Agha Hashr aur unke dramon ka tanqidi mutala'a* (Burhanpur, 1988), 375–80; Miskin Ali Hijazi; *Punjab men Urdu sahafat* (Lahore; 1995), 249–67; and Qurratu'l-'Ain Haidar, *Intikhab Sayyid Haidar Yidirim* (Lahore. 1990), esp. 12–16 and 51.
25. Akmal Ayyubi, 'Urdu ke Turki tarjume' *Nawa-i adab*, 31/2, 11, cited in Erkan Türkmen, 'A Comparative Study of Hayder Yildirim's Translations from Turkish', *Erdem*, 1/3 (Eylül, 1985), 756.
26. Azmi Özcan, 'The Turks in Urdu Literature in the Age of Pan-Islamism', *Journal of the Pakistan Historical Society*, 40/3, (July 1992), 248.
27. See Suriyya Husain (ed.), *Sayyid Hayder Yildirim: majmu'a-i maqalat* (Aligarh, 1981), cited in Özcan, 'The Turks in Urdu Literature in the Age of Pan-Islamism', 247 and 249.
28. Türkmen, 'A Comparative Study of Hayder Yildirim's Translations from Turkish', 755 ff.
29. Published from Lahore in 1907.
30. For *Makhzan* see Hijazi, *Panjab men Urdu sahafat*, 249–67.
31. *Comrade* (Calcutta), 8 July 1911 and 12 Oct. 1912; *Zamindar*, 27 Dec. 1911; and *al-Hilal*, 6 Nov. 1912.
32. See *Kulliyat-i Shibli*, 53–60; Khan Abdullah Khan (ed.), *Maqalat-i Yaum-i Shibli* (Lahore, 1961), 7–17, 27–45 and 122–9 and S.M. Ikram, *Yadgar-i Shibli* (Lahore, 1971), 355–6; and *Zamindar*, 5 Nov., 1912.
33. See Javid Iqbal, 'The Image: of Turkey and Turkish Democracy in Iqbal's Thought and his Concept of a Modern Islamic State', *Iqbal Review*, 28/3 (1987), 27; and F.M. Malik, 'Islam as a Social and Political Ideal: The Role of Muhammad Iqbal in Muslim Reawakening', in Andre Wink (ed.), *Islam, Politics and Society in South Asia* (Delhi, 1991), 9. The text of the '*Jawab-i Shikwa*' is available in Muhammad Iqbal, *Bang-i Dara* (Lahore, 1982; 1st edn. 1924), 222–4.
34. See studies by Niemeijer, Minault, and Qureshi, cited earlier. For the impact of political poetry during the Khilafat Movement, see Gail Minault, 'Urdu Political Poetry during the Khilafat Movement', *Modern Asian Studies*, 8/4 (Oct. 1974), 459–71.
35. *Khilafat*, 16 Nov. 1922. Eng. tr. mine.
36. Ibid. Eng. tr. mine. The word 'victory' refers to the Qur'anic verse 'Help from Allah and a speedy victory', Surah lxi, 13.
37. Ibid., 21 Dec. 1922.

38. Ibid., 24 Dec. 1922. Eng. tr. mine.
39. Ibid.
40. Ibid.
41. Sadiq, *A History of Urdu Literature*, 616–17.
42. Ibid., 490.
43. Quoted by Ghulam Husain Zulfikar, 'Jadid Turki ke bani—Mustafa Kemal Pasha: Zafar aur Iqbal ki nazar men', in id., *Iqbal: ek mutala'a* (Lahore, 1987), 181–2. Eng. tr. mine.
44. Ibid. Also see *Zamindar*; 4 Mar. 1934. Eng. tr. mine.
45. Ibid., 182. Eng. tr. mine.
46. Ibid., 183.
47. Zafar Ali Khan, *Baharistan* (Lahore, n.d.), 283. Eng. tr. mine.
48. Sadiq, *A History of Urdu Literature*, 462.
49. Iqbal, *Bang-i Dara*, 257.
50. Ibid., 264.
51. Ibid., 265.
52. Ibid., 266.
53. Ibid., 266.
54. Sadiq, *A History of Urdu Literature*, 84.
55. Iqbal, *Bang-i Dara*, 267.
56. Muhammad Munawar, *Dimensions of Iqbal* (Lahore, 1986), 102.
57. Iqbal, *Bang-i Dara*, 268.
58. Ibid., 271.
59. Mohammad Iqbal, *Bal-i Jibril* (Lahore, 1982; 1st edn. 1935), 79.
60. See Iqbal, *The Reconstruction of Religious Thought in Islam*, 121 ff.
61. Bakhtiyar, Bano 'Wazahati fehrist *Humayun*', MA thesis (Lahore, 1965).
62. Ibid.
63. Ibid.
64. *Humayun*, 17/4 (April 1930), 332–44.
65. Ibid., 335–6. Eng. tr. mine.
66. Ibid., 336–7.
67. Ibid., 337–44.
68. Ibid., 351–6.
69. Ibid., 351–2.
70. Ibid., 353.
71. Ibid., 354.
72. Ibid., 354–6.
73. Ibid.
74. Ibid.

75. Ibid. Eng. tr. mine.
76. *Zamindar*, 4 Mar. 1934. Eng. tr. below mine.
77. Ibid.
78. All references are to the 8th edn., Lahore, 1938.
79. Ibid., 16.
80. Ibid., 77–8.
81. Ibid., 78.
82. Ibid., 79.
83. Ibid., 79–80.
84. Ibid., 80–1.
85. Ibid., 81–2. Eng. tr. mine.
86. Bolitho, Hector, *Jinnah, Creator of Pakistan*, 102.
87. Jamil-ud-din Ahmad (ed.), *Speeches and Writings of Mr. Jinnah*, i, 72–3.
88. Bano 'Wazahati fehrist *Humayun*', ii.
89. Parveen Rozina (ed.), *Jam'iyyatu'l-'Ulama-i Hind*, ii (Islamabad, 1981) 633.
90. Zafar Ali Khan, *Chamnistan* (Lahore, 1944), 206. Eng. tr. mine.
91. Bano, 'Wazahati fehrist *Humayun*', iii.
92. Ibid., June and Dec. 1950.
93. Ibid.
94. Ibid.

7

Armstrong's Grey Wolf and the 'Real' Atatürk*

In October 1932, when H.C. Armstrong (1892–1943) wrote *Grey Wolf*, its skewed portrayal of Mustafa Kemal Atatürk almost created a diplomatic row between Turkey and Britain. But the impact of its sensationalist drift and fiction-like narrative was such that it immediately caught the imagination of the British public and became a bestseller. Four editions appeared within four months of its first publication and the demand never seemed to cease. The publishers, Arthur Barker of London, were very pleased with their venture as it brought them unexpected money and fame and also good reviews. Armstrong's unrestrained tone was so attuned to the British tastes of the 1930s that even Mohammad Ali Jinnah, later the founder of Pakistan and then living in London in self-exile, read *Grey Wolf* with much interest and talked about it for days with much passion. Hector Bolitho, Jinnah's biographer, notes that: 'For many days afterwards he talked of Kemal Atatürk; so much that his daughter [Dina] chaffed him and nicknamed him 'Grey Wolf'. . . . It is interesting to read the story of Kemal Atatürk again and imagine the

---

*Originally published as 'Atatürk and Armstrong's *Grey Wolf*: Myth and Reality' in the *Proceedings of The Fifth International Congress on Atatürk, 8–12 December 2003*, ii (Ankara, 2005), 973–90.

influence the book must have had on Mohammed Ali Jinnah's mind. Like "Grey Wolf", Jinnah was to create a nation out of a perplexed multitude of Muslim People; but in character—one a libertine, and the other a puritan—they were as different as any two men could be.'[1]

This chapter attempts to analyse Armstrong's account, and sets apart the myth from the reality. This is imperative because the author carried controversial wartime baggage and it evoked hostile retorts from well known Turkish critics such as Necmeddin Sadak (1932), Sadi Borak (1955), and later from, Ergun Hiçyilmaz (1997), in addition to translations and comments by Peyami Safa (1955), Gül Çağali Güven (1996), and Ahmet Çuhadir (2001). Captain Harold Courtenay Armstrong (1892–1943), OBE, the author of *Grey Wolf*, was educated at King's School in Worcester and at Oxford University (BA), before he joined the British Indian Army (67th Punjabis). During the First World War, he served with the British Expeditionary Force in Iraq (Mesopotamia) that surrendered at Kut al-Amara. Captured by the Turks as a prisoner-of-war, he was made to march from the south of Arabia through Syria to Turkey. After the war, because of his experience in military intelligence, he found himself posted back to Turkey at the British Embassy in Istanbul, and later served with the Allied occupation forces. Still later, he was entrusted with the supervision of the Turkish Gendarmeries. Thus, Armstrong had ample opportunity to witness the post-war chaos in Turkey and meet Mustafa Kemal as well as many other important leaders which helped him to comment, in some detail, on the country and its dynamic new leader.[2] However, abundance of detail is never a guarantee for accuracy in scientific historiography; an author's objectivity is more crucial and its essence lies in not being influenced by personal feelings. Authors who display sympathy or antipathy for a nation, a country, or a person are most likely to lose objectivity. Inaccuracies occur due to a variety of reasons: a tendency to exaggerate, group prejudice, conflicting theories, or simply impaired observation. In the case of Armstrong, his humiliation as a POW had turned him into a bitter critic of the Turks and their new leader. *Grey Wolf* was just his way of seeking retribution for the alleged hurt. The book is full of unkind remarks and warped depiction of men and matters in Turkey. The very subtitle of the book, 'An Intimate Study of a Dictator', tells a lot about the mind-set of the author.

In his 334-page text, Armstrong races at an almost breathless speed from Mustafa Kemal's birth to his rise to power and stops only when he takes his subject to the apex of his career in the early 1930s. The book is divided into twelve sections and seventy-five unequal chapters that shred the story into disjointed bits. The style is narrative and absorbing, and the text is interspersed with insinuations and caustic remarks. But the author does not attempt to provide verifiable identification of informants and sources. Armstrong claims that all quotations, with the exception of two, were supplied by Mustafa Kemal himself or were obtained from documentary or verbal sources, but he gives no precise information to confirm the veracity of the claim, particularly when his comments are sated with predispositions. This places the objective reader in the most intriguing predicament. It is also irritating that the author seldom gives the dates of events, hence leaving the reader guessing as to the exact chronology. The appendix on the 'Outline History of Period' is a poor substitution because one cannot turn to it regularly to fix one's bearings.

Armstrong presents young Mustafa Kemal as an 'inherently thin-skinned', 'ill-natured' and 'unpopular' loner with a 'tough constitution' and 'unlimited vitality'.[3] He was never sentimental or romantic; he was rather 'oriental in his mentality'.[4] After getting a commission in the Ottoman army, he joined the revolutionary branch of the *Vatan*. 'Fundamentally he was a revolutionary', says Armstrong, 'with no respect for God, man or institution.' For this, he was constantly kept under surveillance by the sultan but he mostly managed to elude his pursuers.[5] Since he was a man of action, he did not appreciate the abstract notions of CUP leaders like Enver Paşa, Cemal Paşa, and Talat Paşa, whom he contemptuously dismissed as 'puny little men, unfit to rule'. In turn, he was distrusted by them and was never initiated into their inner circle. Thus, when the 'Young Turk' revolution took place in 1908, Mustafa Kemal and his friends were purposely kept out.[6]

According to Armstrong, Mustafa Kemal's attitude changed when he became a senior officer. He grew more expansive, and even congenial, to those who listened to him. He was against foreign influences on Turkey. 'Turkey for Turks!' was his war cry. Like soldiers everywhere, 'he sneered at politics' and despised politicians.[7] During the Tripolitan and Balkan Wars (1911–13), he showed his prowess as a military leader but was often at loggerheads with his seniors, especially Enver. The gulf between the two widened when Enver entrusted the reorganization of the army to the Germans. Mustafa Kemal was banished to Sofia as military attaché. 'Touchy and sensitive', says Armstrong, Mustafa Kemal became more 'lofty and aloof', but found himself comfortable with 'loose women of the capital' in whose company 'he drank and revelled night after night far into the dawn' in shoddy cafés and brothels.[8] The veracity of such comments, to which the author returns repeatedly with obvious relish, is difficult to establish, especially when he gives no authentic references or sources of information.

During the First World War, Mustafa Kemal wanted his country to remain neutral but the triumvirate was pro-German and decided to support Germany. To push him out of his way, Enver sent him to the Çanakkale peninsula in southern Turkey under Otto Liman von Sanders, the German general. There, Mustafa Kemal commanded and fought extremely well, and Armstrong praises him profusely for his military skill, his organizational ability, and his indomitable courage and tenacity of purpose. The author tells us that he fought in the front lines with his men, never taking cover under fire. 'He was convinced, absolutely and completely sure, that no bullet could hit him. It made him utterly fearless.'[9] Armstrong believes that it was Mustafa Kemal's 'driving personality' that gave the Turks their victory and saved the peninsula and the capital. Kemal's differences with Enver and Talat pushed him to the Caucasus front and then to Diyarbekir, where he was fortunate to have Ismet (Inönü) as his chief of staff and Kazim Karabekir as the second in command.[10] Next, he was sent to the Syrian front where General Erich von Falkenhayn, the German commander, had no idea at all how to handle this 'headstrong, insubordinate, but exceedingly capable Turk'.[11] After a brief interlude in Germany with Crown Prince Vehideddin in July 1918, he found himself on the Syrian front again where conditions were indeed pitiable. In spite of his illness, Mustafa Kemal swung into action, re-organized his troops, and planned the strategic withdrawal following the British attack. He was still fighting when news of the Armistice at Mudros arrived. A month later, he returned to Istanbul which, in the meantime, had been occupied by the Allied forces.[12]

Armstrong believes that fate had marked Mustafa Kemal out for greater deeds. While the English were planning to arrest him for deportation and internment in Malta, the sultan thought he was the man who could put an end to the resistance in Anatolia. This gave Mustafa Kemal the opportunity he was looking for—to organize resistance unhindered. The Greek occupation of Smyrna in May 1919, says Armstrong, was a clear signal that Turkey had been damned to ruination. Resistance was the only hope left for Turkey. Kemal hurried out of the capital in time to escape the sultan's change of mind.[13] Armstrong is at his best when he tells us how Mustafa Kemal organized the national resistance against the Allies. One may disagree with Armstrong's tendency to lampoon everyone that he portrays, but his characters in the drama, good or bad, appear extraordinarily authentic. They live and breathe before one's eyes as if in a hologram. Mustafa Kemal is shown to dominate everyone else. With his focused vision, tenacity of purpose, and an unshakable faith in the will of the Turkish people and his own destiny, he lunged forward to convert and organize a demoralized and weary people for resistance.

He toured the villages, lecturing, berating, and preaching resistance. Armstrong thinks that Kemal delivered a master stroke by not taking on the sultan at that point. He saved the situation by suggesting that the sultan was behaving awkwardly because he was a captive in the hands of his advisers and the Allied occupation army. Later, however, when their differences intensified, the sultan, fearing a backlash, decided not to resist and fled the country.[14]

According to Armstrong, Mustafa Kemal's greatest asset was his ability, charisma, and clarity of thought. To him, 'democracy was the rule of the many-headed, the muddle-headed, the fools; the only sound form of government was the absolute rule of one man'.[15] None, even those who had stood by him in the early days of the revolution, escaped his scathing criticism. He 'sneered at and ripped to pieces', says Armstrong, 'all the accepted ideals and morals: morals were a cover for hypocrites or the folly of fools; ideals were dust in the mouth'.[16] Subsequently, the author takes a sudden somersault and, without mincing words, shows Mustafa Kemal as someone who had no fine feelings and 'no loyalties for men, ideas or institutions'. He was 'more animal than man: the wolf, hard, without sentiment or scruples, without morals or guiding principles of conduct except his animal desires'.[17] His 'mood decided his outlook; he was more often ill-natured than pleasant, and, if displeased, would be harsh and merciless'.[18] Armstrong is one of the few writers who examine the relationship between Kemal's ill-health and politics, and this is his forte. His insight into the leader's ill-health and its impact is vivid. He writes: 'His doctor repeatedly warned him that he must go slow … work and drink less, and lead a regular life with someone to look after him; he was living on his nerves: even his energy and the stout constitution inherited from clean-living parents could not stand the strain indefinitely. The old kidney trouble came back repeatedly. He suffered from malaria, which came up from the marshes round Angora.'[19] It was Fikriye, a distant relative who had been entrusted to his care, who saved him from a complete breakdown. The second woman in his life was Latife, an upper-class, educated, girl, who replaced Fikriye and whom Kemal eventually married, but he allowed neither of them to have any control over him.[20]

The last decisive battle with the Greeks began in August 1921. Armstrong thinks Sakarya gave the Turks their first 'real' victory. The decisive encounter was yet to come.[21] The interval slowed down the momentum and exasperated Kemal who took to drinking heavily again. 'The drink', maintains Armstrong, 'stimulated him, gave him energy, but [also] increased his irritability'. Then the author proceeds to make by far the most damaging indictment without giving the source of his information: 'Both in private and public he was sarcastic, brutal and abrupt', maintains Armstrong. 'He flared up at the least criticism. He cut short all attempts to reason with him. He flew into a passion at the least opposition. He would neither confide in nor co-operate with anyone. When one politician gave him advice, he roughly told him to get out. When a venerable member of the Cabinet suggested that it was unseemly for Turkish ladies to dance in public, he threw a Koran at him and chased him out of his office with a stick'.[22] At another place Armstrong highlights Kemal's credulity. 'Irreligious, scoffer at all beliefs, all gods, Mustafa Kemal was yet doubly superstitious. He was afraid of Fate and Chance.'[23]

After defeating the Greeks and the Armistice of Mudania, says Armstrong, Mustafa Kemal was at the apex of his power. He now publicly stated the terms on which Turkey would make peace. They were virtually the same as set forth in the National Pact in January 1920: Turkey must be an independent sovereign state within its own borders, and free from all foreign intrusion. Armstrong praises Mustafa Kemal: 'A smaller man might have increased his demands, been blown up with new ambitions, dreamt dreams of conquest, for from every Islamic country—from India, Africa, from the Malay States, Russia, Afghanistan, Persia and China, even from Christian Hungary, came addresses of congratulation, swords of honour, telegrams of praise: praise on fulsome praise, enough to turn any man's head. . . . They saw in this Moslem general, who had defeated all the might of Europe, the spearhead of their advance towards freedom from the white man and the Christian. . . . But, as ever, though revelling in the praise, drinking in all the flattery, strutting down the centre of the stage, Mustafa Kemal remained level-headed, steady in his judgement, clear in his aims. He had no delusions. . . . He was not going adventuring with dreams of empire or foreign conquest. The Ottoman Empire was dead and broken up: good riddance to it. . . . Enough of that! He would not revive any Ottoman empire.'[24]

Armstrong also recalls Mustafa Kemal's address to the GNA where he supposedly told the members: 'I am neither a believer in a league of all the nations of Islam, nor even in a league of the Turkish peoples. Each of us has the right to hold on to his ideals, but the Government must be stable with a fixed policy, grounded on facts, and with one view and one alone—to safeguard the life and the independence of the nation within its natural frontiers. Neither sentiment nor illusion must influence our policy. Away with dreams and shadows! They have cost us dear in the past.'[25] On another occasion, Armstrong writes, Mustafa Kemal proclaimed loudly that he would not lead Turkey into the folly of championing the East against the West or Islam against Christianity. He reiterated: 'We have but one principle: to see all problems through Turkish eyes and to guard Turkish interests.' The author maintains that Mustafa Kemal thought 'he, and he alone, could create and organize this new Turkey and bring to it success and prosperity'.[26]

Armstrong gives a detailed account of Mustafa Kemal's confrontation with the sultan. The struggle had two phases: in the first stage, he separated the sultanate and the caliphate and, in the second, he abolished the caliphate altogether. The author maintains that though Mustafa Kemal was ruthless and without scruples in obtaining his objectives, he waited for the opportune time to strike. His chance came when the British, rather clumsily, invited the sultan—and not Ankara—to send delegates to the Peace Conference. The reaction was naturally strong and Mustafa Kemal decided to act at once. He proposed to the GNA that the sultanate and the caliphate be separated. The special committee, to which the matter was referred, was hesitant but they hastened to fall in line when Mustafa Kemal threatened them with dire consequences.[27] The GNA sat at once and a vote was forced on it by a show of hands. Although only few hands went up, the chairman declared the vote 'unanimous'. There was an uproar and pandemonium but the law was passed. The sultan, fearing for his life, took shelter with the British on board a battleship. His nephew, Abdülmecid, was made the caliph but the title bestowed only allowed him spiritual powers.[28]

The final clash occurred when Turkey became a republic, with Mustafa Kemal as the president. His friends from the War of Independence, Rauf (Orbay), Rahmi (Evrenos), Adnan (Adivar), the four great military Paşas—Kazim Karabekir, Refet (Bele), Ali Fuad, and Nureddin—and others did not like the change and broke away. Mustafa Kemal was now the 'legal autocrat'. 'He was', says Armstrong, 'President of the Republic with power to appoint his Prime Minister and ministers. He was also President of the Council of Ministers, of the assembly and of the People's Party, which very soon was to be the ruling machine of the country. He was the Commander-in-Chief and held the army and the people in his hands.'[29] For the people of Turkey, Mustafa Kemal was a hero: to them the form of government he introduced did not matter so long as there was peace, enough to eat, and somewhere to live and sleep.[30]

This heralded the end of the caliphate. According to Armstrong, Mustafa Kemal had confided to his friends that 'he would root out religion from Turkey'. 'Religion was for him', says the author, 'the cold, clogging lava that held down below its crust the flaming soul of the nation. He would tear that crust aside and release the volcanic energy of the people. It was a poison that had rotted the body politic. He would purge the state of that poison. Until religion was gone, he could not make of Turkey a vigorous modern nation.' Armstrong goes on to quote Mustafa Kemal: 'Islam, this theology of an immoral Arab, is a dead thing', suggesting thereby that it might have suited the tribal nomads of the desert but not a modern progressive state.[31] Armstrong alleges that Mustafa Kemal denied the existence of God, saying that it was one of the chains by which priests and bad rulers bound people down. In any case, '[a] ruler who needed religion to help him rule is a weakling. No weakling should rule. . . . So far as the priests were concerned, they were like parasites and the people would chase them out of their mosques and monasteries to work like men'.[32]

These are hard-hitting statements but Armstrong does not bother to give us a clue as to how or from whom he obtained this information. Most probably, he was echoing the opinions of Mustafa Kemal's enemies who were itching to get back at him. There is no denying the fact that opposition to Mustafa Kemal had grown considerably and the centre of gravity was none other than the good caliph in Istanbul. According to the author, Abdülmecid II was without political ambition but he had begun to take his office rather seriously. He had revived the pomp and protocol of his predecessors at public ceremonies, and received ambassadors and dignitaries at his court, but more disturbing to Ankara was the fact that 'he attracted all the discontented elements in Turkey like a magnet. All the debris of the dead Ottoman Empire, the priest, the hojas, the ulemas, the palace officials out of work, the dismissed officers of the old régime, the disgruntled people of Constantinople which had now ceased to be the capital, flocked round him'.[33] Worse still, Kemal's political opponents—Rauf, Adnan, Refet, and Karabekir— came running to make Abdülmecid a constitutional sovereign with themselves as the ministers. 'Abdul Mejid', writes the author, 'against all his wishes and inclinations, found himself the centre and weapon of the opposition to Mustafa Kemal and Angora: the quiet, cultured, well-bred gentleman against the raging beast of Angora'.[34]

The curtain came down in November 1923, when the Aga Khan and Syed Ameer Ali, the two Indian Muslim leaders who lived in England, wrote to Ismet conveying the fears of the Muslim world vis-á-vis the uncertain position of the caliph and pleaded with him to restore the latter's powers. The letter was taken to be a sinister conspiracy engineered by the wily British against Ankara. There was an outcry; the GNA was convened in a secret session where speaker after speaker condemned the 'conspirators', the priests, and the caliph. It was agreed that the time had come for Turkey to look after its own interests, ignore the Indians and the Arabs, and divest itself of the leadership of Islam. Intense propaganda made the caliph look like a scoundrel. The army and the party were sounded out and they agreed. The opponents were threatened with dire consequences. Some begged Mustafa Kemal to become the caliph himself: but he was clear about following through with his next step. On 3 March 1924, he presented a bill in the GNA that in essence meant the abolition of the caliphate, the religious courts, codes, and schools. The opponents were cowed down by threats and the bill was passed without debate. The same night, Abdülmecid was banished from Turkey along with his family. 'There was no demonstration, protest or resistance', maintains Armstrong. Mustafa Kemal had won.[35]

Mustafa Kemal was now supreme. But he was ill and tired. The old kidney trouble weighed him down. Armstrong adds: 'To dull the pain he drank heavily which made him morose and irritable. . . . In the hour of success he went slack. Fits of depression carried him down to black depths of despair, where he lost belief in himself, his mission and his star. . . . His private life gave him no relief. He had no one in whom he would open up his intimate self and so get peace of mind.'[36] His mother was dead, differences with Latife would soon result in divorce, and Fikriye would commit suicide. After that, claims Armstrong, Mustafa

Kemal 'became shameless. He drank deeper than ever. He started a number of open affairs with women, and with men. . . . Power brought out in him the brute and the beast, the throw-back to the coarse savage Tartar—the wolf-stock of the central steppes of Asia.'[37] Then, suddenly, a change occurred. 'He became reserved, secluded, and difficult to see.' It happened, when devastated by years of incessant wars, Turkey lay in ruins, the economy was in tatters, and discontent spiralled rapidly. The opposition grew bolder and began to attack Mustafa Kemal himself. It appeared that he was losing his grip. 'Tired, ill, debauched and besotted with drink', Mustafa Kemal's opponents were sure 'he was done'. But the Kurdish revolt flung him back into action. Once more he was in the driving seat. He laid the blame at the door of the British who had stirred trouble with an eye on oil in Mosul.[38]

Next, he turned to his political opponents and sought their impeachment. But, since the GNA and the Party were divided, the matter was deferred. Mustafa Kemal, according to Armstrong, 'had a fanatical belief, a great driving faith in that indefinable personality, the people of Turkey, and in his mission to create out of it a great nation'. He quotes the 'Ghazi' saying, 'I am Turkey. To destroy Me is to destroy Turkey.'[39] The author believes that 'A vast system of secret police, spies, plain-clothes men, agent-provocateurs covered Turkey' to collect evidence and implicate the opposition leaders who were arrested, tried, and hanged. Among them were his old friends (Mehmed) Arif and (Mehmed) Cavid. 'He would allow no memories or sentiments to soften his will.' The four military Paşas, however, were pardoned. In this way, says the author, Mustafa Kemal's success was complete. 'His enemies were banished, broken or dead.'[40] Thus, he emerged 'from the rebellious boy, the revolutionary cadet, the ambitious, disgruntled officer into a ruthless and strong dictator. . . . He was ruthless because with the concentration of a fanatic he believed in himself and his mission. His mission was to make Turkey prosperous, civilized and rich.'[41]

Armstrong then explains the reforms that Mustafa Kemal planned to introduce. 'He must cut Turkey away from the corrupting past; he must clear away all the debris. He had already torn up the whole political fabric, changed a monarchy into a republic, reduced an empire down to a country, made a religious State into a lay republic, ejected the Sultan, the Caliph, and repudiated all connection with the Ottoman Empire. Now he set out to change the whole mentality of the people—their old ideas, their habits, their dress, manners, customs, ways of talking, all the most intimate details of their lives, which linked them with the past and their Oriental upbringing.'[42] Armstrong quotes Kemal as saying: 'All our troubles come from the misuse of religion in the State. . . . It is a weak man who needs religion to bolster up his rule.' He ordered the state to be secularized. He firmly believed, says the author, that 'Religion is a personal matter; each citizen of the Republic may decide his religion for himself.' He sneered openly at religion. 'He made it clear that for him the religious man, the man who went to the mosque and prayed, must be a knave or a fool, and, in either case, useless.' Since Mustafa Kemal's opinions were the faith of the People's Party, 'it became fashionable', says the author, 'to sneer at religion and unwise and even dangerous to practise it. The men went no more to the mosques. Religion went out of fashion.'[43] In line with this, the dervishes and monastic orders had to go. Through a law passed by the GNA in a single night, he closed the monasteries, dissolved their organizations, and turned the dervishes into the streets. As such, 'the whole religious basis and outlook of the Turkish state and people' was changed and an era of reconstruction launched.[44]

Armstrong says that after destroying the old laws and social life based on the religion of Islam and the dictates of the *shari'at*, Mustafa Kemal invited European experts and adopted German commercial, Italian penal, and the Swiss civil, codes across the board. 'They changed', continues the author, 'the whole legal structure. The Swiss Codes revolutionized the status of the family and the rights of ownership, forbade polygamy and the harem, and radically adjusted the position of women who ceased to be chattels owned by their husbands: they became individuals and free citizens.'[45] Next, he turned to making Turkey completely Turkish. From his early days, he had believed in 'Turkey for the Turks'. Now, he started to implement it fully. The Turkish language was purified of Arabic and Persian words, and Tartar made the basis of the language reform. The Qur'an and the New Testament were translated into Turkish, and orders were passed for prayers to be said in Turkish. Foreign schools were discouraged, especially those run by missionaries. In business, each firm was supposed to have a high percentage of Turkish shares. Many professions, such as medicine and law, were closed to foreigners. Although most of the innovations had been borrowed from Europe, in some cases he surpassed even the Europeans.[46] This was followed by language reforms, which he launched with the enthusiasm of a teacher. Then he turned to the arts and western music as 'the criterion of the civilized'. This was followed by the emancipation of women—for which he was the first in the Muslim world in recent history. He also regulated the employment of children.[47]

In Armstrong's opinion, Mustafa Kemal gradually relaxed his control over his country's affairs. He retired to Çankaya, 'shut himself away, became elusive and rarely seen by anyone except his intimates, his women, and a few Government officials, leaving Ismet to deal with the routine of government'. In spite of the wide-ranging reforms that Kemal introduced, Armstrong sees no change in him. 'His outlook was oriental', says the author, 'his life wild and bizarre'. He was now forty-seven and showed signs of middle age. 'His health, varied rapidly. For nights at a time he suffered from insomnia. He would be attacked by the fits of black depression; the old kidney trouble gave him acute pain. As suddenly he became alive and vital. One day he might be seen walking like an old man, and the next hale and hearty.' Nonetheless, 'his immense vitality showed no signs of failing'. Sometimes, he worked with tremendous energy. On one occasion, he delivered a speech reviewing the whole history of the nationalist revolution that took him 'seven whole nights to prepare and all the working hours of six continuous days to deliver'. Only during the last few hours did his voice grow a little hoarse from the prolonged strain. After such flurries of activity, he would stay cloistered at home, 'inaccessible, drinking, gambling, debauching the whole night through and much of the day, with his intimates—his 'desperadoes' and his women'.[48] After this tirade, Armstrong suddenly turns to praise Mustafa Kemal. 'Without doubt, despite his faults and his egoism', says the author, 'the man was a patriot. Much that he said and did was illogical, untrue, even unsound to stupidity, but he believed passionately in his work and its success.' From then on '[h]e was a changed man. He became more pompous and prosy, and waxed eloquent in truisms.'[49]

Armstrong suggests that Mustafa Kemal loved flattery. He demanded that his intimates 'should follow his every mood. If he was irritated, they must be sad. If he smiled, they must be gay. With them his life was wild and unclean. He drank and gambled with them in the smoke-filled rooms, the floors littered with cigarette ends, the table strewn with cards and money. He was at home in the stench of stale spilt liquor, the foul breaths, the coarse laughter of coarse women, the oaths and the bestialities.'[50] Armstrong claims, 'The scandal of his private life was known to all, but it only made him the more popular. The Turks were crude orientals and they understood Mustafa Kemal: He was their ideal of a ruler; he might be cruel, vicious, brutal and spiteful, but despite this he was strong and decided; he was a soldier-ruler and a conqueror. His chief vice was the national vice. Lechery had been the oldest boast of their ancestors. They preferred his robust, crude vitality to the placid domestic virtues.'[51]

Armstrong calls Mustafa Kemal's private life a 'cafe-brothel-like'.[52] And that was the cause of his ill-health: 'Twice he had severe fainting fits with a heart-attack. The heavy drinking was telling on him. His doctor warned him again that he must go slow and that a change of air would do him good.' Moreover, he was out of touch with his people and had loosened his control over state affairs too freely. 'Many even said that already he was a back number, a mere figurehead; that the Grey Wolf had been muzzled and chained up in Chan Kaya; and that Ismet and his ministers were the real rulers.'[53] But all of a sudden, he surprised everyone by making a startling comeback, 'a dramatic attention-catching return, into the limelight.' 'He became more restrained and decorous in public and private. He spent less time with the 'desperadoes' and the women. He drank and gambled less and slept better. His health improved. He was at work again and happy.'[54]

Armstrong asserts that Mustafa Kemal's differences with Ismet came to a head in the summer of 1930 when the latter became openly defiant. Kemal thought that the best way to cut Ismet down to size was to create an opposition party. The result was the emergence of the Republican Liberal Party, with Fethi (Okyar) as its nominal head, and himself its mentor. But the experiment did not work as no one understood how to make the parliamentary system work properly.[55] Mustafa Kemal realized that the people were not yet ready for change. Then, says the author, Mustafa Kemal decided to reassert himself. 'The Grey Wolf showed his teeth. He was the ruler of a brutal, primitive people in a brutal, hard land. He must be strong and brutal.'[56] As a result, he imposed martial law, censorship of press and speech, punished his critics and made up with Ismet. 'He needed the merciless, hard, little man, the rigid staff officer, the martinet', says the author.[57] Once more, there was peace and quiet. Now he came up with a clear plan: the only kind of government that was feasible at the time was 'a benevolent, educating, guiding dictatorship'. He shut down the opposition, drastically purged the People's Party, and arranged elections in a way that the GNA would return a percentage of members from the grassroots with a few independents to criticize the government. 'His faith, his driving faith, in the Nation was as strong as ever. He would educate the people until they were ready. He would lead his people to success.'[58]

ARMSTRONG'S GREY WOLF AND THE 'REAL' ATATÜRK

In the final chapter of his book, Armstrong gives an overview of Mustafa Kemal and, like an oracle, attempts to surmise in his typically indiscreet manner:

> Mustafa Kemal, alive and vibrating with vitality, is the Dictator of Turkey.
>
> He is a man born out of due season, an anachronism, a throw-back to the Tartars of the Steppes, a fierce elemental force of a man.
>
> Had he been born in the centuries when all Central Asia was on the move he would have ridden out with Sulyman Shah under the banner of the Grey Wolf, and with the heart and instincts of a Grey Wolf.
>
> With his military genius, and his ruthless determination unweakened by sentiments, loyalties or moralities, he might well have been a Tamerlane or a Jenghis Khan riding at the head of great hordes of wild horsemen, conquering countries, devouring and destroying cities, and filling in the intervals of peace between campaigns with wild and hideous orgies of wine and women.[59]

The author goes on to write:

> With the mind of an Emperor he lives in brutal royalty in a suburban villa in the poor village of Chan Kaya: a primitive chieftain in a morning-coat with a piece of chalk and a blackboard for his weapons.
>
> His greatness has lain in his knowledge and his acceptance of the narrow limits of his opportunities.
>
> Above all he is great in a great Faith—Faith in the splendid future of his people.[60]

Finally, Armstrong ends his study with the following statement:

> He [Mustafa Kemal] is a Dictator. The future lies in his strong hands. If they fail, grow flabby, tremble, if though strong to destroy they cannot build, then Turkey dies.
>
> A lone man without family, without friends, he has made the people of Turkey the heirs to his private possessions and to his power.

He is Dictator in order that it may be impossible ever again that there should be in Turkey a Dictator.[61]

It is apparent that while Armstrong grudgingly acknowledges Mustafa Kemal's manifold qualities, he goes too far in parading the personal shortcomings of the Turk. Mustafa Kemal is portrayed as a two-faced, reckless drunken debauch and a gambler who enjoyed the company of lowly men and women of easy virtue. When necessary, he could plead, cajole, and concede to win support but would brook no opposition or nonsense and could even sign the death warrant of a close friend and confidante without remorse. Armstrong repeatedly uses derogatory language for Mustafa Kemal, Ismet, and other leaders, as well as for the Turkish nation as a whole. His reasons to revile Atatürk and the Turks are not difficult to discern. Apparently, the author was so devastated by his humiliation as a POW in Turkey that he developed an utter dislike for the Turks. This personal grudge together with his position as an intelligence officer in occupied Turkey shaped his outlook. Another reason, as Roger Norman suggests, was perhaps his excessive reliance on Turkish exiles for information.[62] Whatever the reasons, Armstrong probably thought that the only way to settle the score was to paint Mustafa Kemal in the blackest of colours. Naturally, such work was bound to invite comment and arouse controversy from contemporary opinion-makers. The *Daily Telegraph* of London, for instance, carried a review by Campbell Dixon who tried to balance Armstrong's libel of Mustafa Kemal with Brigadier-General Aspinall-Oglander's tributes in *The Official History of the Gallipoli Campaign*.[63] Dixon recognized in him an 'inspired visionary' as well as a 'hard-headed organizer of victory' for whom the modernization of Turkey was a serious challenge.[64] Even the reviewer of an academic journal like *The Times Literary Supplement* of London, while recognizing 'the legal autocracy' and 'absolutism' of the Ghazi of Ankara and the needless meanderings of the 'puppet "Opposition"', could not help noticing Armstrong's rather frequent references to Mustafa Kemal's private life. And, though he praised

Armstrong's minute description of Kemal as a morose and ferocious man and as a successful military commander, he found the text 'irritatingly breathless and disconnected'.[65]

The *Grey Wolf* also created a stir in the British Foreign Office where officials got worried about its likely impact on Britain's delicate relations with Turkey. Colin Cathcart of the *Daily Express* had forewarned the Foreign Office about the book's likely impact for its explosive content.[66] A.K. Helm at the Foreign Office agreed with Cathcart—that the book was likely to upset the Turks. He thought that instead of being an intimate study of the Turkish president, the book was 'full of contradictions, exaggerations, and impossibilities'.[67] It only gave a biased and a twisted picture of the Turkish president, 'stressing the wild and vicious side of his character and passing over the more agreeable side in silence'.[68] However, he thought that in the midst of the sensational stuff there was a good deal of solid substance that indicated access to some reliable information. Since Armstrong had held a sort of an official position while in Turkey, and had used verbatim certain passages from the official despatches, it was feared that this might create a diplomatic row.[69] What is more, Armstrong had the temerity to send some advertisement postcards to Sir Lancelot Oliphant (1881–1965), assistant under-secretary at the Foreign Office, for distribution among friends, which the latter decided to ignore.[70] Helm was of the opinion that the British government could do nothing to counteract the book's effect but at least their ambassador in Ankara could tell the Turks that it had 'neither official inspiration nor blessing.'[71] On 10 November, James Morgan, counsellor at the British Embassy in Ankara, informed his Foreign Office that there was an apparent calm and the storm over the book had not yet broken.[72] This was probably due to the fact that the book had been banned in Turkey and its translation forbidden.

Initially, Atatürk's response to Armstrong's book was also guarded. 'This man knows me too well!', he is reported to have exclaimed when he had the book read out to him by one of his secretaries.⁷³ Another account suggests that he stated, 'That fellow has made too little of our pleasures'.⁷⁴ He also saw no reason for Ismet's government to impose a ban on the book and wanted it published in Turkish after he had given his own account.⁷⁵ However, towards the end of November 1932, James Morgan reported from Ankara that Atatürk was furious about the book. He was offended, partly because of the distortions and slanders, but mainly due to the fact that Armstrong had failed to live up to the Turkish ideal of a British biographer who would be objective and truthful.⁷⁶ But, instead of giving a public response, Atatürk arranged with Necmeddin Sadak, the proprietor of the *Akşam* newspaper and the ruling party deputy from Sivas, to serialize a sharp retort. He is even said to have dictated the riposte that appeared in several articles between 8 and 20 December 1932.⁷⁷ The whole case was built on the assertion that Armstrong was a member of the British intelligence service and had been sent to Turkey specifically to promote propaganda against Atatürk and the War of Independence.⁷⁸ The articles maintained that Armstrong, along with his two other British accomplices, was a malingerer who spent much time drinking, gambling, and womanizing, thus insinuating that such a person's testimony was unreliable and his motives in writing the book and attacking Atatürk were clearly ulterior.⁷⁹

Necmeddin Sadak asserted that Armstrong, unlike other British writers, had indulged in lies and contradictions simply to increase the sales of his book. And, in the process, he had clubbed the entire Turkish nation as primitive and barbarous and all Ottoman sultans as rebellious animals. Such irresponsible statements, wrote Sadak, had made a rebuttal necessary, and he went on to give several instances where Armstrong was factually wrong.⁸⁰ He pointed out that Atatürk came from pure Turkish stock and was not an Albanian. He never indulged in wild orgies nor was his life wicked, as painted by Armstrong.⁸¹ As to Mustafa Kemal's treatment of his opponents after the revolution, Sadak maintained that the author had it all wrong. He was never close to Arif nor had he signed his (Arif's) or anyone else's death warrant. The authority to do that rested solely with the GNA. Mustafa Kemal never left his friends like Karabekir and Rauf; rather, they had left him. Sadak maintained that when Armstrong found nothing substantial on Mustafa Kemal, he resorted to defaming his character by inventing wild stories. Of course, Atatürk used to drink and he never attempted to hide it. But Armstrong had tried to make a scandal out of it for nothing. He certainly liked women but certainly not the loose and 'painted' type. Mustafa Kemal was very polite and courteous towards women and his detractors maligned him out of spite. Armstrong had no real information about Atatürk and, as a result, he had ended up relying only on gossip.[82]

As to the allegation that Mustafa Kemal was intolerant of criticism, Sadak asserted that he had restrained only those who were known to be against the country and the nation, especially the bad-mouthed politicians. He never turned out any minister by force: the scenario painted by Armstrong was a figment of his imagination. Sadak also contradicted Armstrong for believing that Kemal was superstitious. He maintained that it was out of Atatürk's character to be credulous.[83] Sadak had a different story about Fikriye and Latife as well, which was devoid of the lust and debauchery that finds place in Armstrong's account. He denied that there was any emotion involved in his marriage to Latife, and that it had been consummated merely to provide protection to her. Contrary to what Armstrong claimed, he certainly did not drag her out of her house to get married by the first mullah that he came across. The wedding took place properly at her father's house in the presence of many guests. The fact that they were a mismatch and could not remain together for long was the reason why, Sadak asserted, Mustafa Kemal would spend most of his time drinking with his friends.[84] As a heavy drinker himself, Armstrong should have known better—that kidney trouble does not allow one to indulge in heavy drinking. In the circumstances, his contention about Kemal's excesses was anything but factual.[85]

Sadak further argued that, throughout his book, Armstrong cursed and mortified the Turkish nation as 'rude' and 'uncivilized', and its leader as 'brutal'. But, since he could not deny the force of Kemal's personality, he had ended up in contradictions: sometimes parading him as a schoolteacher, at other times as a genius who had infused new life into a dead nation, and at yet another time as someone akin to Tamerlane and Genghis Khan.[86] Sadak refuted the allegation that Kemal was rude and impolite, saying that he would even treat an ordinary person as if he were the head of a state. He maintained that Atatürk's favourite pastime and greatest pleasure was talking to friends on military and other issues, and that he (Sadak) himself was a witness to that. In those meetings, he would only drink *raki* and would never hide it from anyone. The stories of his drinking and womanizing escapades were purely fictional, based on images of merrymaking among the European nobility. Surely, claimed Sadak, Armstrong did not understand either Turkey or Mustafa Kemal. Atatürk was not friendless; the entire Turkish nation was his friend and relative and they were ready to sacrifice their lives for him. His own intention in writing this refutation, asserted Sadak, was to put the record straight in response to Armstrong's distortions. The Englishman had tried to win fame by linking his name with that of Atatürk. He had selected a fine topic but his tragedy was that he tried, needlessly, to denigrate the life of a great leader. Fortunately, he did not succeed because Atatürk's greatness was rooted firmly in the pages of history.[87]

It is obvious, from the foregoing, that Armstrong's *Grey Wolf* stirred up considerable controversy in the academic and political circles in Britain, Turkey, and British India. In Britain, it remained a bestseller for several months because, as Andrew Mango suggests, its unrestrained tone was quite savoury to the British public of the time.[88] That it did not create a diplomatic row between Turkey and England, the credit goes to Mustafa Kemal and his associates who displayed remarkable prudence and forbearance.[89] Jinnah's extraordinary interest in the *Grey Wolf* has already been noticed. In spite of the apparent dissimilarities between

Jinnah and Mustafa Kemal, the former found much to appreciate in the latter though, when the time came, he did not make Pakistan a truly secular state on the pattern of Atatürk's Turkey. His model was a modernist, progressive state and society where the rule of law and collective good were the ultimate goals.

The controversy over the *Grey Wolf*, however, kept surfacing whenever there was a comment or reference in some book, or on the Internet in recent times.[90] A particular aspect of this debate was Armstrong's unabashed dubbing of Atatürk as the 'Dictator' with a capital 'D'. Anyhow, if the Ismet cabinet banned the book in 1932, the Menderes government went one step further in 1951 by passing a law that declared disparagement of Atatürk a cognizable offence. This was done to ward off more assaults on the president, à la *Grey Wolf*.[91] For the same reason, the book was never translated in its entirety. In 1955, Peyami Safa, a popular writer, raked up controversy by translating a third of the *Grey Wolf*, omitting the controversial portions as well as the irritating subtitle. The same year, Sadi Borak, another prolific writer, joined in the debate by publishing Necmeddin Sadak's *Akşam* articles in book form with additional notes and comments.[92] The idea was to present a fresh rebuttal to Armstrong's book which, as Mehmet Bedri Gültekin points out in his preface to the 1997 edition, was still considered, in Turkey, to be a part of a 'psychological war' aimed at degrading Atatürk and the republican revolution.'[93] In support of his contention, Sadi Borak also reproduced contributions by Madam Spanuidi, a Greek writer, and Monsieur Herriot, a former French prime minister, who had painted positive pictures of the Turkish leader.[94] The Frenchman, in particular, extolled Atatürk's reforms which seemed to display a strong French influence.[95]

After the 1955 renditions, more than forty years were to elapse before Gül Çağali Güven (1996), Ergun Hiçyilmaz (1997), and Ahmet Çuhadir (2001) brought out their versions of the book while still excluding the offensive parts.[96] Meanwhile, Armstrong's book continued to rankle with the Turks and evoke strong emotions. As compared to him, other British biographers of Atatürk, Lord Kinross, and Andrew Mango, in particular, have been more judicious and objective and have disavowed Armstrong's subjective assessment. While Kinross does not mention Armstrong even in his bibliography, Mango dismisses him in just one short paragraph.[97] Myths, no doubt, are an 'occupational' hazard of great men and Kemal Atatürk was no exception. But reality always manages to seep out through the misty horizon to reveal itself. No impartial observer can deny that in spite of *Grey Wolf*, 'Atatürk was a great man' in all facets of his personality.[98] Armstrong's protagonist was indeed based on a case of mistaken identity.

NOTES

1. See Hector Bolitho, *Jinnah: Creator of Pakistan*, 102–3.
2. See *Who Was Who, iv* (London, 1980), 32; and H.C. Armstrong, *Ibn Saud: Lord of Arabia* (London, 1939),—inside flap.
3. H.C. Armstrong, *Grey Wolf—Mustafa Kemal: An Intimate Study of a Dictator* (London, 1932), 30–1.
4. Ibid., 27.
5. Ibid., 33–5.
6. Ibid., 36–43.
7. Ibid., 41–6.
8. Ibid., 60–3.
9. Ibid., 64–74.
10. Ibid., 75–88.
11. Ibid., 89.
12. Ibid., 98–101.
13. Ibid., 113–28.
14. Ibid., 129–34.
15. Ibid., 168–70.
16. Ibid., 171–2.
17. Ibid., 172.
18. Ibid., 173–4.
19. Ibid., 174.
20. Ibid., 174–5, and 199 ff.

21. Ibid., 176–83.
22. Ibid., 190.
23. Ibid., 193.
24. Ibid., 217–18.
25. Ibid., 218–19.
26. Ibid., 219.
27. Ibid., 225–7.
28. Ibid., 227–9.
29. Ibid., 239.
30. Ibid., 240.
31. Ibid., 241.
32. Ibid., 241–2.
33. Ibid., 245.
34. Ibid., 245.
35. Ibid., 246–50.
36. Ibid., 251.
37. Ibid., 251–4.
38. Ibid., 260–9.
39. Ibid., 270.
40. Ibid., 271–9.
41. Ibid., 285.
42. Ibid., 287.
43. Ibid., 290.
44. Ibid., 290.
45. Ibid., 291.
46. Ibid., 291–3.
47. Ibid., 307–13.
48. Ibid., 294–7.
49. Ibid., 297.
50. Ibid., 300.
51. Ibid., 300–1.
52. Ibid., 301.
53. Ibid., 303.
54. Ibid., 303–7.
55. Ibid., 314–25.
56. Ibid., 326.
57. Ibid., 326.
58. Ibid., 328.
59. Ibid., 333.

60. Ibid., 333–4.
61. Ibid., 334.
62. Roger Norman, 'H.C. Armstrong, Patrick Kinross and Mustafa Kemal', in *Turkish Daily News*, Electronic Edition, 6 May 1997, 2.
63. *Daily Telegraph* (London), 24 Oct. 1932.
64. Ibid.
65. *The Times Literary Supplement* (London), 19 Nov. 1932, 826.
66. Salahi R. Sonyel, *Atatürk—The Founder of Modern Turkey* (Ankara, 1989), 163.
67. See PRO, FO 395/469 in ibid., 164.
68. Ibid., 165.
69. Ibid.
70. Ibid.
71. FO 395/469/P 2199 in ibid., 165–6.
72. Ibid., 166.
73. Norman, 'H.C. Armstrong, Patrick Kinross and Mustafa Kemal', 2.
74. Andrew Mango, *Atatürk* (London, 1999), 506.
75. See Gül Çağali Güven's preface to the translation of Armstrong's (*Bozkurt: Kemal Atatürk'un Yasami*, Istanbul, 1996), viii–ix; Mango, *Atatürk*, 506; and Norman, 'H.C. Armstrong, Patrick Kinross and Mustafa Kemal', 2.
76. Sonyel, *Atatürk*, 166–8.
77. See special note in Sadi Borak (ed.), *Atatürk'un Armstrong'a Cevabi*, 3rd edn. (Istanbul, 1997), 17. Also see Sonyel, *Atatürk*, 168.
78. A convenient place to look at Necmeddin Sadak's contributions is Borak's *Atatürk'un Armstrong'a Cevabi*, 23 and 30–1.
79. Ibid., 31 and 34–8.
80. Ibid., 41–6.
81. Ibid., 47–57.
82. Ibid., 58–62.
83. Ibid., 64–5.
84. Ibid., 63 and 66–8.
85. Ibid., 69.
86. Ibid., 70–2.
87. Ibid., 73–6.
88. See Mango, *Atatürk*, 617, n.53.
89. Martin Gilbert, *Sir Harold Rumbold—Portrait of a Diplomat* (London, 1973), 283 and 288.
90. See, for instance, 'Kemal Atatürk—Hailed as a "Liberator of Turkey". We take a second look at his Life and Works', http://www.guidedones.com/issues/women/Atatürk10.htm, 'Life of a Wayward—Kemal Atatürk', (Accessed: 19 Aug. 2003).

91. See Güven's preface to *Bozkurt*, viii–ix.
92. Sadi Borak's original title was *Armstrong'tan Bozkurt: Mustafa Kemal ve Iftirlara Cevap* (Istanbul, 1955). All references here, however, are to the 1997 edition.
93. Borak, *Atatürk'un Armstrong'a Cevabi*, 7.
94. Ibid., 77–84 and 84–122.
95. Ibid., 100–3.
96. For Güven, see n. 70, above. Ergun Hiçyilmaz called his book *"Bozkurt" Yazari ajan Armstrong ve Casusu Örgütlari* (Istanbul, 1997); and Ahmet Çuhadir dubbed his translation *Bozkurt: Kemal Atatürk'un Yasami* (Istanbul, 2001).
97. The Kinross volume, *Atatürk: The Rebirth of a Nation*, was published from London in 1964. For Mango, see n. 69, above.
98. Uluğ Igdemir, E.Z. Karal, et al., *Atatürk*. Eng. Tr. A.J. Mango (Ankara, 1981), esp., 215.

8

Atatürk's Reforms and the Muslim World Bordering South Asia*

Atatürk's crowning achievement was the creation of a sovereign unitary nation state out of the devastation and confusion resulting from the First World War.[1] His success looks even more astounding because he accomplished his objective within a decade despite enormous difficulties. By the time he died, in November 1938, the country had been transformed from a multi-ethnic traditional dispensation into a 'state of the people' through Kemalism—Turkey's pragmatic approach to secular modernization. This chapter examines the broad contours of Atatürk's reforms and traces their impact on South Asia and its Muslim neighbours.

Reform was not new to Turkey, though the enthusiasts of the Turkish 'Historical Thesis' would like to stretch its roots to a much earlier period.[2] A more plausible starting point seems to be the *Tanzimat* period with its moorings in the fifteenth and sixteenth centuries.[3] Usually, external

---

* Originally published as 'Atatürk's Reforms and their Impact on the Muslim World', in *Doğumunun 125. Yilinda Mustafa Kemal Atatürk* (Ankara: Atatürk Araştirma Merkezi, 2011), 523–42. The International Symposium, on Atatürk's 125th Birth Anniversary, was held in Ankara on 15–18 May 2006.

factors are highlighted to explain the modernization of the Ottoman State,[4] but Kemal Karpat finds 'internal' stimuli more important than 'outside' influences.[5] The patterns of social stratification which emerged out of this intricate mesh led to ideas eventually symbolized in the writings of intellectuals like Namik Kemal, Tevfik Fikret, Ahmet Mithat, Halit Ziya, and others. They gave a new meaning to the concept of the *vatan* (fatherland), which helped to create a new form of identity and a new political culture.[6] These ideas later seeped into the writings of Ziya Gökalp and, as with the thinkers of the *Tanzimat* and *Meşrutiyet* eras, provided the intellectual stimulus to nationalist revolution, especially in 'de-Arabising' Islam in Turkey.[7] Likewise, Mustafa Kemal is believed to have been inspired by Abdullah Cevdet in his drive towards westernization, by Celâl Nuri Heri in his reform of the alphabet, and by Hakki Kiliçoğlu in his reform of women's rights.[8] In addition, there was the impact of a sense of history which Mustafa Kemal developed from his appraisal of the works of both Turkish and foreign historians and philosophers.[9] Enver Ziya Karal counts at least four European thinkers whose works interested Mustafa Kemal the most: Jean-Jacques Rousseau, Émile Durkheim, Auguste Mignet, and, more particularly, Auguste Comte.[10] Kemal's collaborators, particularly among the military officers, also evinced strong ideological and intellectual tendencies with secular-nationalist and etatist preferences.[11]

Whatever the intellectual-philosophical basis of Kemalism (*Atatürkçhülük*), it evidently grew out of Mustafa Kemal's declarations and actions and was not the result of any philosophical-dogmatic system. Indeed, Ismet Giritli considers Kemalism as 'a flexible amalgam of secularism, realism, empirical rationalism, and nationalism', opposed to 'rigid ideologies' such as Marxism and National Socialism.[12] Its objective was geared to ensuring that Turkish society changed structurally into a modern, civilized society.[13] However, the Kemalist *inkilab* did not advocate a sudden and total break with the Ottoman past; rather, its aim was to radicalize the culmination of that process which had been taking place for over a century.¹⁴ The fundamentals of Kemalism (announced in a manifesto in April 1931) stressed on six principles: (i) *Republicanism*, which incorporated the concept of national sovereignty that Kemal had absorbed from his younger days; (ii) *Nationalism*, which was partly aroused by writings on the subject but mostly by the tribulations of the state, and which found a renewed expression in Turkey's redefined boundaries as a sociological-psychological concept disavowing discrimination of race or religion; (iii) *Populism*, which centred on the 'people' as a source of democratic rights and favoured liberal political democracy in the sense of the people being in ultimate control of the state; (iv) *Étatism*, which visualized state participation in vital sectors of a mixed economy, aimed at definite and measurable targets and results through a comprehensive and systematic strategy; (v) *Laicism/Lâiklik*, which meant freedom of mind along with separation of religion from the state without subscribing to atheism; and, lastly, (vi) *Revolutionism*, which underscored the other five principles.¹⁵ These edicts were fully guaranteed in the republic's constitution and formed the essence of the Turkish revolution.

Mustafa Kemal had started implementing his reforms the moment he felt he was in a position to do so. At every step, the opposition put up stiff resistance but was either brushed aside, intimidated, or simply won over. Employing the prestige and charisma that he had acquired since his bold stand against the Allies, Mustafa Kemal moved resolutely and took a series of calculated yet bold steps to overhaul the entire state structure. Technically, the first step in that direction was the law of November 1922 that separated the 'church' and the state. Though the *'ulama* never accepted the decision, the law was consistent with the age-old Ottoman practice of indulging in 'extra-Şer'i' procedures.¹⁶ The logical next step that confirmed this disconnection was the abolition of the caliphate in March 1924. To significantly reduce the power of the 'ecclesiastics' (comprising both the *'ulama* and the Sufis), he nudged the GNA into passing the Law of Educational Unity that closed down the madrasas and opened the doors for the teaching of western curricula in schools. Next to go were the ministry of *shari'at*, the office of the shaikhu'l-Islam, as well as the *shari'at* courts. These laws were meant to prevent the misuse of religion as a political tool; and the 1924 constitution saw to it that the freedom of thought and action were fully guaranteed.[17] In September 1925, the dervish orders, intertwined with Sufism, were abolished and visits to the *takya*s forbidden. Simultaneously, in phased strokes, religion was made a matter of individual conscience: first, by striking out the clause that proclaimed Islam as the state religion from the constitution (April 1925) and, then, by removing any reference to it altogether (April 1928). Finally, the Turkish state was described as secular, and state sovereignty was vested in the name of the people (February 1937). However, this did not imply a shift towards atheism; it was only an attempt to keep religion and state apart as the religious orders had continued to show open defiance to the new reforms.[18]

The social reforms, on the other hand, were intended to break the age-old taboos and make Turkey 'an integral part of the Western civilization'.[19] The veil and the red fez were banned and all civil servants were asked to wear western clothes and hats. In 1926, the Swiss civil code was adapted to Turkish needs to preclude unilateral divorces and check polygamy. The Islamic calendar gave way to the Gregorian calendar.[20] The same year, the Perso-Arabic script was abandoned in favour of the Latin script.[21] Other legal reforms included the adoption of a penal code modelled on Italian laws, and a business code that was copied from Germany.[22] In 1932, the *azan* was rendered into Turkish, and in 1934 the law of surnames was passed. A year later, Friday ceased to be a holiday and the weekend shifted to Saturday-Sunday.[23] And, though state grants and *waqf*s were still utilized for the upkeep of religious infrastructure, Turkey was thoroughly westernized—epitomized in the declaration that Turks were part of western civilization (1934). The men who controlled Turkey's destiny were committed nationalists, and yet they chose to fashion the Turkish society in the European cultural matrix. More importantly, the reforms incorporated not just the West's worldview but also its symbols and values.[24] All these changes point to Mustafa Kemal's absolute realism and sense of timing.[25]

Several trends are discernible in Mustafa Kemal's movement for reform. First, he never attacked Islam directly; his tirades were reserved for the 'ecclesiastics' whose power he was, eventually, able to destroy.[26] In fact, at times, he would stand up to argue his case in sermons at Friday prayers, and invariably surprised the audience with his 'astounding knowledge of the Qur'an'.[27] The idea behind Kemal's reforms was not to 'Turkify' Islam for the sake of Turkish nationalism but rather to initiate religious enlightenment and freedom.[28] The break with the traditional concept of a politico-religious state, suggests Fazlur Rahman, was not a secular but a 'quasi-secular' measure because Islam continued to be the term of reference in Turkey.[29] As such, it would be wrong to conclude, as some do, that Mustafa Kemal had practically 'carried his Turkism into irreligion'.[30] Second, his approach was practical rather than doctrinaire and was born of Turkey's practical needs. For instance, state control was not the outcome of any socialist or fascist theory but simply a product of modernism. Third, it is argued, his reforms were brought about not just by force but also by means of persuasion through patient reasoning. Invariably, legislation would follow an elaborate exercise in winning public support. Fourth, he arrived at a decision through a process of trial and error and if he felt that his edicts had been outstretched, as in 1935 over the language reform, he would call a halt and advise moderation. Lastly, his reforms were not a continuous revolutionary movement but a result of the rapidly changing times between 1923 and 1930. The subsequent period was mostly spent in perfecting the system through a positivist-radical approach, especially in economic and cultural matters.[31] Mustafa Kemal's reforms largely succeeded because they were intrinsically sound and had the stamp of his charisma which was based on his defence of the Turkish soil 'inch-by-inch'.[32] Besides, the government over which he presided was strong, efficient, and popular.

ATATÜRK'S REFORMS AND THE MUSLIM WORLD

And, whatever the purists in revolutionary theory might say, the reforms did bring about a fundamental and lasting change in Turkey.[33]

The impact of the Kemalist revolution beyond republican Turkey must be measured cautiously because the 'Muslim world' in the 1920s and 1930s was a misnomer for the ramshackle collection of communities and countries that had survived the western imperial spoliation. The Arabs, for instance, had chosen to break away from the Ottoman connection but ended up under British and French tutelage. Thus, Palestine, Transjordan, and Iraq went to the British as mandated territories, in addition to their control of Egypt, while Lebanon and Syria were assigned to the French in addition to their suzerainty over Algeria, Morocco, and Tunisia. Later, most of Palestine was handed over to the Jews as blood money for their ill-treatment at the hands of Christian Europe, creating perpetual rifts between the Arabs and the Zionists. Only the Hashemite Hejaz was left 'independent', and it was soon taken over by the ultra-conservative Nejdis. The Gulf 'states', though a subdued part of the Muslim world, did not count whereas Central Asia, having been devoured by Soviet Russia, had virtually moved out of the Islamic orbit. In the Far East, the Indonesians were experiencing Dutch imperialism while Malaya was a British colony. India, too, was under the British and, though its Muslims had supported the Turks with the massive Khilafat movement, times had changed. Only the intellectuals and idealists among the Indians now supported Mustafa Kemal and his reforms. The pan-Islamists had largely become wary of the Turkish Nationalists for discarding the caliphate. Technically, therefore, only neighbouring Iran and Afghanistan were the two 'independent' Muslim countries where reform, particularly the Kemalist version, found an appreciative nod from the ruling élite; the reaction, elsewhere, was mixed.

The most ardent devotee of Mustafa Kemal was King Amanullah Khan of Afghanistan, who had, not long ago, won his independence, following the Third Afghan War against the British. Fired by an intense passion for nationalism, the young ruler was intent on imitating Mustafa Kemal in every way. He had inherited this enthusiasm for modernization partly from his mother who had a liberal outlook, and partly from the example of Turkey.[34] With the rise of Mustafa Kemal and his nationalists, Turco-Afghan relations took a more meaningful turn; and the Turks promised to help Afghans develop educationally and militarily.

Amanullah's reforms span two unequal periods: 1919–27 and 1928–9. During the preliminary phase, his drive for modernization comprised different strands for which he hired Egyptian, Turkish, and Indian experts in areas such as education, communications, health, economy, and administration. He built state-sponsored schools for boys and girls, sent students abroad for training, and redesigned curricula to ensure better and more enlightened talent.[35] Amanullah was passionate about the emancipation of women and he encouraged young girls to acquire education and discard the veil (*purdah*).[36] He also helped Queen Soraya, who had an enlightened upbringing in Damascus (Syria), to launch exclusive journals for the enlightenment of women, and encouraged the press generally.[37] As for public works, Amanullah regulated the health services and improved hygiene and sanitation. He also developed communications by building roads and expanding telephone and telegraph systems. To improve the legal-administrative set-up, he tried to inculcate efficiency and eradicate corruption.[38] In order to improve the economy, he regulated and strengthened trade and commerce, which were the mainstay of the Afghan financial system. This was particularly important because the country had no industrial base and, with corruption as a major impediment, made little headway towards any improvement. The one particular sphere that received priority was the reorganization of the army. This was done entirely on the basis of the Turkish and German models. Even in their uniforms, the Afghans imitated some of the items worn by Turkish soldiers, such as the *astrakhan* cap and cavalry boots.[39] This, however, does not mean that

Amanullah was able to change Afghanistan overnight or that it had, all of a sudden, become modernized and forward-looking. Far from that, Afghanistan was still a medieval state with a very conservative society. And, though the reforms were coherent and integrated, only the society's upper-class was modernized; deep down it was still tribal and traditional.

The second phase of Amanullah's reforms (1927–9) was more drastic and more controversial than the first one, and came in the wake of his seven-month long grand tour of India, Europe, and the Middle East. The purpose behind that tour was to have first-hand knowledge of the civilizations abroad, especially in Europe. Even before embarking on his tour, he had ordered the most fashionable clothing from Europe which he and his ladies would wear during their European odyssey.[40] Between December 1927 and July 1928, he visited no less than a dozen countries in which the king, the queen, and their small party were given a right royal reception that turned Afghanistan into 'a three-ring circus'.[41] Amanullah was showered with honours and praises. At Oxford, he was even awarded a doctorate *honoris causa* and made an honorary member of the Royal Geographical Society. The climax of his tour, however, was his 'pilgrimage' to Mustafa Kemal's secular Turkey and a visit to Reza Shah's westernized Iran. According to Dr Abdul Ghani, who knew the Afghan king well, Amanullah had 'a special chamber in his heart [for Mustafa Kemal], and looked upon him as a model hero. It was his ambition to be like him, and to succeed like him.'[42] On his arrival in Ankara on 20 May 1928, Amanullah was received with unusual cordiality. At the railway station, Mustafa Kemal kissed him on both cheeks and escorted him to the venue of the talks where, for over an hour, they discussed how they could best bind their people in cultural reforms.[43] In the evening, the Turkish president arranged a grand banquet at the Palace Hotel, where he showered praise on his guest's fierce spirit of independence. He also spoke of the historic bonds of friendly relations between the two countries and the common goals that they had sworn to follow.[44] Amanullah, in his speech, expressed admiration for Mustafa Kemal's work and referred to the Turks as his elder brothers and guides.[45]

Amanullah remained in Ankara for a week, where his knowledge of the Turkish language helped him bond easily with the Turks. Apart from other activities, he watched the proceedings of the GNA while it adopted a bill substituting Europeanized Arab numerals for the old Arabic ciphers.[46] From Ankara, Amanullah was taken to Istanbul where he attended a grand military parade and then sailed to Batum on board the steamer *Izmir*. But the most important event was the signing of a pact of friendship and cooperation between Turkey and Afghanistan whereby each pledged to grant the other the most-favoured-nation status. Apparently, there were no military clauses but Turkey undertook to send military, legal, and scientific experts to Afghanistan. Additionally, the status of the Turkish legation at Kabul was raised to that of an embassy, and Hikmet Bey was nominated as the first Turkish ambassador.[47] On 6 June, Amanullah was seen off from Turkey with costly presents and rare courtesy.[48] This was in sharp contrast to his earlier visit to King Fuad in Egypt (26 December 1927–5 January 1928) which had ended in a fiasco, or later to Reza Shah in Iran (6–20 June 1928), which had aroused the jealousy of his host and the wrath of the *mujtahid*s for not veiling his queen in Meshed.[49]

Was Amanullah imitating Tzar Peter the Great of Russia who had gone to Europe to learn the secrets of modernization first-hand? From his declarations, it seems that his intentions were similar. In his very first speech on returning home, he stated effusively: 'I visited Europe not for pleasure, recreation or the purpose of machinery, but in order that I might explore the real road to progress. . . . Whatever I learned will shortly be laid before the nation. It will then rest with the nation to judge which was my object—the betterment of my country and nation or the personal interests of Amanullah and Queen Soraya.'[50] Apparently, the red carpet receptions he had received from the European royalty had gone to his head and made him lose his sense of proportion. He thought that he could successfully replicate the European model of development in his own country.[51] But, when he realized the enormity of his task he was filled with 'a sense of pessimism and near failure'.[52] Yet, he decided to confront the traditionalists and those he thought would oppose the reforms. In July 1928, the king and queen took an initiative against the veil and the turban and appealed to the Afghans to discard them as they interfered with their progress.[53] Then, in August, the king convened the 'Loya Jirga' of some one thousand notables from all parts of the country, forced western dress on them, and laid bare his programme of rapid socio-economic transformation, including amendments to the constitution.[54] Even this limited programme meant considerable change in the nature and powers of the executive and the legislature within the monarchical system. Mustafa Kemal had advised Amanullah to reform the army before enforcing modernization. The advice was well received but having lost the British subsidy upon independence, Amanullah had no money to do so.[55] To raise that kind of money he would have to impose new taxes which meant placing himself in a no-win situation. The Afghan economy was unable to sustain the reforms. Being a landlocked country, Afghanistan was hugely dependent on transit trade which was at the mercy of the British who controlled the Khyber Pass and other routes to India. The dream of railways, floated by some French and German companies, would take him nowhere because the terrain was difficult and the coffers empty. So Amanullah was back to square one. A few Afghan notables agreed to copy the ways of the king and the queen but the large majority, particularly the traditionalists, were not in support of the innovations. The other contentious issues were: the education of the girls, the limits imposed on the marriageable ages of men and women, and the ban on polygamy. A clash was inevitable.[56]

While Europe honoured the Afghan king, the conservative elements at home got ready to oppose him. Mysterious hands distributed pictures of Queen Soraya unveiled and in western attire at receptions.[57] Already incensed at the loss of their power in educational and legal spheres, the mullahs, to whom Amanullah's reforms were an anathema, prepared for a showdown. They issued a proclamation that the king was a *kafir* who was leading their country away from Islam.[58] Amanullah had failed to heed the warnings heralded by several rebellions that had taken place—most serious of which had been the Khost uprising of 1924—and continued with his programme of unpopular reforms while neglecting his army. The drift was accentuated by his European tour. A very serious revolt which broke out in the Shinwari area, quickly spread to other tribes.[59] His fall and abdication in 1929, however, was not of Pashtun doing. It was spearheaded by a Tajik warlord who captured power as Amir Habibullah II before he, too, was ousted by tribal forces led by Nadir Khan.[60] The episode is symptomatic of a deeper malaise which is outside the scope of the present paper. But, one must refer to Leon Poullada's contention that social reforms were not really the cause of the conflagration as they had grudgingly found acceptance. In his opinion, 'the rebellion was primarily political in nature and was merely an aggravated recurrence of tribal separatism'.[61] In other words, what lay at the bottom of the trouble was the fear, on the part of the tribal leaders, that Amanullah's attempts to create a strong central government would effectively curtail their power and privileges. And they aligned themselves readily with the mullahs who they thought were good propagandists.[62]

Amanullah tried to treat Afghanistan as the state that he was attempting to create rather than the tribal entity that it was.[63] Anyway, the one power that could have saved Amanullah was the British, except they had no wish to bail him out. Perhaps they had realized that by rolling out the red carpet for him, they had backed the wrong horse and must make amends.[64] A rumour was then current that the British were behind the rebellion and that Lawrence of Arabia, who was then serving with the Royal Air Force in Miranshah near Peshawar, under the pseudonym of aircraftsman T.E. Shaw, was organizing it.[65] Starting with a Fleet Street rag, the story was said to have been encouraged by the Turkish and Russian embassies, and the French mission. Officially, the allegation was denied and the explanation appears to be quite satisfactory, for Lawrence had taken 'asylum' in India to recuperate from the disturbed state of his mental health. In any case, the British government thought it fit to whisk him away to England.[66] But Amanullah never forgot the supposed British complicity and chose to live in exile not in India or Britain but in Italy and Switzerland. He visited Ankara in February 1930, and Istanbul in July 1933 where Atatürk received him at the Dolmabahçe Palace, and finally in 1938 to attend the Turkish leader's funeral. When Amanullah died in April 1960, his body was taken home for burial and buried with due honour, in Jalalabad, by the side of his deceased father.[67]

The other fervent enthusiast of Mustafa Kemal's modernizing programme was Reza Shah Pahlavi of Iran. The tall, well-built soldier had come to power through a *coup d'etat* in 1921, when the country badly needed a strong central authority to put down anarchy and possible disintegration. First, he became the prime minister, and later supplanted the Qajar dynasty to claim the throne. The Majlis, though reluctant, accepted the change because there was a broad support for the new shah among the notable *'ulama*, businessmen, feudals and others. Soon, Reza Shah threw his constitutional role overboard, and by 1928 turned his dictatorship into an autocracy with no check on his arbitrary powers. 'All power corrupts and absolute power corrupts absolutely', goes the dictum of Lord Acton, and this was especially true of Reza Shah. Homa Katouzian, in her study of the change from the Qajars to the Pahlavis, makes a nuanced point by dwelling on the shah's gradual transformation from dictatorial but constitutional rule to an autocratic and irresponsible reign—as compared to Atatürk's monoparty but constitutional system that facilitated the latter's claim to legitimacy. Here, she thinks, lies the cause of Reza Shah's ultimate failure and Mustafa Kemal's success.[68]

Reza Shah's accelerated pseudo-modernism was the result of stark realism sharpened by an intense passion for nationalism. It had no ideological inspiration or intellectual content though one finds advocates of westernization among such men as Sayyed Hasan Taqizadeh, Kazemzade-Iranshahr, Amir Alam, and Muhammad Saad, most of whom came with strong religious backgrounds.[69] There was also some affinity of ideas between Mustafa Kemal and Reza Shah, whose official visit to Turkey in June 1934 was an indication of the esteem in which he held the Turkish leader and his reform programme.[70] The *rapprochement* with Turkey had also been prompted by a lurking desire to counterbalance the opposing pressures of Britain and Russia.[71] Reza Shah's reforms had already run a twelve-year course; now, he had come to try and learn from Turkey's experience and gain an ally as well.[72] Quite conscious that he was a role-model for the Iranian public, Mustafa Kemal took great pains to dazzle his guest with the success of his endeavours in Turkey. He was welcomed at the Black Sea port of Trabzon and taken to Samun and then to Ankara where Mustafa Kemal received him at the railway station. In spite of their different disposition, they clicked instantly for they had the same ideals and commitments. In the evening, a gala dinner was held in Reza Shah's honour at Çankaya where an opera, especially composed for the occasion, was performed for him. During the next few days (16–20 June), the shah attended a military review and witnessed the proceedings of the GNA as it passed the law on surnames, for all Turks, which also gave Mustafa Kemal his title of Atatürk.[73] From Ankara, the shah was taken to other parts of the country, including Istanbul, where he was housed at the Dolmabahçe Palace. There, he witnessed military manoeuvres, and then was entertained by a visit to the sensuous Eastern Nights featuring voluptuous belly dancers.[74] Reza Shah was hoping for a military alliance with Turkey but that did not materialize. However, relations between the two countries improved considerably. Reza Shah was greatly impressed by what he saw in Turkey and returned to his home country with many new ideas.[75]

Reza Shah's three-fold reform programme was centred on the cult of 'nationalism, statism, and secularism'. He thought that rapid westernization and development would bring him legitimacy, break the hold of religion, and reduce his vulnerability to imperialist designs.[76] As a prelude to modernization, Reza Shah extended the bureaucracy and created a strong army, winning for it the respect of the people. Thus armed, he took on the *ulama* to break their hold in the legal and administrative domains by redefining their jurisdiction. The focal point was educational reform under which not only did he tighten control of the religious seminaries but also established new state-sponsored free, modern schools for boys and girls. In higher education, he concentrated on disciplines such as law and politics and sent students abroad for advanced training. He created the University of Tehran by amalgamating the existing colleges. Side by side, attention was paid to trade, industry, and agriculture. Trans-Iranian Railway, though economically unnecessary, brought a certain amount of prestige to the regime. An urban rebuilding programme gave a modern look to the cities. Hygiene and sanitation also improved. Among social reforms, he ordered women to discard their veils and men to wear hats. However, Reza Shah lacked the thoroughness required for the success of the reforms. Coercion, inefficiency, haste, and waste alienated many sections of society and created conflicts and tensions. The growth of the civil service resulted in over-bureaucratization and red tape. The expansion of the armed forces cost a big chunk of the budget without any corresponding advantage. Economic difficulties were subordinated to political ambitions. The mishandling of the ban on the veil or *chadar* produced an even greater reaction. The order was brusque and inflexible, and the protests and violence led to fierce repression, especially in Meshed, over orders for men to wear bowler hats. Reza Shah failed to realize that public protest was but symptomatic of the deeper divisions in the society. By the time his exit came in 1941, Reza Shah was left with no committed support—almost exactly what had happened to Amanullah in Afghanistan a decade earlier.[77] The only enduring feature of his reforms was the restructuring of the justice department, which brought credit to the French system that was adopted as a model.[78]

Meanwhile, in Turkey, Atatürk's secular system strengthened itself under the single-party control of the Republican Peoples Party (RPP), with the armed forces and the judiciary acting as its guardians. 'The ideological void', says Erik Zürcher, 'was filled to some extent with the personality cult that grew round Mustafa Kemal during and even more after his lifetime'.[79] In the late 1940s, however, İsmet İnönü opened the floodgates to a competitive multi-party system, though religious parties had to wait until the 1950s when Celal Bayar initiated a new experiment outside the RPP.[80] The role of religion in Turkish society took a new meaning after a liberal constitution (1960) was enacted. Seven years later, an openly Islam-oriented religious party made its first appearance and then continued its ascent through the years that followed under different names, culminating eventually in the 2000s when it came into political power. The armed forces and the judiciary were never reconciled to the new situation and felt free to take power, now and then, to drive home the fact that Kemalism was alive and well. The significant thing about Turkey is that even the Islamists and Muslim democrats do not want to be seen as repudiating Kemalism. They simply want religion to have some space in Turkish society.[81] Atatürk's desire to ensure his country's position as a western nation was partly realized by Turkey's membership of NATO[82], but its affirmation remains elusive because of the tardy negotiations over its admission into the European Union. As for Turkey's place in the Muslim world, it is significant to note that the present secretary-general of the 57–member Organization of Islamic Conference (OIC), Dr Ekmeleddin Ihsanoğlu, is a Turk. But this has to be seen in the context of the OIC continuing as an assorted collection of inert Muslim countries with conflicting interests. The events of 9/11 have, strikingly, put the Muslim societies on the defensive but, sooner or later, when alternatives come up for review, an adaptation of the Turkish model for the Muslim countries might well be the answer.

NOTES

1. See Chapter Nine below.
2. The hypothesis is that when the Turks migrated from their homelands in Central Asia to the regions in the east, south and west, they brought civilization to those settlements. See Ercümend Kuran, 'The Reforms of Atatürk', in Sencer Tonguç (ed.), *The Reforms of Atatürk* (Istanbul, n.d.), 9.
3. Halil Inalcik, 'Atatürk and the Modernisation of Turkey', in Azmi Süslü (ed.), *A Handbook of Kemalist Thought* (Ankara, 2001), 152 ff.
4. See, for instance, Mim Kemal Öke, 'Turkish Decision for Secularization and the Question of Muslim Unity', in Rashid Ahmad (Jullundhri) and Muhammad Afzal Qarshi (eds.), *Islam in South Asia* (Lahore, 1995), 31–45.
5. Kemal H. Karpat, 'The Transformation of the Ottoman State, 1789–1908', in id., *Studies on Ottoman Social and Political History* (Leiden, 2002), 27–74. Also see Ali Kazancigil and Ergun Özbudun, 'Introduction', id., (eds.), *Atatürk*, 2–3.
6. Karpat, 'The Transformation of the Ottoman State, 1789–1908', 48–54; and Kenneth Cragg, *Counsels in Contemporary Islam* (Edinburgh, 1965), 145.
7. Kuran, 'The Reforms of Atatürk', 11–12.
8. Ibid., 12.
9. He described history as the 'defining science'. See Azmi Süslü, 'Atatürk and History', in id. (ed.), *A Handbook of Kemalist Thought*, esp., 169–76.
10. Enver Ziya Karal, 'The Principles of Kemalism', in Kazancigil and Özbudun, (eds.), *Atatürk*, 13–14.
11. S.N. Eisenstadt, 'The Kemalist Regime and Modernization: Some Comparative and Analytical Remarks', in Jacob M. Landau (ed.), *Atatürk and the Modernization of Turkey* (Boulder & Leiden, 1984), 14.
12. Ismet Giritli, 'Kemalism as an Ideology of Modernization', in Landau (ed.), *Atatürk and the Modernization of Turkey*, 251; and id., 'The Superiority of the Kemalist Ideology over Dogmatic Ideologies', in Süslü (ed.), *A Handbook of Kemalist Thought*, 126.
13. Sulhi Dönmezer, 'Atatürk's Revolution and Social Change', in ibid., 6.
14. Ali Kazancigil and Ergun Özbudun, 'Introduction', id., (eds.), *Atatürk*, 2–3; Ali Kazancigil, 'The Ottoman-Turkish State and Kemalism', ibid., 37 ff; and Paul Dumont, 'The Origins of Kemalist Ideology', in Landau (ed.), *Atatürk and the Modernization of Turkey*, 35.

15. See Enver Ziya Karal, 'The Principles of Kemalism', in Kazancigil and Özbudun, (eds.), *Atatürk*, esp., 16–23; and several contributions on Kemalism by Sulhi Dönmezer, Hamza Eroğlu, Turhan Feyzioğlu, Yücel Özkaya, Mustafa Aysan, Ethem Ruhi Fiğlali, Ismet Giritli, Ergun Özbudun, Halil Inalcik, Azmi Süslü, Zeynep Korkmaz, Yahya Akyüz, Bekir Tünay, Emel Doğramaci, Ilker Alp, Mehmet Gönlübol, and Omer Kürkçüoğlu, in Süslü (ed.), *A Handbook of Kemalist Thought*, passim.
16. Şerif Mardin, *The Genesis of Young Ottoman Thought*, 103.
17. See clauses 70, 75, and 80 in light of Mustafa Kemal's pronouncement that: 'Religion is a matter of conscience. Everyone is at liberty to act in accordance with their conscience. We respect religion. We are not opposed to thought and reflection …' quoted in Ethem Ruhi Fiğlali, 'Atatürk, Religion and Laicism', in Süslü (ed.), *A Handbook of Kemalist Thought*, esp., 115–16, citing Sadi Borak, *Atatürk ve Din* (Istanbul, 1962), 57.
18. A series of events, such as the Seyh Sait rebellion, the Menemen incident, and the opposition's role generally, had prompted the action against them. See ibid., 117–18.
19. M.R. Feroze, *Islam and Secularism in Post-Kemalist Turkey* (Islamabad, 1976), 86.
20. Ibid., 87. On secularism also see Alisabeth Özdalga, *The Veiling Issue, Official Secularism and Popular Islam in Modern Turkey* (Richmond, 1998), esp., 17–31.
21. Ibid., 88.
22. Vamik D. Volkan and Norman Itzkowitz, *The Immortal Atatürk* (Chicago, 1984), 258.
23. Feroze, *Islam and Secularism in Post-Kemalist Turkey*, 90–1.
24. Inalcik, 'Atatürk and the Modernisation of Turkey', 154.
25. Jacob M. Landau, 'Atatürk's Achievement: Some Considerations', in id. (ed.), *Atatürk and the Modernization of Turkey*, xi.
26. 'Religion is a necessary institution', he said in 1930. 'There is no possibility for a nation to carry on without religion. There is one point, though, and that is the tie between Allah and slave. The religious intervention of the fanatical Islamists should not be allowed. Those who procure material benefits from religion are detestable. Thus, we are against the situation and we do not allow it …' See Fiğlali, 'Atatürk, Religion and Laicism', esp., 112–13, citing Kiliç Ali, *Atatürk'ün Hususiyetleri* (Ankara, 1930), 116.
27. Detlev H. Khalid, 'A Study of Atatürk's Laicism in the Light of Muslim History', in Tonguç (ed.), *The Reforms of Atatürk*, 61; and Fiğlali, 'Atatürk, Religion and Laicism', 109–10. Dunkwart Rustow provides evidence of a 'strongly religious tinge' in the early stages of the Kemalist movement. See his 'Politics and Islam in Turkey, 1920–1955', in Richard N. Frye (ed.), *Islam and the West*, 71–3.

28. Niyazi Berkes, *The Development of Secularism in Turkey*, 484.
29. See F. Rahman, 'Internal Religious Developments in the Present Century Islam', *Journal of World History*, 2/1 (1954), 876.
30. Cragg definitely believes that he did. See his *Counsels in Contemporary Islam*, 147.
31. Kuran, 'The Reforms of Atatürk', 10–11; and T.B. Millar, 'Turkey', in M. Ayoob, *The Politics of Islamic Reassertion* (London, 1981), 81–94.
32. Abdülhamid had been damned precisely for having failed to do that. See Mardin, *The Genesis of Young Ottoman Thought*, 364–5.
33. Diana Spearman & M. Naim Turfan, 'The Turkish Language Reform', *History Today* (1979), 29/2, 89.
34. In a picture taken around 1905, his father, Amir Habibullah Khan, is seen flanked by his wives, all in western clothes. See Leon B. Poullada, *Reform and Rebellion in Afghanistan, 1919–1929* (Ithaca, 1973), 37.
35. Ibid., 239 ff.
36. Roland Wild, *Amanullah: Ex-King of Afghanistan* (London, 1932), 68; and Abdul Ghani, *A Brief Political History of Afghanistan* (ed.), Abdul Jaleel Najfi (Lahore, 1989), 666–9.
37. Vertan Gregorian, *The Emergence of Modern Afghanistan: Politics of Reform and Modernization, 1880–1946* (California, 1969), 240–4.
38. Ibid., 244–52.
39. Ibid., 252–4; and Abdul Ghani, *A Brief Political History of Afghanistan*, 676.
40. Ibid., 671.
41. Louis Dupree, *Afghanistan*, 3rd edn. (Princeton, 1980), 450.
42. Abdul Ghani, *A Brief Political History of Afghanistan*, 673.
43. *Civil & Military Gazette* (Lahore), 24 May 1928.
44. *Pioneer* (Lucknow), 24 May 1928; and Gregorian, *The Emergence of Modern Afghanistan*, 256–8. Mustafa Kemal's favourite metaphors, which he used at the reception, were: 'The sun which is dawning on the high horizon of the future is the talisman of the nations who have suffered for centuries. This talisman's never again being [sic] enveloped in dark clouds is dependent upon the scrupulous solicitude and self-sacrifice of those nations and their leaders'. See Volkan and Itzkowitz, *The Immortal Atatürk*, citing Utkan Kocatürk, *Atatürk ve Türk devrimi kronolojisi* (Ankara, 1973), 323.
45. Gregorian, *The Emergence of Modern Afghanistan*, 256–8.
46. *Civil & Military Gazette*, 24 May 1928.
47. *Pioneer*, 30 May and 3 June 1928.
48. *Civil & Military Gazette*, 25 May 1928. In Istanbul, Amanullah also visited the Topkapi Palace which housed the sacred relics of the Prophet but when he expressed his desire to step inside the chamber he was politely told that the custodian's key

would not open the hall. See Rhea Talley Stewart, *Fire in Afghanistan, 1914–1929: Faith, Hope and the British Empire* (New York, 1973), 365–6.
49. See Stewart, *Fire in Afghanistan*, 327–8 and 366–8; and Roland Wild, *Amanullah: Ex-King of Afghanistan* (London, 1932), 100–3.
50. Quoted in Stewart, *Fire in Afghanistan*, 369.
51. Wild, *Amanullah*, 99–100, 107 and 119–21. Also see Gregorian, *The Emergence of Modern Afghanistan*, 259.
52. Gregorian, *The Emergence of Modern Afghanistan*, 258.
53. Stewart, *Fire in Afghanistan*, 375–80.
54. Gregorian, *The Emergence of Modern Afghanistan*, 259.
55. See Rob Hager, 'State, Tribes and Empire in Afghan Inter-Polity Relations', in Richard Tapper (ed.), *The Conflict of Tribes and State in Iran and Afghanistan* (London & Canberra, 1983), 105.
56. Gregorian, *The Emergence of Modern Afghanistan*, 260.
57. Dupree, *Afghanistan*, 450.
58. Stewart, *Fire in Afghanistan*, 390–1.
59. Ludwig W. Adamec, *Historical and Political Who's Who of Afghanistan* (Austria, 1975), 118.
60. See Tapper's introduction to his edited work, *The Conflict of Tribes and State in Iran and Afghanistan*, esp., 36–7.
61. Poullada, *Reform and Rebellion in Afghanistan*, 144–52.
62. Ibid., 152–9.
63. Tapper's introduction in *The Conflict of Tribes and State in Iran and Afghanistan*, 37.
64. Wild, *Amanullah*, 119–21.
65. Phillip Knightly and Colin Simpson, *The Secret Lives of Lawrence of Arabia* (London, 1969), 197–9, 232–7.
66. Ibid., 197–9 and 232–7.
67. Adamec, *Historical and Political Who's Who of Afghanistan*, 118–9; and Andrew Mango, *Atatürk* (London, 1999), 488.
68. Homa Katouzian, *State and Society in Iran: The Eclipse of the Qajars and the Emergence of the Pahlavis* (London, 2000), 314.
69. S.M.A. Sayeed, *Iran: Before and After Khomeini* (Karachi, 1999), 87–8.
70. Salim Neysari, 'A Comparison of the Activities Related to the Language and Writing Reforms in Turkey and Iran During the Time of Atatürk and Reza Shah', in Tonguç (ed.), *The Reforms of Atatürk*, 45–6.
71. General Hassan Arfa, *Under Five Shahs* (London, 1964), 243–4.
72. Ibid., 246.
73. Ibid., 248–9.

74. Volkan and Itzkowitz, *The Immortal Atatürk*, 323–5.
75. Arfa, *Under Five Shahs*, 252.
76. Amin Banani, *The Modernization of Iran* (Stanford, 1961), 45.
77. Ibid., 313–33; and Joseph M. Upton, *The History of Modern Iran: An Interpretation* (Cambridge, Massachusetts, 1961), 55–7.
78. Katouzian, *State and Society in Iran*, 313 ff; and Shahrough Akhavi, *Religion and Politics in Contemporary Iran: Clergy-State Relations in Pahlavi Period* (Albany, 1980), 40–3.
79. Zürcher, *Turkey: A Modern History*, 190.
80. Feroz Ahmad, *The Turkish Experiment in Democracy, 1950–1975* (London, 1977), 8 ff.; and David Westerlund and Ingvar Svaberg, *Islam Outside the Arab World* (London, 1999), 140–3.
81. Ilter Turan, 'Religion and Political Culture in Turkey', in Richard Tapper (ed.), *Islam in Modern Turkey: Religion, Politics and Literature in a Secular State* (London & New York, 1991), 31–55.
82. George S. Harris, *Turkey: Coping with Crisis* (Boulder & London, 1985), 180.

9

The Kemalist Model of State and Ayub Khan's Structural Reforms in Pakistan*

The most remarkable achievement of Atatürk was the establishment of a sovereign, homogeneous, and unitary nation state out of a 'devastated country on the edge of a precipice'.[1] Even more extraordinary was its transformation into a modern secular 'state of the people', in sharp contrast to the multi-religious Ottoman Empire from whose ashes it had risen. Atatürk accomplished all this despite heavy odds and in the teeth of very strong opposition from various elements within the country. Between the declaration of Turkey as a republic in October 1923 and the death of Atatürk in November 1938, the political as well as the entire socio-economic and religio-cultural fabric of Turkey underwent a change that was both profound and comprehensive. Within a single generation, the country had been transformed and, in significant respects, elevated from a traditional Islamic community to a modern secular society, at least in the urban areas, through the sweep of Kemalism—Turkey's pragmatic approach to modernization and secularization. The impact of the Kemalist revolution on the

---

*Published originally in the *Proceedings of Fourth Atatürk International Congress, 25–29 October 1999, Turkistan, Kazakhistan* (Ankara, 2000), 1089–99.

THE KEMALIST MODEL OF STATE AND AYUB KHAN'S STRUCTURAL REFORMS

contemporary Muslim world, especially in countries where colonial rule had had a long history, is worth examining. This chapter attempts to study Atatürk's appeal in a latter-day scenario when another military ruler, Ayub Khan of Pakistan, tried to introduce modernization and certain features of secularism in somewhat different circumstances. The intention is to trace points of convergence and divergence in the ideals and aspirations of the two leaders, and to measure the relative success or failure of the two processes of modernization.

Kemalism, to its proponents, had a scientific and philosophical basis; its underlying idea was to root out those institutions that obstructed the progress of the Turkish people, and replace them with ones that facilitated progress. It did not advocate a sudden and total break with the Ottoman past; rather, it was the 'intensification, radicalisation and culmination' of that process, which had been taking place for over a century.[2] Indeed, the Kemalist *inkilab*, instead of being a break with the past, was 'an extension' of the nineteenth century reform movement.[3] Though the Kemalist principles were announced in a manifesto in April 1931, Atatürk had been explaining and implementing them for years. Using his prestige and charisma, he had moved with determination and took a series of calculated but bold steps from the abolition of the caliphate in 1924 to the declaration that Turks were Westerners in 1934. Thus, within a decade, he was able to overhaul the entire state structure by abolishing religious institutions and introducing purely secular ones in their place. Suffice it say that, in a short period of time, Turkey was secularized and religion made a matter of individual conscience—though state grants and *waqf*s were remained in use for the upkeep of religious infrastructure. But since the men who controlled the destiny of Turkey were committed secularists, they assiduously fashioned Turkish society in the European cultural matrix. Those who did not subscribe to this ideal were simply sidelined. This was a tremendous social change and very few countries have ever had a comparable experience.

At least three trends are discernible in Atatürk's progression towards his political goal. First, there is the frequent use of Islamic terminology during the early period in order to convince the people that Islam is compatible with nationalism. Second, he displays ideas of secular nationalism, which have a remarkable resemblance with those of Ziya Gökalp. Lastly, he conveys, particularly during the later years, a positivist and radical line of thinking.[4] But, though Atatürk advocated a break with Turkey's Ottoman past and a total assumption of westernization, he never attacked Islam. His tirades were reserved for the *'ulama* whose power he eventually smashed by abolishing the religious affairs ministry and banning the Sufi orders.[5] Atatürk's reforms succeeded because, among other things, they were directed by a government that was 'strong, efficient and persuasive'.[6] And, whatever the purists in revolutionary theory might say, the reforms commenced a revolution that brought about a fundamental change and left a lasting impression.[7]

The impact of the Kemalist revolution was felt far beyond the political confines of republican Turkey. Not only were the neighbouring Iran, Iraq, and Afghanistan stirred by Atatürk's ideals and principles, but other developing nations of Asia and Africa also came under their influence. Atatürk's modernizing spurt, envisaging a radical transformation of state and society, seemed to attract the ruling élite of these countries in their pursuit of nationalistic goals.[8] In Muslim India, too, the influence of Atatürk had been quite visible though the leaders often had reservations regarding perceptions and methodology. Others, like Mohammad Iqbal, who fully understood and admired the Turkish experiment, held themselves back—but only temporarily, coming out in full support later—because the magnitude of its secular thrust was much too frightening for them.[9]

Nearly a decade after Atatürk's passing away, when Pakistan won its independence in August 1947, there began a long debate on the kind of socio-political framework the new state should adopt. Mohammad Ali

Jinnah, the founder, who had led, in the words of a perceptive writer, 'a secular campaign to create a state based on religion',[10] baulked at the idea of experimenting with the Turkish model. He opted for the continuation of the British 'viceregal system' of governance, hoping that it would one day blossom into a more workable alternative, imbibing the religio-cultural values of Islam.[11] But the traditionalists, both among those who had supported the Pakistan movement and others who had originally opposed it, wanted to turn the country into a kind of 'citadel of Islam' with the *shari'at* as its cornerstone.[12] In the rough and tumble of post-Jinnah Pakistan, most western-educated, modernist élite also became attracted to this ideal. The result was the Objectives Resolution, passed by the Constituent Assembly of Pakistan in March 1949 at Premier Liaquat Ali Khan's bidding which plotted the contours of the country as an 'Islamic' state.[13] Dr Ishtiaq Husain Qureshi, a Cambridge-educated modernist and one of the architects of the original draft, was very clear about the spirit behind the move: 'The moral concepts of our people are based upon the teachings of our religion. If, therefore, the polity of Pakistan is to be based on a firm foundation of a religious ideology, there is no motive force, but that of Islam which can act as the basis.'[14] The Objectives Resolution was adopted by an overwhelming majority, much to the chagrin of the secularists and non-Muslim members of the house, and the liberals, who generally found it difficult to reconcile with it. And yet, in spite of this strong expression of Islamic bias, the constitution of 1956 essentially proclaimed a liberal democratic structure of a western parliamentary type with no hint of any dogmatically theocratic construct.[15] The question of ideological bearings, however, remained a contentious issue and, combined with socio-economic and political factors, became the cause of deep and persistent crises between the divergent groups. In this atmosphere of political chaos, successive governments fell rapidly and, between 1950 and 1958, there were as many as seven prime ministers compared to only one in India who remained in office from 1947 until his death in 1964.

Ayub Khan's ascent to power in 1958 was the direct result of this instability. Born in a small village of the Frontier, Ayub Khan was educated at the Aligarh Muslim University and the Royal Military College, Sandhurst (commissioned, 1928). He held various staff and command positions under the British before rising, in 1951, to be the first native C-in-C of the Pakistan Army. From 1954–55, he had first-hand experience of politics when he served in the cabinet as minister of defence. Apart from his personal considerations, it was the army's disenchantment with the state of affairs in the country that drove him, in 1958, to force President Iskander Mirza to impose martial law.[16] Mirza, realizing that he stood no chance of being re-elected in a parliamentary democracy, willingly obliged. Ayub had his own designs and, in a counter coup a few days later, assumed the presidency himself. In 1960, he manoeuvred to get his position confirmed through a referendum and, in early 1965, was re-elected under the new electoral system that he had created. Gradually, his popularity began to slip, the decline becoming particularly steep after the 1965 Indo-Pakistan War, and, he was forced to resign in March 1969. He spent the rest of his life in retirement in Islamabad, the capital city that he had conceived and built.[17]

Ayub Khan perceived himself as Pakistan's second founder, with a license to reshape his country's structures in every area of national life.[18]. During his ten years in office, Ayub Khan virtually shook the state structure by his modernizing zeal which displayed traces of Atatürk's influence—though some would pick Brigadier Abdul Karim Kassem's coup in Iraq in 1958 as the closest model, historically, and perhaps also in operational terms.[19] The similarities between the Atatürk's Turkish model and Ayub Khan's experiment are to be found essentially in the nature of the respective military oligarchies that they led and in the thrust of their reforms. The difference between the two leaders was that the latter hovered uneasily between secularism and modernism, and that his plans were usually obstructed by his opponents.

THE KEMALIST MODEL OF STATE AND AYUB KHAN'S STRUCTURAL REFORMS

Among the first steps that the military government in Pakistan took, after taking power in 1958, was the abrogation of the 1956 constitution, dismissal of the central and provincial governments, dissolution of the national and provincial assemblies, and the outlawing of political parties—followed moves to restore political stability and sponsor a programme of socio-economic development. Drastic measures were taken against corrupt politicians and civil servants, which included at least two former prime ministers, 150 ex-ministers, about 600 'demobilized' parliamentarians, and as many as 1662 civil servants.[20] Action was also taken against smugglers, tax evaders, black marketers, and corrupt elements generally, enriching national coffers by millions of rupees. The martial law regime also made a bid for uplifting the fortunes of the common man. Prices of commodities of daily use were slashed and re-fixed, rehabilitation of refugees from India was undertaken, sanitation works were completed, land reforms were introduced to break the power of the landed aristocracy, wide-ranging economic improvements with emphasis on private enterprises were initiated, exports were encouraged, and agricultural production was boosted.[21]

Even more profound were the political and social reforms, especially the introduction of the 'Basic Democracies' (1959) and the initiation of the family laws (1961). 'Basic Democracies' was a four-tiered, 'grass-roots' system of local government, rising upward from the village to the divisional level. The members of the union councils, which numbered 80,000, also acted as an electoral college to elect the president and the members of the national and provincial assemblies. It was an indigenous model, based on non-party lines, and not imitative of the Kemalist experiment. Its ultimate collapse was the result, partly, of the structural flaws that compromised the democratic principles and, partly, of the autocratic nature of the bureaucracy that managed the system.[22] Yet, it survived the two elections of 1962 and 1965 and enabled a vast majority of illiterate people to have a taste of the democratic process along with economic development.[23] Ayub Khan hated political parties and tried his best to root them out of the political system through a centralized, authoritative government, committed to accomplishing material progress. But this was not to be. The results of elections to the 'Basic Democracies' indicated that the majority of the legislators were former politicians or their nominees.[24] In fact, within a year after 1962, Ayub Khan was forced to lift the ban on political parties.

The Muslim Family Laws Ordinance, which was meant to check polygamy, proved more enduring, though it initially encountered—as it does even today—considerable opposition from the *ulama* and the traditionalists. The ordinance provided, *inter alia*, for the registration of marriages and divorces, mandatory permission through a legal process for second and subsequent marriages, acknowledgement of the wife's right of divorce and an assurance of adequate maintenance, and the fixing of the legal marriageable age for both, males and females.[25] The attack on this ordinance, dubbed as un-Islamic, was persistent and vociferous and Ayub Khan was never forgiven for his audacity. The principal agents of criticism were the religio-political journals, like the *Shahab* and the *Asia*, which often became targets of official repression, as were the *ulama* and the right-wing politicians. Mian Tufail Muhammad, secretary-general of the Jama'at-i Islami, who published the *ulama*'s *fatwa*s against the Family Laws in book form, became a marked man and was prosecuted and imprisoned for eight and a half months.[26] In another move, Ayub Khan cleverly got the ordinance excluded from review by the courts of law.[27] Quite apart from the criticism against the ordinance, this piece of legislation still remains a testimony to Ayub Khan's modernizing ardour.

After dismantling the old order, Ayub Khan set about rebuilding the state structure in accordance with his own ideas. The most pressing item on his agenda was the designing of the new constitution. He had, of course, one consolation. The Supreme Court had tacitly extended him legitimacy by recognizing the existence of his regime as 'a basic law-creating fact'.²⁸ But, like a benevolent dictator of the medieval times, Ayub Khan sincerely believed that he had been given the inalienable right to proceed with his reforms without consulting the people. As one of his close associates has recalled, he had no concept that real legitimacy stems from the popular mandate or that the decision-making process requires the full and free participation of the people.²⁹ He preferred a strong central government under a presidential system like the French or the Egyptian models. The Turkish model, which has a constitutional role for the army, was glossed over, perhaps for its uncertain utility. But parliamentary democracy was certainly out.³⁰

In January 1960, when he was secure in the saddle as the president, Ayub Khan appointed a constitution commission under Justice Shahabuddin (1895–1971). The commission took about fifteen months to write its report—one that turned out to be what Ayub Khan had desired. The views of the traditionalist *ulama* and defunct politicians were intentionally ignored.³¹ Instead of releasing the report to the press, it was handed over to Manzur Qadir, the leading lawyer in the cabinet, to do the drafting based on the preferences outlined in a 23-page memo from the president. The constitution was promulgated on 1 March 1962, amidst considerable opprobrium from its opponents.³² As expected, the focal point of the system was the president who, though elected indirectly by an electoral college, enjoyed sweeping powers. As the chief executive, the president could appoint cabinet ministers, provincial governors, judges of the Supreme Court, and other high state functionaries. In addition to the executive powers, he enjoyed extensive legislative and financial powers.³³

It is difficult to place the Ayubian 'revolution' in a theoretical straitjacket by classifying it as one of the models of nation-building.³⁴ As a radical military regime, it should have been inspired by the Kemalist example. The position in Pakistan, however, was more complex. The Ayub Khan regime was the product of a power structure in which the army had gradually acquired ascendancy.³⁵ Basically, the regime rested on an alliance between the civil and military bureaucracy, the feudal aristocracy, and the emergent middle class. The path that Ayub Khan took was clearly defined by a policy of political integration, stimulation of national consciousness, and economic development of the country. Like Atatürk, Islam was not his central concern as he proceeded to secularize the processes of government and make them acceptable to the people through modernist interpretations. He criticized the *'ulama* for their obscurantism and hostility towards those demanding a change.[36] But, after an initial spurt of reform when he tried to defy the traditionalists by changing the rules of the game and even altering the official name of the state from the 'Islamic Republic of Pakistan' to just 'Pakistan', Ayub Khan reverted to the familiar path of religious symbolism the moment he realized that the opposition had grown very strong. He began to profess that Pakistan was an ideological state and that its ideology was Islam.[37] Thereafter, unlike Atatürk's policy, it was more a synthesis of religious and secular ideals than a concern for realism, and Khan shifted his weight whenever and wherever it appeared advantageous. The entire structure was geared to legitimizing his regime and subverting the party system.[38] But his secularist tendencies were frustrated by the old guard in the National Assembly, who demanded that he restore the Islamic features of the 1956 constitution. When cornered, Ayub Khan manoeuvred to make sure that the amendments were merely aspirations and not mandatory commands that had to be obeyed without demur.[39] Nevertheless, the fact remains that in spite of the backing of a strong military-civil bureaucratic élite, Ayub Khan was unable to pass himself off to the people as an Atatürk.

Shrewd, intelligent, and steeped in western cultural traditions though he was, Ayub Khan was not a philosopher or an intellectual like Atatürk and, as such, he offered no philosophy. But he was a pragmatist who wished to see his country firmly on the road to modernization. Therefore, he made sure that religion did not encroach on politics. He wanted Islam to be modernized and made compatible with science. If

THE KEMALIST MODEL OF STATE AND AYUB KHAN'S STRUCTURAL REFORMS

Atatürk followed Ziya Gökalp as his philosopher-mentor, no matter how selectively, Ayub Khan interpreted Islam the same way through the writings of Iqbal and Syed Ahmed Khan. He convinced himself that the perimeters of Islam could be limited to 'a recognized corpus of specific writings and doctrine'.[40] He scorned the *'ulama*, particularly Mualana Maududi of the Jama'at-i Isłami, whose demands for an Islamic State with the *shari'at* as the basic law of the land conflicted with his own. As a result he came down rather heavily against the religious opposition and compelled it to retreat, at least for the time being.[41] He pinned his hopes on the Council of Islamic Ideology, as well as the Islamic Research Institute, whose director, Dr Fazlur Rahman, was a modernist, and whom he later reluctantly dismissed only to save himself from the wrath of his religious adversaries.[42] He also encouraged Ghulam Ahmad Parwez, editor of the religious magazine, *Tulu'-i Islam* (Lahore), to support his modernist plans.[43]

In order to bridle the *'ulama*, Ayub Khan did what Atatürk had done in Turkey. He curbed the autonomy of the traditional madrasas by 'nationalizing' them along with the *waqfs*, and bringing them in line with the state policy.[44] A thorough survey of the madrasas was conducted and a policy regarding them was framed. Deprived of their income and autonomy, the *'ulama* tried to organize themselves; but, they were unable to withstand the governments' overwhelming power of coercion and patronage since they were divided doctrinally.[45] In matters of the constitution and the state, also, Ayub was not moved by any doctrinaire considerations; he only followed the notions he was familiar with, i.e., Islamic historical experience tempered by the western experiment. And he tried to assert that, as in Turkey, the army in Pakistan was the only effective vehicle of modernization and he, Ayub Khan, was its sole, strong, and authoritative handler.

If a final comparison was to be drawn between the Pakistani and Turkish situations, one must analyse the objectives and strategies that Ayub Khan and Atatürk followed. As Umit Berkman has suggested, the political goals sought in Pakistan were more radical than those implemented in Turkey but Ayub Khan's government lacked the capacity to follow through with the plans in practical terms. Berkman, like Hasan Askari Rizvi, argues that the reforms in Turkey emanated from the government and in Ayub Khan's case from the military oligarchy.[46] Atatürk's objective in Turkey was to attain a level of civilization that the West had achieved by transforming the socio-political structure of the state and affecting a complete break with the recent past.[47] Ayub Khan's targets and tactics were not much different but he followed, if at all, only a diluted form of the Turkish model. His own vacillations, and resistance from opponents, dissipated even this borrowing. Like Atatürk, he also tried to establish a single-party system but failed to endear himself to the masses. His passion for Turkey was evident from the enthusiasm he displayed in working with Turkey in CENTO where Pakistan, along with Iran, had a key role to play.[48] This affinity, apart from the geo-strategic realities, perhaps had a historical background connected to his unique experience at Aligarh where, he admitted, he learnt to 'feel like a Muslim' and imbibed the spirit of 'equality, brotherhood, and camaraderie'.[49]

When compared with the system that Atatürk had built and which survives even today, Ayub Khan's system was quickly dismantled after him. This was not due to the failure of modernism in Pakistan, which supposedly slipped back in the face of the broader current of Islamic revivalism,[50] but it collapsed because it was not built on secure foundations as in Turkey. Ayub Khan was unable to break away from the religious anchor that supposedly held the two wings of the country together.[51] Even today, when the geography of the country is much more compact, the same predicament defies the solution to the myriad of problems facing the country. Some believe that there can be no end to instability in Pakistan 'unless religion is privatized ... and passions [in whatever form]... eliminated from politics'.[52] With a string of martial law regimes that followed Ayub Khan, a deliberate notion was but insidiously spread that the armed forces were the only effective and efficient instrument of change. This was despite the fact that these regimes had been coercive in nature and autocratic in action. Militarily, also, there had been quite a few blunders—Yahya Khan lost the entire eastern wing, Ziaul Haq conceded almost 3000 kilometres of Siachen region in the Karakoram, and Pervez Musharraf caused a near-disaster by his Kargil misadventure.

Yet, the military regimes managed to thrive through repressive legislations, political collaborations, and catchy slogans like 'reforms', 'accountability', 'Islamization', and 'enlightened moderation'.[53] As to the replication of the Turkish model, the solitary example was that of Musharraf who half-heartedly tried to portray Atatürk as his source of inspiration and thus secure a tangible role for the armed forces in the governing of the country.[54] This evoked angry responses from both the religious right as well as the modernist left. The leaders of the Jama'at-i Islami, in particular, fumed at him for trying to follow secularism of a Turkish hue when the motto of the armed forces was 'faith, piety and *jihad*'.[55] The army reacted by warning the *'ulama* against using the mosque as a political platform.[56] The intermittent military interventions in politics might have been thwarted if the civilian 'interregnums' were strong, upright, and competent. But, deprived of a role for so long and bereft of moral and political grit, the politicians brooded and blundered till another military dictator took over the reigns of the government which happened repeatedly. In Turkey, the civilian dispensation had been able to secure its primacy after much struggle whereas in Pakistan the tussle remains ongoing until a stable political system is finally established.

NOTES

1. See Atatürk's speech of 9 May 1935, in Afetinan, *A History of the Turkish Revolution and Turkish Republic*. Eng. tr. Ahmet E. Uysal (Ankara, 1981), 135.

2. Ali Kazancigil and Ergun Özbudun, 'Introduction', id., (eds.), *Atatürk: Founder of a Modern State*, 2–3; and Ali Kazancigil, 'The Ottoman-Turkish state and Kemalism', ibid., 37 ff.
3. Paul Dumont, 'The Origins of Kemalist Ideology', in Jacob M. Landau (ed.), *Atatürk and the Modernization of Turkey*, 35.
4. M.R. Feroze, *Islam and Secularism in Post-Kemalist Turkey* (Islamabad, 1976), 94.
5. T.B. Millar, 'Turkey', in M. Ayoob, *The Politics of Islamic Reassertion* (London, 1981), 81.
6. Ibid., 81.
7. Diana Spearman & M. Naim Turfan, 'The Turkish Language Reform', *History Today* (1979), 29/2, 89.
8. For the electoral system as it developed in Turkey, see Feroz Ahmad, *The Turkish Experiment in Democracy, 1950–1975* (London, 1977), 3.
9. See Chapter Five.
10. Keith Callard, *Pakistan, a Political Study* (London, 1957), 200.
11. See, e.g., his speech in the Constituent Assembly dated 11 August 1947, in Government of Pakistan, *Quaid-i-Azam Mohammad Ali Jinnah: Speeches and Statements as Governor General of Pakistan, 1947–48* (Islamabad, 1989), 42–7.
12. This debate can be followed in Sharif al Mujahid, *Ideological Orientation of Pakistan* (Islamabad, 1976), esp. 1–104.
13. On 7 March 1949, Liaquat declared on the floor of the Constituent Assembly that in achieving Pakistan, 'the Muslims League has only fulfilled half of its mission. The other half of its mission was to convert Pakistan into a laboratory where we could experiment upon the principles of Islam.' For the full debate on the Resolution, see Constituent Assembly of Pakistan, *Debates: Official Report*, 5/1–5, 1–102. Also see M. Rafique Afzal, *Pakistan: History and Politics, 1947–1971* (Karachi, 2001), 65–7.
14. See his presidential address to the third session of the All-Pakistan Political Science Conference, held at Lahore on 5–7 March 1950, in Aziz Ahmad (ed.), *Proceedings of the First All-Pakistan Political Science Conference, 1950* (Lahore, 1950), 1–5. Also see Sharif al Mujahid, *Ideological Orientation of Pakistan*, esp. 108.
15. Lawrence Ziring, *Pakistan: The Enigma of Political Development* (Boulder, 1980), 35. For the 1956 Constitution, see Government of Pakistan, *Constitutional Documents (Pakistan)*, iii (Karachi, 1964), 171–343.
16. Khalid bin Sayeed, *The Political System of Pakistan* (Boston, 1967), 93.
17. See Mohammad Ayub Khan, *Friends Not Masters: A Political Autobiography* (Karachi, 1967), *passim*; and Altaf Gauhar, *Ayub Khan* (Lahore, 1993), 35–63.

18. See Sir Morrice James, *Pakistan Chronicle* (ed.), Peter Lyon (London, 1993), 171. Sir Morris was the British high commissioner in Pakistan from 1962 to 1965. He compares Ayub Khan with Napoleon for his diligence and capacity for hard work.
19. Mohammad Waseem, *Politics and the State in Pakistan*, 2nd edn. (Islamabad 1994), 142.
20. Sayeed, *The Political System of Pakistan*, 93–4, citing *Pakistan Observer*, 28 June and 11 Aug. 1959.
21. Ibid., 94–8, citing various sources.
22. For details, see George M. Platt, 'Basic Democracies: The Experiment in Local Government', in S.H. Hashmi (ed.), *The Governing Process in Pakistan, 1958–69* (Lahore, 1987), 215–71.
23. Sayeed, *The Political System of Pakistan*, 245 ff.
24. M. Rafique Afzal, *Political Parties in Pakistan, 1958–1969*, ii (Islamabad, 1987), 20–1.
25. Freeland Abbott, 'Pakistan and the Secular State', in Donald E. Smith (ed.), *South Asian Politics and Religion* (Princeton, 1966), 364–5.
26. Rafique Afzal, *Political Parties in Pakistan*, ii, 18.
27. Abbott, 'Pakistan and the Secular State', 366.
28. See State vs. Doso, 1958, PLD 1958, Supreme Court, cited in Gauhar, *Ayub Khan*, 157.
29. Gauhar, *Ayub Khan*, 159–60.
30. Rafique Afzal, *Political Parties in Pakistan*, ii, 22–3.
31. Ibid., 17–18.
32. Ibid., 185–91.
33. For the 1962 constitution, see Government of Pakistan, *Constitutional Documents (Pakistan)*, v (Karachi, 1964), 1–356.
34. Jerzy J. Wiatr, 'Kemalism and the Models of Nation Building', *I. Uluslararasi Atatürk Sempozyumu, 21–23 Eylul 1987* (Ankara, 1994), 567.
35. Waseem, *Politics and the State in Pakistan*, 95–7.
36. Anwar Syed, *Pakistan: Islam, Politics and National Solidarity* (Lahore, 1984), 123.
37. Ibid, 121.
38. For a discussion of the 1962 Constitution, see Afzal Iqbal, *Islamisation of Pakistan* (Delhi, 1984), 75–83. For the politics of the period, see Rafique Afzal, *Political Parties in Pakistan*, ii, *passim*. Also see M. Rafique Afzal, 'Political Parties' in Hashmi (ed.), *The Governing Process in Pakistan*, 174–214
39. Anwar Syed, *Pakistan: Islam, Politics and National Solidarity* (Lahore, 1984), 122–3.
40. Wayne A. Wilcox, 'Ideological Dilemmas in Pakistan's Political Culture', in Smith (ed.), *South Asian Politics and Religion*, 350.

41. See Seyyed Vali Reza Nasr, *Mawdudi and the Making of Islamic Revivalism* (New York, 1996), 44; also see Charles J. Adams, 'The Ideology of Mawlana Mawdudi', in Smith (ed.), *South Asian Politics and Religion*, esp., 390.
42. Anwar Syed, *Pakistan*, 124; and Gauhar, *Ayub Khan*, 425.
43. Gauhar, *Ayub Khan*, 179 ff.
44. Jamal Malik, 'Dynamics Among Traditional Religious Scholars and their Institutions in Contemporary South Asia', *Muslim World*, 87/3–4 (1997), 204.
45. Ibid., 204–5.
46. See Ali Umit Berkman, 'Administrative Reforms in Pakistan and Turkey: A Comparative Analysis', *Journal of South Asian and Middle Eastern Studies* (Villanova), 2/4 (Summer 1979), 5–7; and Hasan Askari Rizvi, *The Military & Politics in Pakistan, 1947–1997*, revised edn. (Lahore, 2000), esp. 14.
47. Bernard Lewis, *The Emergence of Modern Turkey* (London, 1961), 68.
48. Anees Jillani, 'Pakistan and CENTO: An Historical Analysis', *Journal of South Asian and Middle Eastern Studies*, 15/1 (1991), 40–52.
49. Ayub Khan, *Friends Not Masters*, 5–6.
50. Daniel W. Brown, 'Islamic Modernism in South Asia: A Reassessment', *Muslim World*, 87/3–4 (1997), esp., 259.
51. Syed, *Pakistan*, 171.
52. See Anis Y. Shivani, 'Religion and Politics: time to be frank', *Dawn* (Karachi), 23 May 1998.
53. See *News International* (Islamabad), 19 Oct. 1999.
54. The instrument for this was the National Security Council but with one major difference from the Turkish situation. While, in Turkey, the head of state is also the head of the NSC, in Pakistan, the president of the country has been left out of it completely.
55. *News International*, 24 Oct. 1999.
56. Ibid.

Epilogue

The Ottoman Empire that spanned the reigns of thirty-seven sultans from Osman I (r. 1302–24) to Mehmed VI (r. 1918–22)—Abdülmecid II (r. 1922–24), the last of the Ottomans, reigned only as a caliph—was in its heyday a plural and polyglot world that incorporated several racial groups following different religions and speaking different languages. This grand ethnic and religious mosaic lasted over six hundred years—and for at least four hundred years was the home of the Islamic caliphate. In essence, the Ottoman sultans' claims to the 'universal' caliphate, especially from the Treaty of Küçük Kaynarca (1774) onwards, were based on 'the principles of allegiance (*bey'at*), divine will, inheritance, and actual power—all traditionally recognised justifications.'[1] The sultans, chiefly Abdülhamid II, adopted and asserted exalted titles to push their cherished entitlements to the caliphate.[2]

One of the potent instruments of Ottoman foreign policy was *ittihad-i Islam*, though its impact was not always commensurate with its objectives. Abdülhamid II was portrayed, in the West, as its notorious high priest but a careful enquiry has revealed that, contrary to the traditional view, his interest in pan-Islam was erratic and opportunistic, and held only a marginal role in his strategy.³ He was no revisionist; rather, he was a realist. He was, in fact, reacting to the challenges posed by the European powers whom he understood more intimately than he acknowledged.⁴ Nevertheless, the enigma of pan-Islam has remained controversial and, even today, writers tend to hold opposite views depending on their socio-cultural mores and political preferences. Gradually, the vast Ottoman Empire withered in the face of insurmountable challenges, shrinking, finally, into its Anatolian mould with only a small portion left intact in Europe. This metamorphosis, however, was not due to the empire's internal dynamics but rather to factors such as the Ottoman ambition to over-centralize, which pulled the centre and the periphery in opposite directions, thus shifting the socio-economic milieu, the complex process of acculturation in the race for modernization, and the new order that followed the First World War.⁵

The journey to the republic was arduous and painful. It took years of incessant struggle, including hard-fought battles, to arrive at a system that, in essence, was a hybrid with Europe as its model. Mustafa Kemal Atatürk, who was largely responsible for this achievement, set his country on the course to modernization with a state structure that has more or less survived to this day. Pan-Islam ceased to enjoy state patronage and the religious establishment received an unbearable blow. And, though Islam took a back seat, the real objective of the nationalists was to subordinate religion to the authority of the state by separating the two rather than by displacing them. The driving force was not atheism but western concepts. As Ahmet Kuru suggests, Kemalist secularism in Turkey has been consciously excluding religion from the public domain, until the Erdoğan government decided to follow a policy of 'passive secularism' by 'tolerating' religion in the functioning of the state.⁶ However, the fact remains that even the strictest secularist reforms could not obliterate the integrative functions of its Islamic credentials. Deep down, robust 'Turkishness' retained its ethno-religious

EPILOGUE

characteristic. The ineffectiveness of repression to control the influence of an *'alim* like Bediuzzaman Said Nursi (1876–1960), is a case in point. Symbolically, however, state sovereignty passed on to the GNA, where most interest groups had converged to share power. The broom with which the nationalists swept clean the house before splashing it with their own dash of colours was 'Kemalism', a flexible mechanism devised to achieve rapid modernization. It was not an abrupt intrusion but rather the culmination of a process that had started over a century earlier.

The new ideology was only 'a modified, scientifically sanctioned version of the Turkish nationalism' with roots in Turkism.[7] By the time Atatürk died of liver cirrhosis in November 1938, the Republic of Turkey had stabilized under an authoritarian 'monoparty' system, wherein the ruling party and the government were placed together in a formalized embrace, though the army still exercised a dominant role.[8] Over the years, the guardians of Atatürk's bequest have sedulously built, through conscious endeavour, a personality cult around him by erasing his Islamic past and only emphasizing his secularist face. Things have changed since then and, occasionally, one notices odd attempts to look at the Turkish leader more dispassionately.[9]

After Mustafa Kemal, the succession fell to the lot of Ismet Inönü who promised to establish civilian control over the armed forces and allow a 'loyal opposition' to take root. It was not until after the Second World War that a competitive multi-party system really emerged. By that time, the Republican Peoples Party (RPP) had undergone a bitter power struggle that had led to the post-war socio-economic jam in spite of Turkey's designed neutrality. The situation was made worse by frequent bureaucratic inroads into the political system which upset the finely-balanced stability.[10] Then, slowly during the 1950s, religion began to creep back into the socio-political fabric of Turkey. A series of gentle puffs portended a wind of change: religious education re-entered schools as an optional subject, a faculty of divinity found its place at Ankara University, religious literature reappeared in bookshops and on pavements, attendance at mosques multiplied, the *azan* and recitation of the Qur'an reverted to their original Arabic form, thousands of new mosques dotted the skylines, and *hajj* pilgrimages increased significantly.[11]

These steps made little dent at first but then, from the end of the 1960s, religious ideologies began to multiply. One observer puts it down to rapid socio-economic change.[12] Another feels that 'Islam was in their [Turks'] bones, part of their being'. It was 'the swing of the pendulum back towards [the missing balance of] mutual respect between church and state' rather than the resurgence of Islam.[13] Yet another writer views it as 'a cultural politics of identity' that brought about the change.[14] Surely, the Turks were now harking back to their history. Between 1960 and 1980, in spite of the repeated military interventions and tangled politics, several religious ideologists found their way into parliament under the banner of Necmettin Erbakan's (1926–2011) National Order Party (Milli Nizam Partisi or MNP). When shut down in 1971, it reappeared as the National Salvation Party (Milli Selamet Partisi or MSP). Banned again in 1980, the MSP was reincarnated as the Welfare Party (Refah or RP), and it kept coming back whenever suppressed.

Regardless of the labels, the religious-oriented parties worked for the Islamization of life in Turkey and offered an alternative paradigm to the Kemalist model of modernization which, they alleged, was a product of the blind aping of the West.[15] Another feature inherent to their ideology and political discourse was pan-Islam—which symbolized their influence in the Islamic world. By the 1990s, the Islamists, though still divided doctrinally into different *Tarikat*s, were strong enough to pose a challenge to the radical secularists.[16] Then, with the support of 'popular Islam' and certain elements among the diaspora, the RP entered the Turkish parliament and local/provincial bodies as the major player while moving in and out of power.[17] In 1993, a visible spin towards an Islamic lifestyle and the propagation of Islamic ideology was noted. The government of the day, in order to take the wind out of the Islamists' sails, attempted to pamper them with some symbolic actions of support.[18] The last time that any party was shown the door was in June 1997 when a moderate, like Erbakan, was made to resign from the premiership of the coalition in a 'soft coup' by the secularist army. Six months later (January 1998), the constitutional court dissolved the RP and banned Erbakan and six of his colleagues from politics for five years. Erbakan and his friends unsuccessfully contested the closure in the European Court of Human Rights, sitting in Strasbourg, which further encouraged the military-led secularists to curb religious activism. But this did not mean that the power struggle in Turkey was over.[19]

In the post-1997 period, the Islamists re-invented themselves through a new strategy based on the pragmatic analysis of the ground realities that resulted in the 'denationalization' of approaches on domestic and foreign issues, as a 'path-dependent' survival stratagem in reaction to the attacks of the secular establishment. So far the strategy has yielded profitable dividends for the Islamists though the burgeoning Islamic ethos has progressively divided Turkish society. From the turn of the twenty-first century, public opinion in Turkey has become increasingly polarized 'between its loyalty to the Kemalist secularist uniformity and a growing Islamic ethos based on rediscovery'.[20] And, indeed, Turkey is at the crossroads: socio-economic realities and pragmatism require it to claim its place in Europe while tradition and history beckon it to embrace pan-Islam. No immediate solution is in sight because Europe is reluctant to embrace a Muslim country out of sheer 'Islamphobia', among other reasons, while Turkey feels no particular urge to give up its Islamic essence except for a pledge to continue with Kemalism. Meanwhile, the divisions within Turkish society have deepened since Recep Erdoğan's AKP came to power in November 2002 with a thumping two-thirds majority.

The AKP is, in fact, a makeover from the Fazilet Partisi (FP)—also known as the RP—with its roots in Islamic revival. Their performance was even better in the 2007 elections and, in spite of stiff opposition from the secularists they were able to put up their own man, Abdullah Gül (with a headscarf-wearing first lady), in the presidency—which till then had been the bastion of secularism. The lines were drawn irreverently between the government on one side and the armed forces and judiciary on the other, confronting each other eyeball to eyeball.[21] But the AKP, buoyed by its achievements in introducing good governance and achieving a robust economy, refused to blink. Erdoğan cleverly used Europe to undermine the traditional pillars of secularism while, at the same time, he resorted to religious populism to prop up his power base.[22] Fethullah Gülen's spiritual movement and the leadership of the AKP were, at one point, closely allied, but that period of enthusiastic goodwill has come to an end. Erdoğan, a consummate politician, knows when to stop playing to the gallery.[23] His policy of passive secularism that assigns a tolerant public role to religion has earned him and Abdullah Gül respect not only in Europe and the United States but also in the modern Muslim societies.[24] However, the secularists were not sitting idle. They held massive rallies in Ankara and Istanbul, alleging that the AKP was pursuing a hidden Islamic agenda in order to root out secularism. In summer 2008, they stealthily tried to use the constitutional court to oust the AKP—as a repeat performance of 1998 when they had the RP thrown out. Ten years on, they forgot that the situation had changed drastically. Driven by domestic considerations and international pressure, the constitutional court desisted from forcing the issue.[25] Erdoğan now hit back and, in an unprecedented move, arrested some top serving and retired armed forces generals and officers on charges of fomenting a coup in 2003 and put them on trial. Though the opposition was humbled and deep tensions were created, in the end the will of the government prevailed.

Armed with two successive victories at the polls, and a 'yes' vote in the referendum on constitutional amendments, Erdoğan stridently moved forward to curb the military's power, re-shape the judiciary, and re-write the constitution, ostensibly to bring Turkey closer to European standards.

He won the elections a third time in a row in 2011, by the largest vote share yet, and put 'the dominant party system' in place.[26] The defining moment in civil-military relationship in Turkey arrived when the chiefs of all the three armed forces resigned over the government's decision to proceed with the scheduled trials of the arrested officers for the alleged coup plots. It was a clear sign that the military, which had staged four coups between 1960 and 1997, had grudgingly accepted its subservience to civilian rule—which augurs well for the democratic process of the country.[27] A reliable analysis suggests that unless there is a substantial weakening in the AKP's overall performance or a credible opposition emerges, no significant electoral shift is likely to take place in the near future.[28]

But Erdoğan may be pushing his luck too far. In a recent development, he has put Ilker Başbuğ, his former chief of the general staff, on trial for an alleged bid to topple the government as part of the clandestine 'Ergenekon' network, a radical nationalist group that sprang from within the armed forces. Next in the dock are the ailing retired generals, Kenan Evren (94), and Tahsin Şahinkaya (86), for their part in the staging of the 1980 coup. Evren, who led the bloodiest coup in the republic's history, later occupied the presidency for more than eight years.[29] Erdoğan's supporters perceive this as an attempt to right the past 'wrongs' through the judicial process in order to prevent their recurrence. But, to his opponents, it is vindictiveness, plain and simple, and that, too, politically-motivated, which is a clear sign of a slide towards 'authoritarianism'. Even the liberals have begun to air muffled voices of disapproval about his supposed 'intolerance of dissent', alleged human rights violations, and detention of scores of journalists and countless Kurdish rebels.[30] It remains to be seen how long Erdoğan's charisma will stand him in good stead now that the trial court has returned its verdict putting an end to the two-year-old much-publicized legal wrangle. As many as 322 serving and retired army officers have been handed down various terms of imprisonment and only 34 out of 365 defendants stand acquitted. The ringleaders of the plot—two retired generals and one retired admiral—have been given life terms. All of them have the right to appeal.[31]

The recent wave of anti-government unrest (May-June 2013) that engulfed Istanbul and then spilled over to Ankara and other cities may have been sparked by the government's audacious plans for a mosque complex and a piazza in the Gezi Park section of the Taksim Square, but certainly it was not an isolated event. Deep down it reflects the jagged divisions that exist in Turkish society over the broader issues of identity, religion, social class and politics. It also represents a challenge to the AKP's nostalgia for Turkey's Ottoman and Islamic past and its version of political reform, which includes a possible switch from parliamentary to presidential system. No doubt, the opposition took the occasion as a godsend opportunity to vent their feelings in violent protests against the AKP and its leader. Staggered by protests, Erdoğan chose to strike a defiant note but when he realized that his use of excessive force had alienated even the liberals among his supporters, he offered compromise as a tactical move. But when defied, he resorted to an even harsher crackdown in which hundreds were hurt and an equal number arrested. Further, he rallied his supporters to send a strong message. This was in stark contrast to the conciliatory tone adopted by President Abdullah Gül. Critics, including those linked to Fethtullah Gülen's Islamic movement, read in Erdoğan's angry response an intimidating manifestation of his authoritarian leadership style. However, the premier is confident that 'our democracy has been tested again and came out victoriously'. It is not easy to predict the outcome of the unrest, and the hide-and-seek between the protestors and the police are likely to continue for some time. But Erdoğan seems ready to fight it out to the end with the help of his supporters.[32]

In another arena, Erdoğan is consciously taking Turkey towards the East, which betrays its frustration with Europe. There is a growing empathy for the Muslim world, but of greater significance has been his 'victory lap' to North Africa and Egypt following the 'Arab Spring', where he flaunted the Turkish model of Islam with emphasis on the secular path.[33] But, despite the exit of at least four entrenched dictators—Zine El Abidine bin Ali of Tunisia, Hosni Mubarak of Egypt, Muammar Gaddafi of Libya, and Ali Abdullah Saleh of the Yemen—the situation in the Arab world, is still fluid and dangerous. Ankara's stance vis-à-vis Syria, is hardening over Bashar al-Assad's crackdown on the armed rebels who have Turkey's support.[34] One has to ponder over the comment made by a Lebanese Maronite that 'violence and bloodshed is turning the "Arab Spring" into winter'.[35] However, it is unlikely that the new regimes will benefit from Turkey's experience. Ankara's relations with Tehran are also problematic.[36] Erdoğan's enthusiasm for a Palestinian sovereign state has brought him on a collision course with Israel as well, especially after the Jewish state refused to apologize for the killings of unarmed Turks in May 2010, during a commando raid on a Gaza-bound aid flotilla in international waters. Since then Edoğan has been openly critical of Israel as a threat to the region and for not honouring 89 resolutions of the UN Security Council and 247 of the General Assembly and then appointed a veteran diplomat as Turkey's first ambassador to Palestine more as a symbolic gesture.[37] Rapprochement with Armenia and the Kurds is also in the offing, though no particular guarantee is forthcoming. On the contrary, the French lawmakers' attempt to outlaw the denial of the Aremenian 'genocide' of 1915 strained Turkey's relations with Nicolas Sarkozy's government in France.[38] What will happen under his successor, Francois Hollande, is yet to be seen.

One subject on which the secularists and the pro-Islamic majority seem to converge, however, is Turkey's decades-old desire to enter the European Union (EU) because, apart from economic and political advantages to be gained from it, the Turks strongly feel that they are

'Europeans' and Europe is where they rightfully belong. This feeling is the legacy of Atatürk who fashioned the modern Turkish society in the European cultural matrix; with the exception of the diehards who fear the loss of an Islamic identity, few wish to disregard it. Even the AKP has staked its reputation on this issue; Erdoğan cleverly dismisses the notion of the EU as an exclusive 'Christian Club' overlooking the fact that despite pockets of opinion wanting total religious neutrality Europe is steeped in Christianity.[39] If Turkey looks too European to most of the Muslim countries (except perhaps the Central Asian republics) to acknowledge it as an 'Islamic model', the Europeans dismiss it as too 'Islamic' and 'eastern' to qualify as a member of their club; and are not willing to accept the Turks as Europeans. The arduous ten-year process of entry, with a long checklist that the Turks must achieve to qualify, began in October 2005, but thus far the door to their entry has remained firmly shut in their face.

The alternative suggestion of a 'privileged partnership' is unacceptable to Turkey. History continues to haunt Europe. Earlier, Frits Bolkestein (b. 1933), the Dutch EU commissioner, summed up the general apprehension among the Europeans when he said that Turkey's entry meant that the repulsion of Ottoman forces from the gates of Vienna in 1683 would have been in vain.[40] Another diplomat was unhappy to note that what the Turks could not achieve in the seventeenth century, they were now about to accomplish by climbing the ramparts of Europe through the back door.[41] The fear of seventy million Muslim Turks overwhelming Christian Europe seems too dreadful a scenario for many on the Continent to swallow. This may seem a much-generalized basis for rejection, as there are a number of complex and problematic issues involved in the process, but the stigma of the 'new barbarism' of the so-called 'Islamic terror' has been lurking behind the hard-line conservatives' polemics to keep Turkey at bay.[42] The unfortunate remarks by Pope Benedict XVI (b. 1927) that linked Islam with violence, the resurrection of the Armenian massacres of 1915 in the US and Europe, and the rise of neo-Orientalism in the West, generally, have clouded Europe's relations with Turkey and the Muslim world at large still further.[43] The perception of Turkey as Europe's 'Other' has to end one day for it does have a place in the region and a stake in the western Balkans.[44] Responding to the West's fear of an Islamic Turkey, two Zirve University academics think that 'the AKP's policies are not incompatible with Kemalism', rather the ruling party has become 'Ataturk's last defender', adding a tongue-in-cheek title to their contribution— 'Kemalism Is Dead, Long Live Kemalism'.[45] Incidentally, there are those among the EU members who would like to welcome Turkey, if only for the egotistic reason of exorcising the spectre of the 'clash of civilizations' and removing the credibility deficit in the Muslim world after 9/11.[46] Moreover, a dejected, desperate Turkey might move away from the West to the East. However, one thing is certain: Turkey has changed irrevocably. Far-reaching structural changes, an economic boom, and a mature progressive outlook, have given Turkey a new-found confidence which, according to a UN report, is nothing short of a 'silent revolution'.[47]

How did the Muslims of South Asia react to the developments in Turkey all this time? To be sure, those who had grown up contemporaneous with the events were quite familiar with the fabled caliph in distant Istanbul and, as such, held him in awe as the spiritual head of all Muslims. Such collective recognition apart, the attachment to the caliphate was part of their history and inherent in their psyche. In other words, pan-Islam was woven into their shared ethos. The onset of the colonial hegemony in the mid-nineteenth century, following the fall of the Timurids, gave way to an uneasy duality of allegiance: 'temporal' duty to the British crown and 'spiritual' adherence to the caliph in Istanbul. This evoked no problems until British and Turkish interests began to pull them in opposite directions. The pan-Islamic fervour, which reignited with the troubles of the Ottoman Empire in the nineteenth century, reached a crescendo in the early part of the twentieth.

EPILOGUE

The First World War was the watershed that presaged the dismemberment of the Ottoman Empire and, by corollary, set off a chain reaction among the Muslims of South Asia that produced a political backlash in the form of the Khilafat movement. Its executive body, the CKC, became far more representative and active than either the Congress or the Muslim League. For six long years, the British Indian Muslims conducted this pro-Turkish agitation in concert with their Hindu compatriots for the dual objectives of saving the Ottoman Empire and pulling off *swaraj* for India. The preceding chapters of the book comprehensively explain the deep involvement of Muslims with the Ottoman Empire and, later, with republican Turkey. The failure to achieve either objective was offset by the success of the Kemalist nationalists in Turkey. But things went awry when the nationalists' passion for broad reforms found but few supporters from among the South Asian pan-Islamists. The generality of Muslims though, after some initial hesitancy, accepted the Turkish right to change direction. Iqbal and Jinnah, in particular, lauded Mustafa Kemal as the foremost leader of the Islamic world and welcomed his reforms. However, when South Asia split into the two countries of India and Pakistan in 1947, Jinnah neither replicated the Turkish model for his new state nor succumbed to the *'ulama*'s pressure to turn Pakistan into an ideal Islamic state. He inaugurated a liberal-modernist set-up based on the rule of law with religious freedom for all. Thus, the concept of a nation-state within the Islamic polity became an ideal model instead of the usual obsession with the 'universal' caliphate. No doubt, Jinnah used Islamic symbols for his political movement and called his new state 'Islamic' but he firmly resisted demands for the promulgation of *shari'at* as the source for the law and the constitution, and concentrated more on 'the well-being of the people, especially of the masses and the poor'.[48]

This is not to say, however, that sympathy for Turkey and its leaders had evaporated after the demise of the caliphate. From my own childhood memories, I can recall framed pictures of Turkish personalities embellishing the walls of houses and shops in most towns long after Pakistan's establishment. However, after Jinnah, the differences between the religious and political forces stood out in sharp contrast to the milder disagreements of the earlier period. As time passed, the rise of the traditionalist forces was assured because the westernized élite and the landed aristocracy, who ran the 'highly centralized patriarchal and authoritarian structure of the state and the forces that sustain[ed] this structure', failed to provide the much-needed political stability and economic robustness.[49] Cold War pressures from the major international players complicated the situation still further. The preamble of the 1956 constitution placed the sovereignty of the state in God Almighty, to be exercised through the chosen representatives of the people. All laws repugnant to the Qur'an and *sunnat* were to be struck down or made compatible with the *shari'at*. The use of Islamic symbols and expressions of Islamic identity abounded in the literature of the period.

Even Ayub Khan's military regime, after some twists and turns to break free of the Islamic mould, had to fall back on the Islamic ethos and recognize the 'deep and historical [pan-Islamic] ties' with Turkey which always had 'a warm place in our hearts'.[50] Following East Pakistan's secession as Bangladesh in 1971, Z. A. Bhutto (1928–79) introduced populism and 'Islamic socialism' as his panacea for the malaise following the debacle, but chose to retain the preamble of the abrogated constitution of 1956 in the new one he introduced in 1973. But, none surpasses Ziaul Haq in exploiting the slogan of 'Islam' so blatantly. In the early part of his regime, perhaps misreading the nature and motivation of military interventions in Turkey, he even toyed with the idea of a 'Turkish model' for Pakistan, in the early part of his regime. However, he failed to realize that the Turkish intrusions were intended to prevent the secular 'democratic' system from 'going off the track', whereas the Pakistani coups were largely oligarchic in nature.[51]

Zia ruled through the civil-military bureaucratic partnership[52], though his despotic tendencies found the Islamic ideology as a more useful tool for political mileage. His tragic decision to push Pakistan into the Afghan quagmire unwittingly sowed the seeds of Islamic militancy and sectarianism, the two most debilitating afflictions that have consumed the country ever since. And, what is more distressing is that the West targeted Pakistan for something that they themselves had initiated through Zia.[53] In Turkey, the armed forces have always been well-respected as the bastion of Kemalist secularism whereas, in Pakistan, they are confused, and have often been bogged down with catastrophic consequences for the internal affairs of the country.[54] Of the two civilian rulers that succeeded Zia one after the other, Benazir Bhutto (1953–2007) and Nawaz Sharif (b. 1949), the latter tried to follow the course set by his mentor, Ziaul Haq, but was shown the door by his successor when he crossed swords with the armed forces. Pervez Musharraf, who planted himself in a military coup, thought he could play Atatürk and lead the country to 'enlightened modernism' but retreated when he got snubbed by the religious right. Due to the absence of legitimacy for his coup, Musharraf began to use the Islamic card and manoeuvred visits to Saudi Arabia, the Gulf countries, Turkey, and Iran, almost imposing himself on his hosts.[55] He came back energetically after 9/11, but was dragged deeper and deeper into the mire by the self-serving American-led invasions of Iraq, Afghanistan, and incursions into Pakistan's north-west.

Public opinion in Pakistan has always been widely interested in the events of the Muslim world. The educated élite, in particular, had a better understanding of Turkey's pro-West secular reform; however, in March 1997, when the Turkish establishment imposed tighter restrictions on the Islamic-rooted RP of Necmettin Erbakan, it encountered widespread disapproval in Pakistan. There were critical comments in the Pakistani press.[56] In January 1998, when the constitutional court banned the ruling RP, it evoked a chorus of condemnation, paradoxically, from the far right lobby, which, ideologically, was closer to the ultra-conservative Saudi Arabia. Prominent among the critics was Qazi Hussain Ahmed (b. 1938), the then chief of the Jama'at-i Islami, who called the ban a negation of democracy. He claimed that the West was behind the ban because it was not willing to loosen its grip on the Turkish people. In his opinion, Adnan Menderes (1899–1961), in spite

EPILOGUE

of being a secularist, was the first to pay with his life for launching the movement for Islamic renaissance in Turkey, and now it was Erbakan's turn to be forced into political oblivion for doing the same.[57] Dozens of placard-carrying men and women staged demonstrations against the ban. In Islamabad, some of the placards at a protest meeting organized by human rights activists read: 'Do not kill people's will', 'Is secularism against democracy?', and 'We love Turkish people—do not oppress them'.[58] Though the Pakistani government did not comment on the ban, the English language daily, *News International*, editorially opined that such an action would be counter-productive, and would strengthen Islamic radicalism instead of obstructing it.[59] Another popular daily, *Dawn*, stated that the Turkish secularists would be well advised to draw their opponents into the political mainstream instead of suppressing them.[60]

Musharraf's exit also saw the fading out of his 'enlightened moderation', a concoction invented to charm the West by suggesting the inauguration of a new Islamic society to attain socio-economic uplift based on pluralism, openness, and tolerance. It had achieved little and was dismissed as being 'neither enlightened nor moderate'.[61] Before his exit, his main rival, Benazir Bhutto, died a violent death in 2007 in a suicide bombing at a public meeting at Rawalpindi. Her party returned to power, but, like most Pakistani regimes in the recent past, performed erratically, pandering to narrow self-interest rather than working for national priorities. The stand-off between the government and the higher judiciary, and later, the military in the wake of the embarrassing Osama bin Laden affair and the government's alleged SOS to the US for help, heightened feelings of frustration and alienation. The drama that unfolded subsequent to the disclosures, and the storm over the role of the intelligence agencies, politically created a default situation where everything, from governance to the economy to security to foreign relations to the 'war on terror', got all messed up. Even more self-destructing was the PPP government's defiance of the Supreme Court that cost it the ouster of a prime minister and the narrow escape of another for a similar contempt, which was a bad omen for a fledgling democracy. Worse still, as one analyst lamented, was the absence of sound thinking on the future of the country, to recreate something of Jinnah's Pakistan with its pronounced 'de-conflation between religion and politics'.[62] Meanwhile, the return of Nawaz Sharif to power for the unprecedented third time in the 2013 general elections has changed the political scenario once again. He seems to have matured enough to weather the storm but, the intellectually ossified religious militants on the right, and the well-nigh sterile secular activists on the left, continue to live in the world that they have reconstructed for themselves according to their respective tastes.

Such are the dynamics of power in Pakistan, where authority has swung like a pendulum between the military and civilian dispensations thus rendering the system of governance hollow from inside. But even then, there is a body of Muslim opinion in Pakistan today—and to some extent in India and Bangladesh as well—that thinks that 'Turkey, under the AK[P] government, presents to the world a face of an Islamic country that is moderate, tolerant, progressive, and democratic, and that at the same time proudly adheres to its Islamic faith and traditions'. It could well serve as 'a model for the Islamic world'.[63] This, however, is not likely to happen in the foreseeable future. Even with the weight of the Jeddah-based 57-member OIC in the hands of a Turk, Ekmeleddin Ihsanoğlu (secretary-general), its plausibility seems remote. Of course, pan-Islam will live on in the minds and hearts of the South Asians as, indeed, among Muslims of the world. But the Muslims are far too divided with their own peculiar historical and political baggage, and authoritarian regimes to contend with, to allow the adoption of a common model. Though it is too early to predict because the situation in the Middle East is still unsettled, and various groups from the far right to the far left are engaged in a power struggle, the recent wave of popular dissent does not seem to have precipitated any reflection on how to change the basic structure of those societies. Besides, the stigma of

EPILOGUE

'Islamic terror' hangs like the proverbial sword of Damocles over Muslims everywhere. As for Pakistan and Turkey, there is, as one of Pakistan's former ambassadors to Turkey suggests, a 'qualitative difference in the texture of the two nations'. In his opinion, the Turks do not wear their religion on their sleeve nor propagate it from rooftops. Therefore, he doubts that this example will ever find adherents in Pakistan.[64] If an efficient group like the military could not successfully replicate Kemal's modernizing model, it is even less plausible for an ineffectual civilian dispensation with no sense of nationalism to attempt thus.[65] The rise of Islamic militancy is not a by-product of pan-Islam, and whatever its apologists might say the union of the Muslim world is more of an illusion than a fact. Several Muslim countries are at daggers drawn with each other—Turkey vs. Iran and Syria, Afghanistan vs. Pakistan, Tajikistan vs. Uzbekistan, Saudi Arabia vs. Iran and Syria, and so on. This is in addition to the internal socio-political upheavals and violent disruptions threatening the so called *daru'l-Islam*. The recent military coup in Egypt and the brazen ouster of the democratically-elected president, Mohamed Morsi (b. 1951), followed by a witch-hunt of the Muslim Brotherhood is a case in point. Worst still, the coup, which had a tacit nod from the West, tends to send a clear message that 'political Islam' has no place in the power game even through a democratic process.[66] The tendency among Muslims to indulge in self-destructive behaviour, as shown by the violent reaction following the exhibition of a blasphemous film produced in the United States, often predisposes them to do things that militate against the very spirit of Islam. Turkey, once the centre of gravity for the Muslim world, has no ambitions to reclaim its primacy. Rather, it sees its interests 'anchored to the West'—a stance that invites jibes, especially from Iran, that Ankara is promoting an 'American Islam' across the region.[67] This has really complicated matters. The reasons for the present phase of radicalism among Muslims are to be found in the West's extraordinary activism against Islam, with its roots embedded in history, a sense of economic deprivation, socio-political pressures, and injustices under undemocratic or quasi-democratic dispensations in their own societies that do not seem to fade away.

NOTES

1. Buzpinar, 'The Question of Caliphate Under the Last Ottoman Sultans', 17–21.
2. Ş. Tufan Buzpinar, 'Hilafet Meselesi', in Coskun Yilmaz (ed.), *II. Abdülhamid: Modernleşme Sürecinde İstanbul* (Istanbul, 2010), 114–20.
3. F. A. K. Yasamee, *Ottoman Diplomacy: Abdülhamid II and the Great Powers, 1878–1888* (Istanbul, 1996), 29.
4. Ibid., 41–52.
5. M. Şükrü Haniolğu, *A Brief History of the Late Ottoman Empire* (Princeton, 2008), 2–5.
6. See Ahmet T. Kuru, 'Passive and Assertive Secularism: Historical, Ideological Struggles, and State Policies Toward Religion', *World Politics*, 59/4 (July 2007), 568–94; and id., *Secularism and State Policies Toward Religion: The United States, France, and Turkey* (Cambridge, 2009), *passim*. Also see Ahmed Kuru and Alfred Stepan (eds.), *Democracy, Islam, and Secularism in Turkey: Religion, Culture and Public Life* (New York, 2012), esp. chap. 4.
7. Id., *Atatürk: An Intellectual Biography* (Princeton, 2011), 161.
8. See Feroz Ahmad, *The Turkish Experiment in Democracy*, 1–8; Erik J. Zürcher, *Turkey: A Modern History* (London & New York, 1993), 184–95; Ilter Turan, 'Religion and Political Culture in Turkey', in Richard Tapper (ed.), *Islam in Modern Turkey: Religion, Politics and Literature In Secular State* (London & New York, 1991), 37–44; Özdalga, *The Veiling Issue, Official Secularism and Popular Islam in Modern Turkey* (Richmond, 1998), 17 ff; and Şükran Vahide, *Islam in Modern Turkey: An Intellectual Biography of Bediuzzaman Said Nursi* (ed.), Ibrahim M. Abu-Rabi' (Albany, New York, 2005), 208 ff.
9. In 2008, for instance, film director, Can Dundar, made a documentary that portrayed Atatürk as a leader with merits as well as flaws. See Ibon Villelabeitia, 'Movie of "Human" Atatürk Stirs Emotions in Turkey', *Dawn*, 11 Nov. 2008.
10. Feroz Ahmad, *The Turkish Experiment in Democracy*, 9 ff.
11. Millar, 'Turkey', in Ayoob (ed.), *The Politics of Islamic Reassertion*, 83. Many observers have noted the visible change that has taken place in Turkey. See, for instance, Col (r) Masud A. Shaikh, 'Re-visiting Turkey', in *News International*, 26 Aug. 1994.
12. Turan, 'Religion and Political Culture in Turkey', 45.
13. Millar, 'Turkey', in Ayoob (ed.), *The Politics of Islamic Reassertion*, 82.

14. Haldun Gülalp, 'Political Islam in Turkey: The Rise and Fall of the Refah Party', *Muslim World*, 89/1 (Jan. 1999), 23.
15. Turan, 'Religion and Political Culture in Turkey', 45–6; and Gülalp, 'Political Islam in Turkey, 23 ff. and 41.
16. The main factions ranged from the traditionalist *Tarikat*s like the Naqshbandis and Suleymancis to the left-of-centre Bektashis and the Mevlevis (Whirling Dervishes), with several intermediate groups in-between who would not shirk even from using violence to achieve their objectives. See Jenny B. White, 'Islam and Democracy: The Turkish Experience', *Current History*, 94/588 (Jan. 1995), 9.
17. Ibid., 10–12. Also see Gülalp, 'Political Islam in Turkey', 35 ff.
18. It was reported 'that Islamic-style beards and veiled women have proliferated in Turkey, that mosques are drawing even larger crowds, and that some bookstores are overflowing with books and journals, cassettes, compact disks and videos glorifying Islamic history, precepts and way of life and exalting the Ottoman Empire's role in preserving the values of the Prophet Muhammad [*sal'am*]'. The report added that 'no fewer than 290 publishing houses and printing presses, 300 publications including four dailies, some hundred unlicensed radio stations and about 30 likewise unlicensed television channels were propagating Islamic ideology'. Eric Rouleau, 'The Challenge to Turkey', *Foreign Affairs*, 72 (Nov./Dec. 1993), 119 and 120–1, quoted in Samuel P. Huntington, *The Clash of Civilizations and Remaking of the World Order*. (New York, 1996). 147. Also see Huntington's comment in ibid., 148.
19. *News* (Islamabad), 17 and 20 Jan., 1998.
20. Iftikhar H. Malik, 'Turkey at the Crossroads: Encountering Modernity and Tradition', *Journal of South Asian and Middle Eastern Studies*, 24/2 (Winter 2001), esp. 32.
21. One of the leading belligerents, Gen. Ilker Basbug, warned that the danger of Islamism in Turkey had reached 'alarming' levels and that the top brass still saw itself as the ultimate arbiter of the country's secularist constitution. See report filed by Ian Traynor in the *Guardian*, 27 Sept. 2006.
22. Ian Traynor, 'Secular Turks and Islamists fight for supremacy in the courts and streets', ibid., 12 June 2006.
23. For a comprehensive account of the Gülen Movement, see contributions, besides those of the editors, by John Voll, Yasin Aktay, and Ahmet Kuru in M. Hakan Yuvaz and John L. Esposito (eds.), *Turkish Islam and the Secular State* (Syracuse, 2003), *passim*.
24. See Tanvir Ahmad Khan, 'Islam in Turkish Politics', *Dawn*, 17 October 2005; and Jacques N. Couvas, 'What the wife wears matters for Turkey's presidential post', ibid., 15 Aug. 2007.

25. This is evident from the relief the European Union felt at the decision. See *Dawn*, 31 July and 1 Aug. 2008.
26. Ali Çarkoğlu, 'Turkey's 2011 General Elections: Towards a Dominant Party System?', *Insight Turkey*, 13/3 (2011), 45–6.
27. Safak Timur, 'Mass resignations may mark end of era for Turkey military', *Tengri News*, at http://en.tengrinews.kz/politics_sub/3530/ (Accessed: 8 Nov. 2011).
28. Çarkoğlu, 'Turkey's 2011 General Elections: Towards a Dominant Party System?', 60.
29. As many as fifty people were reportedly executed and half a million arrested, hundreds died in jail, and many more disappeared during the dictator's rule. *Dawn*, 11 Jan. and 5 Apr. 2012.
30. David Gardner and Daniel Dombey, 'Erdogan's Turkey: A rule more ruthless', *Financial Times*, 28 Mar. 2012.
31. *Express Tribune*, 22 Sept. 2012.
32. See *International Herald Tribune*, 4–21 June 2013, esp. contributions by Tim Arango, Seyla Benhabib, Daron Acemoğlu and Graham E. Fuller.
33. Mohamed Argoubi and Sylvia Westall, 'Islam can exist with democracy, says Turkish PM', *Reuters*, 15 Sept. 2011, at http://af.reuters.com/article/tunisiaNews/idAFL5E7KF2N420110915 (Accessed: 8 Nov. 2011); and Gönül Tol and Alex Vatanka, 'Arab Spring Creates New Rifts between Turkey and Iran', *Frontline*, 30 Oct. 2011, at http://www.mei.edu/Scholars/G%C3%B6n%C3%BClTol/tabid/557/ctl/Detail/mid/2216/xmid/ 2189/xmfid/13/ Default.aspx (Accessed: 8 Nov. 2011).
34. Constanze Letsch, 'Tough times for Turks on borders with Syria', *Guardian*, 25 April 2012.
35. The comment came from the head of the Maronite Church in Lebenon. See Samia Nakhoul's feed dated 4 Mar. 2012 at *Reuters*' website at http://blogs.reuters.com/samia-nakhoul/ (Accessed: 3 Apr. 2012).
36. Sinan Ülgen, 'Turkey, Iran, and the Bomb', *EurActive*, 26 Mar. 2012, at http://www.euractiv.com/global-europe/turkey-bomb-analysis-511752 (Accessed: 3 Apr. 2012); and Huma Yusuf, 'Turkey-Iran factor', *Dawn*, 7 Nov. 2011.
37. Jean-Jacques Cornish, 'Israel a "threat" to region as it has N-bomb: Erdogan', *Dawn*, 6 Oct. 2011; and Mike Giglio, 'Turkey's Man in Palestine', *The Daily Beast*, 8 May 2013 at http://www.thedailybeast.com/ articles/2013/05/08/turkey-s-man-in-palestine.html (Accessed: 8 May 2013).
38. *Dawn*, 23 and 24 Dec. 2011.
39. See Andrew Higgins in *Internationa Herald Tribune*, 19 June 2013.
40. Quoted in Shadaba Islam, 'Turkish entry: EU's reservations', in ibid., 14 Dec. 2004.
41. Cited in Karamatullah K. Ghori, 'Many bridges to cross', ibid., 20 Dec. 2004.

42. In a way, this is the revival of the old Renaissance period view of the Muslim world, especially the Ottomans—the 'Barbarians at the Gates'. See Margaret Meserve, *Empires of Islam in Renaissance Historical Thought* (Cambridge, Mass., 2008), esp. 65–116 and 282–300.
43. The Pope, in his speech at Regensburg University, had quoted from a passage written originally in 1391 as an expression of the views of the Byzantine emperor, Manuel II Paleologus. It went as follows: 'Show me just what Muhammad brought that was new and there you will find things only evil and inhuman, such as his command to spread by the sword the faith he preached.' Earlier, as Cardinal Ratzinger, he had opposed Turkey's bid to join the EU, saying it belonged to a different cultural sphere. He also admonished Muslim leaders in Germany for failing to steer their youth away from what he described as 'the darkness of a new barbarism'. See BBC NEWS, websites at http://news.bbc.co.uk/2/hi/europe/5349808.stm; and http://news.bbc.co.uk/2/hi/europe/5348456.stm (Accessed: 18 Feb. 2009). For the Armenians see Robert Fisk, 'Armenian Genocide is no secret', *Dawn*, 17 Oct. 2006.
44. David Lovell, 'Turkey in Europe: Record, Challenges and the Future', *Insight Turkey*, 13/3 (2011), 186–7; and Erhan Türbedar, 'Turkey's New Activism in the Western Balkans: Ambitions and Obstacles', ibid., 139–58.
45. Dariush Zahedi and Gokhan Bacik, 'Kemalism Is Dead, Long Live Kemalism', in *Foreign Affairs*, 23 April 2010, at http://www.foreignaffairs.com/articles/66391/dariush-zahedi-and-gokhan-bacik/kemalism-is-dead-long-live-kemalism (Accessed: 21 May 2012).
46. Madaleine Bunting, 'Regime Change, European-Style', *Guardian*, 26 Sept. 2005.
47. Cited in *Dawn*, 6 Dec. 2006.
48. See Jinnah's presidential speech to the Constituent Assembly of Pakistan at Karachi on 11 August 1947 in Ministry of Information and Broadcasting, Government of Pakistan, *Quaid-i-Azam Mohammad Ali Jinnah: Speeches and Statements as Governor General of Pakistan, 1947–48* (Islamabad, 1989), 42–7; and Afzal Iqbal, *Islamisation of Pakistan* (Delhi, 1984), 33–41.
49 Hassan N. Gardezi, 'Democracy and Dictatorship in Pakistan: Evaluating Public Opinion', *News International*, 16 Jan. 2000.
50 Field Marshal Mohammad Ayub Khan, *Speeches and Statements*, i (Karachi, n.d.), 54; and id., ii (Karachi, n.d.), 64.
51 Mushahid Hussain, 'Pakistan: trying out different "models"', *Nation*, 14 Aug. 1988.
52 Robert LaPorte, Jr., 'Administrative Restructuring During the Zia Period', in Shahid Javed Burki and Craig Baxter (eds.), *Pakistan Under the Military* (Boulder, 1991), 128.

53 M. Naeem Qureshi, 'Islamic Resurgence in Contemporary Pakistan', in Tatsuro Yamamoto (ed.), *Proceedings of the Thirty-First International Congress of Human Sciences in Asia and North Africa*, i (Tokyo, 1984), pp. 309–11.
54 See Irfan Husain, 'A tale of two armies', *Dawn*, 5 May 2005; Syed Aziz-al Ahsan, 'State, Legitimacy, and Succession: Sunni Political Traditions and Colonial Heritage', *Journal of South Asian and Middle Eastern Studies*, 16/3 (Spring, 1993), esp. 24; and Bilal Hashmi, 'Dragon Seed: Military in the State', in Hasan Gardezi & Jamil Rashid (eds.), *Pakistan: The Roots of Dictatorship* (London, 1983), 148–72. For a more intimate account, see Shuja Nawaz, *Crossed Swords: Pakistan, its Army, and the Wars Within* (Karachi, 2008), esp. 122 ff.
55 *News International*, 6 and 9 Nov. 1999; and Riffat Hussain, 'Continuation with a difference', in ibid., 16 Jan. 2000.
56 See, for instance, communication from Faiz Shehabi in ibid., 28 Mar. 1997.
57 See statement in ibid., 18 Jan. 1998.
58 In ibid., 20 Jan. 1998.
59 Ibid.
60 Ibid.
61 Anwer Mooraj, 'Neither enlightened nor moderate', *Dawn*, 16 Jan. 2006.
62 Mohammad Waseem, 'Rethinking the discourse', ibid., 24 Jan. 2012.
63 Dr Syed Amir, 'Turkey—a model for the Islamic World', *Dawn Review*, 24–30 May 2007, 14–15.
64 Karamatullah K. Ghori, 'Turkish example offers a lesson to our politicians', *Dawn*, 8 Aug. 2008.
65 Anatol Lieven, 'Military Exceptionalism in Pakistan', *Survival*, 53/4 (2011), 66. Adapted from id., *Pakistan: A Hard Country* (London: Allen Lane, 2011).
66 See Shadi Hamid, 'Demoting democracy in Egypt', *International Herald Tribune*, 6–7 July 2013.
67 Gönül Tol and Alex Vatanka, 'Arab Spring Creates New Rifts between Turkey and Iran', *Frontline*, 30 Oct. 2011, at the Middle East Institute website at http://www.mei.edu/Scholars/G%C3%B6n%C3%BClTol /tabid/557/ctl/Detail/mid/2216/xmid/2189/xmfid/13/ Default.aspx (Accessed: 8 Nov. 2011).

Appendix 1

Misak-ı Milli, 28 January 1920

The members of the Ottoman Chamber of Deputies recognize and affirm that the independence of the State and the future of the Nation can be assured by an absolute adherence to the following principles, which represent the maximum of sacrifices which can be endured to achieve a just and lasting peace, and that the continued existence of a stable Ottoman Sultanate and society is impossible if we do not adhere to the said principles:

Article 1: Inasmuch as it is necessary that the destinies of the portions of the Turkish Empire which are peopled by Arab majorities, and which on the conclusion of the Armistice of October 30, 1918, were under occupation by enemy forces, should be determined in accordance with a free plebiscite of the inhabitants, all such territories (whether within or outside the lines of the said Armistice) which are inhabited by an Ottoman Muslim majority, who are united in religion in race and in aim, are imbued with sentiments of mutual regard, are prepared for individual sacrifice, and have an absolute respect for one another's racial rights and for social circumstances, form a whole which does not admit of division for any reason in truth or in law.

Article 2: We are willing that, in the case of the three *sancak*s [of Kars, Ardahan and Batum] which united themselves by ... a general vote to the mother country when they were first free, recourse would again be that, if necessary, to a free popular vote.

Article 3: The determination also of the juridical status of Western Thrace, which has been made dependent on the Turkish peace, must be effected in accordance with a vote which shall be given by the inhabitants, incomplete freedom.

Article 4: The security of the city of Istanbul (which is the seat of the Kalifate [Caliphate] of Islam, the capital of the Sultanate, and the headquarters of the Ottoman Government) and likewise the security of the Sea of Marmara must be protected from every danger. Provided this principle is maintained, whatever decision may be arrived at jointly by us and all other Governments concerned, regarding the opening of the Bosphorus to the commerce and traffic of the world, shall be valid.

Article 5: The rights of Minorities as defined in the treaties concluded between the Entente powers and their enemies and certain of their associates shall be confirmed and assured by us—in reliance on the belief that the Muslim minorities in neighbouring countries will also be given the benefit of the same rights.

Article 6: It is a fundamental condition of our life and continued existence that we, like every country, should enjoy complete independence and liberty in the matter of assuring the means of our development in order that our national and economic development may be so rendered possible, that it should be possible to conduct our affairs in the form of a more modern and regular administration.

For this reason we are opposed to restrictions inimical to our development in political, judicial, financial, and other fields.

The conditions of settlements of what our indebtedness shall be shown to be, shall likewise not be contrary to such principles.

Source: A.L. Macfie, *The Eastern Question, 1774–1923*, Revised Edition (London & New York: Longman, 1996), 124–5.

Appendix II

Brief Diary of the Khilafat Delegation's Proceedings, 1920

(Part IV of the Memorandum by Political Intelligence Officer Attached to India Office)

Feb. 1st.—Moh[ame]d. Ali, Maulana Syed Suleiman Nadvi, Syed Hussein, sailed for Marseilles.

22nd.—Landed at Venice.

29th.—Dined with [Marmaduke] Pickthall, whose help he [Mohamed Ali] enlisted.

March 2nd.—Received by Mr Fisher on behalf of the Secretary of State for India.

5th.—Spoke at 3, Campden Hill Road. "If opponent uses force to crush the Muslems by superior arms these Muslems must draw the sword and fight to the last."

8th.—Lunched with Captain Bennet, who is very friendly with Amir Ali, and responsible for pro-Turkish advertisements in the Press. Spoke at meeting of Minerva Café, concluded his speech with threat of force against force. Discussion: Bolshevism and Nationalism.

15th.—Left for Curzon Hotel.

17th.—Present at the formation of the "Persian Association".

19th.—Interview with the Prime Minister.

APPENDIX II

	21st.—At the Woking Mosque.
	30th.—Visited Labour Executive, but interview not very encouraging.
	31st.—Two hours with George Lansbury.
April	13th.—Left London for Paris.
	15th.—Interview with Longuet at office of *Le Populaire*.

22nd.—Meeting in the Kingsway Hall, information publishes interview with Sayed Hussein.

23rd.—Meeting with Pickthall.

24th.—M.A. meets Senators, Deputies, and ex-Ministers.

25th.—Visited Taalby Abdul Aziz, a Tunisian, and Mon. Cauvain, editor of [*Journal des*] *Débates*.

27th.—Visited by Longuet, Le Coconnier, Secretary of *La France at l'Islam*. Visited by Dr Richard and Burde.

28th.—Left for Edinburgh.

29th.—Spoke at Edinburgh.

30th.—Spoke at Manchester. No longer wished to be under foreign subjugation. A king who was antagonistic to their religious convictions could not receive their homage and respect.

May   2nd.—Letter to *Daily Telegraph*, "The Khilafat claim".

8th.—Arrived Paris.

9th.—Saw members [of] Turkish Delegation at Versailles.

10th.—Telegram to Sultan, visited a Deputy at 10, Av. Dugnesne in company of Mlle. Pureau.

11th.—Called at *Le Populaire* and *Le Temps*. Telegram from Tewfik, member of Turkish Delegation, telling him to address himself to Hamid Bey of the Red Crescent, Constantinople.

12th.—Called at *Le Journal*.

14th.—Visited by Baron L.P. Lormain and M. Stoiloff.

15th.—Called on M. Leon Barthou, Deputy, well-known Anglophobe. Visit of utmost importance and M. Riza. Telegram

APPENDIX II

from Bombay, '3,000 cabled International strong non-co-operation Surat movement started."

16th.—Received a letter from M. Riza in which D'Esperey's name occurs. Telephoned to Comité Bulgare.

17th.—Present at conference attended by many politicians and journalists. Among them Rene Le Comte, Du Menil, Thoret, Gen. Chefíls D'Estailleur, Hardemarde, Terff, Jules Roche, Baron de Lormain, Le Coconnier, Jean Meila.

18th.—8, Rue al Pouttach.

19th.—L'Ordre Public, called at 8, Rue de Ponthien Mr Haidar, Shouman, Perin.

20th.—Rained all day.

21st.—Received Lieut.-Col. Azan.

22nd.—Assisted at conference at the College de France.

23rd.—Assisted at a fête at the Trocadero.

24th.—Bank holiday. Walked near hotel.

25th.—Visited office *of Populaire*

26th.—Visited office *of Populaire*

27th.—Meeting at Salle De Sociétés Savantes; speeches by Longuet, Marcel Cachin, Le Coconnier, Secretary wentalone to Turkish Delegation at Versailles.

29th.—Left Paris for London.

30th.—Arrived Oxford.

June   6th.—Conference at the Salle des Ingénieurs Civils organized by *La France at l'Islam*. Speeches by Le Coconnier, De Kerguezec and Claude Farrere, de Mouzie, Senator.

7th.—Went to Bureau Islamique at 2.15; at 4.40 went to Palais de Justice.

8th.—Dined with M. Fealbi, took Arabic newspapers of political interests.

APPENDIX II

9th.—Went to Versailles, and at 8.50 to Salle des Indigéniens. Present at meeting held at the sale des Indigéniens. Revision of Peace Treaty with Turkey.

11th.—Letter from Alitcha Zade Harun, confederate of Djavid Bey and Djemal Pasha, asking M.A. to meet an important personage now in Berlin. Talat. Went to Cooks 2.30; went 9, Quai du Quatre Septembre; 9.0 went to Salle Gaveau.

12th.—Left Paris for London on receipt of a telegram from London from Horniman, "Very urgent. You should be here Saturday without fail."

24th.—Left for Paris.

25th.—Meeting at Salle Wagram under auspices of the Comité France et Islam. The Peace Treaty with Turkey, and interests of France in the East. Present: M. Bourdarie, Director of *Revue Indigène*, M. de Monzie, Senator, Xavier de Magollon, Déptués Le Coconnier, Pillon, Secretary of the Comité France at Islam, S.R. Bomanji.

July 4th.—In Paris.

7th.—Met Petinax.

10th.—Kidwai arrives in Paris from India.

11th.—Abul Kasem and Sayed Hussain left Paris for London.

23rd.—Arrived in Rome. Interviewed Italian Premier and Dr Nikoli, President of the Italian Chamber.

24th.—Met Turati, Italian Socialist.

25th.—Attended meeting of League of oppressed Nations.

30th.—Received by the Pope.

31st.—Arrived Montreux (Territet).

Aug. 1st.—Meeting in his rooms.

2nd.—Retuned to Paris from Geneva.

3rd.—(Talat holds meeting at Lucern. Union of C.U.P. and Nationalists complete, he says) Versailles to see Turkish delegation.

5th.—Returned to Geneva.

APPENDIX II

        6th.—Had long interview with Talat.

        7th.—Returned to London from Paris.

        11th.—Interview with M. Millerand.

        12th.—Returned to England.

        13th.—In England; wrote to Montagu.

        22nd.—Members of Delegation present at Labour meeting in Trafalgar Square.

        30th.—Left for Paris.

Sept.   1st.—Arrived Paris.

        3rd.—Left for Rome.

        17th.—Left Brindisi for India.

Oct.   13th.—Arrived in India.

India Office,
10th January 1921.

Source: Oriental & India Office Collection, Political & Secret Memoranda, B. 361.

Appendix III

Extracts from Mohammad Iqbal's Sixth Lecture

The Principle of Movement in the Structure of Islam

As a cultural movement Islam rejects the old static view of the universe, and reaches a dynamic view. As an emotional system of unification it recognizes the worth of the individual as such, and rejects blood-relationship as a basis of human unity. Blood-relationship is earth-rootedness. The search for a purely psychological foundation of human unity becomes possible only with the perception that all human life is spiritual in its origin. Such a perception is creative of fresh loyalties without any ceremonial to keep them alive, and makes it possible for man to emancipate himself from the earth. . . .

The new culture finds the foundation of world-unity in the principle of 'Tauhid'. Islam, as a polity, is only a practical means of making this principle a living factor in the intellectual and emotional life of mankind. It demands loyalty to God, not to thrones. And since God is the ultimate spiritual basis of all life, loyalty to God virtually amounts to man's loyalty to his own ideal nature. The ultimate spiritual basis of all life, as conceived by Islam, is eternal and reveals itself in variety and change. A society based on such a conception of Reality must reconcile, in its life, the categories of permanence and change. It must possess eternal principles to regulate its collective life, for the eternal gives us a foothold in the world of perpetual change. But eternal principles when they are understood to exclude all possibilities of change which, according to the Quran, is one of the greatest 'signs' of God, tend to immobilize what is

APPENDIX III

essentially mobile in its nature. The failure of Europe in political and social science illustrates the former principle, the immobility of Islam during the last 500 years illustrates the latter. What then is the principle of movement in the nature of Islam? This is known as 'Ijtihad'.

The word literally means to exert. In the terminology of the Islamic law it means to exert with a view to form an independent judgment on a legal question. The idea, I believe, has its origin in a well-known verse of the Quran—'And to those who exert We show Our path.' We find it more definitely adumbrated in a tradition of the Holy Prophet. . . . The student of the history of Islam, however, is well aware that with the political expansion Islam systematic legal thought became an absolute necessity, and our early doctors of law, both of Arabian and non-Arabian descent, worked ceaselessly until all the accumulated wealth of legal thought found a final expression in our recognized schools of law. These schools of law recognize three degrees of Ijtihad: (1) complete authority in legislation which is practically confined to the founders of schools, (2) relative authority which is to be exercised within the limits of a particular school, and (3) special authority which relates to the determining of the law applicable to a particular case left undetermined by the founders. In this paper I am concerned with the first degree of Ijtihad only, *i.e.*, complete authority in legislation. The theoretical possibility of this degree of Ijtihad is admitted by the Sunnis, but in practice it has always been denied ever since the establishment of the schools, inasmuch as the idea of complete Ijtihad is hedged round by conditions which are well-nigh impossible of realization in a single individual. Such an attitude seems exceedingly strange in a system of law based mainly on the groundwork provided by the Quran which embodies an essentially dynamic outlook on life. It is, therefore, necessary, before we proceed further, to discover the causes of this intellectual attitude which has reduced the Law of Islam practically to a state of immobility. Some European writers think that the stationary character of the Law of Islam is due to the influence of the Turks. This is an entirely superficial view, for the legal; schools of Islam had been finally established long before the Turkish influence began to work in the history of Islam. The real causes are, in my opinion, as follows:

1. We are all familiar with the Rationalist movement which appeared in the church of Islam during the early days of the Abbasides [*sic*], and the bitter

controversies which it raised. Take for instance the one important point of controversy between the two camps—the conservative dogma of the eternity of Quran. The Rationalists denied it because they thought that this was only another form of the Christian dogma of the eternity of the world; on the other hand the conservative thinkers whom the later Abbasides [*sic*], fearing the political implications of Rationalism, gave their support, thought that by denying the eternity of the Quran the Rationalists were undermining the very foundations of Muslim society. Nazzam, for instance, practically rejected the traditions, and openly declared Abu Huraira to be an untrustworthy reporter. Thus, partly owing to a misunderstanding of the ultimate motives of Rationalism, and partly owing to the unrestrained thought of particular Rationalists, conservative thinkers regarded this movement as a force of disintegration, and considered it a danger to the stability of Islam as a social polity. Their main purpose, therefore, was to preserve the social integrity of Islam, and to realize this the only course open to them was to utilize the binding force of Shari'at and to make the structure of their legal system as rigorous as possible.

2. The rising growth of ascetic Sufism which gradually developed under influences of a non-Islamic character, a purely speculative side, is to a large extent responsible for this attitude. On its purely religious side Sufism fostered a kind of revolt against the verbal quibbles of our early doctors. The case of Sufyan Sauri is an instance in point. He was one of the acutest legal minds of his time and was nearly the founder of a school of law; but being also intensely spiritual, the dry-as-dust subtleties of contemporary legists drove him to ascetic Sufism. On its speculative side, which developed later, Sufism is a form of free thought and in alliance with Rationalism. The emphasis that it laid on the distinction of *zahir* and *batin* (Appearance and Reality) created an attitude of indifference to all that applies to Appearance and not to Reality. . . . The Muslim State was thus left generally in the hands of intellectual mediocrities, and the unthinking masses of Islam, having no personalities of a higher calibre to guide them, found their security only in blindly following the schools.

3. On top of all this came the destruction of Baghdad—the centre of Muslim intellectual life—in the middle of the thirteenth century. This was indeed a great blow, and all the contemporary historians of the invasion of Tartars

describe the havoc of Baghdad with a half-suppressed pessimism about the future of Islam. For fear of further disintegration, which is only natural in such a period of political decay, the conservative thinkers of Islam focussed all their efforts on the one point of preserving a uniform social life for the people by a jealous exclusion of all innovations in the law of Shari'at as expounded by the early doctors of Islam. Their leading idea was social order, and there is no doubt that they were partly right, because organization does to a certain extent counteract the forces of decay. But they did not see, and our modern Ulema do not see, that the ultimate fate of a people does not depend so much on organization as on the worth and power of individual men. In an over-organized society the individual is altogether crushed out of existence. He gains the whole lot of wealth of social thought around him and loses his own soul. Thus a false reverence for past history and its artificial resurrection constitute no remedy for a people's decay. 'The verdict of history', as a modern writer has happily put it, 'is that worn-out ideas have never risen to power among a people who have worn them out.' The only effective power, therefore, that counteracts the forces of decay in a people is the rearing of self-concentrated individuals. Such individuals alone reveal the depth of life. They disclose new standards in the light of which we begin to see that our environment is not wholly inviolable and requires vision. The tendency to over-organization by a false reverence of the past, as manifested in the legists of Islam in the thirteenth century and later, was contrary to the inner impulses of Islam, and consequently evoked the powerful reaction of Ibn-i-Taimiyya, one of the most indefatigable writers and preachers of Islam, who was born in 1263, five years after the destruction of Baghdad.

Ibn-i-Taimiyya was brought up in Hambalite tradition. Claiming freedom of Ijtihad for himself he rose in revolt against the finality of the schools, and went back to first principles in order to make a fresh start. Like Ibn-i-Hazm—the founder of Zahiri school of law—he rejected the Hanafite principle of reasoning by analogy and Ijma as understood by older legists; for he thought agreement was the basis of all superstition. And there is no doubt that, considering the moral and intellectual decrepitude of his times, he was right in doing so. In the sixteenth century Suyuti claimed the same privilege of Ijtihad to which he added the idea of a renovator at the beginning of each century. But the spirit of Ibn-i-Taimiyya's teaching found a fuller expression in a movement of immense potentialities which arose in the eighteenth century, from the sands of Nejd, described by Macdonald as the 'cleanest spot in the decadent world of Islam.' It is really the first throb of life in modern Islam. To the inspiration of this movement are traceable, directly, or indirectly, nearly all the great modern movements of Muslim Asia and Africa, *e.g.,* the Sennusi movement, the Pan-Islamic movement, the Babi movement, which is only a Persian reflex of Arabian Protestantism. The great puritan reformer, Mohammad Ibn-i-Abdul Wahab, who was born in 1700, studied in Medina, travelled in Persia, and finally succeeded in spreading the fire of his restless soul throughout the whole [sic] world of Islam. He was similar in spirit to Ghazali's disciple, Mohammad Ibn-i-Tumart—the Berber puritan reformer of Islam who appeared amidst the decay of Muslim Spain, and gave her a fresh inspiration. We, are, however, not concerned with the political career of this movement which was terminated by the armies of Mohammad Ali Pasha. The essential thing to note is the spirit of freedom manifested in it: though inwardly this movement, too, is conservative in its own fashion. While it rises in revolt against the finality of schools, and vigorously asserts the right of private judgment, its vision of the past is wholly uncritical, and in matters of law it mainly falls back on the traditions of the Prophet.

Passing on to Turkey, we find that the idea of Ijtihad, reinforced and broadened by modern philosophical ideas, has long been working in the religious and political thought of the Turkish nation. This is clear from Halim Sabit's new theory of Mohammedan Law, grounded on modern sociological concepts. If the renaissance of Islam is a fact, and I believe it is a fact, we too one day, like the Turks, will have to re-evaluate our intellectual inheritance. And if we cannot make any original contribution to the general thought of Islam, we may, by healthy conservative criticism, serve at least as a check on the rapid movement of liberalism in the world of Islam.

I now proceed to give you some idea of religio-political thought in Turkey which will indicate to you how the power of Ijtihad is manifested in recent thought and activity in that country. There were, a short time ago, two main lines of thought in Turkey represented by the Nationalist Party and the Party of Religious Reform. The point of supreme interest with the Nationalist Party is above all the State and not Religion. With these thinkers religion as such has

APPENDIX III

no independent function. The State is the essential factor in national life which determines the character and function of all other factors. They, therefore, reject old ideas about the function of State and Religion, and accentuate the separation of Church and State. Now the structure of Islam as a religio-political system, no doubt, does permit such a view, though personally I think it is a mistake to suppose that the idea of state is more dominant and rules all other ideas embodied in the system of Islam. In Islam the spiritual and the temporal are not two distinct domains, and the nature of an act, however secular in its import, is determined by the attitude of mind with which the agent does it. It is the invisible mental background of the act which ultimately determines its character. An act is temporal or profane if it is done in a spirit of detachment from the infinite complexity of life behind it; it is spiritual if it is inspired by that complexity. In Islam it is the same reality which appears as Church looked at from one point of view and State from another. It is not true to say that Church and State are two sides or facets of the same thing. Islam is a single unanalysable reality which is one or the other as your point of view varies. The point is extremely far-reaching and a full elucidation of it will involve us in a highly philosophical discussion. Suffice it to say that this ancient mistake arose out of the bifurcation of the unity of man into two distinct and separate realities which somehow have a point of contact, but which are in essence opposed to each other. The truth, however, is that matter is spirit in space-time reference. The unity called man is body when you look at it as acting in regard to what we call the external world; it is mind or soul when you look at it as acting in regard to the ultimate aim and ideal of such acting. The essence of 'Tauhid' as a working idea is equality, solidarity, and freedom. The State, from the Islamic standpoint, is an endeavour to transform these ideal principles into space-time forces, an aspiration to realize them in a definite human organization. It is in this sense alone that the state in Islam is a theocracy, not in the sense that it is headed by a representative of God on earth who can always screen his despotic will behind his supposed infallibility. The critics of Islam have lost sight of this important consideration. The ultimate Reality, according to the Quran, is spiritual, and its life consists in its temporal activity. The spirit finds its opportunities in the natural, the material, the secular. All that is secular is, therefore, sacred in the roots of its being. The greatest service that modern thought has rendered to Islam, and as a matter of fact to all religion, consists in its criticism of what we call material or natural—a criticism which discloses

APPENDIX III

that the merely material has no substance until we discover it rooted in the spiritual. There is no such thing as a profane world. All this immensity of matter constitutes a scope for the self-realization of spirit. All is holy ground. As the Prophet so beautifully puts it: 'The whole of this earth is a mosque.' The State, according to Islam, is only an effort to realize the spiritual in a human organization. But in this sense all State, not based on mere domination and aiming at the realization of ideal principles, is theocratic.

The truth is that the Turkish Nationalists assimilated the idea of the separation of Church and State from the history of European political ideas. Primitive Christianity was founded, not as a political or civil unit, but as a monastic order in a profane world, having nothing to do with civil affairs, and obeying the Roman authority practically in all matters. The result of this was that when the State became Christian, State and Church confronted each other as distinct powers with interminable boundary disputes between them. Such a thing could never happen in Islam; for Islam was from the very beginning a civil society, having received from the Quran a set of simple legal principles which, like the twelve tables of the Romans, carried, as experience subsequently proved, great potentialities of expansion and development by interpretation. The Nationalist theory of state, therefore, is misleading inasmuch as it suggests a dualism which does not exist in Islam.

The Religious Reform Party, on the other hand, led by Said Halim Pasha, insisted on the fundamental fact that Islam is a harmony of idealism and positivism; and, as a unity of the eternal verities of freedom, equality, and solidarity, has no fatherland. 'As there is no English Mathematics, German Astronomy or French Chemistry,' says the Grand Vizier, 'so there is no Turkish, Arabian, Persian or Indian Islam. Just as the universal character of scientific truths engenders varieties of scientific national cultures which in their totality represent human knowledge, much in the same way the universal character of Islamic verities creates varieties of national, moral and social ideals.' Modern culture based as it is on national egoism is, according to this keen-sighted writer, only another form of barbarism. It is the result of an over-developed industrialism through which men satisfy their primitive instincts and inclinations. He, however, deplores that during the course of history the moral and social ideals of Islam have been gradually de-Islamized through the influence of local character, and pre-Islamic superstitions of Muslim nations. These ideals today are more Iranian, Turkish, or Arabian than Islamic. The pure brow of the principle of Tauhid has received more or less an impress of heathenism, and the universal and impersonal character of the ethical ideals of Islam has been lost through a process of localization. The only alternative open to us, then, is to tear off from Islam the hard crust which has immobilized an essentially dynamic outlook on life, and to rediscover the original verities of freedom, equality, and solidarity with a view to rebuild our moral, social, and political ideals out of their original simplicity and universality. Such are the views of the Grand Vizier of Turkey. You will see that following a line of thought more in tune with the spirit of Islam, he reaches practically the same conclusion as the Nationalist Party, that is to say, the freedom of Ijtihad with a view to rebuild the laws of Shari'at in the light of modern thought and experience.

Let us now see how the Grand National Assembly has exercised this power of Ijtihad in regard to the institution of Khilafat. According to Sunni Law, the appointment of an Imam or Khalifa is absolutely indispensable. The first question that arises in this connexion is this: Should the Caliphate be vested in a single person? Turkey's Ijtihad is that according to the spirit of Islam the Caliphate or Imamate can be vested in a body of persons, or an elected Assembly. The religious doctors of Islam in Egypt and India, as far as I know, have not yet expressed themselves on this point. Personally, I believe the Turkish view is perfectly sound. It is hardly necessary to argue this point. The republican form of government is not only thoroughly consistent with the spirit of Islam, but has also become a necessity in view of the new forces that are set free in the world of Islam.

In order to understand the Turkish view let us seek the guidance of Ibn Khaldun—the first philosophical historian of Islam. Ibn Khaldun, in his famous 'Prolegomena', mentions three distinct views of the idea of Universal Caliphate in Islam: (1) That Universal Imamate is a Divine institution, and is consequently indispensable. (2) That it is merely a matter of expediency. (3) That there is no need of such an institution. The last view was taken by the Khawarij. It seems that modern Turkey has shifted from the first to the second view, i.e., to the view of the Mu'tazilla who regarded Universal Imamate as a matter of expediency only. The Turks argue that in our political thinking we must be guided by our past political experience which points unmistakably to the fact that the idea of Universal Imamate has failed in practice. It was a workable idea when the Empire of Islam was intact. Since the break-up of this Empire independent political units have arisen. The idea has ceased to be operative and cannot work as a living factor in the organization of modern Islam. Far from serving any useful purpose it has really stood in the way of a reunion of independent Muslim States. Persia has stood aloof from the Turks in view of her doctrinal differences regarding the Khilafat; Morocco has always looked askance at them, and Arabia has cherished private ambition. And all these ruptures in Islam for the sake of a mere symbol of a power which departed long ago. Why should we not, they can further argue, learn from experience in our political thinking? Did not Qazi Abu Bakr Baqilani drop the condition of Qarshiyat in the Khalifa in view of the facts of experience, i.e., the political fall of the Qureish and their consequent inability to rule the world of Islam? Centuries ago Ibn Khaldun, who personally believed in the condition of Qarshiyat in the Khalifa, argued much in the same way. Since the power of the Qureish, he says, has gone, there is no alternative but to accept the most powerful man as Imam in the country where he happens to be powerful. Thus Ibn Khaldun, realizing the hard logic of facts, suggests a view which may be regarded as the first dim vision of an International Islam fairly in sight today. Such is the attitude of the modern Turk, inspired as he is by the realities of experience, and not by the scholastic reasoning of jurists who lived and thought under different conditions of life.

To my mind these arguments, if rightly appreciated, indicate the birth of an International ideal which, though forming the very essence of Islam, has been hitherto overshadowed or rather displaced by Arabian Imperialism of the earlier centuries of Islam. This new ideal is clearly reflected in the work of the great nationalist poet Zi[y]a [Gökalp] whose songs, inspired by the philosophy of Auguste Comte, have done a great deal in shaping the present thought of Turkey. I reproduce the substance of one of his poems from Professor Fisher's German translation:

'In order to create a really effective political unity of Islam, all Moslem countries must first become independent: and then in their totality they should range themselves under the caliph. Is such a thing possible at the present moment? If not to-day, one must wait. In the meantime the Caliph must reduce his own house to order and lay the foundations of a workable modern State.

'In the international world the weak find no sympathy; power alone deserves respect'.

These lines clearly indicate the trend of modern Islam. For the present every Muslim nation must sink into her own deeper self, temporarily focus her vision on herself alone, until all are strong and powerful to form a living family of republics. A true and living unity, according to the nationalist thinkers, is not so easy as to be achieved by a merely symbolical overlordship. It is truly manifested in a multiplicity of free independent units whose racial rivalries are adjusted and harmonized by the unifying bond of a common spiritual aspiration. It seems to me that God is slowly bringing home to us the truth that Islam is neither Nationalism nor Imperialism but a League of Nations which recognizes artificial boundaries and racial distinctions for facility of reference only, and not for restricting the social horizon of its members.

From the same poet the following passage . . . determines the poet's attitude towards the position of Arabic in the educational system of Turkey. He says:

> 'The land where the call to prayer resounds in Turkish, where those who pray understand the meaning of their religion; the land where the Quran is learnt in Turkish; where every man, big or small, knows full well the command of God; O Son of Turkey! That land is thy fatherland!'

If the aim of religion is the spiritualization of the heart, then it must penetrate the soul of man, according to the poet, only if its spiritualising ideas are clothed in his mother-tongue. Most people in India will condemn this displacement of Arabic by Turkish. For reasons which will appear later the poet's Ijtihad is open to grave objections, but it must be admitted that the reform suggested by him is not without a parallel in the past history of Islam. We find that when Mohammad Ibn-i-Tumart—the Mehdi of Muslim Spain—who was a Berber by nationality, came to power, and established the pontifical rule of the Muwahidin, he ordered for the sake of the illiterate Berbers, that the Quran should be translated and read in the Berber language; that the call to prayer should be given in Berber; and that all the functionaries of the Church must know the Berber language. . . .

APPENDIX III

The truth is that among the Muslim nations of today, Turkey alone has shaken off its dogmatic slumber, and attained to self-consciousness. She alone has claimed her right of intellectual freedom; she alone has passed from the ideal to the real—a transition which entails keen intellectual and moral struggle. To her the growing complexities of a mobile and broadening life are sure to bring new situations suggesting new points of view, and necessitating fresh interpretations of principles which are only of an academic interest to a people who have never experienced the joy of spiritual expansion. It is, I think, the English thinker Hobbes who makes this acute observation that to have a succession of identical thoughts and feelings is to have no thoughts and feelings at all. Such is the lot of most Muslim countries today. They are mechanically repeating old values, whereas the Turk is on the way to creating new values. He has passed through great experiences which have revealed his deeper self to him. In him life has begun to move, change, and amplify, giving birth to new desires, bringing new difficulties and suggesting new interpretations. The question which confronts him today, and which is likely to confront other Muslim countries in the near future is whether the Law of Islam is capable of evolution—a question which will require great intellectual effort, and is sure to be answered in the affirmative, provided the world of Islam approaches it in the spirit of Omar—the first critical and independent mind in Islam who, at the last moments of the Prophet, had the moral courage to utter these remarkable words: 'The Book of God is sufficient for us.'

We heartily welcome the liberal movement in modern Islam, but it must also be admitted that the appearance of liberal ideas in Islam constitutes also the most critical moment in the history of Islam. Liberalism has a tendency to act as a force of disintegration, and the race-idea which appears to be working in modern Islam with greater force than ever may ultimately wipe off the broad human outlook which Muslim people have imbibed from their religion. Further, our religious and political reformers in their zeal for liberalism may overstep the proper limits of reform in the absence of check on their youthful fervour. We are today passing through a period similar to that of the Protestant revolution in Europe, and the lesson which the rise and outcome of Luther's movement teaches should not be lost on us. A careful reading of history shows that the Reformation was essentially a political movement, and the net result of it in Europe was a gradual displacement of the universal ethics of Christianity by systems of national ethics. The result of this tendency we have seen with our own eyes in the Great European War which, far from bringing any workable synthesis of the two opposing systems of ethics, has made the European situation still more intolerable. It is the duty of the leaders of the world of Islam today to understand the real meaning of what has happened in Europe, and then to move forward with self-control and a clear insight into the ultimate aims of Islam as a social policy. . . .

This brief discussion, I hope, will make it clear to you that neither in the foundational principles nor in the structure of our systems, as we find them today, is there anything to justify the present attitude. Equipped with penetrative thought and fresh experience the world of Islam should courageously proceed to the work of reconstruction before them. This work of reconstruction, however, has a far more serious aspect than mere adjustment to modern conditions of life. The Great European War bringing in its wake the awakening on Turkey—the element of stability in the world of Islam, as a French writer has recently described her—and the new economic experiment tried in the neighbourhood of Muslim Asia, must open our eyes to the inner meaning and destiny of Islam. Humanity needs three things today—a spiritual interpretation of the universe, spiritual emancipation of the individual, and basic principles of a universal import directing the evolution of human society on a spiritual basis. Modern Europe has, no doubt, built idealistic systems on these lines, but experience shows that truth revealed through pure reason is incapable of bringing that fire of living conviction which personal revelation alone can bring. This is the reason why pure thought has so little influenced men, while religion has always elevated individuals, and transformed whole societies. The idealism of Europe never became a living factor in her life, and the result is a perverted ego seeking itself through mutually intolerant democracies whose sole function is to exploit the poor in the interest of the rich. Believe me, Europe today is the greatest hindrance in the way of man's ethical advancement. The Muslim, on the other hand, is in possession of these ultimate ideas of the basis of a revelation, which, speaking from the inmost depths of life, internalizes its own apparent externality. With him the spiritual basis of life is a matter of conviction for which even the least enlightened man among us can easily lay down his life; and in view of the basic idea of Islam that there can be no further revelation binding on man, we ought to be spiritually one of the most emancipated peoples on earth. Early Muslims emerging out of the spiritual slavery of pre-Islamic Asia were not in a position to realize the true significance of this basic idea. Let the Muslim of today appreciate his position, reconstruct his social life in the light of ultimate principles, and evolve, out of the hitherto partially revealed purpose of Islam, that spiritual democracy which is the ultimate aim of Islam.

Source: Sir Mohammed Iqbal, *The Reconstruction of Religious Thought in Islam* (Lahore, 1982; 1st edn. London, 1934), 146–80.

Appendix IV

M.A. Jinnah's Tribute To Atatürk

10 November 1938

Bombay, Nov. 10: Interviewed on the death of Kemal Atatürk, Mr M.A. Jinnah, President of the All India Muslim League, said:

'He was the greatest Musalman in the modern Islamic world and I am sure that the entire Musalman world will deeply mourn his passing away.

'It is impossible to express adequately in a press interview one's appreciation of his remarkable and varied services as the builder and maker of modern Turkey and an example to the rest of the world, especially to the Musalman states in the Near East. The remarkable way in which he rescued and built up his people against all odds has no parallel in history of the world. He must have derived the greatest sense of satisfaction that he fully accomplished his mission during his lifetime and left his people and his country consolidated, united and a powerful nation. In him, not only the Musalmans have lost, but the whole world has lost, one of the greatest men that ever lived.'—Associated Press.

Source: *Civil & Military Gazette* (Lahore), 11 November 1938.

Glossary

anjuman: a political or non-political association; a society.

Auqaf (pl. of *waqf* [q.v.]): charitable endowments.

azan: Muslim call to prayer, customarily performed from the minaret of a mosque.

chadar (*chador* in Farsi): a covering; unlike the veil, it does not hide the face.

daru'l-harb: 'land of war'; a country not under Islamic rule or law.

daru'l-Islam: 'land of peace'; a country under Islamic rule or law.

'Eid: a Muslim festival, especially *'Idu'l-fitr*—celebrated to mark the end of the month of Ramazan—and *'Idu'l-azha*—commemorated in Prophet Ibrahim's sacrificial tradition.

falasifa (pl. of *falsafi*): philosophers.

fatwa (pl. *fatawa*) (*fetva*, in Turkish): a ruling on a point of Islamic law on any issue given by a *mufti* or a learned *'alim* or a body of *'ulama* (q.v.) in response to an *istifta'*. In this study, the plural used is *fatwa*s.

fez: a cylindrical, red, brimless, felt hat, with or without tassel, worn in Ottoman Turkey and Egypt and by Muslims of British India, especially by the students of the Aligarh Muslim University.

hadis (pl. *ahadis*): an accurate narration (as far as possible) of what the Prophet Muhammad [*sal'am*] said, did, or tacitly approved, from sources considered authentic by the largest body of learned Muslims, and accepted as such after a very careful scrutiny by experts/*'ulama*.

hajj: annual pilgrimage to Makkah; the fifth of the five 'pillars' of Islam.

hijab: a veil.

hijrat (*hijra*, in Arabic): lit. to abandon, to break ties with someone, or to migrate; voluntary withdrawal on religious grounds from *daru'l-harb* to *daru'l-Islam*.

Hindu: lit. an adherent of Hinduism, one of the oldest living religions.

ijma: general agreement or consensus on a point of Islamic religious law.

ijtihad: in Islamic jurisprudence, the use of individual reasoning based on doctrine.

imam: a supreme leader of the Muslims; the leader of prayer. In Shi'a doctrine, the hereditary claimant to the headship of the community through the Prophet's daughter Fatima and son-in-law Ali; in Sunni usage, it is interchangeable with khalifa or caliph.

imamat: the office of an *imam* (q.v.).

inkilab (*inqilap*, in Turkish): a revolution or change; here, it refers to Mustafa Kemal's radical reforms.

ittihad-i Islam: union of Islam or pan-Islam.

Jaziratu'l-'Arab: Arabian Peninsula, Arabia, Palestine, and Iraq, as delimited by Muslim geographers.

jihad: 'utmost endeavour' or struggle, mainly used for taking up arms in a religious cause or in the defence of the *daru'l-Islam*; a war for the defence of Islam and Muslims.

kafir: unbeliever, used for non-Muslims, especially for those who are not the 'people of the Book'.

khalifa: lit. a successor, a vicegerent, or a deputy; typically, the caliph (the anglicized form), the supreme head of the Muslim community, the *imam* (q.v.); as vicegerent of the Prophet he is vested with absolute authority in all matters of state, both civil and religious, as long as he rules in conformity with the laws of the Qur'an and *hadis* (q.v.).

Khalifat-Allah: vicegerent of God. Title adopted by the Umayyads and Abasids.

Khalifatu'r-Rasul-Allah: vicegerent of the Prophet of God. Title adopted by Hazrat Abu Bakr Siddiq (R.A.)

khilafat: the office of the *khalifa* (q.v.), the caliphate.

Khilafat-i Ilahiya: God's Caliphate.

khutba: public sermon, especially that delivered before the Friday or after the 'Eid congregational prayers by the imam or the ruler.

madrasah: same as *daru'l-'ulum* (q.v.) but particularly means a collegiate mosque.

millet (*millat* in Urdu): a community, especially the religious community of Islam.

muhajirin: pl. of *muhajir*, one who undertakes or carries out a *hijrat* (q.v.).

mujtahid: a Muslim jurist.

mullah: a learned man; often used in British India for a dogmatic preacher.

namaz: ritual prayers to be offered five times a day as prescribed by Muslim law.

nikah: Muslim marriage ceremony.

Qur'an: the revealed book of the Muslims. Its original language is Arabic.

risalat: Prophethood.

sal'am: a shortened version of 'peace be upon him' used for Muhammad, the Prophet of Islam.

shaikhu'l-Islam (*şeyhülislam* in Turkish): an honorific title of a jurist par excellence, applied especially to the Mufti of Istanbul, the chief religious dignitary and *fatwa*-giver of the Ottomans. In March 1924, the nationalists abolished this office along with the Caliphate.

shari'at (*shari'a* in Arabic and *şeriat*, in Turkish): moral and religious law of Islam.

Shia: One of the two main branches of Islam. Followers of this sect regard Ali, the son-in-law of the Prophet, and his descendants as the only legitimate *imam*s (q.v.) of the Muslim community after the Prophet.

shura: consultation; deliberation.

Sufi: a Muslim mystic.

Sunni: One of the two main branches of Islam. Those who belong to this branch acknowledge the authority of the *sunnat*, and accept the first four caliphs as rightful successors of Muhammad (*sal'am*).

sunnat: Traditions of the Prophet of Islam.

swaraj: self-rule, self-government, independence.

tajdid: renewal of Islamic thought; revival; renaissance.

tanzimat: the reforms taken up in the Ottoman Empire during 1839–76.

tauhid: the divine unity; declaring God to be one.

takya: the abode of a *faqir* or a saint.

'ulama (pl. of *'alim*): a man of Islamic religious learning.

ulu'l-amr: one in authority.

GLOSSARY

ummat (*umma* in Arabic and *ümmet* in Turkish): world-wide Muslim polity.
Urdu: language of Muslim South Asia (today of Pakistan and parts of India) developed from a mixture of Farsi, Arabic, and Turkish words, upon a base of Hindi, Sanskrit, and local dialects but written in Arabic characters.
vilayet: realm; a province in the Ottoman Empire.
waqf: a pious foundation; a charitable endowment.

Biographical Sketches

(Based on *Who Was Who*, *Islam Ansiklopedisi*, *Encyclopaedia Brittanica*, and Ahmad Saeed's *Muslim India: A Biographical Dictionary*. The abbreviations are standard, used in these works and *The Oxford Writers Dictionary*)

(Ahmed) Cemal Paşa (1872–1922): one of the CUP triumvirs of the Ottoman Govt. during the First World War; Military Gov., Istanbul, 1913; Navy Minister, 1914; doubled as Comdr. 4th Army and Gov.-Gen., Syria, 1914; repressed Syrian plotters, 1917; fled to Germany with Enver and Talat Paşas after the Armistice, 1918; plotted against the British in Central Asia and Afghanistan; assassinated by an Armenian in Tiblisi (Georgia).

(Ismail) Enver Paşa (1881–1922): another of the CUP triumvirs of the Ottoman Govt. during the First World War; educ., Military School, Manastir, and Staff College, Istanbul, 1902; fought against the Italians, 1911; Conqueror of Edirne, 1913; married Sultan's niece; War Minister and Chief of the Gen.-Staff, 1914; acting C-in-C during the War; fled to Germany, 1918; worked with the Soviets to raise Muslims against the British; split with the Soviets and died fighting alongside the Basmachis against the Red Army in Central Asia.

(Mehmed) Talat Paşa (1874–1921): humble beginnings but rose gradually after joining the CUP in Edirne; prepared ground for the CUP takeover, 1908; elected MP, Edirne, and Deputy Speaker, Ottoman Parliament; held various Ministerial posts, including that of the Interior Minister during the Armenian deportations, 1915; Grand Vizier, 1917; fled to Germany with

Cemal and Enver Paşas, 1918; plotted against the British with Soviet help, 1918–21; assassinated by an Armenian.

(Mustafa) Ismet (Inönü) (1884–1973): Turkish General, statesman and second President of the Republic; graduated Staff College, 1906; served in Yemen, the Balkans and, later, on the Syrian front during the First World War; joined Mustafa Kemal as Chief of the Gen.-staff of the nationalist forces in the War of Independence, 1919–22; named Foreign Minister, 1922; negotiated the Treaty of Lausanne, 1923; PM with interruptions, 1923–1937; elected Second Pres. of the Republic, 1938.

Abdul Bari, Maulana Qayyam-ud-din Mohammad (1878–1926): leading *Pir* and pan-Islamist *'alim* from Farangi Mahal, Lucknow; son of Maulawi Abdul Wahab, Shaikh of Farangi Mahal; educ., Farangi Mahal and the Hejaz; founded the Madrasa Nizamiyya, Farangi Mahal, 1908; Pres., Majlis-i Muidu'l-Islam, Lucknow, 1910; Pres., Anjuman-i Khuddam-i-Ka'ba, 1913; played a leading role in organizing the Lucknow Muslim Conference and the Jam'iyyatu'l-'Ulama-i Hind, 1919; Founder-Member, CKC, 1919–26; opposed *hijrat* to Afghanistan, 1920; opposed Ibn Saud during the Hejaz crisis, 1924–26.

Abdul Qayyum, Malik (1892–1956): pan-Islamist barrister and, later, Principal University Law College, Lahore; son of Malik Ghulam Mohyuddin of Lahore; educ., Islamia College, Lahore, MAO College, Aligarh, and Gray's Inn, London (Bar-at-Law); Member, Aligarh Muslim University Court, 1926–47; Pakistan Delegation, Commonwealth Relations Conference, 1954; Pakistan Press Commission, 1954; Editor, *Islamic Review* (London), 1916–19, *Muslim Outlook* (London), and *Muslim Standard* (London); taught law at the University Law College, Lahore, 1932–47; Principal, 1947–56.

Abdulmecid II (1868–1944): thirty-seventh and last Ottoman Caliph who reigned from 19 Nov. 1922 to 3 Mar. 1924; son of the Sultan Abdülaziz; educ., privately; elected Caliph by the GNA at Ankara following the deposition of his cousin Mehmed VI, 1 Nov. 1922; shorn of his temporal powers, he became a rallying-point for the anti-nationalist forces which resulted in the abolition of the Caliphate and his expulsion from Turkey with the rest of his family; his daughter, Princess Dürrühşehvar, was married to Azam Jah, son of the last Nizam of Hyderabad; he died in Paris and was buried in Madinah.

Abul Kasem, Moulvi (1871–1936): Member, Indian Khilafat Delegation to Europe, 1920; opposed the Partition of Bengal, 1905; took part in the *Swadeshi* Movement, 1906; Sec., Bengal Mohammedan Association, 1906; Editor, English weekly *Mussalman* (Calcutta); Member, AICC; Vice-Pres., Bengal Provincial ML, 1917; Chm., Reception com., AIML, Howra Session, 1933.

Aga Khan, The, Aga Sultan Sir Mohamed Shah (1877–1957): 3rd Head of the Nazari Isma'ili Sect of Shi'a Muslims; succeeded his father, 1885; educ., privately; Member, Legislative Council, 1902–4; led Muslim (Simla) deputation to Lord Minto, 1906; Pres., AIML, 1906–13; granted salute of 11-guns in recognition of loyal services during the First World War; pleaded Indian Muslim case *re* Khilafat before the Council of Four at Paris, 1919; opposed the non-cooperation experiment; Member, non-official Khilafat Delegation to Britain, 1921.

Ali, Mohamed (1878–1931): leading pan-Islamic journalist and politician from Rampur and younger brother of Shaukat Ali; son of Abdul Ali Khan; educ., MAO College, Aligarh, and Lincoln College, Oxford; graduated, 1902; Chief Educ. Officer, Rampur, 1902–4; Founder-Member, AIML; Editor, *Comrade* (Calcutta/Delhi), 1911; and *Hamdard* (Calutta/Delhi), 1913; interned for pro-Turkish activities, 1915–19; Member, CKC, 1919–28; led the Khilafat Delegation to Europe, 1920; interned for the Karachi Resolutions, 1921–23; Pres., INC, 1923; CKC delegate to the Makkah Congress, 1926; participated in first RTC, 1930–31.

Ali, Shaukat (1873–1938): pan-Islamist journalist and politician from Rampur and elder brother of Mohamed Ali; son of Abdul Ali Khan; educ., MAO College, Aligarh; Sub-Deputy Opium Agent in Opium Dept. till 1912; Founder-Member, AIML; helped found Anjuman-i Khuddam-i Ka'ba, 1913; interned with Mohamed Ali, 1915–19; Hon. Sec., Pres., CKC, with two interruptions, 1923–38; delegate of the CKC to World Muslim Congress, Makkah, 1926.

BIOGRAPHICAL SKETCHES

Amanullah Khan (1892–1960): ruler of Afghanistan first as the Amir (1919–26) and then as Shah (1926–29); third son of Amir Habibullah Khan; seized power after the assassination of his father, 1919; fought the Third Anglo-Afghan War, May 1919; encouraged Indian *hijrat* to Afghanistan as a bargaining chip with the British, 1920; gained independence, 1921; used his influence to modernize the country, which produced a backlash resulting in the Khost Rebellion, 1924; opposition to his rule increased when he travelled to Europe to display his modernity, 1927; uprising in Jalalabd culminated in his ouster by Habibullah Kalakani, a warlord known as Bacha Sakao, soon to be replaced by Nadir Khan; Amanullah abdicated in 1929 and settled first in Italy and, later, in Switzerland.

Ameer Ali, Syed (1849–1928): Calcutta Barrister and Judge; educ., Hoogley College, Calcutta, and Inner Temple, London; called to Bar, 1873; Lecturer on Mahomedan Law, Presidency College, Calcutta, 1873–78; Magistrate and Chief Magistrate, Calcutta, 1878–81; MLC, Bengal, 1878–83; MILC, 1883–85; Judge, High Court of Judicature, Bengal, 1890–1904; settled in Britain, 1904; helped found the London ML, 1908; Member, Judicial Com. of the Privy Council, 1909–28; published extensively on Islam and Islamic history.

Ansari, Dr Mukhtar Ahmad (1880–1936): leading medical practitioner and politician from Ghazipur settled in Delhi; educ., Muir Central College, Allahabad, Edinburgh and London; led the Red Crescent Medical Mission to Turkey, 1912–13; Member, AIML Council; Chm. Reception Com., AIML Delhi Session, 1918; Member, AICC for eight years from 1919; Member, CKC, 1919–28: led the Khilafat Deputation to the Viceroy, 1920; Member, non-official Khilafat Delegation to Britain, 1921; Pres., Khilafat Conference, Gaya, 1922.

Azad, Maulana Feroz Bakht Muhyi-ud-din Ahmad Abul Kalam (1888–1958): leading *'alim* and pan-Islamic journalist settled in Calcutta; born at Makkah of an Arab mother and Indian father; educ., Dars-i Nizamia, Calcutta, and Nadwatu'l-'Ulama, Lucknow; Editor, *Vakil* (Amritsar), 1907 and *al-Nadwah* (Lucknow), 1911; started weekly *al-Hilal* (Calcutta), 1912; and, on its suppression, *al-Balagh* (Calcutta), 1913; interned for pro-Turkish activities, 1916–20; Member, CKC and Jam'iyyatu'l-'Ulama; issued a *fatwa* in support of the *hijrat*, 1920; Member, Non-cooperation Com. of the CKC, 1920–21; interned, 1921–23; Pres., INC, 1923; Pres., CKC, 1925; supported Ibn Saud, 1924–26.

Baig, Mirza Sir Abbas Ali (1859–1932): prominent Indian Muslim and former Member of the Council of India; educ., Wilson College, Bombay (BA, 1878), and Glasgow (LLB, 1912); awarded CSI (1912) and KCIE (1917); Bombay Education Service, 1882–89; Asst. Collector, Thana, 1890–92; Presidency Magistrate, Bombay, 1893; Special Duty, Junagarh State, 1906–10; Member, Council of India, 1910–17; Special Duty, Egypt, 1914–15; Revenue & Finance Member, Baroda State, 1928–31.

Benedict XV, Giacomo della Chiesa (1854–1922): Pope of Rome, 1914–22; made Archbishop of Bologna, 1907; Cardinal, 1914; elected as Pope, 1914; maintained strictest neutrality during the First World War; initiated several proposals for peace; founded the Vatican Service for POWs; France and England resumed diplomatic relations with the Holy See during his pontificate; gave a controversial audience to the Indian Khilafat Delegation, 1920.

Bryce, Viscout James (1838–1922): British jurist, historian and politician; educ., Belfast Academy, Glasgow University, and Trinity College, Oxford; Fellow of Oriel, 1862; Regius Prof. of Civil Law, Oxford, 1870–93; Liberal MP, 1880–1907; Under-Sec. of State for Foreign Affairs, 1885–92; Minister, 1894–95; Chief Sec. for Ireland, 1905–7; Ambassador to the US, 1907–13; Member of the House of Lords, 1913; produced official report on Armenian massacres with the assistance of Toynbee, 1916; served at the International Court at The Hague; supported the establishment of the League of Nations.

Cecil, Lord Robert (1864–1958): British lawyer, politician, and diplomat and one the architects of the League of Nations; awarded Nobel Peace Prize, 1937; son of Marquess of Salisbury; educ., at home, Eton College, and University College, Oxford; admitted to the Bar, 1887; appointed a Queen's Counsel, June 1899; MP, 1906–23; Under-Sec., of State for Foreign Affairs, 1915–19; vehement critic of Turkey, 1919–20; Lord Privy Seal, 1923–24;

British Rep., Paris Peace Conference, 1920; Minister for the League affairs, 1923–27.

Chelmsford, Frederic John Napier Thesiger, 3rd Baron and Ist Viscount (1868–1933): Viceroy of India; educ., Winchester, and Magdalen College, Oxford; called to the Bar, 1893; Gov. of Queensland, 1905–9; Gov. of New South Wales, 1909–13; Viceroy of India, 1916–21; repression against Indian nationalists leading to the massacre of Amritsar by Brig.-Gen. Dyer, 1919; unsympathetic towards the Khilafatists, 1918–24; First Lord of Admiralty, 1924; Warden of All Souls, 1931–33.

Chotani, Seth Mian Muhammad Hajee Jan Muhammad (1873–1932): millionaire timber merchant and supporter of pan-Islam from Bombay and President of the Central Khilafat Committee (CKC); head office in Podoni (Bombay) and branches all over India; closely associated with Abdul Bari through his (Chotani's) *Pir*, Sayyid Ibrahim Saif-ud-din, a friend of the former; helped to establish the Khilafat Funds; Pres., CKC, 1919–23; Member, AICC, 1920–21; Member, non-official Khilafat Delegation to Britain, 1921; Pres., Khilafat Civil Disobedience Enquiry Com., 1922; resigned from the presidency of the CKC owing to the funds scandal, 1923, and retired to live a secluded life with virtually no money; last days spent in Madinah.

Curzon of Kedleston, George Nathaniel Curzon, 1st marquess (1859–1925): Sec. of State for Foreign Affairs; educ., Eton, and Balliol College, Oxford; Fellow of All Souls, 1883–1925; Conservative MP for Southport, 1886–98; Privy Councillor, 1895; Under-Sec. of State for India, 1891–1922; Viceroy of India, 1899–1904; Lord Privy Seal, 1915–16; Lord Pres. of the Council, 1916–19; Sec. State for Foreign Affairs, 1919–24; passed over in favour of Stanley Baldwin as PM but stayed on at the Foreign Office, May 1923; negotiated the Treaties of Versailles (1919) and Lausanne (1923); extremely anti-Turk.

Faisal ibn Hussein, Emir (1885–1933): King of Greater Syria (1920) and later of Iraq (1921–33); third son of Hussein bin Ali, Sharif of Makkah; organized, with T.E. Lawrence, the Arab revolt against the Ottomans during First World War; demanded Arab independence at the Paris Peace

BIOGRAPHICAL SKETCHES

Conference, 1919; conditionally signed the Faisal-Weizmann Agreement accepting the Balfour Declaration in exchange for Britain fulfilling wartime promises of Arab independence; King of Greater Syria and, after expulsion, of Iraq, 1920–33; he died in Berne, Switzerland.

Fuad I, King of Egypt (1868–1936): King of Egypt and Sudan; seventh son of Ismail Pasha and great-grandson of Muhammad Ali Pasha who was of Albanian descent; after Egyptian independence (1922), struggled with the Wafd Party throughout his reign; abrogated the 1923 Constitution, replacing it with a new one that limited the role of the Parliament to an advisory status, 1930; large scale public dissatisfaction compelled him to restore the earlier Constitution, 1935.

Gandhi, Mohandas Karamchand (1869–1948): Gujarati Hindu barrister, journalist, and politician; Editor, *Young India*; educ., Rajkot, Bhavagar, and London; called to the Bar, 1889; practiced in South Africa for seventeen years; gave up practice to lead the 'Passive Resistance' campaign on behalf of the Indian settlers, 1908; returned to India, 1915; supported the Khilafat Movement, 1918–24; leading figure of the INC till his assassination.

Giolitti, Giovanni (1842–1928): Italian statesman and five times Prime Minister of Italy between 1892 and 1921; elected to the Lower House of Parliament, 1882; Treasury Minister in the Depretis and Crispi Cabinets, 1889–92; PM, 1892–93, 1903–5, 1906–9, 1911–14 and 1920–21; opposed Italy's entry into the First World War on grounds that Italy was militarily unprepared; yet agreed to serve PM during 1920–21; enjoyed the support of the Fascist Squadristi and did not try to stop their forceful incursions against their political opponents; initially supported Mussolini but withdrew later, 1924.

Hasan, Yakub (1875–1940): journalist and politician from Madras; educ., MAO College, Aligarh; for few years published an Urdu weekly, *Qaumi Halchal*, and an English weekly, *Muslim Patriot*; Member, AIML deputation to Britain *re* reforms and Khilafat, 1919; managed Islamic Information Bureau and its journal, *Muslim Outlook* (London), along with Kidwai and Ispahani; returned to India, 1920; was imprisoned twice.

BIOGRAPHICAL SKETCHES

Hayat, Hasan Muhammad (1882–1955): pan-Islamist and Member-Sec. of the Khilafat Delegation to Europe, 1920; educ., MAO College, Aligarh; Registrar, Jamia Millia Islamia, Delhi; Sec., Nawab of Bhopal, 1949.

Hossain, Syud (1886–1949): pan-Islamic journalist from Bihar and Member of the Khilafat Delegation to Europe; son of Nawab Syed Mohammad; educ., MAO College, Aligarh, and England; Member, Council of AIML; Sub-Editor, *Bombay Chronicle*, 1917–19; Editor, *Independent* (Allahabad), 1918; Editor, *Nawa-i Watan* (USA); Member, AIML; Prof. of Indian & Islamic Civilizations, University of South Carolina (USA), 1937; Indian Ambassador to Egypt.

Hussein ibn Ali, Sayyid (1853–1931): Sharif/Emir of Makkah (1908–17) and the last of the Hashamite king of the Hejaz; remained loyal to the Ottomans during the early stages of the First World War, 1914–16; led the British-instigated Arab Revolt, 1916–18; refused to sign the Treaty of Sevrès (1920) because of the Allied failure to fulfil promises about Arab independence; the only reward came when his sons were made the kings of Transjordan, Syria, and later, Iraq; proclaimed himself Caliph, Mar. 1924; this led to his defeat and expulsion at the hands of Abdul Aziz al-Saud, 1924; abdicated in favour of his eldest son Ali and fled to Cyprus and then settled in Amman, Transjordan, where his son Abdullah was King; he is buried in Jerusalem.

Ibn Saud, Abdul Aziz (1876–1953): the 'Wahabi' ruler of the Nejd and King of Saudi Arabia; grew up in exile in Kuwait; recaptured Riyadh and recovered his family heritage, 1902–4; consolidated control over the Nejd, 1904–12; founded the Ikhwan, a militant religious organization; entered into treaties with the British, 1915 and 1922; conquered the Hejaz, ending Hussein's Hashamite control of the Holy Places, 1925; proclaimed himself King raising controversy in India, 1926; the British recognized his independence, 1927; founded the unified nation of Saudi Arabia, 1932.

Iqbal, Dr (Sir) Mohammed (1876–1938): Barrister, poet-philosopher, and politician, settled in Lahore; educ., Scotch Mission College, Sialkot; Govt. College, Lahore (BA, 1897, MA, 1899), Trinity College, Cambridge (BA Hons., 1907), Munich University (Ph.D., 1907), and Lincolns Inn, London

(Bar-at-Law, 1908); on the faculty of the Oriental College, Lahore, 1899–1903 (with breaks); Govt. College, Lahore, 1903–5 and 1909–10; resigned to practice law at Lahore High Court; Sec., Punjab Khilafat Committee, 1919; but opposed Non-Cooperation; MLC, Punjab, 1926; Pres., AIML, Allahabad Session, 1930; RTCs in London, 1931–32.

Jinnah, Mohammad Ali (1876–1948): Barrister and politician from Bombay; educ., Sind Madrasatul Islam and Mission School, Karachi, and Lincoln's Inn, London; called to Bar, 1896; practiced first at Karachi and then enrolled as an advocate at Bombay High Court, 1897; MILC, 1910; joined AIML, 1913; principal negotiator of the Lucknow Pact with the INC, 1916; Pres., AIML, 1916, 1920 and 1934–48; Pres., Home Rule League, Bombay, 1917–20; leader, AIML Delegation to Britain regarding Reforms and Khilafat, 1919; first Gov.-Gen. of Pakistan, 1947–48.

Kamaluddin, Khwaja (1870–1932): Head of the Ahmadiayya Mission in Woking (Surrey), UK; took over the Shah Jahan Mosque, established by Dr G.W. Leitner in 1889 with funds from the Nizam of Hyderabad and the Begum of Bhopal; established the Woking Muslim Mission & Literay Trust with the help of the British Muslim, Lord Headley al-Farooq, 1912; helped Mohamed Ali and his Khilafat Delegation to Europe, 1920; contributed to the the Woking Mission's journal, the *Islamic Review*.

Khan, Hakim Ajmal (1865–1927): leading practitioner of the *unani* system of medicine, and pan-Islamic politician from Delhi; son of Mahmud Khan; educ., privately; Founder-Member, AIML: helped strengthen political alignment between the politicians and the *'ulama*, 1906–19; Pres., AIML, 1919; Vice-Pres., CKC, 1919–25; Pres., INC, 1921; Member, Congress and Khilafat Civil Disobedience Eenquiry Coms., 1922; travelled to Europe, and Near and Middle East, 1925–26.

Khan, Muhammad Ayub (1907–74): Commander-in-Chief of the Pakistan Army and President of Pakistan; son of Mir Dad Khan Tareen, an NCO of the British Indian Army; educ., Aligarh Muslim University, 1922; joined the Royal Military Academy, Sandhurst (UK); Com., 1928; served in the Second World War; after Partition joined the fledgling Pakistan Army, 1947; became its Chief, 1951; Defence Minister, 1954; Chief Martial Law Administrator,

7 Oct. 1958; deposed Pres. Iskandar Mirza in a coup, 27 Oct. 1958; Pres. of Pakistan, 1958–69; appointed himself Field Marshal during the mid-1960s; introduced far-reaching socio-economic and structural reforms; forced to hand over control as the ruler of Pakistan to Gen. Yahya Khan, 1969.

Kidwai (of Gadia), Moshir Husain (1878–1938): Barrister, zamindar, and pan-Islamic politician from Barabanki (UP); educ., Lucknow and London; Sec., Pan-Islamic Society of London, 1903–7, and later, of the Central Islamic Society, 1907–20; closely associated with Abdul Bari through his *Pir*, Haji Waris Ali Shah, a friend of the former; helped establish Anjuman-i-Khuddam-i Ka'bah, 1913; conducted the Islamic Information Bureau and managed the *Muslim Outlook* (London); joined the Khilafat Delegation in London, 1920; Pres., Oudh Khilafat Com. since 1920; supported King Hussein's claim to the Caliphate, 1924.

Lansbury, George (1859–1940): British Socialist, Pacifist and an unusually popular politician; began career with the Liberal Party, 1886; joined Independent Labour Party, 1903; MP, 1910–12; helped found the *Daily Herald*, 1912; supported the Suffragette Movement; charged with sedition and jailed, 1913; opposed the First World War; returned to Parliament, 1922–40; Chm. Parliamentary Labour Party, 1927–28; Leader of the Labour Party, 1932–35; increasingly at odds with the official foreign policy of the Party for which he resigned, 1935.

Lloyd George, David (later 1st earl Lloyd George of Dwyfor) (1863–1945): Prime Minister of Britain; educ., Llanystumdwy Church School and privately; Solicitor, 1884; Liberal MP, 1890–1931; Pres. of the Board of Trade, 1905–8; Minister of Munitions, 1915–16; Sec. of State for War, 1916; PM, 1916–22; anti-Turk and pro-Greek in his views; supported Gladstone's 'bag and baggage' policy against the Turks; despised the Indian agaitation to help save the Ottoman Empire after the First World War.

Longuet, Jean (1876–1938): French Socialist lawyer and a grandson of Karl Marx; son of Charles and Jenny Longuet; held a pacifist position during the First World War, but invariably voted for War Credits; Founder-Editor, *Le Populaire*; his policy was adopted by the majority of the Socialist Party at the Strasbourg Congress, 1918; supported the minority after the Tours Congress where the Communists gained majority, 1920; joined the centrist 'Vienna Union', 1920; supported by the Commintern, 1927.

MacDonald, Ramsay (1866–1937): British politician and Labour Prime Minister; illegitimate son of John Macdonald, a farm labourer; educ., village Church and Drainie Parish Schools, 1875–81; became a Radical Socialist, 1885; Editor, *Socialist Review*, 1892; Labour MP, 1906–18; Party Leader, 1911–14; accused of treason and deceit by the right-wing; lost his seat, 1918; failed to give support to the Indian Khilafat Delegation, 1920; returned as MP and elected Leader of Opposition, 1922; PM, Jan.–Nov. 1924, 1929–31 and 1931–35; Lord Pres. of the Council, 1935–37.

Mahmud, Dr Syed (1889–1971): prominent nationalist leader from Patna; educ., MAO College, Aligarh, Cambridge University, Lincoln's Inn, London (Bar-at-Law), and Munster University, Germany (Ph.D., 1911); started legal practice in Patna, 1913; participated in Kanpur Mosque Affair, 1913; and the Khilafat Movement; 1918–24; Sec., CKC, 1921–26; Gen.-Sec, AICC, 1923, 1930–36 and Working Com., 1940–45; participated in the Congress Civil Disobedience, 1930; Member, Bihar Legislative Assembly, 1927; Minister of Education, Bihar, 1937–42; Minister for Development, 1946–52; Member, Indian Parl., 1952–57.

Mehmed V, Sultan Reşad (1844–1918): thirty-fifth Ottoman Sultan (r. 1909–18); son of Sultan Abdülmecid I; educ., privately; became an acclaimed poet; actual decisions of the State were made by various Members of the Ottoman Govt. and, during the First World, War by the triumvirate of the Paşas; his only significant political act was to formally declare *jihad* against the Allies with no noticeable effect on the War, 11 Nov. 1914; hosted Kaiser Wilhelm II in Istanbul, Oct. 1917.

Mehmed VI, Sultan Vahideddin (1861–1926): thirty-sixth and last Ottoman Sultan (r. 1918–22); brother of Mehmed V; after the defeat in the First World War, his reps. signed the Treaty of Sèvres, severely reducing the territorial extent of Turkey, 1920; angered, the nationalists formed a new Government and an Assmbly (GNA) in Ankara under Mustafa Kemal, Apr. 1920; as a consequence, the Sultanate was abolished, 1 Nov. 1922; fearing for his life, Mehmed fled aboard a British naval ship for Malta; later went to live on the Italian Riviera; he died in San Remo, Italy, and was buried in Damascus.

Millerand, Etienne Alexandre (1859–1943): French Socialist politician, Prime Minister and President of France; educ., made his reputation as a defence lawyer; Editor, *La Justice*; elected to the Chamber of Deputies as a Radical Socialist, 1885; influence grew as Chief of the Socialist faction, and Editor, *La Petite République*, until 1896, and *La Lanterne*, 1898; Minister of Commerce, 1899; moved away from Marxism that led to his expulsion from the group, 1903; continued to move to the right on being appointed PM, Jan.–Sept. 1920, and Pres., 1920–24.

Montagu, Edwin (Samuel) (1879–1924): Secretary of State for India; educ., Clifton, City of London School, and Trinity College, Cambridge; Liberal MP, 1906–22; parl. Under-Sec. of State for India, 1910–14; Financial Sec. to the Treasury, 1914–16; Minister of Munitions, 1916; Sec. of State for India, 1917–22; Jewish but anti-Zionist; one of the few Ministers who understood Muslim apprehensions over the Khilafat question; despised by Lloyd George for his pleadings on their behalf.

Mustafa Kemal Paşa (1881–1938): Ottoman General and, later, President of Turkey; son of Ali Riza and Zübeyde, middle-class Turkish settlers in Ottoman Macedonia; educ., Şemsi Efendi School, Salonika, Salonika Military School, Manastir Military High School, and the Ottoman Military Academy; showed competence during the Young Turk period, 1908–18; opposed Turkey's entry in the First World War but fought gallantly to win laurels at Gallipoli, 1915; shifted to Anatolia and organized resistance, 1919–21; emerged victorious and forced the Allies to renegotiate the Peace Treaty that resulted in Turkish sovereignty through the Treaty of Lausanne, 1923; elected Pres. of the Turkish Republic, October 1923; initiated reforms which came to be referred to as 'Kemalism' that aimed at transforming Turkey into a modern society, 1924–38; developed differences with the CKC and the Indian Muslims over his handling of the Caliphate and its final abolition, 1922–24.

BIOGRAPHICAL SKETCHES

Nitti, Saverio Francesco (1868–1953): left-wing liberal Italian statesman who became Prime Minister for the critical year after the First World War; started career as a journalist and Professor of Economics; elected Deputy, 1904; Minister, 1911–14 and 1917–19; succeeded Vittorio Orlando as the PM, June 1919; inherited serious political, economic, and fiscal problems; rise of the Fascists under Mussolini further undermined his govt.; resigned, June 1920; re-elected, 1921–24; remained in exile in France; arrested by the Germans during the Second World War and interned in Austria, Aug. 1943; freed after the Allied victory, 1945; became Senator, June 1948.

Pickthall, (Mohammed) Marmaduke (1875–1936): British scholar of Islam and a noted translator of the Qur'an into English; born into a comfortable, middle-class English family; educ., at Harrow; converted to Islam, 1917; published his translation of the Qur'an authorized by the Al-Azhar University, Cairo; challenged the anti-Turkish propaganda in Britain, 1915–24; supported the Indian Khilafat Movement, 1918–24; Editor, the pro-Khilafat, *Bombay Chronicle*; assisted the Indian Khilafat Delegation to Europe, 1920.

Reza Shah Pahlavi (1878–1944): King of Iran; son of Abbas Ali, a member of the regional army; joined the Persian Cossaks and rose to be a Brig.-Gen.; staged a coup to counter Bolshevik inroads, Feb. 1921; became Army Chief and Minister of War, Apr. 1921; overthrew Ahmad Shah Qajar, the last Shah of the dynasty and founded his own Pahlavi dynasty, Oct. 1923; forced the Majlis to recognize him as Shah, Dec. 1925; coronation, Apr. 1926; wide-ranging programme of modernization invited strong opposition from the conservatives; repression against his opponents made him unpopular; played the Soviet Union off against Britain, but the plan misfired when they jointly occupied Iran and forced Reza Shah to abdicate in favour of his son, Aug. 1941.

Toynbee, Arnold Joseph (1889–1975): British historian who, along with Lord Bryce, prepared the official report on the Armenian massacres, 1916; educ., Winchester and Balliol, Oxford; Fellow of Balliol, 1912; positions at the King's College, London, the LSE and the Royal Institute of International Affairs (RIIA) in Chatham House, 1925–55; worked for the Intelligence

Department of the British Foreign Office during the First World War and served as a Delegate to the Paris Peace Conference, 1919; co-edited RIIA's annual *Survey of International Affairs*; best-known for his twelve-volume analysis of the rise and fall of civilizations in *A Study of History* (1934–61), a synthesis of world history and metahistory based on universal rhythms of the rise and fall of the civilizations.

Venizelos, Eleftherios (1864–1936): Greek statesman and Prime Minister several times with breaks during 1910–15, 1917–20, 1924 and 1928–32 and 1933; son of Kyriakos Venizelos, a Cretan revolutionary; educ., in Ermoupolis (1880), and University of Athens (degree in Law); Minister of Justice, 1899–1901; catalytic role in the creation of the Balkan League, 1912–13; brought Greece into the First World War on the side of the Allies; took part in the Paris Peace Conference, 1919; direct conflict with the monarchy, 1917–20; withdrawal from politics and self-exile in Paris after defeat in the Graeco-Turkish War, 1922; came out of retirement to negotiate peace terms with the Turks at Lausanne, July 1923; returned to power with breaks, 1924–33; reconciliation with Turkey, Apr. 1930; supported the Military coup that weakened the Republic he had created, 1935; left Greece once more and sentenced to death *in absentia*.

Selected Bibliography

Unpublished Sources

(i) PRIVATE PAPERS:

Chelmsford Papers. Papers of the First Viscount Chelmsford as Viceroy of India, 1916–21. OIOC, MSS Eur. E. 264.

Curzon Papers. Papers of the Marquess Curzon of Kedleston as Secretary of State for Foreign Affairs, 1919–24. PRO, FO 800.

Hardinge Papers. Cambridge University Library, Cambridge.

Lloyd George Papers. Papers of David Lloyd George as Prime Minister of Britain, 1916–22, Beaverbrook Library, London.

Lytton Papers. Papers of the First Earl of Lytton as Viceroy of India, 1876–80. OIOC, MSS Eur, E. 218.

Montagu Papers. Papers of Edwin S. Montagu as Secretary of State for India, 1917–22. OIOC, MSS Eur. D. 523.

Reading Papers. Papers of the First Marquess of Reading as Viceroy of India, 1921–6. OIOC, MSS Eur. E. 238.

(ii) OFFICIAL RECORDS:

Britain:

(a) Oriental and India Office Collections, British Library (formerly India Office Library), London (OIOC):

Records of the Goverment of India and the India Office:

L/P&S/3 and L/P&S/7, Political and Secret Letters and Enclosures Received from India; L/P&S/10, Political and Secret Subject Files; L/P&S/11, Political

SELECTED BIBLIOGRAPHY

and Secret Department Regular Series Files; L/P&S/18 and L/P&S/20 Political and Secret Memoranda; Political and Secret Department Library Series; L/P&J/6 and L/P&J/7, Judicial and Public Department Files, 1919–24; ICH(P)P, India Confidential Home Political Proceedings; and L/R/5, Record Department: Native Newspaper Reports.

(b) National Archives (formerly Public Record Office), London (NA):
Records of the British Cabinet and the Foreign Office:
Cabinet Files, Series CAB, 23 (Cabinet Minutes and Conclusions); 27 (Cabinet Committees: General Series); 29 (War Cabinet: Allied and International Conferences); and 42 (War Cabinet: Papers of the War Council, Dardanelles Committee and War Committee).
Foreign Office Files, Series 78 (Turkey: General Correspondence); 141 (Egypt: Embassy and Consular Archives); and 371 (General Correspondence: Political).

Pakistan:
(a) National Archives of Pakistan (NAP), (Islamabad):
All India Muslim League Records, previously housed in the Archives of the Freedom Movement (AFP), University of Karachi (Karachi).

(b) Special Branch Records (Lahore):
Punjab Police Abstracts of Intelligence, 1912–47.

Turkey:
Başbakanlık Osmanlı Arşivi, Istanbul:
Irade 1294, Hariciye 16873.
BEO, 4173/312901–1–10 dated 2, 5, 8, 14, 17 and 20 May 1913.
Türkiye Kızılay Derneği Kütüphanesi, Istanbul
PUBLISHED SOURCES

(i) OFFICIAL PUBLICATIONS:
(a) India:
Bamford, P.C., *The Histories of the Non-co-operation and Khilafat Movements* (Delhi, 1925).

SELECTED BIBLIOGRAPHY

(b) Italy:

Foreign Office:

Nallino, C.A., *Appunti sulla natura del 'Califfato' in genere e sul presento 'Califfato Ottomano'* (Rome, 1916). Eng. tr. *Notes on the Nature of the 'Caliphate' in general and on the alleged 'Ottoman Caliphate'* (Rome, 1919).

(c) Pakistan:

Ministry of Information, *Turkey and Pakistan: Relations Between Turkey and Muslims of Indo-Pakistan Sub-continent* (Karachi, n.d.).

Ministry of Law, *Constitutional Documents (Pakistan)*, i–vii (Karachi, 1964).

Ministry of Information, *Quaid-i-Azam Mohammad Ali Jinnah: Speeches and Statements as Governor General of Pakistan, 1947–48* (Islamabad, 1989).

— *Field Marshal Mohammad Ayub Khan: Speeches and Statements*, i–ii (Karachi, n.d.).

(d) Britain:

Parliamentary Papers:

1916, Cmd. 8325, *The Treatment of Armenians in the Ottoman Empire, 1915–16.*

1920, Cmd. 964, *Treaty of Peace with Turkey, Treaty Series No. 11 (1920).*

1923, Cmd. 1841, *Lausanne Conference on Near Eastern Affairs, 1922–23. Records of Proceedings and Draft Terms of Peace.*

Hansard, Parliamentary Debates of the House of Lords and the House of Commons.

(ii) NON-OFFICIAL PUBLICATIONS:

(a) British Labour Party:

Report of the Twentieth Annual Conference of The Labour Party, Scarborough, 1920 (London, 1920).

(b) Central Khilafat Committee:

Honorary Secretaries, CKC, *Kar rawa'i ijlas jama'at-i 'amila* [held on 27 February 1923, at Allahabad] (Bombay, 1923).

Khatri, Ahmad Haji Siddik, *Hisabat wafd-i Khilafat yurup* (Bombay, 1923).

SELECTED BIBLIOGRAPHY

(c) Indian Khilafat Delegation:

The Turkish Settlement and the Muslim and Indian Attitude, pub. no. I (London, 1920).
The Secretary of State for India and the Indian Khilafat Delegation, pub. no. 2 (London, 1920).
The Prime Minister and the Indian Delegation, pub. no. 3 (London, 1920).
The Case for Turkey and the Khilafat, pub. no. 4 (London, 1920).
Atrocities Committed by the Greeks in Smyrna, pub. no. 5 (London, 1920).
Justice to Islam and Turkey, pub. no. 6 (London, 1920).
India's Verdict on Turkish Treaty, pub. no. 7 (London, 1920).

(d) Mahomedan Literary Society, Calcutta (Kolkata):

Abstract of Proceedings of the Mahomedan Literary Society of Calcutta. Lecture by Moulvie Karamat Ali (of Jounpore) on a question of Mahomedan law Involving the Duty of Mahomedans in British India towards the Ruling Power (Calcutta, 1871).

(e) All India Muslim League:

S. Shamsul Hasan (ed.), *Presidential Address of Quid-e-Azam M.A. Jinnah delivered at the sessions of the All India Muslim League* (Delhi, 1946).

(iii) NEWSPAPERS AND JOURNALS:
(a) Daily:

English:
Amrita Bazar Patrika (Calcutta, now Kolkata)
Bombay Chronicle (Bombay, now Mumbai)
Bombay Gazette (Bombay)
Civil and Military Gazette (Lahore)
Comrade (Calcutta/Delhi)
Daily Herald (London)
Daily Telegraph (London)
Dawn (Karachi/Islamabad)
Englishman (Calcutta)
Express Tribune (Islamabad)
Independent (Allahabad)
Madras Mail (Madras, now Chennai)

Urdu:
Akhbar-i 'Am (Lahore)
Al-Hilal (Calcutta)
Khilafat (Bombay)
Paisa Akhbar (Lahore)
Vakil (Amritsar)
Zamindar (Lahore)

SELECTED BIBLIOGRAPHY

Morning Post (London)
News International (Islamabad)
Pioneer (Lucknow)
Punch (London)
The Times (London)
Times of India (Bombay)

(b) Weekly/Fortnightly/ Periodical:

English:

Asiatic Quarterly Review (Woking)
Asiatic Review (London)
Comrade (Delhi)
Hindu (Madras, now Chennai)
India (London)
Islamic Culture (Hyderabad)
Islamic News (London)
Islamic Review and Muslim India (London)
Muslim Outlook (London)
Nation (London)
New Europe (London)
Theosophist (Madras)
The Times Literary Supplement (London)

Urdu:

Ahsanu'l-Akhbar (Allahabad)
Al-Hilal (Calcutta)
Akhbar-i 'Am (Lahore)
Humayun (Lahore)
Nuqush (Lahore)
Qaisaru'l-Akhbar-i Hind (Allahabad)
Rahbar-i Hind (Lahore)
Sada-i Hind (Lahore)

(c) Others:

Annual Register, 1920–1924 (London, 1920).
Nuqush (Lahore), 109 (Apr./May, 1968) [Contains letters of Abdul Bari and other prominent leaders].
Nuqush (Lahore), 50–1 (Nov. 1954) [Contains a selection of letters of 155 prominent Indian leaders, writers, poets and intellectuals].
Who Was Who, iv (London, 1980).

(iv) BOOKS, TRACTS, AND ARTICLES:

Abbasi, M.Y., 'Jauhar is Outspoken as Ever: The 1913 Episode', *Pakistan Times* (Rawalpindi), 22 Dec. 1978.

——, *London Muslim League (1908–1928): An Historical Study* (Islamabad, 1988).

Abbot, Freeland, *Islam and Pakistan* (Ithaca, 1968).

——, 'Pakistan and the Secular State', in Donald E. Smith (ed.), *South Asian Politics and Religion* (Princeton, 1966), 352–70.

Abdul Aziz, Shah, *Fatawa-i 'Aziziyya*, i (Delhi, 1904).

Abdul Ghaffar, Qazi Muhammad, *Asar-i Jamalu'd-Din Afghani* (Delhi, 1940).

Abdul Ghani, *A Brief Political History of Afghanistan*, (ed.), Abdul Jaleel Najfi (Lahore, 1989).

Abdul Hakim, Khalifa, *Islamic Ideology*, 3rd edn. (Lahore, 1980).

Abdul Hayy, Shah, *al-Khilafah* (Delhi, 1909).

Abdur Rahim, 'Mughal Diplomacy: Akbar–Aurangzeb', unpublished PhD thesis (London, 1932).

Abdul Vahid, Syed (ed.), *Thoughts and Reflections of Iqbal* (Lahore, 1967).

Adamec, Ludwig W., *Historical and Political Who's Who of Afghanistan* (Austria, 1975).

Adams, Charles J., 'The Ideology of Mawlana Mawdudi', in Smith (ed.), *South Asian Politics and Religion*, 371–97.

Afetinan, [A.], *A History of the Turkish Revolution and Turkish Republic*. Eng. tr. Ahmet E. Uysal (Ankara, 1981).

Afzal, M. Rafique, *Political Parties in Pakistan, 1958–1969*, i–ii (Islamabad, 1987).

——, 'Political Parties', in S.H. Hashmi (ed.), *The Governing Process in Pakistan, 1958–69* (Lahore, 1987), 174–214.

——, *Pakistan: History and Politics, 1947–1971* (Karachi, 2001).

Ahmad, Aziz, 'Sayyid Ahmad Khan, Jamal al-Din al-Afghani and Muslim India', *Studia Islamica*, 13 (1960), 55–78.

——, *Studies in Islamic Culture in the Indian Environment* (Oxford, 1964).

——, *Islamic Modernism in India and Pakistan, 1857–1964* (London, 1967).

——, 'An Eighteenth-Century Theory of Caliphate', *Studia Islamica* (Paris), 28 (1968), 135–44.

——, 'Afghani's Indian Contacts', *Journal of the American Oriental Society* (Boston), 89/3 (1969), 476–504.

SELECTED BIBLIOGRAPHY

———, 'Shrinking Frontiers of Dar al-Islam', *Quaid-i-Azam Memorial Lectures*, (limited circulation), (Islamabad, 1975), 1–32.

Ahmad, Aziz (ed.), *Proceedings of the First All-Pakistan Political Science Conference, 1950* (Lahore, 1950).

Ahmad, Feroz, *The Young Turks: The Committee of Union and Progress in Turkish Politics, 1908–14* (Oxford, 1969).

———, *The Turkish Experiment in Democracy, 1950–1975* (London, 1977).

———, 'The Late Ottoman Empire', in Marian Kent (ed.), *The Great Powers and the End of the Ottoman Empire* (London, 1989), 5–30.

———, *The Making of Modern Turkey* (London & New York, 1993).

Ahmad, Jamil-ud-din (ed.), *Speeches and Writings of Mr. Jinnah*, i (Lahore, 1960).

Ahmad, Mirza Ghulam, *Gornamint angrezi aur jihad* (Qadian, 1900). Eng. Tr. *Jehad and the British Government* (Lahore, n.d.). The later version was published as *The British Government and Jehad*.

Ahmad, Qeyamuddin, *The Wahabi Movement in India* (Calcutta, 1966).

Ahmad, Rafiuddin, 'Is the British "Raj" in Danger?', *Nineteenth Century*, 42/247 (1897), 493–500.

———, 'A Moslem's View of the Pan-Islamic Revival', *Nineteenth Century* (London), 42/248 (1897), 517–26.

Akhavi, Shahrough, *Religion and Politics in Contemporary Iran: Clergy-State Relations in Pahlavi Period* (Albany, 1980).

Akhtar, Raja Sultan Zahur, *Shikwah, Jawab-i-Shikwah (Representation and Reply)* (Lahore, 1998).

Aksan, Akil, *Quotations from Mustafa Kemal Atatürk*. Eng. tr. Yilmaz Öz (Ankara, 1982).

Alam, Mahbub, *Safarnama: yurup bilad-i Rum Sham wa Misr* (n.p., 1908).

Ali, (Maulawi) Muhammad, *The Khilafat in Islam* (Lahore, 1920).

Ali, Mohamed, *My Life: A Fragment* (ed.), Afzal Iqbal (Lahore, 1942).

Ali, Rahman, *Tazkira-i 'ulama-i Hind* (Lucknow, 1914). Urdu tr. Muhammad Ayub Qadiri (Karachi, 1961).

Ali, Shaukat, *Pan-Movements in the Third World* (Lahore, 1976).

Ali Reis Effendi, Sidi, *Mir'at al-Mumalik* (ed.), Jevdet (Istanbul, 1895). Eng. tr. A. Vambéry (London, 1899).

SELECTED BIBLIOGRAPHY

Ambassador for Cultural Affairs, Turkish Centre, New York, *Atatürk's Republic of Turkey* (New York, 1981).Ameer Ali, (Syed), 'Pan-Islamism', *The Times*, 11 January 1912.

―――, 'Moslem Feeling', in Sir Thomas Barclay, *The Turco-Italian War and its Problems* (London, 1912).

―――, 'The Caliphate, a Historical and Juridical Sketch', *Contemporary Review* (London), 107/594 (1915), 681–94.

―――, 'Memoirs of the late Rt. Hon'ble Syed Ameer Ali', *Islamic Culture* (Hyderabad), 5 (1931), 508–42 and 6 (1932), 1–19, 163–82, 333–62, and 503–25.

Amir, Dr Syed, 'Turkey—a model for the Islamic World', *Dawn Review*, 24–30 May 2007, 14–15.

Anderson, M.A., *The Eastern Question, 1774–1923* (New York, 1966).

Andonian, Aram (Comp.), *The Memoirs of Naim Bey* (London, 1920).

Anjum, Khaliq, *Maulana Abu'l-Kalam Azad: shakhsiyyat aur karname* (Karachi, 1988).

Anon., *The Memoirs of Naim Bey*, published by Aram Anoonian (London, 1920).

―――, *Muhammad Ali: His Life, Services and Trial* (Madras, 1922).

Anon., *Turkey and Pakistan: Relations Between Turkey and Muslims of Indo-Pakistan Sub-continent*, Govt. of Pakistan, (Karachi, n.d.).

Anwar, Saiyid Hasan Musana, 'Imam Ahmad Riza: ek mazlum Islami mufaqqir', *al-Mizan*, 6/6–8 (1976), 249–59.

Arfa, General Hassan, *Under Five Shahs* (London, 1964).

Armstrong, H.C., *Turkey in Travail: The Birth of a New Nation* (London, 1925).

―――, *Grey Wolf—Mustafa Kemal: An Intimate Study of a Dictator* (London, 1932).

―――, *Ibn Saud: Lord of Arabia* (London, 1939).

Arnold, T.W., *The Caliphate* (Oxford, 1924).

―――, 'Khalifa', *Encyclopaedia of Islam*, ii (Leiden, 1927), 881–85.

―――, *Bozkurt: Kemal Atatürk'un Yasami*, (Istanbul, 1996).

Askari, Hasan, *Society and State in Islam* (Lahore, 1979).

Asrar, N. Ahmet, 'The Myth About the Transfer of the Caliphate to the Ottomans', *Journal of the Regional Cultural Institute* (Tehran), 5/2–3, (1972), 111–20.

Ataullah, Shaikh (ed.), *Maktibat-i Iqbal*, i–ii (Lahore, 1945).

———, *Iqbalnama*, i–ii (Lahore, n.d.).

Atwan, Abdel Bari, *The Secret History of al Qaeda* (Berkeley & Los Angeles, 2006).

Aubert, Roger, 'Papacy–VII: The 19th and 20th Centuries', *Encyclopaedia Britannica*, xvi, 1972, 271.

Aybek, Zafar Hasan, *Ap biti*, i–iii (Lahore, [1964]).

Ayyubi, N. Akmal, 'Urdu men Turki zaban ke alfaz', *Ma'araf* (Azamgarh), 104/6 (1969), 460–5.

———, 'A Proposal for Research on Indo-Turkish Relations', *Belleten*, Turk Tarikh Kurumu (Ankara), 46/181 (1982), 67–72.

Azad, Abul Kalam, *Mas'ala-i Khilafat wa Jazira-i 'Arab*, (Calcutta, 1920).

———, *Khutbat-i Azad* (ed.), Shorish Kashmiri, 3rd edn. (Lahore, 1944).

Aziz, K.K., *Britain and Muslim India* (London, 1963).

———, (ed.), *Ameer Ali: His Life and Work* (Lahore, 1968).

Aziz-al Ahsan, Syed, 'State, Legitimacy, and Succession: Sunni Political Traditions and Colonial Heritage', *Journal of South Asian and Middle Eastern Studies*, 16/3, (Spring 1993), 1–24.

Bacik, Gokhan, 'Denationalisation as a Key Concept in Understanding the Success of Islam in Tuksih Politics', in Maqsudul Hasan Nuri, et al (eds.), *Islam and State: Practice and Perceptions in Pakistan and the Contemporary Muslim World* (Islamabad, 2012), 106–22.

Badger, George Percy, 'The Precedents and Usages Regulating the Muslim Khalifate', *Nineteenth Century*, 2/9 (1877), 274–82.

Baird, J.G.A. (ed.), *Private Letters of the Marquess of Dalhousie* (London, 1910).

Bamford, P.C., *The Histories of the Non-Co-operation and Khilafat Movements*, Government of India (New Delhi, 1925).

Banani, Amin, *The Modernization of Iran* (Stanford, 1961).

Bano, Bakhtiyar, 'Wazahati fehrist *Humayun*', MA thesis (Lahore, 1965).

Barakatullah (maulavie), Mohammad, *The Khilafet* (London, 1924).

Barclay, Sir Thomas, 'England and Islam', *Asiatic Review* (London), 15 Aug. 1914.

Barthold, Wilhelm, 'Khalif i Sultan', *Mir Islama* (St Petersburg), i (1912), 202–26 and 345–400.

Batalwi, Ashiq Husain, *Chand yaden chand ta'assurat*, (Lahore, 1969).

Bayur, Y. Hikmet, 'Maysor Sultani Tipu ile Osmanli Padşahlarindan I Abdul Hamid ve III Selim arasindaki Mektuplasma', *Belleten*, 47 (1948), 619–54.

SELECTED BIBLIOGRAPHY

Baxter, W.E., *England and Russia in Asia* (London, 1885).

Becker, Carl H., 'Panislamismus', *Archiv fur Religionswissenschaft* (Leipzig), 7 (1904), 169–92.

Bennigsen, Alexander, and Broxup, Marie, *The Islamic Threat to the Soviet State* (London, 1983).

Berkes, Niyazi, *The Development of Secularism in Turkey* (Montreal, 1964).

Berkman, Ali Umit, 'Administrative Reforms in Pakistan and Turkey: A Comparative Analysis', *Journal of South Asian and Middle Eastern Studies* (Villanova), 2/4 (Summer 1979), 3–17.

Binder, Leonard, 'Al-Ghazali's Theory of Islamic Government', *Moslem World*, 45/3, (1955), 229–41.

Blunt, W.S., 'The Future of Islam', *Fortnightly Review*, 30 (Aug.-Nov. 1881), 204–23, 315–32, 441–58 and 585–602, and 31 (Jan. 1882), 32–48.

———, *The Future of Islam* (London, 1882).

———, *Secret History of the English Occupation of Egypt: Being a Personal Narrative of Events*, (London, 1907).

———, *India Under Ripon* (London, 1909).

Bolitho, Hector, *Jinnah: Creator of Pakistan* (London, 1954).

Borak, Sadi (ed.), *Armstrong'tan Bozkurt: Mustafa Kemal ve Iftirlara Cevap* (Istanbul, 1955).

———, *Atatürk ve Din* (Istanbul, 1962).

———, *Atatürk'un Armstrong'a Cevabi*, 3rd edn. (Istanbul, 1997).

Boulger, Demetrius Charles, *England and Russia in Central Asia*, i–ii (London, 1879).

Brand, Carl F., *The British Labour Party: A Short History* (London. 1965).

Brogan, D.W., *The Development of Modern France (1870–1939)*, 4th edn. (London, 1943).

Brown, Daniel W., 'Islamic Modernism in South Asia: A Reassessment', *Muslim World*, 87/3-4 (1997), 258–71.

Browne, Edward G., 'Pan-Islamism', in F.A. Kirkpatric (ed.), *Lectures on the History of the Nineteenth Century* (Cambridge, 1904), 306–30.

———, *The Persian Revolution of 1905–1909* (Cambridge, 1910).

Bryce, Lord, 'The Settlement of the Near East', *Contemporary Review* (London), Jan. 1920.

Buckler, F.W., 'The Historical Antecedents of the Khilafat Movement', *Contemporary Review*, 121/677 (1922), 603–11.

Bunting, Madaleine, 'Regime Change, European-Style', *Guardian*, 26 Sept. 2005.
Bury, G. Wyman, *Pan-Islam* (London, 1919).
Bury, J.P.T., *France, 1814–1940,* 6th edn. (London, 1962).
Buzpinar, Ş. Tufan, 'The Question of Caliphate Under the Last Ottoman Sultans', in Itzchak Weismann and Fruma Zachs (eds.), *Ottoman Reform and Muslim Regeneration: Studies in Honour of Butrus Abu-Manneh* (London & New York, 2005), 17–36.
_____, 'Hilafet Meselesi', in Coskun Yilmaz (ed.), *II. Abdülhamid: Modernleşme Sürecinde İstanbul* (Istanbul, 2010), 113–29.
Caldarola, Carlo, *Religion and Societies: Asia and the Middle East* (Berlin, 1982).
Callard, Keith, *Pakistan: a Political Study* (London, 1957).
Cash, W. Wilson, *The Moslem World in Revolution* (London, 1925).
Caskel, Werner, 'Western Impact and Islamic Civilization', in G.E. von Grunebaum (ed.), *Unity and Variety in Muslim Civilization* (Chicago, 1955), 335–60.
Cheragh Ali, Moulavi, *The Proposed Political, Legal, and Social Reforms in the Ottoman Empire and Other Mohammadan States* (Bombay, 1883).
_____, *A Critical Exposition of the Popular Jihad* (Calcutta, 1885).
Chirol, Valentine, 'Pan-Islamism', *Proceedings of the Central Asian Society* (London), 14 Nov. 1906, 1–28.
Cirakman, Asli, *From the 'Terror of the World' to the 'Sickman of Europe': European Images of the Ottoman Empire and Society from the Sixteenth Century to the Nineteenth* (New York, 2001).
Cole, D.G.H., *A History of Socialist Thought: Communism and Social Democracy, 1914–1931*, i–ii and iv (London, 1958).
Colquhoun, A.R., 'Pan-Islam', *North American Review* (Boston), 182/6 (1906) 906–18.
Cornish, Jean-Jacques, 'Israel a "threat" to region as it has N-bomb: Erdogan', *Dawn*, 6 Oct. 2011.
Couvas, Jacques N., 'What the wife wears matters for Turkey's presidential post', *Dawn*, 15 Aug. 2007.
Cragg, Kenneth, *Counsels in Contemporary Islam* (Edinburgh, 1965).
Creagh, General Sir O'Moore, *The Autobiography of General Sir O'Moore Creagh* (London, 1924).

SELECTED BIBLIOGRAPHY

Cunningham, Allan, 'The Wrong Horse?—A Study of Anglo-Turkish Relations Before the First World War', in Albert Hourani (ed.), *St. Anthony's Papers No.17, Middle Eastern Affairs, Number Four*, i (Oxford, 1965), 56–76.

Çarkoğlu, Ali, 'Turkey's 2011 General Elections: Towards a Dominant Party System?', *Insight Turkey*, 13/3 (2011), 43–60.

Çuhadir, Ahmet, *Bozkurt: Kemal Atatürk'un Yasami* (Istanbul, 2001).

Daryabadi, Abdul Majid (ed.), *Khutut-i mashahir* (Lahore, [1944]). [Letters of Mohamed Ali, Akbar Allahabadi and Shibli Nu'mani addressed to the editor.]

Dar, B.A., *A Study in Iqbal's Philosophy* (Lahore, 1971).

Degras, Jane (ed.), *The Communist International, 1919–1943: Documents*, i (London, 1956).

de Hammer, Josef, (von Hammer-Purgstall), 'Memoir on the Diplomatic relations between the Courts of Delhi and Constantinople in the Sixteenth and Seventeenth Centuries', *Transactions of the Royal Asiatic Society*, 2 (London, 1830).

de Tassy, Garcin, *La Langue et la litterature hindoustanies en 1871* (Paris, 1872).

d'Ohsson, Mouradges, *Tableau general de l'Empire Ottoman* (Paris, 1778).

Dolu, F. Halidé, 'Some Similarities in the Turkish and Urdu Languages', *Peshawar University Review* (Peshawar), 1/1 (1974–5), 78–110.

Dönmezer, Sulhi, 'Atatürk's Revolution and Social Change', in Azmi Süslü (ed.), *A Handbook of Kemalist Thought*. Eng. tr. Ayşegül A. Yeşilbursa (Ankara, 2001), 1–16.

Douglas, Ian, *Abul Kalam Azad: An Intellectual and Religious Biography* (ed.), Gail Minault (Delhi, 1988).

Dumon, Paul, 'The Origins of Kemalist Ideology', in Jacob M. Landau (ed.), *Atatürk and the Modernization of Turkey* (Boulder & Leiden, 1984), 25–44.

Dupree, Louis, *Afghanistan*, 3rd edn. (Princeton, 1980).

Dyer, Gwynne, 'The Young Turks', *Dawn*, 9 July 2008.

Edib, Halidé, *Inside India* (London, 1937).

Eisenstadt, S.N., 'The Kemalist Revolution in Comparative Perspective', Ali Kazancigil and Erghun Özbadun (eds.), *Atatürk: Founder of a Modern State* (London, 1981), 127–42.

———, 'The Kemalist Regime and Modernization: Some Comparative and Analytical Remarks', in Jacob M. Landau (ed.), *Atatürk and the Modernization of Turkey*, 3–15.

Elkholy, Abdo A., 'The Concept of Community in Islam', in Khurshid Ahmad and Zafar Ishaq Ansari (eds.), *Islamic Perspectives* (London, 1979), 171–81.

Emecen, Feridun, 'Osmnlilar', *Islam Ansiklopedisi*, xxxiii, 487–96.

Emin, Ahmed, *Turkey in the World War* (New Haven, 1930).

Eraslan, Cezmi, *II. Abdülhamid ve Islam Birliği* (Istanbul, 1992).

Farah, Caesar E., *Abdulhamid II and the Muslim World* (Istanbul, 2008).

Faroqhi, Suraiya, *The Ottoman Empire and the World Around It* (London & New York, 2004).

Farooqi, Naimur Rahman, 'Pan-Islamism in the Nineteenth Century', *Islamic Culture* (Hyderabad), 57/4 (1983), 283–96.

Feroze, M.R., *Islam and Secularism in Post-Kemalist Turkey* (Islamabad, 1976).

Ferrer, M.L., 'India', in H.A.R. Gibb (ed.), *Whither Islam?* (London, 1932).

Fığlali, Ethem Ruhi, 'Atatürk, Religion and Laicism', in Süslü (ed.), *A Handbook of Kemalist Thought*, 109–24.

Findley, C.V., 'The Advent of Ideology in the Islamic Middle East', *Studia Islamica*, 55 (1982), 140–51.

Fisk, Robert, 'Armenian Genocide is no secret', *Dawn*, 17 Oct. 2006.

Frechtling, L.E., 'Anglo-Russian Rivalry in Eastern Turkistan, 1863–1881', *Journal of Royal Central Asian Society* (London), 26/3 (1939), 471–98.

Gardet, L., 'Islam', *Encyclopaedia of Islam*, iv, 1978, 171–4.

Gardezi, Hassan N., 'Democracy and Dictatorship in Pakistan: Evaluating Public Opinion', *News International*, 16 Jan. 2000.

Gardner, David, and Dombey, Daniel, 'Erdogan's Turkey: A rule more ruthless', *Financial Times*, 28 Mar. 2012.

Gauhar, Altaf, *Ayub Khan: Pakistan's First Military Ruler* (Lahore, 1993).

Ghauri, Iftikhar Ahmad, 'The Sunni Theory of Caliphate and its Impact on the Muslim History of India', *Journal of the Punjab University Historical Society*, 13 (Dec. 1961), 93–9.

Al-Ghazali, Abu Hamid Muhammad, *Nasihat al-Muluk*. Arabic tr. *al-Tibr al-Masbuk* Eng. tr. F.R.C. Bagley, *Ghazali's Book of Counsel for Kings* (London, 1964).

———, *Ihya 'ulum al-din*. Fr. tr. G.H. Bousquet (Paris, 1953). German tr. H. Kindermann, (Leiden, 1962).

Ghori, Karamatullah K., 'Many bridges to cross', *Dawn*, 20 Dec. 2004.

———, 'Turkish example offers a lesson to our politicians', *Dawn*, 8 Aug. 2008.

Gibb, H.A.R., *Whither Islam?* (London, 1932).

———, 'Al-Mawardi's Theory of the Khalifa', *Islamic Culture*, 11/3, (1937), 291–302.

———, 'Some Considerations on the Sunni Theory of the Caliphate', *Archives d'historie du droit oriental* (Wetteren-Paris), 3 (1948), 401–10.

———, *Islam* (Oxford, 1975).

Gibbons, Herbert Adams, *The Blackest Page in Modern History: Armenian Events of 1915* (New York, 1916).

Gilbert, Martin, *Sir Harold Rumbold—Portrait of a Diplomat* (London, 1973).

Giritli, Ismet, 'Kemalism as an Ideology of Modernization', in Landau (ed.), *Atatürk and the Modernization of Turkey*, 251–3.

———, 'The Superiority of the Kemalist Ideology over Dogmatic Ideologies', in Süslü (ed.), *A Handbook of Kemalist Thought*, 125–35.

Goldzieher, Ignaz, 'Djamal al-Din al-Afghani', *Encyclopaedia of Islam* (Leiden), i (1913), 1008–11.

Gregorian, Vertan, *The Emergence of Modern Afghanistan: Politics of Reform and Modernization, 1880–1946* (California, 1969).

Gülalp, Haldun, 'Political Islam in Turkey: The Rise and Fall of the Refah Party', *Muslim World*, 89/1 (Jan. 1999), 22–41.

Hager, Rob, 'State, Tribes and Empire in Afghan Inter-Polity Relations', in Richard Tapper (ed.), *The Conflict of Tribes and State in Iran and Afghanistan* (London & Canberra, 1983), 83–118.

Haidar, Qurratu'l-'Ain, *Intikhab Sayyid Haidar Yildirim* (Lahore, 1990).

Hairi, Shamsu'l-'Ulama Allama, *Khilafat-i Qur'ani* (Lahore, 1927).

Hali, Altaf Husain, *Madd-o Jazar-i Islam* known as *Musaddas-i Hali* (Delhi, 1879).

Hambly, G.R.G., 'Unrest in Northern India During the Viceroyalty of Lord Mayo, 1869–72', *Journal of the Royal Central Asian Society* (London), 48/1, (1961), 37–55.

Hameed, Syeda Saiyidain, *Islamic Seal on India's Independence: Abul Kalam Azad—A Fresh Look* (Karachi, 1998).

Hammer-Purgstall, Joseph, Freiherr von, 'Memoir on the Diplomatic relations between the Courts of Delhi and Constantinople in the Sixteenth and Seventeenth Centuries', *Transactions of the Royal Asiatic Society*, 2 (London, 1830).

Hanioğlu, M. Şükrü, 'Ittihat ve Terakki Cemiyeti', *Islam Ansiklopedisi*, xxiii, 476–84.

— *Preparation for a Revolution: The Young Turks, 1902–1908* (Oxford, 2001).

— *A Brief History of the Late Ottoman Empire* (Princeton, 2008).

— *Atatürk: An Intellectual Biography* (Princeton, 2011).

Hardy, P., *The Muslims of British India* (Cambridge, 1972).

Harris, George S., *Turkey: Coping with Crisis* (Boulder & London, 1985).

Hasan, Sayyid Nasim, *Istikhlaf* (Amroha, 1919).

Hashmi, Bilal, 'Dragon Seed: Military in the State', in Hasan Gardezi & Jamil Rashid (eds.), *Pakistan: The Roots of Dictatorship* (London, 1983), 148–72.

Hassaan, M.R., 'Indian Politics and the British Right, 1914–1922', Ph.D. thesis (London, 1963).

Henderson, Arthur, *Labour and Foreign Affairs* (London, 1922).

Heyd, Uriel, 'The Later Ottoman Empire in Rumelia and Anatolia' in P.M. Holt, Ann K.S. Lambton and Bernard Lewis (eds.), *The Cambridge History of Islam*, i (Cambridge, 1970), 354–73.

Hiçylmaz, Ergun, *"Bozkurt" Yazari ajan Armstrong ve Casusu Örgütlari* (Istanbul, 1997).

Hijazi, Miskin Ali, *Punjab men Urdu sahafat* (Lahore, 1995).

Holt, P.M., 'The Later Ottoman Empire in Egypt and the Fertile Crescent' in id., Lambton and Lewis (ed.), *The Cambridge History of Islam*, i, 374–93.

Hostler, C.W., *Turkism and the Soviets: The Turks of the World and their Political Objectives* (London, 1957)

Hottinger, Arnold, *The Arabs: Their History, Culture and Place in the Modern World* (London, 1963).

Hourani, Albert, *The Emergence of Modern Middle East* (London, 1981).

Howard, H.N., *The Partition of Turkey: A Diplomatic History, 1913–1923* (Norman, 1931).

Huntington, Samuel P., *The Clash of Civilizations and Remaking of the World Order* (New York, 1996).

Hurgronje, Snouck C., 'Over Panislamisme', *Archives du Musée Teyler* (Haarlem), 3rd Series, i (1912), 87–105.

Husain, Irfan, 'A tale of two armies', *Dawn*, 5 May 2005.
Husain, S. Abid, *The National Culture of India* (Bombay, 1956).
———, *The Destiny of Indian Muslim* (London, 1965).
Husain, Sadiq (ed.), *Anmol moti*, ii (Lahore, 1968).
Husain, Suriyya (ed.), *Sayyid Hayder Yildirim: majmuʻa-i maqalat* (Aligarh, 1981).
Hussain, Mushahid, 'Pakistan: trying out different "models"', *Nation*, 14 Aug. 1988.
Hussain, Riffat, 'Continuation with a difference', in *News International*, 16 Jan. 2000.
Hülagü, Metin, *Islam Birliği ve Mustafa Kemal* (Istanbul, 2008).
Ibn Iyas, *Bada-i al-Zahur fi waqaʻ-i al-duhur* (Boulak, 1893–95). Eng. tr. W.H. Salmon, *An Account of the Ottoman Conquest of Egypt in the Year A.H. 922 (A.D. 1516)* (London, 1921).
Igdemir, Ulug, Karal, E.Z., et al., *Atatürk*. Eng. tr. A.J. Mango (Ankara, 1981).
Ikram, S.M., *Modern Muslim India and the Birth of Pakistan*, 2nd edn. (Lahore, 1970).
———, *Yadgar-i Shibli* (Lahore, 1971).
Imam, Zafar, *Colonialism in East-West Relations: A Study of Soviet Policy Towards India and Anglo-Soviet Relations, 1917–1947* (New Delhi, 1969).
Inalcik, Halil, 'The Rise of the Ottoman Empire', *The Cambridge History of Islam*, i, 295–323.
———, 'The Heyday and Decline of the Ottoman Empire', in ibid., i, 324–53.
———, 'Atatürk and the Modernisation of Turkey', in Süslü (ed.), *A Handbook of Kemalist Thought*, 151–9.
The Indian Annual Register, 1920 (ed.), H.N. Mitra (Calcutta, 1920).
Inshaullah, Muhammad, *The History of the Hamidia Hedjaz Railway Project* (Lahore, 1908).
Iqbal, Afzal (ed.), *Select Writings and Speeches of Maulana Mohamed Ali* (Lahore, 1944).
———, *The Life and Times of Mohamed Ali* (Lahore, 1974).
———, *Islamisation of Pakistan* (Delhi, 1984).
Iqbal, Javid, 'The Image of Turkey and Turkish Democracy in Iqbal's Thought and his Concept of a Modern Islamic State', *Iqbal Review* (Lahore), 28/3, (1987), 25–39.
Iqbal, Dr (Sir) Mohammed, *Bang-i Dara* (Lahore, n.d.).

SELECTED BIBLIOGRAPHY

———, *Khilafat-i Islamiyya*. Urdu tr. Choudhry Muhammad Husain (Lahore, 1923).

———, *The Reconstruction of Religious Thought in Islam*, reprinted (Lahore, 1982, 1st edn. London, 1934).

———, 'Javid Nama', in *Kulliyat* (ed.), Ahmad Saroosh (Tehran, 1343 A.H. [shamsi]).

———, *Bal-i Jibril* (Lahore, 1982, 1st edn. 1935).

———, *Bang-i Dara* (Lahore, n.d.).

Isa, Qazi Faez, 'Islam-Christianity relationship', *Dawn*, 31 Oct. 2006.

Islam, Shadaba, 'Turkish entry: EU's reservations', *Dawn*, 14 Dec. 2004.

Itzkowitz, Norman, (See Volkan, Vamik D. and Norman Itzkowtiz, below).

Jackson, J. Hampden, *Jean Jaurès: His Life and Work* (London, 1943).

Jafari (Nadwi), Rais Ahmad, *Sirat-i Mohamed 'Ali*, 2nd edn. (Delhi, 1932).

———, (ed.), *'Ali Baradaran* (Lahore, 1963).

———, (ed.), *Selections from Moulana Mohamed Ali's Comrade* (Lahore, 1965).

———, (ed.), *Auraq-i Gumgashta* (Lahore, 1968).

Jalal, Ayesha, *Self and Sovereignty: Individual and Community in South Asian Islam Since 1850* (London & New York, 2000).

Jalaluddin, Mirza, 'Mera Iqbal', in Mahmud Nizami (ed.), *Malfuzat* (Lahore, n.d.).

James, Sir Morrice, *Pakistan Chronicle* (ed.), Peter Lyon (London, 1993).

Jelavich, Barbara, *History of the Balkans*, ii (Cambridge, 1983).

Jennings, Sir Ivor, *Party Politics*, i–ii (Cambridge, 1960–1).

Jillani, Anees, 'Pakistan and CENTO: An Historical Analysis', *Journal of South Asian and Middle Eastern Studies*, 15/1 (1991), 40–52.

Jomier, J., 'Islam', *Encyclopaedia of Islam*, iv, 174–7.

Jones, Thomas, *Lloyd George* (London, 1951).

Kamil Paşa, Mustafa, *Mas'ala-i sharqiyya* (Cairo, 1898). Urdu tr. (from Arabic) Maulana Niyaz Muhammad Khan Niyaz Fatehpuri (Pindi Bahawuddin, n.d.).

Kansu, Aykut, *The Revolution of 1908 in Turkey* (Leiden, 1997).

Karal, Enver Ziya, 'The Principles of Kemalism', in Kazancigil and Özbadun (eds.), *Atatürk*, 11–35.

Karim, K.M., 'Pakistan's Historical and Cultural Ties with Iran and Turkey through the Ages', *Journal of the Regional Cultural Institute* (Tehran), 2/2 (1969), 91–5.

Karpat, Kemal H., (ed.), *Political and Social Thought in the Contemporary Middle East* (New York, 1982).

⎯⎯⎯, 'Historical Continuity and Identity Change or How to be Modern Muslim, Ottoman and Turk', in id. (ed.), *Ottoman Past and Today's Turkey* (Leiden, 2000), 1–28.

⎯⎯⎯, (ed.), *Studies on Ottoman Social and Political History* (Leiden, 2002).

⎯⎯⎯, 'The Transformation of the Ottoman State, 1789–1908', in ibid., 27–74.

Katouzian, Homa, *State and Society in Iran: The Eclipse of the Qajars and the Emergence of the Pahlavis* (London, 2000).

Kayani, Muhammed Han, 'Mezarlikta Çürüyen Tarihimiz', *Izlenim*, 20 (Nisan, 1995), 52–4.

Kazancigil, Ali, 'The Ottoman-Turkish State and Kemalism', in Kazancigil, Ali and Özbadun, Erghun (eds.), *Atatürk: Founder of a Modern State* (London, 1981), 37–56.

⎯⎯⎯, and Özbadun, Erghun, 'Introduction', in id. (eds.), *Atatürk: Founder of a Modern State*, 1–7.

Keddie, Nikki R., *An Islamic Response to Imperialism: Political and Religious Writings of Sayyid Jamal ad-Din 'al-Afghani'* (Berkeley and Los Angeles, 1968).

⎯⎯⎯, 'Pan-Islam as Proto-Nationalism', *Journal of Modern History* (Chicago), 40/1 (1969), 17–28

⎯⎯⎯, *Sayyid Jamal ad-Din "al-Afghani": A Political Biography* (Los Angeles, 1972).

Kedourie, Elie, 'Egypt and the Caliphate 1915–1946', *Journal of the Royal Asiatic Society* (London), Parts 3–4 (1963), 208–48.

Khadduri, Majid, 'Pan-Islamism', *Encyclopaedia Britannica*, xvii (Chicago, 1966), 227–28.

Khalid, Detlev H., 'A Study of Atatürk's Laicism in the Light of Muslim History', in Sencer Tonguç, (ed.), *The Reforms of Atatürk* (Istanbul, n.d.), 49–72.

Khalid, Khalil, *The Diary of a Turk* (London, 1903).

⎯⎯⎯, *The Crescent Versus the Cross* (London, 1907).

Khaliquzzaman, Choudhry, *Pathway to Pakistan* (Lahore, 1961).

Khan, Khan Abdullah (ed.), *Maqalat yaum-i Shibli* (Lahore, 1961).

Khan, M. Anwar, *England, Russia and Central Asia (A Study in Diplomacy), 1857–1878* (Peshawar, 1963).

Khan, M.H., *History of Tipu Sultan* (Calcutta, 1951).

Khan, Mohammad Ayub, *Friends Not Masters: A Political Autobiography* (Karachi, 1967).

Khan, Sir Syed Ahmed, *Review on Dr Hunter's Indian Musalmans: Are They Bound in Consceince to Rebel Against the Queen?* (Lahore, n.d., 1st edn. Benares, 1872).

———, 'Khutba men Badshah ka nam', *Tahzibu'l-Akhlaq* (Aligarh), 7/11 (1876), 154–5.

———, *Akhiri mazamin* (Lahore, 1898).

———, *The Truth About Khilafat*. Eng. tr. Kazi Siraj-ud-din Ahmad (Lahore, 1916).

Khan, Tanvir Ahmad, 'Islam in Turkish Politics', *Dawn*, 17 October 2005.

Khan, Zafar Ali, 'Indian Musalmans and Pan-Islamism', *Comrade*, 14 June 1913.

———, *Chamnistan* (Lahore, 1944).

———, *Baharistan* (Lahore, n.d.).

Khuda Bukhsh, S., *Studies: Indian and Islamic* (London, 1927).

Khurshid, Abdus Salam, *Sahafat: Hind-o-Pak Men* (Lahore, 1963).

Kidwai (of Gadia), Shaikh Mushir Hosain, *Pan-Islamism* (London, 1908).

Kinross, Lord, *Atatürk: The Rebirth of a Nation* (London, 1964).

Knightly, Philip, and Simpson, Colin, *The Secret Lives of Lawrence of Arabia* (London, 1969).

Kocabaşoğlu, Uygur, 'Punch', *Tarih ve Toplum* (June 1992), 17/102, 332–50.

Kohn, Hans, *A History of Nationalism in the East* (London, 1929).

Kocatürk, Utkan, *Atatürk ve Türk devrimi kronolojisi* (Ankara, 1973).

Kremer, F.A. von, *Geschichte der Herrschenden Ideen des Islams* (Leipzig, 1868).

———, *Culturgeschichte des Orients unter den Chalifen*, i–ii (Vienna, 1875–77). Eng. tr. S. Khuda Bukhsh, *The Orient Under the Caliphs* (Calcutta, 1920).

Kuran, Ercümend, 'The Reforms of Atatürk', in Sencer Tonguç (ed.), *The Reforms of Atatürk* (Istanbul, n.d.), 7–12.

Kuru, Ahmet T., 'Passive and Assertive Secularism: Historical, Ideological Struggles, and State Policies Toward Religion', *World Politics*, 59/4 (July 2007), 568–94.

———, *Secularism and State Policies Toward Religion: The United States, France, and Turkey* (Cambridge, 2009).

———, and Alfred Stepan (eds.), *Democracy, Islam, and Secularism in Turkey: Religion, Culture and Public Life* (New York, 2012).

Küçükcan, Talip, 'Atatürk ve Din', *Islam Ansiklopedisi*, xxxi, 337–9.

Lambton, A.K.S., 'The Theory of Kingship in the Nisihat ul-Mulk of Ghazali', *Islamic Quarterly* (London), 1/1 (1954), 47–55.

Landau, Jacob M., 'Atatürk's Achievement: Some Considerations', in id. (ed.), *Atatürk and the Modernization of Turkey*, xi–xiii.

———, 'al-Afghani's Pan-Islamic Project', *Islamic Culture* (Hyderabad), 26/3 (1952), 50–4.

———, *Politics of Pan-Islam: Ideology and Organization* (Oxford, 1990).

Landauer, Carl, *European Socialism*, i (Berkeley & Los Angeles, 1959).

Lane-Poole, Stanley, 'The Caliphate', *Quarterly Review*, 224/444 (1915), 162–77.

LaPorte, Jr., Robert, 'Administrative Restructuring During the Zia Period', in Shahid Javed Burki and Craig Baxter (eds.), *Pakistan Under the Military* (Boulder, 1991).

Lee, Dwight E., 'The Origins of Pan-Islamism', *American Historical Review* (Washington DC), 47/2 (1942), 278–87.

Letsch, Constanze, 'Tough times for Turks on borders with Syria', *Guardian*, 25 April 2012.

Levy, Reuben, *The Social Structure of Islam*, 2nd edn. (Cambridge, 1979).

Lewis, Bernard, *The Emergence of Modern Turkey*, 2nd edn. (London, 1968; 1st edn. 1961).

———, *The Middle East and the West* (London, 1963–4).

———, 'The Ottoman Empire in the Mid-Nineteenth Century: A Review', *Middle Eastern Studies* (London), 1/3 (1965), 283–95.

———, *The Assassins: A Radical Sect in Islam* (London, 1967).

———, 'The Mughals and the Ottomans', *Pakistan Quarterly* (Karachi), 8/2 (1968), 4–5.

Lieven, Anatol, *Pakistan: A Hard Country* (London, 2011).

———, 'Military Exceptionalism in Pakistan', *Survival*, 53/4 (2011), 53–68.

Lovell, David, 'Turkey in Europe: Record, Challenges and the Future', *Insight Turkey*, 13/3 (2011), 173–90.

Lybyer, A.H., 'Caliphate', *Encyclopaedia of the Social Sciences*, iii (New York, 1935), 145–49.

MacColl, Malcolm, 'The Musalmans of India and the Sultan', *Contemporary Review*, 71/374 (1897), 280–94.

MacDonald, D.B., *Development of Muslim Theology, Jurisprudence, and Constitutional Theory* (New York, 1903).

MacDonald, Ramsay, 'Turkey and Constantinople', in *Foreign Affairs*, Apr. 1920.

Mahmud Sahib, Syed, *Khilafat aur Inglistan*, 3rd edn. (Patna, [1921]).

Malik, Aziz, *Sahafat aur tahrik-i azadi* (Lahore, 1984).

Malik, F.M., 'Islam as a Social and Political Ideal: The Role of Muhammad Iqbal in Muslim Reawakening', in Andre Wink (ed.), *Islam, Politics and Society in South Asia* (Delhi, 1991), 1–17.

Malik, Iftikhar H., 'Turkey at the Crossroads: Encountering Modernity and Tradition', *Journal of South Asian and Middle Eastern Studies*, 24/2 (Winter 2001), 1–32.

Malik, Ikram Ali, (ed.), *Punjab Muslim Press and the Muslim World, 1888–1911* (Lahore, 1974).

Malik, Jamal, 'Dynamics Among Traditional Religious Scholars and their Institutions in Contemporary South Asia', *Muslim World*, 87/3–4 (1997), 199–220.

Malirkotli, M.M.K. Shihab, 'Maulana 'Abdu'l-Halim Sharar ke nawal', *Humayun* (Lahore), 44/6, (1943), 466–9.

Mango, Andrew, *Atatürk* (London, 1999).

Marchand, H., 'Un coup d'oeil sur l'Islam: Pan Islamisme et modernisme', *Renseignements Coloniaux et Documents* (Paris), 7 (Suppl. to *L' Afrique Francaise*, July 1909), 146–52.

Mardin, Şerif, *The Genesis of Young Ottoman Thought: A Study in the Modernization of Turkish Political Ideas* (Syracuse, 2000; 1st edn. Princeton, 1962).

———, 'Religion and Secularism in Turkey', in Kazancigil and Özbadun (eds.), *Atatürk*, 191–219.

———, 'Turkish Islamic Exceptionalism Yesterday and Today: Continuity, Rupture and Reconstruction in Operational Codes', in Ali Çarkoğlu and Barry Rubin (eds.), *Religion and Politics in Turkey* (London & New York, 2006), 3–24. Also in *Turkish Studies*, 6/2 (2005), 145–65.

Margoliouth, D.S., 'Pan-Islamism', *Proceedings of the Central Asian Society* (London), 12 Jan. 1912.

_____, 'The Caliphate', *New Europe* (London), 14/182 (1920), 294–300.

_____, 'The Caliphate, Yesterday, Today and Tomorrow', in J.R. Mott (ed.), *The Moslem World of To-day* (London, 1925), 31–44.

Marriot, J.A.R., *The Eastern Question: An Historical Study in European Diplomacy* (London, 1917).

Martin, [R.] M., *The Despatches, Minutes, and Correspondence of the Marquess Wellesley, K.G., During his Administration in India*, i–v (London, 1836–7).

Matiur Rahman, *From Consultation to Confrontation: A Study of Muslim League in British Indian Politics, 1906–1912* (London, 1970).

Maududi, Sayyid Abul-Ala, *Islamic Law and Constitution* (tr. and ed.), Khurshid Ahmad (Lahore, 1960).

_____, *Khilafat wa Mulukiyyat* (Lahore, 1966).

_____, *A Short History of the Revivalist Movement in Islam*, 2nd Eng. edn. (Lahore, 1972).

al-Mawardi, Ali ibn Muhammad, *Ihkam al-Sultaniyya* (Cairo, 1881).

McLane, John R., *Indian Nationalism and the Early Congress* (Princeton, 1977).

al-Mehdi, Sadiq, 'The Concept of an Islamic State', in Altaf Gauhar (ed.), *The Challenge of Islam* (London, 1978), 115–33.

Mehrotra, S.R., *The Emergence of the Indian National Congress* (Delhi, 1971).

Meserve, Margaret, *Empires of Islam in Renaissance Historical Thought* (Cambridge, Mass., 2008).

Mihr, Ghulam Rasul, *Sayyid Ahmad Shahid* (Lahore, 1952).

_____, *Jama'at-i mujahidin* (Lahore, 1955).

_____, *Sarguzasht-i mujahidin* (Lahore, 1956).

_____, (ed.), *Tabarrukat-i Azad* (Lahore, [1959]).

Miliband, Ralph, *Parliamentary Socialism: A Study in the Politics of Labour* (London, 1961).

Millar, T.B., 'Turkey', in M. Ayoob (ed.), *The Politics of Islamic Reassertion* (London, 1981), 81–94.

Minault, Gail (Graham), 'Urdu Political Poetry during the Khilafat Movement', *Modern Asian Studies*, 8/4 (1974), 459–71.

_____, 'The Khilafat Movement: A Study of Indian Muslim Leadership, 1919–1914', unpublished Ph.D. thesis, (Pennsylvania, 1972).

SELECTED BIBLIOGRAPHY

———, *The Khilafat Movement: Religious Symbolism and Political Mobilization in India* (New York, 1982).

Miyan, Muhammad (ed.), *'Ulama-i Haq* (Muradabad, n.d.).

———, *'Ulama-i Hind ka shandar mazi*, i–iv (Delhi, 1957–60).

Mooraj, Anwer, 'Neither enlightened nor moderate', *Dawn*, 16 Jan. 2006.

Mosley, Leonard, *Curzon: The End of an Epoch* (London, 1960).

Mourad, Kanizé, *Memoirs of an Ottoman Princess*. Tr. Sabine Destrée and Anna Williams (Islamabad, 2001).

Muhammad, Shan (ed.), *Unpublished Letters of Ali Brothers* (Lahore, 1986).

Mujeeb, Muhammad, *The Indian Muslims* (London, 1967).

Müller, August, *Der Islam* (Berlin, 1885–87).

Munawwar, Mohammad *Dimensions of Iqbal* (Lahore, 1986).

———, and Jalil, Rakhshanda, *Partners in Freedom: Jamia Millia Islamia* (New Delhi, 2006).

Mushirul Hasan (ed.), *Muslims and the Congress: Select Correspondence of Dr M.A. Ansari, 1912–1935* (Lahore, 1980).

———, (ed.), *Mohamed Ali in Indian Politics: Select Writings*, i (Delhi, 1985).

Nadwi, Maulana Abu'l-Hasanat, *Khilafat-i 'Usmaniyya aur Turk* (Delhi, 1920).

Nadwi, Sayyid Sulaiman, 'Khilafat and the Koreish', *Foreign Affairs* (London), 2 (July 1920), Special Supplement, vi–ix.

———, *Khilafat aur Hindustan* (Azamgarh, 1921)

———, *Barid-i Farang* (Karachi, 1952). [Letters of Syed Sulaiman Nadvi written from Europe to Abdul Bari, Abdul Majid Daryabadi and others.]

Najjar, Fauzi M., 'Democracy in Islamic Political Philosophy', *Studia Islamica*, 51 (1980), 107–22.

Najmul Hasan, Maulana Sayyid, *al-Nabuwwat-wa'l-Khilafat*, Eng. tr. L.A. Haidari (Lucknow, 1924).

Nallino, C.A., *Appunti sulla natura del 'Califfato' in genere e sul presento 'Califfato Ottomano'* (Rome, 1916). Eng. tr. *Notes on the Nature of the 'Caliphate' in general and on the Alleged 'Ottoman Caliphate'* (Rome, 1919).

Nasr, Seyyed Hossein, *Ideals and Realities of Islam*, 2nd edn. (London, 1975).

Nasr, Seyyed Vali Reza, *Mawdudi and the Making of Islamic Revivalism* (New York, 1996).

Nawaz, Shuja, *Crossed Swords: Pakistan, its Army, and the Wars Within* (Karachi, 2008).

Nevakivi, Jukka, *Britain, France and the Arab Middle East, 1914–1920* (London, 1969).
Neysari, Salim, 'A Comparison of the Activities Related to the Language and Writing Reforms in Turkey and Iran During the Time of Atatürk and Reza Shah', in Tonguç (ed.), *The Reforms of Atatürk*, 43–8.
Niemeijer, A.C., *The Khilafat Movement in India, 1919–1924* (The Hague, 1972).
Nomani, Shibli, *Safarnama-i Rum-o Sham* (Agra, 1894).
Norman, Roger, 'H.C. Armstrong, Patrick Kinross and Mustafa Kemal', in *Turkish Daily News*, Electronic Edition, 6 May 1997.
———, *Kulliyat-i Shibli*, 4th edn. (Azamgarh, 1954).
———, *Maqalat-i Shibli*, i–iv (Azamgarh, 1954).
Nuri Bey, Celal, *Ittihad-i Islam* (Istanbul, 1912).
Oman, Sir C.W., 'East and West', *Transactions of the Royal Historical Society*, 4/3 (London, 1920).
Öke, Mim Kemal, *Tahrik-i Khilafat*. Urdu tr. Nisar Ahmad Asrar (Karachi, 1991).
———, *Hilafet Hareketleri* (Ankara, 1988).
———, 'Turkish Decision for Secularization and the Question of Muslim Unity', in Rashid Ahmad (Jullundhri) and Muhammad Afzal Qarshi (eds.), *Islam in South Asia* (Lahore, 1995), 31–45.
Özcan, Azmi, 'The Turks in Urdu Literature in the Age of Pan-Islamism', *Journal of the Pakistan Historical Society*, 40/3, (July 1992), 245–50.
———, 'The Press and Anglo-Ottoman Relations, 1876–1909', *Middle Eastern Studies*, 29/1 (1993), 111–17.
———, *Pan-Islamism: Indian Muslims, the Ottomans & Britain (1877–1924)* (Leiden, 1997).
Özdalga, Alisabeth, *The Veiling Issue, Official Secularism and Popular Islam in Modern Turkey* (Richmond, 1998).
Palgrave, W.G., *Essays on Eastern Question* (London, 1872).
Panipati, Muhammad Ismail (ed.), *Maqalat-i sar Sayyid*, i–xvi (Lahore, 1963).
———, (ed.), *Maktubat-i Sar Sayyid*, i (Lahore, 1976).
Pears, Sir Edwin, *Life of Abdul Hamid* (London, 1917).
Pelling, Henry, *A Short History of the Labour Party* (London & New York, 1965).

Peters, W.H., 'Benedict XV', in *New Catholic Encyclopaedia,* II (New York & London, 1967), 280.

Philips, C.H., (ed.), *The Correspondence of Lord William Cavendish Bentinck, Governor-General of India, 1825–1835,* i–ii (Oxford, 1977).

Pickthall, Marmaduke, 'Massacres and the Turks: The Other Side', *Foreign Affairs* (London), July 1920.

Pirzada, Syed Sharifuddin (ed.), *Foundations of Pakistan: All India Muslim League Documents, 1906–1947,* i–iii (Karachi, 1969).

Platt, George M., 'Basic Democracies: The Experiment in Local Government', in Hashmi (ed.), *The Governing Process in Pakistan, 1958–69,* 215–71.

Poullada, Leon B., *Reform and Rebellion in Afghanistan, 1919–1929* (Ithaca, 1973).

'Q', 'Self-determination and the Turkish Treaty', *Foreign Affairs,* 2 (July 1920), Spec. Suppl. xvi–xxiv.

Qadiri, Mufti M. Habibur Rahman, *Ayat-i Khilafat* (Badaun, [1922]).

Quataert, Donald, *The Ottoman Empire, 1700–1922* (Cambridge, 2000).

Qureshi, I.H., 'Two Newspapers of pre-Mutiny Delhi', *Indian Historical Records Commission. Proceedings of Meetings,* XVIII, *(Eighteenth Meeting Held at Mysore, January 1942)* (Delhi, 1942), 258–60.

———, 'The Purpose of Tipu Sultan's Embassy to Constantinople', *Journal of Indian History,* 24 (1945), 77–84.

———, *The Muslim Community of the Indo-Pakistan Subcontinent (610–1947)* (The Hague, 1962).

———, *Ulema in Politics* (Karachi: Ma'are Limited, [1974]).

Qureshi, M. Naeem, 'The Khilafat Movement in India, 1919–1924', unpublished PhD thesis (London, 1973).

———, 'The Indian Khilafat Movement (1918–1924)', *Journal of Asian History,* 12/2 (1978), 152–68.

———, *Mohamed Ali's Khilafat Delegation to Europe (February–October 1920)* (Karachi, 1980).

———, '(Quaid-i-Azam) Jinnah and the Khilafat Movement (1918–1924)', in A.H. Dani (ed.), *World Scholars on Quaid-i-Azam Mohammad Ali Jinnah* (Islamabad, 1979), 151–70.

———, 'Bibliographic Soundings in Nineteenth Century Pan-Islam in South Asia', *Islamic Quarterly* (London) 24/1–2 (1980), 22–34.

———, 'The Rise of Atatürk and its Imapact on Contemporary Muslim India: The Early Phase', *Proceedings; International Conference on Atatürk*, iii (Istanbul, 1981), 55/1–9.

———, 'Islamic Resurgence in Contemporary Pakistan', in Tatsuro Yamamoto (ed.), *Proceedings of the Thirty-First International Congress of Human Sciences in Asia and North Africa,* i (Tokyo, 1984), pp. 309–11.

———, 'Muslims of British India and the Kemalist Reform in Turkey: Iqbal, Jinnah and Atatürk, 1924–1938', in *Atatürk Araştirma Merkezi Dergisi* (Ankara), 12/35 (1996), 379–86.

———, 'Images of Atatürk and Turkey in Urdu Literature', in *Third International Symposium on Atatürk* (Ankara, 1998), 257–82.

———, *Pan-Islam in British India: The Politics of the Khilafat Movement, 1918–1924* (Karachi, 2009; 1st edn. Leiden, 1999).

———, 'The Kemalist Model of State and Ayub Khan's Reforms in Pakistan' in *Atatürk 4. Uluslararasi Kongresi*, ii (Ankara, 2001), 1089–99.

———, 'Atatürk and Armstrong's *Grey Wolf*: Myth and Reality', *The Fifth International Congress on Atatürk, December 8–12, 2003, Ankara*, ii (Anakara, 2005), 973–90.

———, 'The Kemalist Reform and its Impact on Contemporary Muslim World', paper presented at Doğumunun 125. Yilinda Mustafa Kemal Atatürk Uluslararasi Sempozyumu, 15–18 May 2006, Ankara.

Rahman, F[azlur]., 'Internal Religious Developments in the Present Century Islam', *Journal of World History* (Paris), 2/1 (1954), 862–79.

———, *Islam*, Encyclopaedia Britannica, 2nd edn., Chicago, 1979.

———, 'Islam: Challenges and Opportunities', in Alford T. Welch and Pierre Cachia (eds.), *Islam: Past Influence and Present Challenge* (Edinburgh, 1979), 315–30.

———, 'Islam', *Encyclopaedia Britannica*, ix, 1981, 911–26

———, 'Roots of Islamic Neo-Fundamentalism', in Philip H. Stoddard (ed.), *Change and the Muslim World* (Syracuse, 1981), 23–35.

Ramsaur, Jr., E.E., *The Young Turks: The Prelude to the Revolution of 1908* (Beirut: Khayats, 1965).

Redhouse, J.W., *A Vindication of the Ottoman Sultan's Title of 'Caliph', Shewing Its Antiquity, Validity, and Universal Acceptance* (London, 1877).

Reid, Anthony, 'Nineteenth Century Pan-Islam in Indonesia and Malaysia', *Journal of Asian Studies*, 26/2 (1967), 267–83.

SELECTED BIBLIOGRAPHY

Rizvi, Hasan Askari, *The Military & Politics in Pakistan, 1947–1997*, revised edn. (Lahore, 2000).

Robinson, Francis, 'The Leadership of the Professional Politicians in Muslim Politics, 1911–1923', paper presented in October 1973 at the Centre of South Asian Studies, School of Oriental and African Studies, University of London.

———, *The 'Ulama of Farangi Mahall and Islamic Culture in South Asia* (Lahore, 2002).

Ronaldshay, Earl of, *The Life of Lord Curzon*, i–iii (London, 1928).

Rose, J. Holland, '1815 and 1915', *Contemporary Review*, 107 (Jan. 1915), 12–18.

Rosenthal, Erwin I.J., *Political Thought in Medieval Islam* (Cambridge, 1958).

Rozina, Parveen (ed.), *Jam'iyyatu'l-'Ulama-i Hind*, i–ii (Islamabad, 1980–1).

Rustow, Dankwart A., 'Politics and Islam in Turkey, 1920–1955', in Frye (ed.), *Islam and the West*, 69–107.

———, 'Atatürk as an Institution Builder', in Kazancigil and Özbudun (eds.), *Atatürk*, 57–77.

Sadiq, Muhammad, *A History of Urdu Literature*, 2nd edn. (Karachi, 1985).

Saeed, Ahmad, *Anjuman-i Islamiyya Amritsar* (Lahore, 1986).

———, *Muslim India: A Biographical Dictionary* (Lahore, [1997]).

Saksena, Banarsi Prasad, *History of Shahjahan of Dihli* (Allahabad, 1932).

Saksena, Ram Babu, *A History of Urdu Literature* (Lahore, 1927).

Salahi, R.S., *Turkish Diplomacy, 1918–1923* (Abingdon, 1975).

Salmoné, H.A., 'Is the Sultan of Turkey the True Khaliph of Islam?' *Nineteenth Century*, 39/227 (1896), 173–80.

Sarwar, Muhammad, (ed.), *Maulana Mohamed 'Ali ke yurup ke safar (khud unke apne qalam se)* (Lahore, 1941). [Letters by Mohamed Ali, written from Europe to his friends and relatives.]

———, (ed.), *Maulana Mohamed 'Ali* (Lahore, 1962).

Sayeed, Khalid bin, *The Political System of Pakistan* (Boston, 1967).

Sayeed, S.M.A., *Iran: Before and After Khomeini* (Karachi, 1999).

Scatchard, F.R., 'Armenian Atrocities and Some Sceptics, *Asiatic Review*, Jan. 1916.

Schulze, Reinhard, *A Modern History of the Islamic World*. Tr. Azizeh Azodi (London & New York, 2000).

SELECTED BIBLIOGRAPHY

Shafi, Muhammad, *Agha Hashr aur unke dramon ka tanqidi mutala'a* (Burhanpur, 1988).
Shafique, Khurram Ali, *Iqbal: An Illustrated Biography*, 2nd edn. (Lahore, 2007).
Shahabi, Mufti Intizamullah, *Ist Indiya kampni aur baghi 'ulama* (Delhi, n.d.).
Shahjahanpuri, Abu Salman, *Maulana Muhammad 'Ali aur unki Sahafat* (Karachi, 1983).
———, *Ghazi 'Abdu'r-Rahman shahid Peshawari* (Karachi, 1979).
Shaidai, Iqbal, 'Memoirs', *Imroze* (Lahore), Jan.–May 1969.
Shaikh, Col (r) Masud A., 'Re-visiting Turkey', in *News International*, 26 Aug. 1994.
Sharif al Mujahid, 'Pan-Islamism', *A History of the Freedom Movement*, iii, Part i (Karachi, 1961), 88–117.
———, *Ideological Orientation of Pakistan* (Islamabad, 1976).
Shaw, Stanford J., 'Ottoman Empire', in John L. Esposito (ed.), *The Oxford Encyclopedia of the Modern Islamic World* (New York & Oxford, 1995), 269–76.
Sherwani, H.K., *Studies in the History of Early Muslim Political Thought and Administration* (Lahore, 1942).
———, *Studies in Muslim Political Thought and Administration* (Lahore, 1945).
Shirani, Hafiz Mahmud, *Panjab men Urdu* (Lahore, 1928).
Shirani, Mazhar Mahmud (ed.), *Maqalat-i Hafiz Mahmud Shirani*, i–ii (Lahore, 1966).
Shivani, Anis Y., 'Religion and Politics: time to be frank', *Dawn* (Karachi), 23 May 1998.
Sindhi, Ubaidullah, *Shah Waliu'llah aur unki siyasi tahrik* (Lahore, 1952).
Singh, Khushwant, 'Pax Islamica (A Study of Pan-Islamic Movements)', *Journal of the Punjab University Historical Society* (Lahore), 9 (Apr. 1946), 27–42.
Smith, Wilfred Cantwell, *Modern Islam in India: A Social Analysis*, 2nd edn. (London, 1946).
———, *Islam in Modern History* (Princeton, 1957).
Sonyel, Salahi R., *The Ottoman Armenians* (London, 1987).
———, *Atatürk—The Founder of Modern Turkey* (Ankara, 1989).
Spearman, Diana, & Turfan, M. Naim, 'The Turkish Language Reform', *History Today* (1979), 29/2, 88–97.
Spies, Otto, 'Turkisches Sprachgut im Hindustani', *Studia Indologica* (1955), 321–43.

SELECTED BIBLIOGRAPHY

Stewart, Rhea Talley, *Fire in Afghanistan, 1914–1929: Faith, Hope and the British Empire* (New York, 1973).

Stoddard, Lothrop, *The New World of Islam* (London, 1921).

Stoddard, Philip H. (ed.), *Change and the Muslim World* (Syracuse, 1981).

Storrs, Sir Ronald, *Orientation* (London, 1937).

Stripling, G.W.P., *The Ottoman Turks and the Arabs, 1511–1574* (Philadelphia, 1942).

Sumner, Benedict H., *Russia and the Balkans, 1870–1880* (Oxford, 1937).

Svaberg, Ingvar (See Westerlund, David, below).

Syed, Anwar, *Pakistan: Islam, Politics and National Solidarity* (Lahore, 1984).

Süslü, Azmi, 'Atatürk and History', in id. (ed.), *A Handbook of Kemalist Thought*, 161–87.

Talha, Maulawi Muhammad, *Mas'ala-i Khilafat aur ahkam-i shari'yyat* (Lucknow, 1922).

Tapper, Richard (ed.), *Islam in Modern Turkey: Religion, Politics and Literature in a Secular State* (London & New York, 1991).

———, (ed.), *The Conflict of Tribes and State in Iran and Afghanistan* (London & Canberra, 1983).

Terentyef, M.A., *Russia and England in Central Asia*. Eng. tr. F.C. Daukes (Calcutta, 1876).

Thadani R.V. (ed.), *The Historical State Trial of the Ali Brothers and Five Others* (Karachi, 1921).

Tibi, Bassam, *Arab Nationalism*. Eng. tr. Marion Farouk-Sluglett and Peter Sluglett (London, 1981).

Titus, Murray, 'The Reaction of Moslem India to Western Islam', J.R. Mott (ed.), *The Moslem World of To-day* (London, 1925).

Tonapetean, P., *The Sultan is Not Caliph* (London, 1920).

Tonguç, Sencer (ed.), *The Reforms of Atatürk* (Istanbul, n.d.).

Toynbee, Arnold J., 'A Review of the Turkish Problem', *New Europe*, 14/170 (1920), 1–5.

———, 'The Meaning of the Constantinople Decision', *New Europe*, 14/175 (1920), 129–31.

———, 'Mr Montagu's Pound of Flesh', *New Europe*, 14/176 (1920).145–9.

———, 'The Question of the Caliphate', *Contemporary Review*, 127 (Feb. 1920), 192–6.

———, 'The Indian Moslem Delegation', *New Europe*, 15/185 (1920), 145–61.

——, *Survey of International Affairs, 1925*, i (London, 1927).
Traynor, Ian, 'Secular Turks and Islamists fight for supremacy in the courts and streets', *Guardian*, 12 June 2006.
Tufail, Malik Muhammad, *al-Khilafat* (Badaun, 1922).
Turan, Ilter, 'Religion and Political Culture in Turkey', in Tapper (ed.), *Islam in Modern Turkey*, 31–55.
Turan, Şerafettin, 'Mustafa Kemal Atatürk', *Islam Ansiklopedisi*, xxxi, 310–31.
Türkmen, Erkan, 'A Comparative Study of Hayder Yildirim's Translations from Turkish', *Erdem*, 1/3 (Eylül, 1985).
——, 'Turkish Elements in Urdu', *Journal of Ottoman Studies*, 6 (1986), 1–30.
Türbedar, Erhan, 'Turkey's New Activism in the Western Balkans: Ambitions and Obstacles', *Insight Turkey*, 13/3 (2011), 139–58.
Upton, Joseph M., *The History of Modern Iran: An Interpretation* (Cambridge, Mass., 1961).
Vahide, Şükran, *Islam in Modern Turkey: An Intellectual Biography of Bediuzzaman Said Nursi* (ed.), Ibrahim M. Abu-Rabi' (Albany, NY, 2005).
Valyi, Felix, *Spiritual and Political Revolutions in Islam* (London, 1925).
Vambéry, Armenius, *Western Culture in Eastern Lands* (London, 1906).
——, 'Pan-Islamism', *Nineteenth Century and After*, 60 (July–Dec. 1906), 547–58; and 61 (Jan.–June 1907), 860–72.
——, 'Pan-Islamism and the Sultan of Turkey', *Asiatic Quarterly Review and Oriental and Colonial Record* (London), 23/45 (1907), 1–11.
Villelabeitia, Ibon, 'Movie of "Human" Atatürk Stirs Emotions in Turkey', *Dawn*, 11 Nov. 2008.
Vitkus, Daniel J., 'Early Modern Orientalism: Representations of Islam in Sixteenth-and Seventeenth-Century Europe', in Michael Frassetto and David R. Blanks (eds.), *Western Views of Islam in Medieval and Early Modern Europe: Perception of Other* (Houndmills & London, 1999), 207–30.
Volkan, Vamik D., and Itzkowitz, Norman, *The Immortal Atatürk* (Chicago, 1984).
Voll, J.O., *Islam: Continuity and Change in the Modern World* (Boulder, 1982).
Yusuf, Huma, 'Turkey-Iran factor', *Dawn*, 7 Nov. 2011.
Wahby Bey, Behdjet, 'Pan-Islamism', *Nineteenth Century and After*, 61/363 (1907), 860–72.
Waley, S.D., *Edwin Montagu: A Memoir* (Bombay, 1964).

Waliullah, Shah, *Tafhimat-i Ilahiya* (Delhi, 1906).

Walker, Denis, 'Pan-Islam as a Modern Ideology in Egyptian Independence Movement of Mustafa Kamil', *Hamdard Islamicus*, 17/1 (Spring 1994), 57–109.

Waseem, Mohammad, *Politics and the State in Pakistan*, 2nd edn. (Islamabad, 1994).

——, 'Rethinking the discourse', *Dawn*, 24 Jan. 2012.

Webster, Richard A., *Christian Democracy in Italy, 1860–1960* (London, 1961).

Weil, G., *Geschichte des Abbasidenchalifats in Egypten*, ii (Stuttgart, 1860).

Werner, Franz von, (Murad Effendi, pseud.), *Turkische Skizzen* (Leipzig, 1877).

Westerlund, David, and Svaberg, Ingvar, *Islam Outside the Arab World* (London, 1999).

White, Jenny B., 'Islam and Democracy: The Turkish Experience', *Current History*, 94/588 (Jan. 1995), 7–12.

Wiatr, Jerzy J., 'Kemalism and the Models of Nation Building', *I. Uluslararasi Atatürk Sempozyumu, 21–23 Eylul 1987* (Ankara, 1994), 567–73.

Wilcox, Wayne A., 'Ideological Dilemmas in Pakistan's Political Culture', in Smith (ed.), *South Asian Politics and Religion*, 339–51.

Wild, Roland, *Amanullah: Ex-King of Afghanistan* (London, 1932).

Wilson, S.G., *Modern Movements Among Moslems* (New York, 1916).

Wirth, Albrecht, 'Panislamismus', *Deutsche Rundschau* (Berlin), 163 (1915), 429–40.

'X' (Sayyid Hasan Taqizadeh), 'Le panislamisme et le panturqisme', *Revue du Monde Musulman*, 22 (1913), 179–220.

Yasamee, F.A.K., *Ottoman Diplomacy: Abdülhamid II and the Great Powers, 1878–1888* (Istanbul, 1996).

Young, George, 'Pan-Islamism', *Encyclopaedia of the Social Sciences*, 11 (1935), 542–4.

Yuvaz, M. Hakan, and Esposito, John L. (eds.), *Turkish Islam and the Secular State* (Syracuse, 2003).

Zakaria, Rafiq, *Rise of Muslims in Indian Politics: An Analysis of Developments from 1885 to 1906* (Bombay, 1970).

Zenkovsky, S.A., *Pan-Turkism and Islam in Russia* (Cambridge, 1960).

Ziring, Lawrence, *Pakistan: The Enigma of Political Development* (Boulder, 1980).

Zulfikar, Ghulam Husain, 'Iqbal aur Turki', *Mah-i Nau* (Nov. 1986).

———, 'Urdu Language in the Background of Pak-Turkish Cultural Relations', *Journal of the Research Society of Pakistan*, 23/4, (1986), 1–10.

———, 'Jadid Turki ke bani—Mustafa Kemal Pasha: Zafar aur Iqbal ki nazar men', in id., *Iqbal: ek mut'ali'a* (Lahore, 1987), 179–95.

———, *Maulana Zafar 'Ali Khan: hayat, khidmat-o asar* (Lahore, 1993).

Zurayk, Constantine K., 'The National and International Relations of the Arab States', in T. Cuyler Young (ed.), *Near Eastern Culture and Society* (Princeton, 1951), 205–24.

Zürcher, Erik Jan, *Turkey: A Modern History*, 3rd edn. (London & New York, 2004).

———, 'Young Turks, Ottoman Muslims and Turkish Nationalists: Identity Politics, 1908–1938', in Kemal H. Karpat (ed.), *Ottoman Past and Today's Turkey* (Leiden, 2000), esp. 150–79.

(v) INTERNET WEBSITES:

Argoubi, Mohamed and Westall, Sylvia, 'Islam can exist with democracy, says Turkish PM', *Reuters*, 15 Sept. 2011, http://af.reuters.com/article/tunisiaNews/idAFL5E7KF2N 42011 0915 (Accessed: 8 Nov. 2011).

BBC News, 'Pope Benedict XVI and Islam', http://news.bbc.co.uk/2/hi/europe/5349808.stm (Accessed: 18 Feb. 2009).

———, 'Key Exerpts: Bavaria Speech', http://news.bbc.co.uk/2/hi/europe/5348456.stm (Accessed: 18 Feb. 2009).

Giglio, Mike, 'Turkey's Man in Palestine', The Daily Beast, 8 May 2013 at http://www.thedailybeast.com/articles/2013/05/08/turkey-s-man-in-palestine.html (Accessed: 8 May 2013).

Kuru, Ahmet, 'Passive and Assertive Secularism', interview with Molly Pesce at http://www.youtube.com/watch?v=YdkkRT9Veh8 (Accessed: 27 April 2012).

'Life of a Wayward—Kemal Atatürk', 'Kemal Atatürk—Hailed as a "Liberator of Turkey". We take a second look at his Life and Works', http://www.guidedones.com/issues/women/Atatürk10.htm (Accessed: 19 Aug. 2003).

Nakhoul, Samia, feed in *Reuters*, dated 4 Mar. 2012 at http://blogs.reuters.com/samia-nakhoul/ (Accessed: 3 Apr. 2012).

Timur, Safak, 'Mass resignations may mark end of era for Turkey military', *Tengri News*, http://en.tengrinews.kz/politics_sub/3530/ (Accessed: 8 Nov. 2011).

SELECTED BIBLIOGRAPHY

Tol, Gönül, and Vatanka, Alex, 'Arab Spring Creates New Rifts between Turkey and Iran', *Frontline*, 30 Oct. 2011, at http://www.mei.edu/Scholars/G%C3%B6n%C3%BClTol /tabid/557/ctl/Detail/mid/2216/xmid/2189/xmfid/13/ Default.aspx (Accessed: 8 Nov. 2011).

Ülgen, Sinan, 'Turkey, Iran, and the Bomb', *EurActive*, 26 Mar. 2012, at http://www.euractiv.com/global-europe/turkey-bomb-analysis-511752 (Accessed: 3 Apr. 2012).

Zahedi, Dariush, and Bacik, Gokhan, 'Kemalism Is Dead, Long Live Kemalism', in *Foreign Affairs*, 23 April 2010, at http://www.foreignaffairs.com/articles/66391/ dariush-zahedi-and-gokhan-bacik/kemalism-is-dead-long-live-kemalism (Accessed: 21 May 2012).

Index

A

Abbasid(s) (caliphs of Baghdad), 4, 28, 49, 50, 58, 82

Abd al-Raziq, Ali (1888–1966, Egyptian scholar of Islam, jurist at al-Azhar and politician who advanced justification for Political Secularism in Islam), xxvi, 68–69

Abdul Aziz, Shah (1746–1824, Sunni scholar of Islam and son and successor of Shah Waliullah), 7

Abdul Bari, (1878–1926, Indian Muslim pan-Islamic *'alim* who provided theoretical basis to the Khilafat movement), xxviii, 30, 40, 66, 76–77, 79, 95–96, 117, 122, 145

Abdul Ghaffar, Qazi (1894–1956, Indian Muslim journalist), 3

Abdul Ghani, Dr (1864–1943, Indian Muslim in the service of the Afghan government), 223

Abdul Hakim, Khalifa (1896–1959, Indian/Pakistani Muslim philosopher, poet and author), 52

Abdul Hayy, Shah (d. 1828, Islamic scholar and son-in-law of Shah Abdul Aziz), 4

Abdul Majid, Syed (b. 1868, founder-member Muslim League), 87

Abdul Qadir, Shaikh (Sir) (1874–1950, Indian Muslim leader and journalist), 165

Abdul Qayyum, Malik (1892–1956, editor of the *Muslim Outlook*), 88

Abdul Saleh, Ali, 258

Abdülaziz (1830–76, Ottoman Sultan, r. 1861–76), xxiv, 59, 64, 164

Abdülhamid I (1725-89, Ottoman Sultan, r. 1774–89), xxiv, 28

Abdülhamid II (1842–1918, Ottoman Sultan, r. 1876–1909), xxiv, xxix, 10–11, 25–26, 28, 60, 71, 104, 251

Abdülmecid (1823–61, Ottoman Sultan, r. 1839–61), 58, 198

Abdülmecid II (1862–1944, Ottoman Sultan, r. 1922–24), xix, 64, 251

INDEX

Abingdon, Montagu Arthur Bertie, Seventh Earl of (1836–1928, an English peer), 86

Abu Bakr (RA), (573–634, companion of the Prophet of Islam and first caliph), 181

Abdur Rahim (Indian Muslim historian), 6

Acton, John Emerich Edward, First Baron, Lord (1834–1902, British politician and historian), 227

Aden, 79, 119

Adivar, Adnan (1882–1955, Turkish politician), 197–98

Adriatic, 79

Aegean Islands, 27

Afghan War, Third, 222

Afghanistan, xxxi, xxxiv, xxxv, 70, 116, 156, 161, 166, 195, 221, 223–26, 229, 238, 263, 266

Africa, xv, 9, 23, 26, 47, 69, 108, 122, 195, 238

Afzal, Rafique (b. 1941, Pakistani historian), xiii

Aga Khan III, The, Sir Sultan Muhammad Shah (Third Head of the Nizari Ismaili community, 1877–1957), 33–34, 65, 71–72, 87, 97, 148, 199

Ahmad, Aziz (1913–78, Canada-based Pakistani professor and historian), 3, 5–7, 10, 50

Ahmad, Mansur, xxxiii, 175–76

Ahmad, Mian Bashir (1893–1971, Pakistan's ambassador to Turkey, 1951–3), xxxiii, 174–75, 182–83

Ahmad, Qeyamuddin (Muslim author), 12

Ahmad, Rafiuddin (1865–1954, barrister and Muslim politician), 13

Ahmed III (1673–1736, Ottoman Sultan, r. 1703–30), 59

Ahmed, Qazi Hussain (1938–2013, former head of the Jama'at-i Islami), 264

Ahmedabad, 145

Ahsanu'l Akhbar (Allahabad-based newspaper), 10, 163

Aidin (Smyrna), 94

Akhbar Daru'l-Khilafat (Turkish newspaper), 165

Akhbar-i Am (Lahore-based newspaper), 12, 163

Akhiri Mazamin, 10, 12–13

Akmalu'l-Akhbar (Dehli newspaper), 164

AKP, xxiii, xxiv, 255–57, 259, 260 *see also* Justice and Development Party

Akşam (Turkish evening daily), xxxiv, 208, 211

al Mujahid, Sharif (b. 1926, Pakistani author), xiii, 2

al-Afghani, Jamaluddin (1838–97, Iran-born pan-Islamist revolutionary), xxix, 3, 10, 26, 56–57

Alam, Amir, 228

Alam, Maulawi Mahbub (1863–1933, editor of the *Paisa Akhbar*), 29, 37, 164

al-Assad, Bashar (b. 1965, president of Syria), 258

al-Azhar University, 68–69

al-Azhari, Shaikh Razzaq, 181

Albania, xix, 26–27

Aleppo, 66, 83

Alexandria, 35, 80

Algeria, xix, xxi, 69, 221

al-Ghazali/al-Ghazzali (1058–1111, philosopher of Sunni Islam), 3, 49

'al-Ghazali's Theory of Islamic Government', 3

Algiers, 23

al-Hilal (Abul Kalam Azad's newspaper), xxviii, 29, 30, 32–33, 40, 165

INDEX

Ali brothers, 40, 70, 78–79, 146

Ali, Maulawi Muhammad, (1874–1951, head of the Lahori Ahmadis), 4

Ali, Mohamed (1878–1931, Indian pan-Islamist journalist and Khilafatist), xxx, xxxi, xxxvii, 29, 33, 35, 37, 77–79, 81–82, 89, 90–91, 94–99, 103–05, 107–09, 110–19, 120–22, 145–46, 165, 180

Ali, Rahman (Indian Muslim author), 8

Ali, Shaukat (1873–1938, Indian pan-Islamist and Khilafatist), 33–35, 71, 77–79, 95, 145, 149

Ali, Syed Reza (1880–1949, Indian Muslim politician), 78

Ali Paşa, Muhammad (1769–1849, Ottoman viceroy of Egypt, 1805–48), 113

Ali Reis, Sidi (1498–1563, Ottoman admiral), 6, 28

Aligarh Institute Gazette, 163

Aligarh Muslim University, 33, 240

Aligarh, 29, 35, 78, 85, 168, 246

al-Islam wa usul al-hukm, 68

al-jawaib (newspaper), 165

al-Khilafah, 4

al-Khilafat, 4

Allahabad, 163, 167

al-Maraghi, Muhammad Mustafa (1881–1945, grand imam of al-Azhar, 1935–45), 69, 71

al-Mawardi, Abu al-Hasan Ali (974–1058, Muslim jurist of Shafi'i school), 3, 49

al-Muqid, 181

al-Mutawakkil (822–61, Cairene Abbasid ruler, r. 846–61), 4

al-Nabuwwat wa'l-Khilafat, 4

al-Nadwa (Azamgarh-based journal), 78

Alsace Lorraine, 94

al-tibr al-masbuk, 3

Amasaya, 61

Ameer Ali, Syed (1849–1928, Indian Muslim jurist and politician), 4, 12, 25, 32, 34, 37, 65, 87, 89, 96, 148, 199

America, 83, 102, 118 *see also* United States

Amin, Zahid, xiii

Amin al-Huseini, Mufti (1897–1974, Mufti of Palestine), 71

Amin Effendi, 181

Ampthill, Lord (1869–1935, Governor of Madras, 1899–1906, interim viceroy of India, 1904), 86

Amrita Bazaar Patrika (Calcutta), 95

Amritsar, 77, 121, 164

Anatolia, xxii, xxxi, 9, 38, 62–63, 82, 97, 105, 114, 116, 145–46, 167, 193, 252

Anatolian Peninsula, xix

Andalusia, 48

Anderson, M. A. (*The Eastern Question*), 9

Anglo-Hellenic Society, 82

Anglo-Ottoman Society, 87, 100

Angora, 171, 194, 199

Angora Fund, 146

Angora Legion, 147–48

Anjuman-i Islam/Islamia (1886), 12, 33, 87

Anjuman-i Khuddam-i Ka'ba (1913), 40

Ankara, xxv, xxx, xxxvii, xxxviii, 62, 64–65, 115, 145–48, 167–68, 171, 176, 181, 183, 197–99, 206–08, 223–24, 227–28, 253, 256, 258, 266

Ankara Law of 1922, 64

Ankara University, 253–54

Ansari, Dr Mukhtar Ahmad (1880–1936, Indian pan-Islamist and Khilafatist), xxix, 35–39, 40, 76, 78

Ansari, Dr Naim (Member of the Indian Medical Mission to Turkey), 36

INDEX

Ansari, Tegh (Indian Muslim poet), xxxiii, 167
Arab League, 72
Arab Revolt (1916), 66, 120
'Arab Spring' (2013), 258
Arabia, xix, xxvii, xxix, 8, 26, 53, 70, 92, 120, 170, 190, 226
Arabs: Their History, Culture and Place in the Modern World, The, 3
Aras, Dr Tevfik Rüştü (1883–1972, former Turkish foreign minister under Atatürk and after, 1920–39), 36, 105
Armenia, 47, 62–63, 83–84, 94, 97, 258
Armenian massacre (1915), xxx, 81, 83, 93, 258–59
Armistice, xxii, 36, 61, 63, 66, 147, 193, 195
Armstrong, Harold Courtenay/H. C. (1892–1943, British Indian army officer and author of *Grey Wolf*), xxxiii, xxxiv, xxxvii, 157, 182, 189, 190–99, 200–09, 210–12
Arnold, (Sir) T. W. (1864–1930, British historian and author), 5, 85
Asar-i Jamalu'd-Din Afghani, 3
Asia (Journal), 242
Asia Minor, 47, 63, 82–83, 92–93
Asia, xix, 9, 23, 51, 122, 167, 171, 179, 183, 200, 258
Aspinall-Oglander, Brig. Gen. Cecil Faber (1878–1959, army officer and author), 206
Asquith, Herbert (1852–1928, Britain's Liberal prime minister, 1908–1916), 99
Asrar, N. Ahmet (Pakistani writer based in Turkey), 5
as-Said, Nuri (1888–1958, seven times premier of Iraq during the 1930s to 1950s), 113
Atatürk Araştırma Merkezi (AAM), xii, xxxvii
Atatürk Kültür, xii
Atatürk, Mustafa Kemal Paşa (1881–1938, president of Turkey, 1923–38), xi, xix, xxii, xxiii, xxv, xxvi, xxx, xxxi, xxxii, xxxiii, xxxiv, xxxv, xxxviii, 36, 39, 61–65, 68, 97, 114–17, 143–49, 150–53, 156–57, 163, 166–67, 170–71, 174–79, 180–82, 184, 189, 190–99, 200–06, 208–09, 210–11, 217–18, 220–25, 227–28, 230, 236, 237–38, 240, 244–47, 252–53, 259, 260–01, 263, 265
Atiqi, Abdul Majid, xxxiii, 179, 180–81
Auction of Souls, 83
auqaf, 150
Australia, 113
Austria, xix, 27, 48, 60, 92, 94
Austria-Hungary, Treaty of (1908), 60
Awadh Akhbar (Lucknow newspaper), 163
Awadh Punch (Lucknow newspaper), 163
Ayat-i Khilafat, 4
Aydin, Akif, xii
Azad, Abul Kalam (Indian pan-Islamist *'alim* and Khilafatist, 1888–1958), xxviii, xxxi, 4, 7, 29, 30, 33, 40, 95–96, 145, 165–66
Azamgarh, 78

B

Badger, G. P. (British publicist), 9
Badi'a Hanim, 178
Badshahi Masjid (Lahore), 33
Baghdad, 6, 50, 58
Baig, Mirza Sir Abbas Ali (1858–1932, member, India Council), 78, 88
Baird, J. G. A. (editor of Delhousie's letters), 8

INDEX

Bajwa, Altaf, xiii

Balfour, Arthur James, First Earl of (1848–1930, former British prime minister, 1902–5, and foreign secretary 1916–19), 88

Balkan crisis (1912–1913), xxviii, xxix, xxxviii, 28, 32–33, 38–39, 40, 114

Balkan League, 27, 29, 33

Balkan Peninsula, xix, 9, 23–27, 29, 30, 32, 34, 39, 48, 51, 165, 260

Balkan War(s) (1912–13), xxi, xxiv, xxv, 27, 49, 86, 91, 192 *see also* Balkan crisis

Bangladesh, 262, 265

Barakatullah, Maulavie (1859–1927, Indian Muslim pan-Islamist revolutionary), xxx, 4, 67–69

Bareilly School, 30

Barid-Shahis (dynasty), 161

Barker, Arthur, 189

Baroda, 78

Barthold, Wilhelm (1865–1930, Russian orientalist), 5

Barthou, Jean Louis (1862–1934, former French politician and premier during 1813), 103

Basbakanlik Osmanli Arsivi (BOA), xiii, xiv

Başbuğ, Ilker (b. 1943, former Turkish army chief, 2008–10), 257

Basic Democracies, xxxvi, 241–42

Batum, 224

Baxter, W. E. (British author), 8

Bayar, Celal (1883–1986, Turkish prime minister, 1937–9 and president, 1950–60), 230

Bayur, Yusuf Hikmet (1891–1980, Turkish politician and historian), 6

Becker, Carl H. (1873–1945, American historian), 2, 5

Beg, Chirin, 115

Beirut, 66

Ben Ali, Zine El Abidine (b. 1936, former president of Tunisia), 259

Benedict XV, Pope, Giacomo della Chiesa (1854–1922, served as Pope, 1914–22), 110–12

Benedict XVI, Pope, Joseph Ratzinger (b. 1927, served as Pope, 2005–13), 259

Bengal, partition of (1905), 86

Bennet, Capt. E. N. (1868–1947), 89

Bentinck, Lord William (1774–1839, governor-general of India, 1828–35), 7

Berkes, Niyazi (1908–88, Turkish Cypriot sociologist), 3, 11

Berkman, Umit, 246

Berlin, 114, 116

Berne, 115

Besiret, 59

Beyazit II (1447–1512, Ottoman Sultan, r. 1482–1512), 28

Bhopal, Nawab [Hamidullah Khan (1894–1960)] of, 79

Bhutto, Benazir (1953–2007, two-times Pakistan premier, 1988–90 and 1993–96), 263–64

Bhutto, Z. A. (1928–79, former Pakistan president/premier, 1971–7), 262

Bilecik University (Turkey), xii

Binder, Leonard (b. 1927, American political scientist), 3

Birch, Bishop, 84

Birdwood, George (1832–1917, Anglo-Indian official), 7–9

Bitlis, 61

Black Sea, 228

Blunt, Wilfred Scawen (1840–1922, British writer-poet and traveler), 2–3, 10

INDEX

Bolitho, Hector (1897–1974, New Zealand-born author and author of *Jinnah*), 189
Bolkestein, Frits, 259
Bolshevik, xxxi, 114, 116, 120–21
Bombay (Mumbai), 32, 35, 38, 77, 79, 97, 114, 119
Bombay Chronicle, 89, 94
Bombay Legislative Council, 97
Bonaventura, Cerretti (1872–1933, Italian cardinal of Roman Catholic Church), 112
Borak, Sadi, 190, 211
Bosnia-Herzegovina, xix, xxi, 27
Boulger, D. C. (*England and Russia in Central Asia*), 8
Bourdarie, M., 104
Brindisi, 79, 119
Britain, xiii, xx, xxv, xxviii, 2, 9, 26, 32, 61, 63, 70, 77–79, 81–84, 86–89, 94–96, 100, 102, 106–09, 111, 113, 116, 118–19, 121, 189, 207, 210, 227–28
British Balkan Committee, 34
British Congress Committee, 90, 121
British Expeditionary Force, 190
British Foreign Office, 2, 8, 118, 145, 207
British Indian Army (67th Punjabis), 190
British Military Intelligence, 145, 190, 206, 208
British Parliament, 81, 83, 89, 99
British Red Crescent Mission, 34, 37
Browne, Edward G. (1862–1926, British orientalist), 2–3, 87, 180
Bryce, Viscount James (1838–1922, British academic and jurist), 81, 83
Bucharest, Treaty of (1913), 24
Buckler, F. W. (1859–1927, Turkophobe British historian), 7
Budak, Mustaf, xii
Bulgaria, Treaty of (1913), 60
Bulgaria, xv, xvii, 26–27, 36, 60

Bulgarian tragedy (1890), 29
Bureau d'Islamique, 103, 114
Bursa, 85–86
Bury, G. W. (author of *Pan-Islam*), 2
Buxton, Leland (1884–1967, British barrister of the Inner Temple), 89
Byzantine city, 48

C

Cachin, Marcel (1869–1958, French politician), 103–04
Caesar, 48
Cairo conference, 68–69, 70
Cairo, 68, 70, 72, 79
Calcutta, 29, 30, 33
Caliph/Caliphate/Ottoman Caliphate, xix, xx, xxii, xxiii, xxiv, xxv, xxvii, xxix, xxx, xxxi, xxxvii, 1, 7, 25, 30, 56, 67, 91, 117, 119, 163, 182
Caliphate, a Historical and Juridical Sketch', 'The, 4
Caliphate, The, 5
Caliphate, Yesterday, Today and Tomorrow, The, 5
Cambridge, 101, 239
Canada, 113
Canterbury, 84
Carmichael, Lord (1859–1926, Scottish politician, governor of Madras, 1911–12, and Bengal, 1912–17), 86
Cash, W. W. (*The Moslem World in Revolution*, 11
Caskel, Werner (1896–1970, German historian of Islam), 11
Caspian Sea, xix
Cathcart, Colin, 207
Caucasus, 53, 193
Cauvain, M., 103

INDEX

Cavid Bey, Mehmed (1875–1926, Ottoman politician), 114
Cecil, Lord Robert (1864–1958, British lawyer, politician and diplomat), 80–81
Celil Hanim, Nuzhat, 177
Celaleddin Harzemşah, 165
CENTO, 246
Central Asia, xxvii, 8, 11, 28, 47, 51, 53, 55, 58–9, 161, 205, 221
Central Islamic Society, 87
Central Khilafat Committee (CKC), 70, 77–79, 96, 116–17, 145, 147–49, 166, 261
Cevdet, Abdullah (1869–1932, Ottoman intellectual and medical doctor of Kurdish descent), 217
Chal Balqan Chal, 32
Chamier, Sir Edward (1866–1945, legal advisor to the secretary of state for India, 1920), 106
Charing Cross Hospital (London), 35
Charmes, Gabriel (1850–86, French writer), 2
Chattopadhyaya, V. N. (1883–1937, Indian Hindu revolutionary), 116
Chelmsford, Frederic John Napier Thesiger, First Viscount (1868–1933, viceroy of India, 1916–21), 77, 96–98
Cheragh Ali, Maulawi (1844–95, Indian Muslim author on Islam), 10, 13
Cherif Paşa, General, 71
Chesaro, A. (Italian head of the Colonial Institute in Rome), 108
China, 182, 195
Chindwara, 78
Chinoy, Fazalbhai M., 35
Chirol, Sir Ignatius Valentine (1852–1929, British journalist and diplomat), 2
Chotani, Mian Muhammad Haji Jan Muhammad (1873–1932, president of the Central Khilafat Committee, 1919–23), 35, 77–79, 117, 147–49
Church of England, 84
Churchill, Winston (1874–1965, British statesman and premier, 1940–5 and 1951–5), xxii
Cilesia, 62
CKC, *see also* Central Khilafat Committee
Clifford, Dr John (1826–1923, British Non-conformist minister), 84
Clynes, John Robert (1869–1949, British trade unionist and Labour party politician), 100
Colonial Institute, 108
Colquhoun, A. R. (American author of 'Pan-Islam'), 2
Comité la France et l'Islam, 104
Comité National d'Estudes, 104
Committee of Union and Progress (CUP), xxii, *see also* CUP
Commonwealth (of Britain, Canada, and Australia), 113
Comrade (Mohamed Ali's paper), xxviii, 29, 33–34, 38, 78
Comte, Auguste (1789–1857, French philosopher), 217
Congress of Vienna (1815), xxxv
Congress, Indian National, 32, 67, 145, 261
Constantinople (later renamed Istanbul), 6–7, 48, 80, 84, 94, 198
Constituent Assembly of Pakistan, 239
Constitution (of Pakistan, 1956), 239, 241, 244, 262
Correspondence of Lord William Cavendish Bentinck, Governor–General of India, 1825–1835, The, 7
Council of Islamic Ideology, 245
Crete, xix, 27
Crimea, 51

INDEX

Crimean War (1854), 8, 28, 58
Critical Exposition of Popular Jihad, A, 13
Croatia, xix, 27, 60, 63, 82, 85, 92–93, 105, 168
Cunningham, Allan (1784–1842, Scottish author and poet), 9
CUP, xxii, 26, 114–15, 117, 120, 191
Curzon of Kedleston, Lord (1859–1925, viceroy of India, 1899–1905), 85–86, 109, 112, 171
Cyprus, xix, 63
Cyrenaica, 39
Çanak (Samsun), 61
Çanakkale (Gallipoli), xxii, 36, 144, 147, 192
Çankaya/Chan Kaya, 202, 204–05, 228
Çatalja, 36
Çudahir, Ahmet (Turkish writer), 190, 211

D

D'Ohsson, Mouradgea (1779–1851, Swedish historian and diplomat of Armenian descent), 5
D'Orleans, Duke of (French statesman), 103
Daily Citizen (British newspaper), 101
Daily Express (British daily newspaper launched in 1918), 207
Daily Herald (British daily newspaper, 1912–64), 90, 101
Daily Telegraph (British right-wing newspaper), 106, 206
Dalhousie, Marquess of (1812–69, governor-general of India, 1848–56), 8
Dalmatia, 108
Damascus, 66, 222
Dane, Sir Louis (1856–1946, Lt. Governor of the Punjab, 1908–13), 86

Dardanelles, 36, 48, 63, 105
daru'l-harb, xx, 7, 166
daru'l-Islam, xxi, xxvii, xxix, xx, 1, 9, 23, 40, 48, 50, 56–58, 149, 266
Darwesh, Celal Salma, 178
Davidson, Dr Randall Thomas (1848–1930, Archbishop of Canterbury, 1903–28) 84
Dawn (Karachi based newspaper with branches in other cities), 264
De Kergeuzec, 104
de Lormain, Baron (representative of the Duke d'Orleans), 103–04
de Magallon, Xavier (French politician), 104
de Mouzie, Senator M. (French politician), 104
de Robeck, Admiral Sir John Michael (1862–1928, British High commissioner in Istanbul, 1919), 93
de Salis, John Francis Charles, Seventh Count (1864–1939, British ambassador to the Vatican, 1916–23), 112
de Tassy, Joseph Héliodore Sagesse Vertu Garcin (1794–1878, French orientalist), 10
Deccan, 6, 28
Defence of Women's Right, 176
Delhi, 6–7, 30, 34–35, 76–77, 79, 95, 161, 163
Deoband, 30, 97
Deslailleur, Gen. Cherfils, 104
Destiny of Indian Muslims, The, 6
Development of Muslim Theology, Jurisprudence, and Constitutional Theory, 5
Development of Secularism in Turkey, The, 11
Dil-Godaz (journal), 164
Din, Justice Mian Mohammad Shah (1868–1918, president of the Muslim

INDEX

League and judge of the Punjab chief court), 174
Dixon, Campbell, 206
Diyarbekir, 61, 193
Dodecanese, 63
Dolmabahçe Palace (Istanbul), 227–28
Durkheim, Émile (1858–1917, French sociologist), 217
Dutch Indies, 69

E

Eastern Question, 1774–1924, The, 9
Echo d'Islam (Paris-based journal), 103–04
Edib (Adivar), Halidé (1883–1964, Turkish intellectual and author), 40
Edinburgh, 101
Edirne (Adrianople), 27, 36, 38–39
Educational Unity, Law of, 218
Egerton, Field Marshall Sir Charles (1848–1921, member Council of India, 1907–17), 86
Egypt, xix, xxi, xxx, xxxv, 9, 47, 53, 58, 63, 66, 68–69, 70–71, 85, 109, 115, 156, 181, 183, 221, 224, 258
Elazig, 61
Ellison, Grace, 175–76
Emergence of the Indian National Congress, The, 10
Emin, Ahmed (author of *Turkey in the World War*), 11
Encyclopedia of Islam, 3
England, xxxiv, 84, 87, 199, 210, 227
England and Russia in Asia, 8
England and Russia in Central Asia, 8
England, Russia and Central Asia (A Study in Diplomacy), 8
Enver Paşa, (Ismail) (1881–1922, Ottoman minister, 1914–18), 38, 39, 40, 83, 116, 191–93

Epirus, 27
Eraslan, Cezmi (Turkish historian), xii, xxxviii
Erbakan, Necmettin (1926–2011, former Turkish premier, 1996–7), 254–55, 263–64
Erdoğan, Recep Tayyib (b. 1954, incumbent Turkish premier since 2003), xxiii, 252, 255–59
Eren, Halit, xiii
Ergenekon group, 257
Erzurum, 61–62
Esad Efendi, Mehmed (b. 1847, shaikh of the Naqshbandiyya Sufi order), 59
Escarpa, Dr (secretary of the Colonial Institute, Rome), 108
Essays on Eastern Question, 12
Essex Hall, 100
Europe, xix, xx, xxi, xxii, xxvii, xxviii, xxx, xxxi, xxxv, xxxvii, 23–24, 26–27, 39, 40, 48, 60–61, 63, 77–79, 80–83, 85, 87, 96, 102, 105, 109, 111, 113–15, 119, 121–23, 146, 151, 155, 167, 170–71, 173–74, 178–79, 180, 196, 202, 221, 223–25, 252, 255–56, 258–59, 260
European Court of Human Rights, 255
European Union (EU), 230, 259, 260
Evren, Kenan (b. 1917, seventh president of Turkey, 1980–89), 257

F

Fabricius (author), 5
Fahmy, Mohammad (Egyptian politician), 115
Faisal ibn Hussein, Emir/King (Arab leader and ruler of Iraq, 1883–1933), xxxi, 70, 113, 120
Far East, xxvii, 40, 55, 221
Farabi, 173

INDEX

Farangi Mahal, 30, 66, 76–77
Faridabadi, Saiyid Hashmi, 32
Farooqi, Naimur Rahman, xxvii
Farrère, Claude (1876–1957, French author who supported Atatürk), 104
Farouk, King (1920–65, Egyptian monarch, 1936–52), 71
Fasana-i Azad, 164
Fatihpuri, Niaz (1884-1966, Urdu poet and writer), 32
Fatimids (dynasty, 969–1171), 58
Fazilet Partisi (FP), 256 *see also* Welfare Party
Fazl-i-Husain, Mian (Sir) (1877–1936, Punjab Muslim leader), 78
Fazlul Haq, Abul Kasem (1873–1962, Indian Muslim leader from Bengal), 77–79, 89, 118
Fazlur Rahman (1919–88, scholar of Islam and author), 12, 53, 220, 245
Ferid Paşa, Damad (1853–1923, Ottoman grand vizier, 1919 and 1920), 62
Fethi (Okyar) (1880–1941, prime minister of Turkey, 1924–25), 204
Fevzi, Mustafa (Ottoman minister of religious affairs during the abolition of the caliphate crisis of 1924), 65
Fez, 32, 150, 172, 176, 219
Field, Arthur G., 89, 94
Fikret, Tefvik (1867–1915, Ottoman poet), 217
Fikriye Hanim (nominal cousin of Atatürk with undefined relationship), 194–95, 199, 209
Fisher, H. A. L. (1865–1940, British historian and minister), 90, 92, 95, 98, 102
Foreign Affairs (British journal), 101
Foreign Enlistment Act 1870, 147

Fortnightly Review (influential journal of the nineteenth-century Britain), 2, 180
France, 47–48, 80, 102–05, 107–08, 119, 258
Frechtlings, L. E., 8
French Revolution, xxi
French Socialist Party, 102–03
Fuad (Cebesoy), Ali (1882–1968, Turkish officer, politician and statesman), 197
Fuad, King (ruler of Egypt), 1923–36), xxx, 69, 70, 224
Fulanis, 53
Future of Islam, The, 2

G

Gaddafi, Muammar (1942–2011, former Libyan strongman, 1969–2011), 258
Gaiti Ara (wife of Bashir Ahmad, Pakistan's first ambassador to Turkey), xxxiii, 174, 183–84
Gandhi, M. K. (1869–1948, Hindu leader of the Indian National Congress), 67, 95–96, 117
Gasparri, Cardinal Pietro (1852–1934, Roman Catholic Cardinal), 112
Gaza, 258
Gendarmeries, 190
Geneva, xxxi, 71, 102, 115
German Business Law, 150
German Oriental Bureau, 108–09
Germany, xi, 94, 192–93, 219
Ghauri, Iftikhar Ahmad (late Pakistani historian), 6
Ghaznavids (dynasty), 161
Ghulam Ahmad, Mirza (1839–1908, founder of the Qadiani heterodoxy), 6, 12–13
Gibb, H. A. R. (1895–1971, Scottish historian and orientalist), 2–3, 49

INDEX

Giolitti, Giovanni (1842–1928, five times Italian premier between 1892 and 1921), xxxi, 108–09, 110

Giritli, Ismet, 217

Gladstone, William (1809–98, four-times British premier between 1868 and 1894), 26, 84

Glasgow, 101

Gleichen, Major-Gen. Lord Edward (1863–1937, British army general), 94

GNA, *see also* Grand National Assembly

Gökalp, Ziya (1876–94, Ottoman sociologist, writer, poet, and political activist), 217, 238, 245

Goldziher, Ignáz (1850–1921, Hungarian scholar of Islam), 3

Golra, Pir Mihr Ali Shah (Sufi *pir* and *'alim* of the Punjab, 1859–1939) of, 32

Gornamint angrezi aur jihad, 12

Government of India, 33, 35, 40, 86, 98, 119, 146–47

Grand National Assembly (GNA), xxxiv, 64–65, 147–49, 196–97, 199, 200–01, 204, 209, 218, 224, 228, 253

Greco-Turkish crisis (1919–22), 169

Greece, xix, xxii, 27, 34, 60, 63, 82, 85, 92–93, 105, 168

Greece, Treaty of (1913), 60

Grey Wolf, xxxiii, xxxiv, xxxvii, 157, 182, 189, 190–91, 204–05, 207, 210–12

Gujarat, 6, 28

Gül, Abdullah (b. 1950, eleventh president of Turkey since 2007), 256

Gülen, Fethullah (b. 1941, Turkish writer and religious social reformer), 256

Gultekın, Mehmet Bedri (deputy chairman of the Workers' Party of Turkey), 211

Güven, Gül Çağali (Turkish author), 190, 211

H

Habib, Muhammad, 90

Habibullah II, Amir (1872–1919, ruler of Afghanistan, 1901–19), 226

Hagia Sofia cathedral (CE 532–37), 81

Hairi, Shamsu'l-'Ulama Allama (author of *Khilafat-i Qur'ani*), 4

Hali, Altaf Hussain (1837–1914, Indian Muslim poet), 10, 164

Halk Firkasi (Peoples' Party of Turkey), 65

Hambly, G. R. G. (author on Lord Mayo's period), 12

Hamdam (newspaper), 166

Hamdard (Mohamed Ali's newspaper), 78, 165–66

Hamidia, 40

Hangama-i Balkan, 30, 166

Hansard (official report of proceedings of British Parliament), 9

Hardinge of Penshurst (1858–1944, viceroy of India, 1910–16), 33, 35, 86

Hardy, P., 9, 12

Haristanve Gülistan, 165

Haroon, Seth Haji (Sir) Abdoola (1872–1942, Indian businessman and pan-Islamist), 78

Harun, Alitcha Zade, 114–15

Hasan aur Angelina, 164

Hasan, Mahmud (1851–1920, head of Deoband seminary), 97–98

Hasan, Sayyid Nasim (author of *Istikhlaf*), 4

Hasan, Yakub (1875–1940, Indian pan-Islamists from Madras), 90

Hashemite Hejaz, 221

Hasrat Mohani, Syed Fazl-ul-Hasan (1878–1951, Indian poet, journalist, pan-Islamist and Khilafatist), 32

INDEX

Hayat, Hassan Muhammad (1882–1955, Indian Khilafatist), 78, 108, 111, 118

Hejaz, xxx, 63, 69, 70, 91, 113, 120, 172, 179, 221

Hejaz Railway Project, 29

Hejazi, Selim Bey, 115

Helm, A. K. (British diplomat), 207

Henderson, Arthur (1863–1935, British Labour Party politician and minister), 99

Flight, Omar Henson (British Muslim of the Islamic Society), 87

Herbert, Lt. Col. Aubury (1880–1943, British MP), 86

Herriot, Monsieur, 211

Heyd, Uriel (Jewish author on Turkey), 9

Hiçyalmiz, Ergun (Turkish author), 190, 211

Hijrat, 47, 51, 97, 116, 166

Hikmet Bey (former Turkish ambassador to Kabul), 224

Hilal-i Ahmer, 36–37, 40 *see also* Ottoman Red Crescent Society

Hilmi Paşa, Abbas (1874–1944, Khadive of Egypt, 1892–1914), 113

History of Nationalism in the East, A, 11

History of Shahjahan of Dihli, 6

History of Tipu Sultan, 6

Hollande, Francois (b. 1954, current president of France), 258

Holt, P. M. (1918–2006, historian of the Middle East), 9

Horniman, B. G. (1873–1948, British socialist), 89, 12

Hossain, Syud (Indian Khilafatist, 1888–1949), 78–79, 89, 91, 113, 118

Hostler, C. W. (author of *Turkism and the Soviets*), 2

Hottinger, A. b. 1926, German journalist and publicist), 3

House of Commons, 80–81, 86, 98

Humayun (Lahore-based monthly journal), 174–76, 182–83

Hungary, xix, 23, 48, 60, 92, 195

Hunter Committee Report (1920), 121

Hurgronje, Snouck C. (1857-1936, Dutch orientalist), 2

Husain, Kazim (secretary, London Muslim League), 34, 37

Husain, S. Abid (Indian Muslim writer), 5

Hussein ibn Ali, Sayyid (1853–1931), xxvi, 39, 64, 69, 113, 179

Hutchinson, William (d.1965, chair of the national executive committee of the British Labour Party), 100

Hutton, Rev. William Holden (1860–1930, Dean of Winchester and Reader in Indian History at Oxford, 1920), 81

Hyderabad, 71

I

Ibn Iyas, Muhammad (1448–1552, Egyptian historian), 4

Ibn Saud, Abdul Aziz (1876–1953, ruler of the Nejd and Hejaz, 1932–53), 69, 70, 179

Ibn Taimiyya, Taqi ad-Din Ahmad (1263–1328, Islamic scholar-theologian), 49

Ibret (Namik Kemal's Turkish newspaper), 59

Ihkam al-Sultaniyya, 3

Ihsanoğlu, Dr Ekmeleddin (b. 1943, secretary general of the OIC since 2004), 230, 265

Ihya 'ulum al-din, 3

ijma, 49, 54

ijtihad, xxxii, 52–53, 151

Imam, Syed Hasan (1871–1933, Indian Muslim leader), 78

INDEX

Imros, 63
Inalcik, Halil (b. 1916, Turkish historian), 11
Independent (Allahabad-based newspaper), 78, 95
India, xi, xiv, xxv, xxvii, xxviii, xxix, xxx, xxxi, xxxii, xxxiii, xxxiv, xxxv, xxxvii, 3, 5–7, 9, 10, 12–13, 25–26, 28–29, 33–34, 38–39, 40, 47, 53, 55–56, 58, 66–67, 70–71, 76–79, 80, 85–87, 89, 94–99, 101, 105–06, 109, 112–19, 120, 122, 144–47, 150–52, 156, 161–64, 166, 173, 182–84, 195, 210, 221, 223, 225, 227, 238, 241, 261, 265
India (London-based journal), 90, 94, 101
India Council, 88, 151
India Office, 93, 96, 106, 112
India Under Ripon, 10
Indian Muslims, The, 5
Indian Nationalism and the Early Congress, 12
Indonesia, 11, 25, 58
Indo-Pakistan War 1965, 240
Inshaullah, Muhammad (Indian Muslim journalist who collected funds for the Hejaz Railway project), 29
Ionian Islands, xv
Iqbal, Muhammad (1877–1938, Indian Muslim poet-philosopher), xxxii, xxxiii, xxxvii, 4, 31–32, 53, 96, 144, 151–57, 166, 171, 173–74, 238, 245, 261
Iran, xxxiv, xxxv, 6, 47, 70, 85, 183, 221, 223–24, 227, 238, 246, 263, 266
Iraq, xix, 26, 47, 69, 70, 85, 91, 111, 121, 179, 190, 221, 238, 240, 263
Ishaq, Shah Muhammad (1778-1846, Indian Musim *'alim*), 7
Iskander Mirza, Maj.-Gen. Sahibzada Sayyid (1898–1969, governor-general of Pakistan, 1955–6, and first president 1956–8), 240
Islam Araştirmalari Merkezi (ISAM), xii, xiv
Islamabad, xiii, xiv, 240, 264
Islamic Information Bureau, 79, 88–89, 122
Islamic Modernism in India and Pakistan, 1857–1964, 3, 7
Islamic Research Institute, 245
Islamic Review and Muslim India (later shortened to *Islamic Review*), 88
Ispahani, M. Hashim (hon. Secretary, London Muslim League), 87–89, 90
Ismet Inönü, Mustafa (1884–1973, Turkish premier, 1923–7, president, 1938–), 65, 147–48, 193, 199, 202, 204, 206, 208, 211, 230, 253
Israel, 258
Ist Indya Kampni aur baghi 'ulama, 8
Istanbul, xii, xiii, xiv, xxii, xxv, xxviii, xxix, xxx, xxxii, xxxiv, xxxvii, 7–8, 12, 23, 28–29, 30, 36–39, 48, 58, 60, 62, 64, 68, 80–83, 86, 93–95, 105, 108, 111, 115, 147–48, 165, 168–69, 177–79, 190, 193, 198, 224, 227–28, 256, 260
Istanbul University, xii
Istikhlaf, 4
Italian Penal Code, 150
Italy, 29, 60, 102, 108–09, 119, 120, 165, 227
Italy, Treaty of (1912), 60
ittihad-i Islam, xxi, xxvii, xxix, 1, 25, 29, 30, 251 *see also* pan-Islam
Ittihat ve Terakki Cemiyeti, xxii, *see also* CUP
İzmir, 61
Izmir (steamer), 224
Izzet Paşa, Ahmed (1864–1937, Ottoman general during First World War), 36–37

INDEX

J

Jalalabad, 227
Jam'iyyatu'l- 'Ulama-i Hind, 148, 182
Jama'at-i Islami, 242, 245, 247, 264
Jama'at-i Mujahidin, 12
Jamia Masjid, Delhi, 30
Japan, 102, 118
Jarida-i Rozgar (Madras journal), 163
Jaurès, Jean (1859–1914, French socialist leader), 103
Jawab-i Shikwa/Answer to the Complaint, 31–32
Jaziratu'l-Arab (Island of Arabia), 91, 105, 114, 149
Jeddah, 66, 265
[Jemal] Cemal Paşa, Ahmed (1872–1922, Ottoman minister, 1914–18), 38, 114, 116, 191
Jerusalem, 71, 173
jihad, 13, 30–31, 47, 53, 97, 166
Jinnah, Mohammad Ali (1876–1948, president of All India Muslim League), xxxii, xxxiv, xxxvii, 32, 67, 77, 144, 151–52, 156–57, 182, 189, 190, 210–11, 239, 261–62, 265
Johur, Sultanate of, 69
Jounpuri, Karamat Ali (Indian Muslim *'alim*), 13
Journal des Débats, 103
Jowett, F. W. (1864–1944, British Labour politician), 99
Judicial Committee of the Privy Council, 87
Jung, Nawab W. H. M. (hon. Secretary, Islamic Society, London), 87
Justice and Development Party (Adalet ve Kalkinma Partisi/ AKP of Turkey), xxiii

K

Kabul, 35, 183, 224
Kadirga Hospital, 36
Kairanwi, Rahmatullah (1818–91, Indian Muslim *'alim*), 8
Kaliyar Sharif, Pir of (scion of the Chishtiyya Order of pirs near Hardawar in India), 32
Kamaluddin, Khwaja (head of the Woking Mission, UK), 1870–1930), 88
Kamil Paşa, Mustafa (1874–1908, Egyptian politician), 69
Kamil Paşa (1833–1913, Ottoman statesman of Cypriot origin), 36
Kanpur (Cawnpore) Mosque affair (1913), 78, 105
Karabekir, Musa Kazim (1882–1948, Turkish general and politician), 193, 197, 209
Karachi, 73, 79, 145
Karakoram, 247
Karal, Enver Ziya (1906–82, Turkish historian), 217
Kargil, 247
Karim, Dr K. M. (Indian Muslim historian and author), 6
Karpat, Kemal, 51, 55, 217
Kashgar, 172
Kashmiri, Agha Hashr (1879–1935, Indian playwright,), 165
Kassem, Brig. Abdul Karim (1914–63, former premier of Iraq, 1958–63), 240
Kasur, 31–32
Katouzian, Homa, 227
Kazemzade-Iranshahr, 228
Keddie, Nikki R. (b. 1930, American professor of Iranian history), 2–3
Kemal Bey, Ghalib (Mustafa Kemal's agent in Rome), 109, 114

INDEX

Kemal Day, xxxii

Kemal, Namik (1840–88, Ottoman poet and social reformer), 11, 59, 165, 217

Kemalism, xxiii, xxxiii, 216–18, 230, 236–37, 253, 255, 260

Kennworthy, Lt.-Commander J.J. (1886–1953, British MP), 86

Kerr, Philip (1882–1940, Eleventh Marquess of Lothian, private secretary to Llyod George), 92

Khadduri, Majid (1909–2007, Iraqi-born author and professor of Middle Eastern studies), 2

Khaksar, 70

Khalid, Shaikh, 109

Khalid Bey, Khalil, 114

Khalid bin Walid, (592–642, companion of the Prophet of Islam and commander of his forces), 179

Khalifat-Allah (and not just *Khalifatu'r-Rasul-Allah*), 58

Khaliquzzaman, Choudhry (1889–1973, Indian pan-Islamist and Khilafatist), 35–36, 38

Khaljis (dynasty), 161

Khan, Ahmad Riza (1856–1921, Indian Muslim *'alim* and head of the Barelwi school), 30

Khan, Ayub (1907–74, former Pakistani president, 1958–69), xii, xxxvi, xxxvii, 237, 239, 240–47, 262

Khan, Haji Musa (1872–1944, Muslim League leader), 40

Khan, Hakim Ajmal (1865–1927, Indian pan-Islamist and Khilafatist), 76, 95

Khan, Hakim Muhammad, 164

Khan, Genghis (1162–1227, Mongol leader), 205, 210

Khan, King Amanullah (1892–1960, ruler of Afghanistan, 1919–29), xxxiv, xxxv, 221–27, 229

Khan, Liaquat Ali (1895–1951, Pakistan's first premier, 1947–51), 239

Khan, M. Anwar (historian/vice-chancellor, Peshawar University), 8

Khan, M. H. (Indian Muslim author on Tipu Sultan), 6

Khan, Malik Mubaraz, 32

Khan, Nadir (1883–1933, Afghan ruler, 1829–33), 226

Khan, Sahibzada Aftab Ahmad (1867–1930, Indian Muslim barrister and politician), 151

Khan, Syed Ahmed (1817–98, Indian Muslim reformer), 7, 10, 12–13, 54, 163, 245

Khan, Zafar Ali (1873–1956, pan-Islamist editor/proprietor of the *Zamindar*), xxviii, xxxiii, 25, 29, 31, 35, 38, 165, 169, 170, 178–79, 182

Khilafat (newspaper), 166

Khilafat aur Hindustan, 8

Khilafat aur Inglistan, 8

Khilafat Conference, All-India, 77, 148

Khilafat Day, 88

Khilafat delegation, xxx, xxxvii, 77, 79, 80, 89, 90, 104

Khilafat in Islam, The, 4

Khilafat movement (1918–24), xxv, xxviii, 13, 40, 66–67, 76, 79, 84, 86, 88, 96, 98, 119, 150, 166, 180, 221, 261

Khilafat wa Mulukiyyat, 4

Khilafat-i 'Usmaniyya aur Turk, 4

Khilafat-i Ilahiya, 48

Khilafat-i Islamiyya, 4

Khilafat-i Qur'ani, 4

Khilafatists, xxv, xxx, xxxii, 85, 95–96, 108, 113–14, 117, 119, 121, 145, 147–49
Khilafet, The, 4
Khizr, Prophet, 172
Khizr-i Rah, 171
Khost, 226
Khuda Bakhsh, Prof. (1877–1931, Indian Muslim scholar), 50, 151
Khuhro, Hamida (Pakistani historian and politician), xiii
Khusrau, Amir, Ab'ul Hasan Yamin-ud-din (1255–1325, Medieval Muslim poet and musician), 162
Khyber Pass, 225
Kidwai, Mushir Hosain (1878–1938, Indian pan-Islamist and Khilafatist), xxviii, 2, 30, 40, 79, 86, 88–89, 95–96, 118
Kilçoğlu, Hakki, 217
Kingsway Hall, 100
Kinross, Lord, John Patrick Douglas Balfour, 3rd Baron Kinross (1904–1976, Scottish historian and writer), 212
Kirkareli, 36
Kishore, Munshi Newal (1836–85, Indian publisher of Lucknow), 163
Knox, Edmund Arbuthnott (1847–1937, Bishop of Manchester, 1903–21), 84
Kohn, Hans (1891-1971, Jewish American historian-philosopher), 11
Konya, 86
Kosovo, xix
Kostantiniyye, 7 *see also* Constantinople; Istanbul
Küçük Kaynarca, Treaty of (1774), xxiv, 251
Küçük, Mustafa, xiii
Kurdistan, 63

Kuru, Ahmet (Turkish political scientist in America's San Diego State University), 252
Kut al-Amara, 190

L

L'Avenir de la Turquie: Le Pan-Islamisme, 2
L'Humanité (Paris-based Socialist journal), 102
Labour Party, 80, 99, 100, 119
Lahore, xiii, xiv, xxvi, 29, 31–33, 35, 161, 163, 165, 174
Lahori Ahmadis, 88
Lakshmi (Pandit), Vijaya (née Swarup Kumari, 1900–90, Indian diplomat and politician), 89
Lambton, A. K. S. (1912–2008, British historian), 3
Landau, Jacob M. (b. 1924, Israeli-American political scientist at Hebrew University Jerusalem), xxvii, 2
Lane-Poole, Stanley (1854–1931, British orientalist), 5
Lang, Dr Cosmo Gordon (1864–1945, Archbishop of York, 1908–28, and of Canterbury, 1928–42), 84
Lansbury, George (1859–1940, British politician and social reformer), 89, 90, 99, 100–01, 119
Latife (Uşşaki/Uşakligil), (1895–1975, Sorbonne-educated wife of Mustafa Kemal Atatürk, 1923–25), 195, 199, 209
La Touche, Sir James (1844–1921, former Lt. Governor of the UP), 86
Lausanne, 63–64, 148, 179
Lausanne, Treaty of (1923), xxiii, 60, 64, 147, 167, 170
Lausanne Conference, 148

INDEX

Lawrence of Arabia/Shaw, T. E., T. E. Lawrence (1888–1935, British scholar/army officer known for his role in the Arab Revolt, 1916–18), 226–27
Le Temps (1861–1942, Parisian newspaper), 103
Le Coconnier (French Turkophile), 104
Le Journal (1892–1944, Parisian daily newspaper), 103
Le Populaire (French Socialist daily newspaper), 102
Le Quay d'Orsay (French foreign office in Paris), 105
League of Muslim Nations, 151
League of Nations, 63
Lebanese Maronite, 258
Lebanon, 221
Lecomte, Rene, 104
Lee, Dwight E. (American author), 2
Lenin, V. I. (1870–1924, Russian Communist revolutionary), 103
Léon, H. M. (1856–1932, originally William Henry/Abdullah Quilliam converted to Islam and founded England's first Mosque and Islamic Centre in Liverpool), 87
Lewis, Bernard (b. 1916, British-American historian), 6, 11
Liberal Party, 99
Libya, 39, 53, 63, 258
Life of Abdul Hamid, 11
Ligue des Nations Opprimes de tout l'Orient, 108–09, 116
Lloyd George, David (1863–1945, British prime minister, 1916–22), xxxi, 80, 84–86, 88, 90, 92–97, 99, 100, 106, 111, 146–47, 180
London, xii, xiii, xiv, xxxiv, xxxvii, 8, 10, 12, 33, 35, 37, 67, 77, 79, 80, 82, 84, 87–89, 95, 100, 103, 105, 109, 113, 118, 120, 122, 148, 189, 206
London, Treaty of (1912), 24, 27
London Muslim League, 34, 87–88
Longuet, Charles (1839–1903, French socialist journalist), 102
Longuet, Jean (1876–1938, French socialist and grandson of Karl Marx), 102–04
Lucerne, 115
Lucknow, 30, 33, 76, 163
Lüleburgaz, 36
Lutfi Hanim, 177
Lyallpur, 32
Lybyer, A. H. (1876–1949, scholar of the history of the Middle East), 5

M

MacColl, Malcolm (1831–1907, British clergyman and publicist), 9
MacDonald, D. B. (Canadian political scientist), 5
MacDonald, Ramsay (1866–1937, former British premier, 1924, 1929–31, and 1931–5), 99, 100–01
Macedonia, xix, xxii, xxxviii, 26–27, 38–39
Maclean, Neil (1876–1953, Scottish socialist and Labour MP), 100, 115
Maclean, Sir Donald (1864–1932, British Liberal politician), 80
Madd-o Jazr-i Islam, 10, 164
Madras, 163
Mahdis, 53
Mahmud, Syed (Indian politician, Khilafatist and author), 8
Mahmudabad, Raja of, Sir Mohammad Ali Mohammad (1877–1931, Muslim League leader), 77
Majlis-i Watani, 181

INDEX

Makhzan (Lahore-based Urdu journal), 165
Makkah, 39, 64, 70, 82
Malabar Coast, 28
Malay States, 195
Malaya, 221
Malaysia, 11, 58
Malta, 48, 64, 97, 193
Manchester, 84, 87, 101
Mango, Andrew (b. 1926, British biographer of Atatürk), 210, 212
Maqalat, 12
Maqalat-i sar Sayyid, 10
Maqam-i Khilafat, 165
Marash (Cilicia), 81, 83
Marchand, H. (French author), 2
Margoliouth, D. S. (1858–1940, Oxford professor and orientalist), 2, 5, 81
Marmara Region, xii
Marriot, J. A. R. (1859–1945, British author with a knighthood), 9
Martin, R. (editor of Wellesley's correspondence), 6
Marx, Karl (1818–1901, German philosopher and revolutionary socialist), 102
Mas'ala-i Khilafat aur ahkam-i shari'yyat, 4
Mas'ala-i Khilafat wa Jazira-i 'Arab, 4
Mas'ala-i Sharqiyya, 8
Mashriqi, Inayatullah Khan (1888–1963, founder of the Khaksar movement), 70
Massawa, 79, 119
Maududi, Abul-Ala (1903–79, founder-leader of the Jama'at-i Islami), 4, 52, 245
McLane, J. R. M. (author on nationalism and Congress), 12
Medical Mission, All-India, xxix, 34
Mediterranean, 47
Meeruthi, Ismail (1844–1917, Indian Muslim poet), 164

Mehmed I (1390–1421, Ottoman Sultan, r. 1413–21), xx
Mehmed V, Rişad (1844–1918, Ottoman Sultan, r. 1909–18), 26, 36
Mehmed VI, Vahideddin (1861–1926, Ottoman Crown Prince/Sultan, r. 1918–22, fled after the abolition of Sultanate), 61, 64, 105, 147, 193, 251
Mehmed, Arif (old friend of Atatürk, executed), 200, 209
Mehmed, Cavid (old friend of Atatürk, executed), 200
Mehrotra, S. R. (Indian historian of the Congress party), 10
Meila, Jean, 104
Memoirs of Naim Bey, The, 83
Menderes, Adnan (1899–1961, Turkish premier, 1950–60), 211, 264
Menil, Du (French Turkophile), 104
Meshed, 224, 229
Mesopotamia, 23, 47, 63, 190
Meşrutiyet era, 217
Middle East, 40, 55, 121, 223, 266
Middle East and the West, The, 11
Mignet, François Auguste (1796–1884, French journalist and historian), 217
Mihr, Ghulam Rasul (1895–1971, Pakistani poet, writer and journalist), 12
Milan, 119, 120
Millerand, Alexandre Etienne (1859–1943, French premier, 1920, and president 1920–4), xxxi, 93, 107
millet, xx, 23–24, 59, 172
Milner, Alfred 1st Viscount (1854–1925, British statesman and colonial administrator), 99
Mir'at al-Mumalik, 6
Miranshah, 226

INDEX

Misak-i Milli (National Party), xxii, 62, 117, 175

Mithat, Ahmet (1844–1912, Ottoman intellectual), 217

Miyan, Muhammad (author of *'Ulama-i Haq*), 8

Mochi Gate, 31

Modern Movements among Muslims, 9

Mohammedan Anglo-Oriental College of Aligarh, 85

Mohy-ud-din, Ghulam (1880–1963, Kasur lawyer and social reformer of Anjuman-i Himayat-i Islam), 31

Mohyuddin Hanim, 176

Monghir, 87

Mongols, 50

Montagu, Edwin S. (1879–1924, British secretary of state for India, 1917–22), 80, 90, 93, 96–99, 106, 112, 118

Montenegro, xix, xxi, 25, 27

Montreaux, xxxi, 102, 115

Morgan, James, 207

Morison, Sir Theodore (1863–1936, principal of MAO College, Aligarh, 1899–1905, member, council of India, 1906–16), 86

Morocco, 63, 69, 221

Morsi, Mohamed (b. 1951, toppled fifth president of Egypt), 266

Moscow, 103, 116

Moslem world in Revolution, The, 11

Mosul, 65, 177, 200

Mourad, Kanizé (b. 1940, Turkish journalist of the former Ottoman ruling house), xx

Mowbray, Charles Stourton, Lord Stourton, Segrave, and (1867–1936, ran the Anglo-Ottoman Society of London), 87

Mubarak, Hosni (b. 1928, toppled Egyptian president, 1981–2011), 258

Mudania, 147, 195

Mudros, 193

Mufakkar-i Azam (Great Thinker), 182

Mu'tamar al-Alam al-Islami (World Muslim Congress), 72, 115

Mughals, 6–7, 28, 51, 55, 143, 161

Muhammad (*sal'am*), Abu'l-Qasim Muhammad ibn Abd-Allah (570–622, Prophet of Islam), 31, 47, 49, 68, 91, 122, 168, 171, 179, 180–82

Muhammad, Mian Tufail (1914–2009, Pakistani politician of Jama'at-i Islami), 242

Muhammad, Sheikh Ghulam (proprietor of *Vakil*, Amritsar), 164

Muhammad the Conqueror (Ottoman Sultan r.1451–81), 28

Mujaddad-i Khilafat ('Restorer of the Caliphate', title conferred on Atatürk by Indian Khilafatists), 148

Mujahid-i Akbar (Great Mujahid), 182

Mujeeb, Muhammad (b. 1902, Indian Muslim historian), 5

mujtahids, 224

Murad I (1326–89, Ottoman Sultan r. 1362–89), xxiv

Murad V (1840–1904, Ottoman Sultan r. May-August 1876), xx, 71

Musaddas-i Hali, 10, 164

Musharraf, Pervez (b. 1943, former chief executive and president of Pakistan, 1999–2001 and 2001–8), xii, 247, 263–64

Muslim Community of the Indo-Pakistan subcontinent 610–1947, The, 5

Muslim Family Laws Ordinance, 241–42

Muslim League, All India, 33–34, 40, 67, 77, 87, 156, 174, 182, 261

INDEX

Muslim nationalism, 57
Muslim Outlook (Lahore-based English newspaper), 88, 90, 101, 112
Muslims of British India, The, 9
Mussolini, Benito (1883–1945, Italian dictator, 1922–43), 71
Mustafa III (1717–74, Ottoman Sultan r. 1757–74), 28, 59
Müftüoğlu, Ahmed Hikmet (1870–1927, Turkish diplomat and author), 165
Müller, August (1848–1892, German orientalist), 5
Mysore, 28
Myth About the Transfer of the Caliphate to the Ottomans, The, 5

N

Nadwatu'l 'Ulama, 30
Nadwi, Abul Hasanat (1890–1924, Indian Muslim scholar of Daru'l-Musannifin connection), 4
Nadwi/Nadvi, Abu Najib Anisu'l-Hasan Sayyid/Syed Sulaiman (1884–1953, India *'alim* and member of the Khilafat delegation, 1920), 4, 8, 78–9, 89, 91, 113, 118, 122, 180
Naidu, Sarojini (1879–1949, Indian poet and Congress leader), 89, 116, 121
Najmul Hasan, Sayyid (b. 1911, Shia author and Bihar MLA, 1937-45), 4
Nallino, Carlo A. (1872–1938, Italian orientalist), 5, 82
Naqshbandis, 53
Nasihat al-Mulk, 3
Nasr, Hossein (b. 1933, Iranian scholar of Islamic Studies), 5
Nath, Pandit Gopi (founder of *Akhbar-i Am* of Lahore, 1870), 163

National Culture of India, The, 6
National Mahommedan Association, 87
National Order Party (Milli Nizam Partisi or MNP), 254
National Pact 1920, 195
National Salvation Party (Milli Selamet Partisi or MSP), 254
NATO, 230
Nazim Paşa, (1848–1913, Ottoman chief of the staff during the First Balkan War, 1912), 36 [Done]
Near East, 8, 64, 84, 146
Nehru, Pandit Motilal (1861–1931, Indian lawyer and Congress president, 1919–20 and 1928–9), 78, 89, 95
Nejd, 70
Nekowar Hanim, 178
Nestorians, Patriarch of, 84
New Europe (British journal), 82
New World of Islam, The, 9
New York, 84
News International (Islamabad-based English daily newspaper), 264
Niaz, Ilhan, xiii
Nigeria, 53
Nihad, Prince Ahmed (1883–1954, grandson of Ottoman Sultan Murad V), 71
Nikoli, Dr, 110
Nimrod, 172
Nitti, Saverio (1868–1953, Italian prime minister, 1919–20), 93
Nomani, Shibli (1857–1914, Indian Muslim scholar of Islam during the British Raj), 12, 30, 165–6
Norman, Roger, 206
North Africa, xix, 47, 258
Northcliffe, Alfred Charles William Harmsworth, First Viscount (1865–

INDEX

1922, British newspaper and publishing mogul who also owned *The Times* of London), 82
Nottingham University, 7
Nuncios, 111
Nureddin, 197
Nuri Bey, Aziz (politician working with the Greeks during occupation), 109
Nuri Bey (Ileri), Mehmet Celal (1877–1939, Turkish author), 2, 217
Nursi, Bediuzzaman Said (1876–1960, Sunni Muslim scholar of Kurdish origin), 253

O

O'Connor, T. P. (1848–1929, Irish nationalist, journalist and British MP for nearly half a century), 80
Objectives Resolution, 239
Observer (Lahore-based newspaper), 165
Official History of the Gallipoli Campaign, The, 206
OIC, 41, 265 *see also* Organization of Islamic Conference
Oliphant, Sir Lancelot (1881–1965, British diplomat at the Foreign Office), 207
Oman, Sir Charles (1860–1946, British military historian), 80
Omar (RA, 575–644, second caliph of Islam, 634–44), 181
Organization of Islamic Conference (OIC), 230
Oriental and India Office Collections, xiv, 10, 12
Ormsby-Gore, S.F. (1863–1950, British MP), 80
Osama bin Laden, (1957–2011, Saudi millionaire-turned-*jihadi* and founder of al Qaeda), 265

Osman, House of (dynasty), 64
Osman Ali Khan, Mir, Asaf Jah VII (1886–1967, Nizam of Hyderabad, 1911–48), 71
Osmanlis, xiii, xiv, xxv, xxx
Ottoman Empire, xi, xx, xxi, xxii, xxiv, xxvi, xxx, xxxi, 9, 13, 23–24, 26–27, 29, 32–34, 39, 60–61, 76, 80–81, 86, 88, 92, 105, 109, 147, 165–66, 196, 198, 201, 236, 251–52, 260–61
Ottoman Red Crescent Society (Osmanli Hilal-i Ahmer Cemiyeti), 30, 35–36
Ottoman Salonika, xxii
Ottoman Treasury, 38
Ottoman Turks and the Arabs, 1511–1574, The, 5
Oxford University, 29, 78, 81–82, 174, 190, 223
Ömar Paşa, Dr Besim (1862–1940, head of the Ottoman Red Crescent Society), 36, 40
Ömerli, 36
Özcan, Azmi (b. 1960, Turkish scholar of pan-Islam), xii, xxviii

P

Pahlavi, Reza Shah (1878–1944, Shah of Iran, 1925–41), xxxiv, xxxv, 223–24, 227–29
Paik-i Islam (Nineteenth-century pan-Islamic Turkish newspaper), 165
Paisa Akhbar (Lahore-based daily newspaper), 12, 29, 32, 37, 164, 166
Pakistan, xi, xii, xiii, xiv, xxv, xxxii, xxxiv, xxxvi, xxxvii, 32, 40, 72, 161, 174, 183–84, 189, 211, 237–39, 240–41, 243–47, 261–63, 265–66
Pakistan Army, 240
Pakistan movement, 174, 239

INDEX

Palestine, xix, 47, 63, 69, 71, 91, 111, 121, 179, 221

Palgrave, W. G. (1826–1888, scholar of Arabic), 12

pan-Islam, xii, xxi, xxii, xxiv, xxv, xxvi, xxvii, xxviii, xxix, xxx, xxxi, xxxvii, 1–3, 5, 8–9, 10–11, 13, 25–27, 29, 30, 54–58, 60, 64, 66, 69, 72, 113, 163–64, 166, 179, 251–52, 254–55, 260, 265–66 *see also ittihad-i Islam*

Pan-Islam (London journal), 2

Panipati, Ismail (compiler of Syed Ahmed's works), 10

Pan-Islamic Society of London, 33 *see also* Anjuman-i Islam

Pan-Turkism and Islam in Russia, 11

Paris, 69, 71, 77, 80, 102–07, 113, 115, 118, 122, 146

Partito Popolare (Popular Party), 108

Parwez, Ghulam Ahmad (1903–1985, Pakistani Islamic scholar), 245

Pathe, M., 104

Patmos, John of (author of the *Book of Revelation* which forms part of the *New Testament*), 173

Pax-Islamica, 1–2

Peace Conference, 64, 80, 93, 106, 197

Pears, Edwin (biographer of Abdülhamid II, 11

Peoples' Party (of Turkey), 201, 204 *see also* Halk Firkasi

Perim, 119

Persia, 156, 195

Persian Revolution of 1905–1909, The, 3

Peshawar, 32, 226

Peshawari, Abdur Rahman (1886–1925, Indian pan-Islamist and Turkey's man in Afghanistan), 35, 38

Peter the Great, Tsar (1672–1725, Russian monarch, 1682–1725), 224

Philips, C. H. (1912–2005, historian and vice-chancellor, London University), 7

Pickthall, Muhammad Marmaduke (born (1875–1936, British journalist originally Marmaduke William Pickthall but converted to Islam), 87–89, 90, 100–01

Pillon, 104

Pirbhai, Currimbhai Adamji (1845–1913, Muslim businessman-philanthropist of Bombay), 35

Poitiers, 48

Poland, 69, 100

Political Thought in Medieval Islam, 4

Port Said, 79, 119

Porte, 27, 59, 63

Portland Collection, 7

Portugal, 182

Poullada, Leon (1913–87, American diplomat and author), 226

Powell, Avril Ann (British scholar of Islam), xiii

PPP, 264–65

Private Letters of the Marquess of Dalhousie, 8

Proposed Political, Legal and Social Reforms in the Ottoman Empire and Other Mohammedan States, 10

Punjab, 29, 31, 85

Punjab Police, 31

Q

Qadir, Manzur (1913–74, Pakistani jurist and later foreign minister, 1958–62), 243

Qadiri, Mufti Muhammad Habibur Rahman (author of *Ayat-i Khilafat*), 4

Qaisaru'l-Akhbar Hind (Allahabad-based newspaper), 10, 163

Qajar Dynasty, 227
Qipchaq Steppes, 51
Quetta, 32
Qurashi, Muzaffar Mahmood (former federal secretary), xiii
Qureshi, Ishtiaq Husain/I. H. (1903–81, Pakistani historian and former minister of state), 5–6, 239
Qureshi, Shoaib (1891–1962, Indian pan-Islamist and Khilafatist), 35–36, 38, 90
Qutub-Shahis (dynsty), 161

R

Rahbar-i Hind (Lahore-based newspapaer), 12
Rahimtoola, Sir Ibrahim (1862–1942, member, Governor of Bombay's executive council, 1918–23), 97
Rahmi (Evernos), 197
Rai, Lala Lajpat (1865–1928, Hindu Arya Samaj-Congress leader of), 79
Rampur, 29, 32, 78
Rauf (Orbay), Admiral Hüseyin (1881–1964, Turkish statesman), 40, 61, 197
Rawalpindi, 264
RCD, 41
Reading, Rufus Daniel Isaac, First Marquess of (1860–1935, viceroy of India, 1921–4), 147
Rechad, Dr Nehad (editor of the *Echo d'Islam*, Paris), 103–04
Reconstruction of Religious Thought in Islam, 152
Redhouse, J. W. (1811–92, British author and lexicographer), 8–9
Rees, J. D. (1854–1922, British colonial administrator in India and MP, 1906–10 and 1912–22), 86

Refet (Bele) (1877–1963, Ottoman/Turkish general), 197–98
Reid, Anthony (New Zealand-born historian), 11
Renaudel, Pierre (1871–1935, conservative French socialist), 102
Republica Moslemica, 117
Republican Liberal Party, 204
Republican Peoples' Party (RPP), xxiii, 230, 253
Research Centre for Islamic History, Art and Culture (IRCICA), xiii, xiv
Reuters, 80, 94, 180
Revue de deux Mondes (French monthly journal), 2
Revue Indigéne, 104
Rise of Islam and the Caliphate: The Pan-Islamic Movement, The, 2
Rise of the Ottoman Empire', 'The, 11
Rizvi, Hasan Askari (Pakistani political scientist and author), 246
Roche, Jules (1841–1923, French politician and minister, 1890–2), 104
Romania, xix, xxi, 27
Rome, 82, 102, 108–09, 110, 113–15, 119, 129
Roos-Keppel, Sir George (1866–1921, British army officer and chief commissioner, NWFP, 1908–19), 87
Rose, J. Holland (1855-1942, British historian), 11
Rosenthal, E. I. J. (prolific author on Islam), 4
Rosinus, 5
Rousseau, Jean-Jacques, 217
Royal Geographical Society, 223
Royal Military College, Sandhurst, 240
Royal University of Rome, 82
Rumelia, 9, 27
Russia, xix, 100, 195, 221, 224, 228

INDEX

Russia and England in Central Asia, 8
Russia and The Balkans, 1870–1880, 8
Russo-Turkish War of 1877, 10, 25, 28, 163–64
Rüşti, Halil (Ottoman writer), 165

S

S.S. *Cracovia*, 119
S.S. *Graz*, 119
S.S. *Hungaria*, 79
S.S. *Sardinia*, 35
Saad, Muhammad (Iranian modernist intellectual), 228
Sada'-i Hind (Lahore newspaper), 12
Sadak, Necmeddin (1890–1953, Turkish politician and foreign minister, 1947–50), 190, 208–09, 210–11
Safa, Peyami (1890–1961, Turkish novelist), 190, 211
Safarnama-i Rum-o Sham, 12
Safavid, 51
Safia Hanim, 178
Saghir/Sagir, Mustafa (1877–1921, Indian Muslim agent deputed by the British intelligence to kill Mustafa Kemal), 145
Said, Dr Abdul Hamid (Egyptian pan-Islamist), 109
Saifu'l-Islam ('Sword of Islam', title conferred on Atatürk by Indian Khilafatists), 148
Sakarya University, xii
Sakarya, 195
Saksena/Saxena, Banarsi Prasad (Hindu historian of Muslim period in India), 6
Salafis, 53
Salisbury, Third Marquess of, Robert Arthur Talbot Gascoyne-Cecil (1830–1903, three times Britain's premier,
1885–6, 1886–92 and 1895–1902, and four times foreign secretary), 81
Salle de Ingénieurs Civil, 104
Salle de Sociétés Savantes, 104
Salle Wagram, 104
Salmone, H. A. (author of the Sultan's claim to the caliphate), 9
Samun, 228
San Remo, 97–98
San, Nagai, 118
Sanhoury, A., 69
Sanussi, Sheikh Ahmad Sherif (1873–1933, the supreme leader of the Senussi order in Libya, 1902–1933), 68
Sanussis, 53
Saray, Mehmet (b. 1942, Turkish historian and author), xii, xxxvii
Sarguzasht-i Mujahidin, 12
Sarkozy, Nicolas, 258
Sarshar, Pandit Ratan Nath (1845–1903, Indian novelist of Urdu and editor of the *Avadh Akhbar*, Lucknow), 164
Saudi Arabia, 263–64, 266 *see also* Arabia
Sayyid Ahmad Shahid, 12
Sayyid Jamal ad-Din "al-Afghan": A Political Biography, 3
Scarborough, 100
Scotland Yard, 102
Secret History of the English Occupation of Egypt: Being a Personal Narrative of Events, 3
Selim I (1465–1520, Ottoman Sultan, r. 1512–20), 4, 28
Selim III (1761–1808, Ottoman Sultan, r. 1789–1807), 28
Selim, Prince Mehmed (1870–1937, eldest son of Abdülhamid II), 71
Selma, Princess (granddaughter of Sultan Murad V, married a *taluqdar* of Awadh, UP), xx

INDEX

Serbia, xix, xxi, 25, 27
Sèvres, Treaty of (1920), xxii, xxiii, 60, 63, 107, 113, 118, 166, 169
Sforza, Count Carlo (1872–1952, Italian diplomat), 110
Shafi, Sir Muhammad (1869–1932, Indian Muslim politician), 33, 174
Shah Alam II (1728–1806, Eighteenth Mughal emperor, r.1759–1806), 28
Shah Waliullah aur unki siyasi tahrik, 7
Shah, Qaim, xiii
Shahab (journal), 242
Shahabi, Mufti Intizamullah (author of *Ist Indiya kampni aur baghi 'ulama*, 8
Shahabuddin, Justice Muhammad (1895–1971, chief justice of Pakistan, 1955–60, head of Ayub Khan's constitutional commission), 243
Shahidan-i Dastur (Martys of the Constitution), 180
shaikhu'l-Islam (title of the Ottoman chief religious authority), 219
Shama'-o shair (1912), 165
Shamsu'l Akhbar (Madras-based newspaper), 163
Sharar, Abdul Halim (1860–1926, Indian Muslim writer and historian), 12, 164
Sharar, Sahibzada Mustafa Khan (Indian Muslim poet from Rampur), 32
shari'at, xx, xxiv, 25, 49, 58, 150, 177, 180, 201, 219, 239, 245, 261–62
Sharif, Muhammad Nawaz (b. 1949, Pakistani politician and three times prime minister), 263
Shariff Paşa (a former ADC to Ottoman Sultan Abdülhamid II), 103, 113
Shaw, T. E., 226 *see also* Lawrence of Arabia
Shawish, Abdul Aziz (1872–1929, al-Azhar-educated Egyptian pan-Islamist close to Enver Paşa), 38

Sheldrake, Khalid (born 1888, originally Bertram William Sheldrake, he converted to Islam), 87
Sherwani, Haroon Khan (1891–1980, Indian historian, scholar, and author), 3–4
Shibli Academy, 78
Shikwa/ The Complaint, 31
Shinwari area, 226
Shuneh, 66
Siachen, 247
Sicily, 48, 51
Siddiqui, Abdur Rahman (1887–1953, Indian Muslim pan-Islamist and Khilfatist), 35–36, 38, 90
Sina, 173
Sinar, Archbishop of, 84
Sindhi, Ubaidullah (1872–1944, Indian Muslim *'alim* of Deoband connection and revolutionary), 7
Singh, Khushwant (b. 1915, Indian Sikh journalist and writer), 2
Siraj-ud-din, Kazi (lawyer and translator of Syed Ahmed Khan's *The Truth About the Khilafat*), 10
Sivas, 61–62, 208
Sivas Congress 1919, 62
Siyasat (Lahore-based Urdu newspaper), 166
Slankamen (1691), xxi
Slovenia, xix
Smyrna, 63, 82, 92–94, 105, 146, 167–69, 170, 177, 193
Smyrna Fund, 146
Snowden, Philip, First Viscount (1864–1937, British politician and chancellor exchequer, 1924 and 1929–31), 99
Sofia, 192
Song of Felicitation, The, 168

INDEX

Soraya, Queen (1899–1968, originally Soraya Tarzi she married in 1913 to Amanullah, later King of Afghanistan), 222, 224–25
South Africa, 69
South Asia, xi, xxiv, xxv, xxvi, xxvii, xxviii, xxxvii, 2, 5, 10–11, 47–48, 55, 216, 260–61, 265
South East Asia, 11, 48
Soviet Union, 39
Sowern, Afzal, xiii
Spain, 47–48, 51
Spanuidi, Madame, 211
St. Sophia Church (Istanbul), 86
Stoddard, L. (1850–1931, American writer), 9
Stoiloff, M., 103
Straits, The, 61, 63, 105
Strasbourg, 255
Striplings, G. W. F. (author of books on Ottoman Turkey), 4–5
Studies in Islamic Culture in the Indian Environment, 5
Studies in the History of Early Muslim Political Thought and Administration, 4
Sturzo, Don Luigi (1871–1959, Italian Catholic priest and politician), 108
Sudan, 53, 63
Suez Canal Treaty 1888, 63
Suhail, Iqbal Ahmad (Indian Muslim poet of Aligarh), xxxiii, 168
Suhrawardy, Barrister Abdulla al-Mamun (1875–1935, Indian pan-Islamist barrister), 33
Sultan as Caliph (Nallino), 82
Sultan, Tipu (1750–99, ruler of the Kingdom of Mysore in India, 1782–99), 6, 28
Sumatra, 48

Sumner, Benedict H. (author of *Russia and the Balkans*), 8
Suriyya Hanim, 178
Surtees, Brig.-Gen. H. Conyers (1858–1933, British MP), 86
Survey of International Affairs, 1925, 11
Süleyman/Sulyman 'Kanuni' (1494–1566, tenth Ottoman Sultan, r. 1520–66), xx, 205
Süslü, Azmi (Turkish historian), xii, xxxvii
Swaraj, xxx, 122, 166
Sweden, 116
Swiss Civil Code, 150, 201, 219
Switzerland, 65, 69, 80, 114, 118, 147, 227
Syria, xix, 26, 47, 63, 71, 91, 107, 111, 121, 179, 190, 221–22, 258, 266
Şagufta Hanim, 178
Şahinkaya, Tahsin (b. 1925, former Turkish air force chief, 1978–83), 257
Şevket Paşa, Mahmud (1856–1913, Ottoman general and statesman), 36, 38–39

T

Taalby, Abdul Aziz (Tunisian pan-Islamist), 114
Tabassum, Sufi Ghulam Mustafa (1899–1978, Indian Muslim/Pakistani Urdu poet-writer), xxxiii, 175–78
Tableau general de l'empire Ottoman, 5
Tafhimat-i Ilahiya, 7
Tahzibu'l Akhlaq, 10
Taimurid Mughals (tribe/dynasty), 161
Tajikistan, 266
Talat Paşa, Mehmed (1874–1921, Ottoman minister, 1908–18), xxxi, 38, 83, 114–16, 191, 193

INDEX

Talha, Maulawi Muhammad (author of *Mas'ala-i Khilafat*), 4
Tamerlane (1336–1404, Central Asian conqueror Amir Timur), 205, 210
Tanzimat reforms (1839–76), 24–25, 59, 216–17
Taqizadeh, Sayyed Hasan (1870–1978, Iranian politician), 228
Tarikats, 254
Tashkent, 1 16
Tazkira-i 'ulama-i Hind, 8
Tenedos, 63
Tercuman-i Mashriq (newspaper), 165
Tercuman-i Rum (Turkish newspaper), 165
Terentyef, M. A. (Russian state functionary and author), 8
Territet, xxxi, 65, 102, 115, 118
Tevfik Paşa, Ahmed (1845–1936, the last Ottoman grand vizier, April-May 1909, 1918–19, and 1920-2), 105
The Development of Secularism in Turkey, 3, 11
Theory of Kingship in the *Nasihat ul-Muluk* of Ghazali', 'The, 3
Third International, 103
Thomas Cook (travel agents), 119
Thrace, 27, 63, 92–92, 94–95, 147, 168
Tilak, B. G. (1856–1920, Hindu Congress extremist leader), 95
Times Literary Supplement, The, 206
Times, The (London newspaper of Viscount Northcliffe), 8–9, 34, 82, 90, 94
Timurids, 260
Tokyo, 118
Tonapetean, P. (anti-Turk publicist), 82
Toynbee, Arnold J. (1889–1975, British historian-philosopher), 11, 81, 83, 85
Trabzon, 61, 228
Transcuacasia, 61
Trans-Iranian Railway, 229

Transjordan, 91, 221
Treatment of Armenians in the Ottoman Empire (1915–1916), The, 83
Trebizond, Archbishop of, 84
Tripoli, 109
Tripolitan war (1911), xxix, 27, 29, 34, 86, 165, 192
Truth About the Khilafat, The, 10
Tufail, Malik Muhammad (author of *al-Khilafat*), 4
Tughluqs (dynasty), 161
Tul'u-i Islam, 173
Tunisia, xxi, 63, 69, 109, 221, 258
Tural, Sadik, xii
Turati, Filippo (1857–1932, Italian socialist politician and poet), 108, 110
Turco-Italian crisis 1911, 28
Turkey, xi, xii, xix, xxii, xxiii, xxiv, xxv, xxvi, xxviii, xxix, xxx, xxxi, xxxii, xxxiii, xxxiv, xxxv, xxxvi, xxxvii, xxxviii, 3, 6, 8–9, 30, 31, 33–35, 37–39, 40, 53, 58, 61–66, 68–69, 70, 76–77, 80–83, 85, 86–88, 92–96, 99, 102, 104–06, 109, 110, 115, 117, 120, 121, 143–44, 147–49, 150–57, 161–63, 165–67, 171, 173–79, 180–81, 183–84, 189, 190–93, 195–99, 200–02, 205–08, 210–11, 213, 217–19, 220–24, 228, 230, 236–38, 245–47, 252–55, 257–59, 260–66
Turkey in the World War, 11
Turkan-i Ahrar, 180
Turkische Skizzen, 2
Turkish Relief Fund, 31–32
Turkism and the Soviets, 2
Turkistan, 26
Türkiye Büyük Millet Meclisi, xxxiv *see also* Grand National Assembly (GNA)
Türk-Shahiya (dynasty), 161

INDEX

U

Ulama-i Haq, 8
'Ulama-i Hind ka shandar mazi, 8
ulu'l-amr (those in authority), 54, 58
Umayyad Caliphate (661–750), 49
ummat, 49, 52, 54, 71–72
UN report, 260
UN Security Council, 258
Union of Democratic Control, 101
United Provinces, 32
United States, 77, 91, 117–18, 256, 265 *see also* America
University of London, xiii, xiv
University of Punjab, 85
University of Tehran, 229
Urdu language, xxvi, xxxiii, xxxvii, 4, 32, 162–69, 171, 174, 176, 179, 184
Uruj-i Turki (Rise of Turkey), 180
Uzbekistan, 266

V

Vakil (Amritsar newspaper), 164, 166
Vambéry, Arminius (1832–1913, Hungarian orientalist), 2, 11–12
Van, 61
Vatan (Amritsar-based newspaper), 29, 191
Vatican, 103, 110, 112
Venice, 79, 80, 119
Venizelos, Eleutherios (1864–1936, Greek politician and premier, 1910–20 and 1928–32), 85, 97
Versailles, xxxi, 102
Victoria Docks, 35
Vienna, xx, xxxv, 48, 94, 259
Vilayets, 61
Vindication of the Ottoman Sultan's Title of 'Caliph': Shewing its Antiquity, Validity, and Universal Acceptance, A, 8

Viqarul Mulk, Nawab Mushtaq Hussain (1841–1917, Indian Muslim reformer of the Aligarh movement), 32, 39
von Falkenhayn, Erich (1861–1922, chief of German general staff during First World War), 193
von Hammer-Purgstall, Josef, (1774–1856, Austrian orientalist) 6
von Kremer, F. A. (German orientalist), 5
von Sanders, Otto Liman (1855–1929, German general and head military mission to Turkey, 1913), 192
von Werner, Franz (1836–81, Austrian diplomat and author, better remembered for his pseudonym of Murad Effendi), 2

W

Wahabi, 53
Wahabi Movement in India, 12
Wahby Bey, Behdjet (insightful writer on pan-Islam), 2, 115
Waliullah, Shah (1703–62, Indian Muslim *'alim* and reformer), 7, 53
Waliullahis, 53
Waqat, 177
waqf, 219, 237, 245
Wedgwood, Col. Josiah, 1st Baron (1872–1943, British Liberal and Labour politician, 1924), 86
Weil, G. (German orientalist), 5
Welfare Party (Refah or RP), 254–56, 263–64
Western Culture in Eastern Land, 12
Whither Islam?, 2
Wilhelm II, Kaiser (1859–1941, emperor of Germany, 1888–1918), 11
Wilson, S. G. (author of *Modern Movements Among Muslims*), 9

INDEX

Wilson, Woodrow (1856–1924, American president, 1913–21), 91
Winchester, 81
Winnington-Ingram, Dr Arthur (1858–1946, Bishop of London, 1901–39), 84
Winterton, Edward Turnour, Sixth Earl (1883–1962, British Conservative MP and minister, 1937–9), 86
Wirth, Albrecht (German author), 2
Woking Mosque, 95, 100
Worcester, 190
World War, First, xi, xxii, xxvi, xxx, xxxi, xxxiv, 9, 39, 61, 76, 78, 81, 86, 143, 166, 169, 175–76, 179, 183, 190, 192, 216, 252, 261
World War, Second, 72, 253

Y

Yahya, Imam Muhammad Hamid ed-Din (1869–1948, Imam of the Yemen, 1918), 70
Yahya Khan, Agha Muhammad (1917–80, former president of Pakistan, 1969–71), 247
Yemen, 23, 69, 70, 258
Yildirim, Sajjad Haidar (1880–1930, Indian Muslim writer of Turkish themes), 165
Yildiz Kösk/Palace (Ottoman royal residence in Istanbul), xiii, xiv, 59
Yildizgördü, Necla, xiii
York Diocesan conference 1920, 84

York, Archbishop of, 84
Young Turk revolution (1908–09), 29, 192
Young Turks/ Young Ottomans (1889–1918), xi, xxi, xxii, xxiv, xxv, xxviii, xxix, 11, 24–27, 29, 38, 59, 192
Young, George (political scientist), 2

Z

Zaghloul, Saad Pasha (1859–1927, Egyptian revolutionary political and premier, 1924), 114
Zakrya Hanim, 178
Zaman, Muhammad Qasim (Pakistani historian at Princeton), xiii
Zamindar (Zafar Ali Khan's newspaper), xxviii, 29, 32, 165–66, 178
Zenkovsky, S.A. (author of *Pan-Turkism and Islam in Russia*), 11
Ziaeddin, Prince (eldest son of Sultan Murad V), 71
Ziaul Haq, (1928–88, former military dictator and president of Pakistan, 1977–88), 72, 247, 262–63
Zirve University, 260
Ziya, Halit (1867–1945, Turkish author), 217
Zurayk, Constantine Z. (professor of Syrian origin at Beirut's American University), 11
Zürcher, Erik (1928–2008, Dutch historian at Leiden University), 230